ANTIQUE AND COLLECTIBLE

·DICTIONARY·

COLLECTOR BOOKS

A Division of Schroeder Publishing Co., Inc.

ROBERT & CLAUDETTE REED

Front cover: Madame Alexander bride doll, Cincinnati Reds bobbing head figure, ca. 1970s; vintage amber chemical bottle; autographed photograph of Western star Gene Autry. Vintage playing cards; pie safe; alligator bottle opener; cast iron bell toy, ca. 1890s.

Back cover: Montgomery Ward catalogs from the 1930s. United Cigar Stores premium catalog 1929; Montgomery Ward catalog 1973. Arcade Company toy catalog, 1927; bottle opener and figural; Pepsi Cola bottle, ca. 1950s; Elvis magazine.

Cover design by Beth Summers
Book design by Terri Hunter

COLLECTOR BOOKS
P.O. Box 3009
Paducah, Kentucky 42002-3009

www.collectorbooks.com

Copyright © 2008 Robert and Claudette Reed

The current values in this book should be used only as a guide. They are not intended to set prices, which vary from one section of the country to another. Auction prices as well as dealer prices vary greatly and are affected by condition as well as demand. Neither the authors nor the publisher assumes responsibility for any losses that might be incurred as a result of consulting this guide.

Searching for a Publisher?

We are always looking for people knowledgeable within their fields. If you feel that there is a real need for a book on your collectible subject and have a large comprehensive collection, contact Collector Books.

Acknowledgments

Special thanks to Antiques and Collectibles News Service copy editor Heather Reed for extraordinary efforts in preparing this volume. Deepest appreciation also to the distinguished auction and appraising firm of Skinner Inc. with offices in Bolton and Boston, Massachusetts, for the use of many illustrations over the years. Grateful acknowledgement to the Harris Auction Center in Marshallville, Iowa, for the use of many illustrations. We also appreciate and acknowledge the assistance and encouragement from others including Mary Maley, Nadine Abshire, and Barry and Barbara Carter.

Mission style rocking arm chair designed by Gustav Stickley.
(Skinner Inc.)

About the Authors

Robert and Claudette have operated Antique and Collectible News Service since 1988. Together they have researched and written 15 books, plus some 1,000 articles on antiques and collectibles. The Antique and Collectible News Service has served publications nationwide, as well as in Canada and Australia. Tragically Claudette died as this volume was in its final stages of preparation. Her contribution however remains.

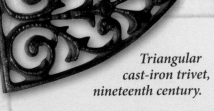

Triangular cast-iron trivet, nineteenth century.

Contents

Framed yard print, early twentieth century.
(Harris Auction Center)

To be informed is to be ever more effective.

Greeting postcard honoring George Washington, early 1900s.

Introduction

From the neighborhood garage sale to the worldwide internet there is a need for individuals to communicate in as specific terms as possible. Buyer, collector, dealer, seller, or someone else in the chain — all benefit from a clear expression of just what (or who) may be the object of their attention.

A firedog does not have four paws and a tail. A lazy susan is not an indifferent person with a common first name. Sandwich glass has nothing to do with food preparation. And as romantic as it might sound the French armoire had nothing to do with love.

To this end we have gathered over the past two decades thousands of antique and collectible terms as well as more than a few of the long lost names of many makers. These entries, more than 5,000 of them, fully extend from

Joseph Aaron and abacus to George Zink and zwiebelmuster.

In a single volume there is access to thousands of proper names, brands, terms, companies, clockmakers, silversmiths, factory operations, names for dolls and toys, and yet more dusty but defining word meanings.

We spent literally 20 years searching through dictionaries, early books on antiques, vintage catalogs, documents, definitions, registers, newspaper clippings, discarded lists, and many other sources as well.

Maybe it won't answer a zillion questions. But it should relatively quickly answer many.

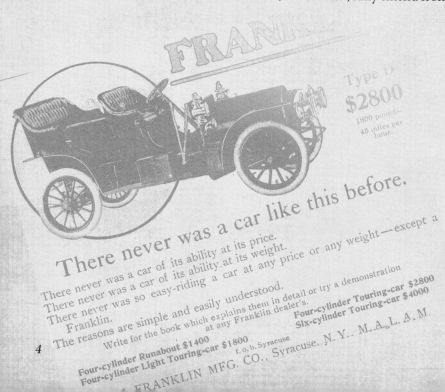

Armoire, eighteenth century, fruitwood.

4

Terms A – Z

Aaron, Joseph: Early 1800s silversmith working in Philadelphia, Pennsylvania.

Abacus: In early furniture the uppermost member of a column capital.

Abattant: Furniture term for early drop-front or fall-front bureau, desk, or secretary.

Abbess watch: Watch worn around the neck, usually made of rock crystal. Made in sixteenth century Switzerland.

Abbott, J. W.: Silversmith operating during the first half of the nineteenth century in Portsmouth, New Hampshire.

Abbott Motor Company: Manufacturer of electric self-starting automobiles in the early 1900s. In 1913 their four-door roadster was priced at $1,700.

ABC Educational Tea Set: Richly lithographed and boxed children's tea sets offered by Butler Brothers in 1921. Made of metal, the sets ranged from six to 20 pieces.

Abdice: An eighteenth century term for a small but sturdy axe.

Abele: Early term sometimes used to designate a white poplar wood.

A.B.R. & Bro.: Listed as a maker of a Confederate bronze howitzer cannon during the Civil War. Located in Vicksburg, Mississippi.

Abrasives (glass): Those gritty substances such as sand and pumice introduced for polishing and cutting glass surfaces.

Abruzzi ware: General term for a specific type of Italian pottery which had the attributes of majolica but also had several different makers.

Acacia: Lovely grained wood of a dull yellow color which was used in fine furniture, mostly as a very sturdy veneer or for inlay. Somewhat similar to the wood of the locust tree. Early cabinet makers considered it stronger yet more elastic than oak, and highly durable.

Acajou: Term used by the French during the colonial era for mahogany wood. A report in 1732 described it as "strong, somewhat light and sometimes reddish, not at all susceptible to worms, and in great demand for making furniture and building ships."

Acanthus leaf: Highly decorative style incorporating the leaf design of the Mediterranean plant of the same name. For a time its intricate detail was craved on fine furniture of the seventeenth and eighteenth centuries, including Chippendale chairs in Philadelphia. Eventually it also accented ceramics, precious metals, and other objects.

Accouterment: Dress or fashion accessory worn or carried, not part of the main clothing or uniform.

Acid etching: Striking process for leaving a permanent image on some types of glass and metal. In the process the background was painted with a protective substance which resisted the effects of acid. Once the background was rinsed off, the original artistic image remained on the surface.

Acier: The name of a remarkable French modeler who crafted many fine figures at the Meissen works in the very early 1800s. Credited with statuettes such as Cries of Paris and the Monkey Orchestra.

Ackerman, David: New York City silversmith working in the 1820s.

Ackermann Co.: Publisher of New York City related postcards, early twentieth century.

Advertising tin, Log Cabin Syrup.

Advertising bank, early 1900s.

Advertising tin, Fatima Cigarettes, early twentieth century.

Advertising postcard for grocery store, 1893.

Ackerman, Rudolph: Noted British publisher of furniture style books of the late eighteenth and early nineteenth centuries, including the Repository.

Ackley, Francis: Silversmith in New York City, ca. 1795.

Acmegraph Co.: Early twentieth century postcard publisher based in Chicago, Illinois.

Acme sifter: Brand of flour sifter sold for 10¢ at S.S. Kresge Co. variety stores during the early twentieth century. The crank offered a japanned handle.

Acorn clock: Distinctive nineteenth century clock with a case fully in the shape of the lowly acorn.

Acorn turning: Notable carved wooden ornament used on many types of furniture and intended to resemble actual nut of the oak tree. It was used chiefly on the backs of Jacobean chairs.

Acroterium: Reference to top corners of highboys, secretaries, and similar colonial furniture in light of the Greek revival among cabinetmakers.

Activated paper dolls: Paper dolls with jointed arms and legs. Makers included Dennison Manufacturing, W. J. Jefferson, and U.S. Toy Manufacturing.

Acton, George: Silversmith doing business in 1790s, New York City.

Acushnet side-wheel steamer toy: Sold for children in the 1880s, complete with steam boiler which would operate for over 30 minutes. Manufacturers advertised "it cannot explode and is perfectly safe."

Adam and Eve needlework: Frequently seen in eighteenth century needlework in America, and even before. Typically the Biblical figures were depicted in contemporary costume on decorative needlecraft of the time.

Adam furniture: Term used to describe the remarkable furniture crafted by Robert Adam and James Adam. The two brothers migrated from Scotland to England where they began furniture making around 1758 in their own shop. Ultimately their work was heavily influenced by their intense study of Italian design. Additionally they revised classical design first seen on early Greek and Roman furniture. It put emphasis on slender straight lines, small tapering legs and narrow moldings. Additionally they incorporated the use of two woods on a single piece of furniture. Ultimately the two brothers were providing elaborate furnishings for entire households using intricate carvings of animals, festoons, and griffins. Generally they refined the tastes in fashionable furniture of the time from the more sublime oak to the more elegant mahogany and satinwood.

Adam, J.: Active silversmith in New York City, ca. 1795.

Adam, John: New Orleans silversmith, active in 1825.

Adams, Emma: (see Columbian)

Adams, Emma (doll): Noted maker of dolls in 1890s Oswego, New York. Early twentieth century production involved Marietta Adams Ruttan.

Adams Glass Company: Early glass operation incorporated in 1812 in the town of Adams, Massachusetts.

Adams, John: Granted a patent in 1865 for a military grenade, Taunton, Massachusetts.

Adams, Jonathan: Silversmith in Philadelphia, Pennsylvania, ca. 1785.

Adams Mass. Arms Co.: Makers of Army and Navy percussion revolvers, patented in 1850s. Located in Chicopee Falls, Massachusetts.

Adams, Pygan: An eighteenth century silversmith based in New London, Connecticut.

Adams, S. G.: Publisher noted for 1904 World's Fair postcards. Based in St. Louis, Missouri.

Adams, Thomas: Noted clockmaker in 1805, Baltimore, Maryland.

Adams Wire Works: A thriving 1820s operation headed by Samuel Adams in Boston which produced a wide-range of wire goods from handy baskets to bird cages.

Addison, George: Baltimore, Maryland, silversmith, ca. 1805.

Adele doll: Distinguished bisque doll of the 1880s, made in France. The 16" figure with blue eyes and long golden hair had a sister doll named Reta. There was also a folding chair accessory.

Adelphia: This term was adopted by the furniture making Adams brothers as their trade mark. Originally it was a Greek word meaning brothers.

Adgate, William: Silversmith operating 1745 to 1780 in Norwich, Connecticut.

Ados clock: Name for an eight-day Swiss-made traveling clock which folded. Also called a camera clock.

Adriance, Edwin: Practicing silversmith during the first half of the nineteenth century in St. Louis, Missouri.

Advertising collectibles: Truly a vast and expanding area of collecting which extends from ashtrays and banks to posters, tins, and even toys. While advertising has been almost as traditional as apple pie, it was not until the advance of lithographic printing techniques late in the nineteenth century that it became really colorful and appealing. The early twentieth century was of course awash with eye-catching treasures from advertising thermometers at general stores to tin-shaped products on the grocer's shelves.

Adz: Rather distinctive hand tool used in early American construction. The tool had a curved blade set hoe-like at right angles with the handle itself. It was used to prepare raw timber for actual building. Experts can sometimes detect the familiar smoothing marks of the adz tool in searching the remains of historic buildings.

Aeolic: Term for use of palm capitals in a classic style of architecture.

Aerial Photography Services: Noted postcard publisher based in Atlanta, Georgia.

Aeriola radio: An early radio produced by Westinghouse. Basically a portable receiving set complete with headphones. Aeriola senior and Aeriola junior were both sold built into wooden cases. Listed in 1923 by Sears, Roebuck and Company.

Aerocar: Automobile produced by the Aerocar Company in early 1900s Detroit, Michigan. The 1906 Aerocar Model A advertised a top speed of 45 miles per hour, cost was $2,800.

Aerodrome: A very early word for flying machine, credited to S. P. Langley in 1896. It was superseded by the word airplane.

Aeronaut: Early term for a balloonist or pilot of a flying machine.

Aetna: (see Billiken)

Affleck, Thomas: Scottish-born cabinet-maker working in Philadelphia in the 1760s.

Agar, Edward: New York City clockmaker, ca. 1765.

Agata glass: A blown glass of the late nineteenth century which was a product of the New England Glass Company in the United States. Such glass had a soft rose color which varied in shade from dark to light. It some ways it was similar to peach blow, but distinguished

Advertising thermometers.

Advertising puzzle, Heinz 57 Varieties, 1920s.

Aerocar advertisement, 1906.

Almanac, Voltaic Belt Company, 1880.

itself with pronounced splattered mottled effect on its glossy surface.

Agate ware: An eighteenth century variety of quartz which involved processing to reach its creamy body and appealing shape. Initially the surface was cleaned with a decorative effect. Later the clays were formed into layers of different colors through a wire cutting process, molded into shape, and fired in a nearby kiln. Much of the ware was attributed to Thomas Whieldon.

Aiguiere: Early term for ewer or pitcher which held water and stood on a table.

Aiken, George: Silversmith of the late eighteenth and early nineteenth centuries in Baltimore, Maryland.

Aikinson, Peabody: A Colonial era clockmaker in 1790s, Concord, Massachusetts.

Ainsworth, Michael: Silversmith located in Fredricksburg, Virginia, ca. 1760.

Aircraft carrier toy: Scale model of aircraft carrier of solid wood which launched planes into the air. Spring-action mechanical action Keystone Toy, middle 1940s.

Airedale (color): Medium dark tan, in 1920s the color of an Airedale dog.

Air-Float face powder: Brand offered ladies of the early 1900s in white or flesh tint. Four ounce box was 10¢.

Airman Limited: Luxury automobile produced by the Franklin Automobile Company in Syracuse, New York. In 1928 it was advertised nationally as "the world's fastest car."

Airship: Term for an elongated dirigible balloon with a propelling system.

Air Ship Los Angeles: German-made mechanical toy of the 1920s showing the airship Los Angeles making trips between German and the United States. It ran on string and clockwork spring, and had a metal base.

Ajoure (furniture): Meaning of pierced design in furniture making or architecture.

Akin, John: Silversmith located in Danville, Kentucky, ca. 1850s.

Akron China Company: Listed as a maker of pottery ware. Established in 1890s Akron, Ohio.

Akron Stoneware Agency: A prolific manufacturer of various lines of stoneware by the 1900s, located in Akron, Ohio. The firm also produced Rockingham and yellow ware. Utilitarian forms included jugs, jars, pitchers, flower pots, bottles, and spittoons.

Alabama Baby (doll): (see Smith, Ella)

Alabama Coon Jigger: Mechanical toy marketed in the 1920s and described in catalogs as a "realistic dancing Negro… in a lively jig." The 10½" toy used a lever-operated spring mechanism.

Alabastron: Depiction of a small, ancient Greek ointment jar in design.

Aladdin Series: Popular 1890s children's book featuring Aladdin and Ali Baba from Arabian Nights, with oil-colored illustrations. Sold in catalogs.

Alamode: A very early term describing fabric used on fine furniture. Typically thin, glossy, black, and silk-like.

Alarum: Term for a very early watch-clock combination which also served as a primitive alarm clock.

Alaska Silverlike: Tableware sold by Sears and Roebuck during the 1920s. A 28-piece set retailed between $5 and $6, depending on the pattern.

Alaska Silverware: Offered by Sears, Roebuck and Company in the early 1900s. It was not plated, but sold as solid metal. The fancy engraved ware was stamped Sears, Roebuck and Co.'s Alaska Silverware. Pieces included forks, knives, and spoons.

Alaska Silver Watch: An open face pocket

watch sold by Sears, Roebuck and Company in 1902. The case was a composition of several metals described as looking like coin silver. Price was $2.40.

Albany slip: So named for the quality clay gleaned from the riverbanks of the Hudson River during the first half of the nineteenth century around Albany, New York. Such material provided a dark brown coloring for stoneware.

Albertype Company: Prolific publisher of postcards featuring fairs and expositions; also regional views. Based in Brooklyn, New York.

Albright, Charles: Maker of 100,000 pairs of military bootees for Federal troops during the Civil War. Located in Mauch Chunk, Pennsylvania.

Alcora: Unique type of chinaware produced by the Count of Aranda and others in Alcora, Spain. A factory began operation in the 1750s. Typically the Alcora porcelain varied in shape but steadfastly had little decoration. It was of high quality but similar to other European ware, and was sometimes misidentified.

Alco Touring Car: Flashy and powerful motor car produced by the American Locomotive Company in 1911. It came with a 60 horsepower engine and a $6,000 price tag.

Alden and Eldridge: Clock making business operated in 1820s, Bristol, Connecticut.

Alden Coffee: A mid-nineteenth century coffee brand which was an early forerunner of dehydrated products. Alden was "cooked" in a paste form after cream and sugar were added. In the 1850s it became known for its familiar glass jar container, and its slogan, "a spoonful makes a cupful."

Alder wood: Whitish wood with pink hue, knots, and curls frequently seen. Staple of eighteenth century country furniture.

Aldis, Charles: New York City silversmith, ca 1815.

Alencon: Finely made lace first crafted in the French town of the same name. Over the years the same richly done lace was duplicated elsewhere in France and Italy. Basically those who crafted it used a very fine thread to weave a design on hexagonal net background. Later flowers and leaves were woven into the basic design using a parchment pattern directly under the net background. Later the process became industrialized and machines replaced the hand-making operation but the overall design was still more or less retained.

Alexander Doll Company: Accomplished maker of Madame Alexander dolls and other quality dolls starting in 1920s, New York City.

Alexander, Isaac: Silversmith operating in New York City in the 1850s.

Alexander, Robert: Noted silversmith, 1820s to 1860s, Rochester, New York.

Alford, Samuel: Listed as a silversmith in 1840, Philadelphia, Pennsylvania.

Alhambra: (see American Encaustic Tiling Co.)

Alice blue (color): Considered medium blue early in the twentieth century.

Alice Daye (doll): Dolls with dried apple heads and cloth bodies. Made by Alice Daye in 1940s and 1950s, Chicago, Illinois.

Alice in Wonderland dishes: Alice in Wonderland, boxed, plastic tea time dishes were produced by Plastic Art in the early 1950s. The 46-piece sets were offered in the Billy and Ruth catalog for $2.98.

Ayer's American Almanac, 1879.

Shaker Almanac of 1886.

Velvet Joe's Almanac, 1922.

Hostetter's Illustrated Almanac, 1910.

Alice in Wonderland doll: China head dolls of the nineteenth century which were not patented by author Lewis Carroll, but simply resembled the little girl in the famed children's book. Hair styles on the dolls were slicked back to a band or circular comb of blue or black. Similar dolls were also made of bisque and wax.

Alice's Adventures in Wonderland game: Boxed game, brightly illustrated, offered in a 1905 holiday catalog for a price of 50¢.

Alkaline glaze (ceramic): Term for using wood ash with clay and water to fire to a certain clear or mottled finish.

Allcock and Allen: Silversmiths based in New York City, 1820s.

Allen, Alexander: Listed in the clock-making trade in 1850s, Rochester, New York.

Allen and Edwards: Silversmith partnership of early 1700s located in Boston, Massachusetts.

Allen, Charles: Colonial silversmith operating in 1760, Boston, Massachusetts.

Allen, Ethan: Granted patent for cartridge making machine, 1861, Worcester, Massachusetts.

Allen, Ethan and Wheelock: Makers of percussion revolvers for U.S. Army and Navy during the Civil War, located in Worcester, Massachusetts.

Allen, Joel: Listed in the 1820s as a silversmith in Middletown, Connecticut.

Allen Motor Company: In 1917 the company produced the Allen automobile for $795. Headquarters of the company was in Fostoria, Ohio.

Allen's Foot Ease: Powered product sold in the 1890s for "nervous feet" and other ills. Produced by Allen Olmsted of Le Roy, New York.

Alligatoring (furniture): Term for alligator-like scaly cracks on furniture caused by the shrinking of previously applied paint or varnish.

Allison furniture: Very fine furniture crafted from early 1800 to the 1830s by Michael Allison, a peer of famed Duncan Phyfe in New York City. Allison, a student of the Sheraton style, was said to have marked some furniture with a punch stamp. Otherwise it was remarkably similar to Phyfe's fine craftsmanship.

Allison, Peter: New York City silversmith doing business in 1790.

Allstate automobile: Short-lived automobile offered by Sears, Roebuck and Company early in the 1950s.

Allwine, Lawrence: Cabinetmaker in late eighteenth century Philadelphia who specialized in Windsor furniture.

Almanacs: America maintained an enduring romance with almanacs for centuries. For countless years they were consumed and saved by Americans in households where there was little else to read. Early almanacs provided information on everything from moon phases for planting to social advice and health care. Over the decades almanacs contained advertising and sometimes were entirely sponsored by a particular product or service. Ultimately there were thousands of different titles, some strikingly colorful in their cover presentations.

Almeria: Regarding textiles, this region in Spain was a great center for silk centuries ago and made the famous tiraz as well as many kinds of striped silk and brocade, in addition to the scarlet silk known as iskalaton.

Almery: Very early term for a relatively small cupboard. During medieval times the almery was a slight cupboard located near the church altar. At the time the enclosed space was used to store items used in religious ceremonies. Llater they were used to used for making donations (alms) to the poor. Such structures, also called alms cupboards or dole cupboards, were put into use in some castles as well.

Almond (color): Listed as light tan in the 1927 Sears and Roebuck catalog.

Almond green (color): Medium light green with grayish cast according to 1920s mail order catalog.

Alms bason: Basically a smaller version of the collection plate used in early American churches. Often decorated, and frequently made of silver.

Aloma (color): Sears and Roebuck catalog of the 1920s listed it as medium tan.

Alpaca: Quality yarn taken from the alpaca goats who were herded in the mountains of South America. Typically such yard was woven with cotton, linen, and silk for a fairly agile and vibrant textile smooth to the touch.

Alphabet blocks: Very prolific wooden toy for children particularly during the last quarter of the nineteenth century. Painted and unpainted, and later embossed and lithographed. Marshall Field and Co. sold elaborate boxed sets with lavish lithographing in the 1890s.

Alphabet ware: Earthenware mugs and plates for children, especially popular for youngsters of the nineteenth century. Such ware was often covered with alphabet patterns, symbols, verses, or combinations of all three.

Alsop, C. R.: Listed as a maker of percussion revolvers, patented in 1860. Located in Middletown, Connecticut.

Also toy auto: Mechanical toy automobile made by Lehmann in Germany. When wound-up, the 4" vehicle ran in circles.

Altmore, Marshall: Noted clockmaker in 1830s, Philadelphia, Pennsylvania.

Aluminum doll: Giebeler-Falk Doll Corporation of New York produced a doll between 1918 and 1920 with aluminum head, hands, and feet. The body was solid wood.

Aluminum match safe: Metal carrier for matches with embossed rose decoration was 10¢ in the 1913 S.S. Kresge Co. variety stores.

Aluminum ware: Offered in many forms for household use in the early 1900s. Retail selections included child's mug, funnel, collapsible drinking cup, salt shaker, jelly mold, and tea percolator.

Amarinth: A type of mahogany found in in Honduras and once imported for making fine furniture. The wood generally ranged from red wine to dark purple in color. Sometimes called Violet wood.

Amber (color): Classified as golden yellow in mail order catalogs of the 1920s.

Amberg, Louis: Founder of Louis Amberg and Son doll making operation early in 1900s, New York City.

Amberina glass: Very fine popular glass produced at the New England Glass Company in Cambridge, Massachusetts. A term credited to Edward Libbey, the glass itself came in a variety shades ranging from amber yellow to ruby red. It was similar to glass later made by the Libbey Glass Company. Some accounts say worker Joseph Lock stumbled upon the process after dropping a ring into a vat of cooling amber glass. Lock patented the process in 1883. Eventually amberina was extended to blown glass and mold pressed glass. The result was an entire line of tableware including pitchers, tumblers, vases, and other items.

Amber onyx (color): Amber color with a so-called marble effect.

Amboina (wood): (see Amboyna)

Seven Barks Almanac, 1887.

Ambrotype of Siamese twins, Civil War era, pressed leather case. (Harris Auction Center)

American Plastic Bricks by Elgo, ca. 1940s.

Amos 'n Andy Fresh Air Taxi toy by Louis Marx Company, ca. 1930s. (Skinner Inc.)

Amboyna: A fine wood used for veneering and inlaying in quality furniture early in America. It was imported from the Spice Islands in the East Indies, where it was cut into thin slices from the burls of the Amboyna tree. Its mottled designed and curly nature left a very distinctive design. Such fine wood, very hard and durable, was put to use in the eighteenth century for inlaying, veneering, and detailed panel work.

Ambrotype: Type of glass background photograph which was developed around 1840 and popular in the decades that followed. The process was named for James Ambrose Cutting, and more or less followed the development of the similar looking daguerreotype. Basically ambrotype involved a square of glass which was treated with chemicals to offer a silvering effect. For full effect the glass photograph had to be viewed at an angle to allow the light to catch various elements of the image.

Ambulantes: The French served tea during the Louis XV era on tables of this type.

Amelung glass: Ware produced by the New Bremen Glass Manufactory which operated over a 10 year period starting in 1784. The factory was founded by John Frederick Amelung in Frederick County, Maryland. Ever the craftsman, Amelung produced a wide range of fine glass items including bottles, bowls, wine glasses, and tableware. Often the pieces included patriotic slogans citing independence and liberty offered by the newly founded United States. The glassware was frequently decorated with engraved crests, monograms, vines, and wreaths. Unlike many American glassmakers of the time, Amelung also went to the trouble of signing and dating many of his engraved glass offerings.

America: Name of a cast iron toy airplane of the early 1930s. "America" was emblazoned across the 17" wing top. Wheels, propeller, and motor shields were nickel-plated.

America Lever: (see Norton, Charles P. and Co.)

American Art Ceramic Company: Began producing pottery in 1901 in Corona, New York.

American Art China Works: Established in 1891 in Trenton, New Jersey. It was formerly known as the Washington Pottery. It crafted what was marketed as American china which featured a thin and translucent body said to resemble Belleek.

American beauty (color): Classified by the 1927 Sears and Roebuck catalog as the color of a deep red rose.

American Card Company: (see Hitchcock, Benjamin)

American China Company: Maker of pottery products. Established in 1897 Toronto, Ohio.

American Crockery Company: A leading producer of stone china, bisque, and white granite goods during the second half of the nineteenth century. A major exhibitor at the Centennial Exhibition of 1876, the prosperous factory was located in Trenton, New Jersey.

American Desiccating Co.: Supplier of military rations for Federal troops during the Civil War, located in 1860s, New York City.

American Doll and Toy Co.: (see Can't Break 'Em doll)

American Eagle toy bank: Striking 8" 1880s mechanical item of iron. Coin in the eagle's beak caused the nest of eaglets to rise, the eagle bent forward and the coin disappeared into the bank.

American Encaustic Tiling Company: Robust factory producing glazed or enameled flooring tiles as early as 1880 in Zanesville, Ohio. Additionally the firm made various relief and embossed tiles. Some of their more elaborate but unglazed tiling was identified by the name Alhambra.

American Flask Company: Maker of percussion caps for Federal troops in 1860s, Waterbury, Connecticut.

American Flint Glass Company: Highly prolific firm which first commenced making glass around 1811 in Boston, Massachusetts. Over the years the factory was relocated to various places, but the output of cut and pressed glass continued in significant numbers. American Flint Glass officially ended its extensive operations in 1870.

American Fork and Hoe Company: (see Evansville Toy)

American Gold Pen Co.: Maker of gold pens for the U.S. government during the Civil War, located in 1860s, New York City.

American Locomotive Co.: (see Alco Touring Car)

American Maid: Popular rag doll sold in the early 1900s by Sears, Roebuck and Company. Costumed and wearing a bonnet, they were offered in sizes ranging from 11" to 16". Price was 25¢ to 50¢.

American plastic bricks: Interlocking toy bricks sold in boxed sets. Made in the early 1950s by Halsam Products Company and retailed at $3.75.

American Porcelain Manufacturing Company: This firm was incorporated in 1854 in Gloucester, New Jersey. Largely experimental, the often translucent and thin wares were usually delicate. Some were marked at the bottom, A.P.M. Co.

American Pottery Manufacturing Company: First organized in 1833, it produced various kinds of pottery early on at Jersey City, New Jersey. It became one of the first American companies to incorporate the English method of transfer printing in decorating its wares.

American Powder Co.: Supplier of gunpowder to Federal troops during the Civil War, located in South Acton, Massachusetts.

American Princess: Lovely doll offered by Montgomery Ward catalog in 1914. Its attributes included long curly hair, white teeth, and closing eyes. The 20" doll sold for 98¢.

American Roadster: Proud product of the American Motor Company in 1913, Indianapolis, Indiana. It offered "underslung" construction involving production while the frame remained upside down. For a time the product line was identified as American Underslung.

American Scout automobile: Automobile priced in 1912 at $1,250 and sold by American Motors in Indianapolis, Indiana.

American Terra-Cotta and Ceramic Company: Located near Chicago in the early 1900s, the firm produced Teco ware. Stamped with the single word of identification, it bore a gray to green tint glaze and relief designs.

American Underslung: (see American Roadster)

American vermilion (color): Listed in the Sears and Roebuck catalog of 1927 as brilliant red.

American Watch Co.: Producer of watches in gold or silver case for the Federal government during the Civil War. The company was located in Waltham, Massachusetts. Other contractors

Arcade card of Janette McDonald, 1940s.

Arcade card of Lana Turner, 1940s.

using the American Watch identification were Appleton, Tracy & Co. of Waltham, Massachusetts; P.S. Barlett, of Waltham, Massachusetts; and William Ellery, of Boston, Massachusetts.

Ames, Horace: Listed in the 1850s as a clockmaker in New York City.

Ames Manufacturing Co.: Supplier of swords and sabers to U.S. forces during the Civil War, located in Chicopee, Massachusetts.

Ames, Nathan: Patented a knife-fork-spoon combination for military use in 1861. Located in Saugus Center, Massachusetts.

Ames, Oliver & Co.: Contracted to provide shovels for Federal troops during the Civil War.

Amethyst: Basically a purplish colored semi-precious stone which was especially popular among the upwardly mobile of England during the nineteenth century. During the Victorian era, Queen Victoria was said to have set the trend by turning from mourning jewelry to the more colorful amethyst. Earrings, necklaces, and brooches were sometimes part of entire sets of amethyst jewelry of the Victorian era.

Amethyst (color): Bluish purple according to the 1920s-era mail order catalogs.

Ameya: Korean potter credited with originating Raku ware used for the ceremony of tea-drinking as early as the sixteenth century. Raku meant enjoyment, and the ware was given a gold seal and special mark.

Amish doll: For two centuries the Amish have crafted cloth dolls for their children inwardly with love and care, but outwardly with faceless features. Oddly there is no written rule for the folk dolls without faces. However both historians and members of the religious sect cite

the biblical commandment forbidding "any graven image, or any likeness of anything that is in heaven above, or that is in the earth beneath…" During the nineteenth century most dolls of this type were of single-piece construction with head and arms being part of the overall torso. The doll's clothing was often made from scraps of the family's garments.

Amish quilt: Perhaps the most appealing of all the historic nineteenth century quilts are those which were rendered bold and bright by the enduring Amish religious sect. The striking designs and strong colors that were applied in such a skillful way make these past works of art highly sought by collectors today.

Amorina (Amorini): Sweet sounding Italian word for cupids or cherubs which once appeared on elaborately carved furniture of the baroque style in that country. During the Renaissance similar highly-detailed images were used to highlight all manner of fine furniture in England.

Amoskeag Manufacturing Co.: Contracted to provide rifled muskets to Federal troops during the Civil War, located in Manchester, New Hampshire.

Amos 'N Andy Taxicab: Billed as the original toy vehicle representing the Fresh Air Taxi Cab Company of America. A wind-up vehicle as well as a wind-up figures of Amos and Andy were produced by Marx in connection to a popular radio show of the 1930s.

Ampas: A richly done textile similar to brocades. Popular for wearing in France during the reign of Louis XII and Louis IV.

Amphora: Gradually the term came to

Arcade, McCormick-Deering Wagon, early twentieth century.

Arcade, Yellow parlor coach, ca. 1927.

define an ornamental vase having an oval-shaped body. Initially it defined a vase with two handles and a curving neck to shoulders body which was clearly tapered and defined. Some place the origin of the amphora container as one used for wine.

Ampol mechanical toy: Cart-like vehicle which came with revolving parasol that displayed a map of the north pole. Made in Germany and sold in the United States during the 1920s.

Amstel: Historic porcelain produced in what was said to be Holland's oldest porcelain factory near Amsterdam. Products of hard paste, somewhat similar in appearance to Dresden works, were made generally from 1764 until 1810.

Amulet: Dating to ancient times, the amulet charm was worn about the neck to ward off real or imagined dangers. At times the specific item ranged from an animal's tooth to a precious gem. Other amulets amounted to polished glass or perhaps a parchment of enclosed paper. In the colonies of New England when witchcraft was a great fear the populace sought protection by wearing assorted amulets.

Anchor Pottery Company: Pottery firm first established during the 1890s in Trenton, New Jersey.

Anderson Carpet: During the 1840s carpets sold by New York dealer Hiram Anderson were marked with his name. Anderson was not a maker of carpets but instead was simply a seller of fine quality carpets, mostly from Europe.

Anderson Clock Company: Ambitious firm which briefly excelled in clock making of the 1820s. Operation was housed in Marietta, Ohio.

Anderson, David D.: Doing business as a clockmaker in 1830s, Marietta, Ohio.

Anderson, Hiram: (see Anderson Carpet)

Anderson, Mary: Commercial artist during the first half of the twentieth century and one of the creators of the Morton Salt girl. Her model in 1921 was niece Dorothy Anderson Tormoehlen.

Andirons: Central to the Colonial fireplace, and sometimes known as firedogs, they were originally crafted of wrought iron. Toward the eighteenth century finer andirons were made of brass. Early examples were often ball topped.

Andras and Richard: Silversmiths located in New York City, around 1795.

Andreas, Abraham: Silversmith in Bethlehem, Pennsylvania, ca. 1780.

Andrews, Benjamin: Provider of army trucks to Federal troops during the Civil War, based in Philadelphia, Pennsylvania.

Andy Gump (toy vehicle): Arcade Manufacturing Company produced an Andy Gump toy car and figure in the late 1920s. Old 348 was bright red with a cast-iron body. Andy was the sport-hat-wearing driver.

Angel: Starting in the seventeenth century, a European pewter maker's mark. The angel was sometimes depicted flying or standing with outstretched arms holding a palm branch or sword. Reportedly the so-called touch mark was only used on metal of the highest quality.

Angel bed: Term for an early children's bed which provided a small, plain frame without posts. It could sometimes be stored under larger beds.

Anglo-American Postcard Company: Noted publisher of holiday postcards early in the twentieth century.

Anglo-Japanese (furniture): Style of

Arcade, toy truck, ca. 1920s.

Arcade, delivery truck from 1927 catalog.

15

Armchair, Chippendale, cherry, upholstered, ca. 1770s. (Skinner Inc.)

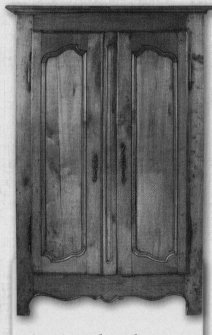

Armoire, eighteenth century, fruitwood. (Skinner Inc.)

decoration which incorporated Japanese design along with certain Gothic images. Developed in 1860s England and further enhanced by the 1876 Centennial Exhibition in Philadelphia.

Anna Pottery: (see Kirkpatrick, C. & W.)

Annealing (glass): Reference to the slow cooling of hot glass to prevent stress within an object's structure.

Annely Pottery: Earthenware of "eight different sorts" produced during the 1750s in Whitestone, New York.

Anniversary clock: Reference to the American manufactured Four Hundred Day clock. Such clocks typically ran for at least one year without winding.

Annular jug: Ceramic drinking vessel of the eighteenth century with a hollow ring or double-hollow ring which could hold two different types of wine at the same time.

Ansco Company: Early twentieth century makers of cameras and Speedex film. Ansco Vest-Pocket No. 2 sold for $18.50 in 1917. Ansco was based in Binghamton, New York.

Ansonia Clock Company: A major manufacturer of clocks in the nineteenth century, located in Ansonia, Connecticut.

Anthemion: A Greek ornament added to early furniture of the Colonial era based upon the foliage and flowery bloom of the aromatic plant, chamomile. Basically a Greek Honeysuckle.

Anthony dump truck (toy): Toy dump truck which actually dumped. Based on the full-sized vehicle made by Anthony Company. Made of cast iron, circa 1920s.

Anthony, L. D.: Listed as a silversmith active in 1805, Providence, Rhode Island.

Anti-Macassar (furniture): Term for a small doily used to protect the back or arms of early upholstered furniture. Used to counteract Macassar hair oil. The term tidy was also used.

Antimony: An element used in some pewter to prevent tarnishing that offered a bluish-white color. The alloy, when used in large amounts, gave the pewter a certain shine. When higher amounts of lead were used, instead the result was a dulling effect.

Antiquarianism: A term for the fad of copying earlier antique styles late in the nineteenth century.

Antique: Truly in the eye of the beholder. The United States Tariff Act, passed in 1930, offered that "works of art, except rugs and carpets, collections in illustrations of the progress of the arts, works in bronze, marble, terra cotta, parian, pottery or porcelain, artistic antiquities and objects of art or ornamental or educational value, which have been made prior to 1830 may enter the United States free of duty." In other words it took 100 years to qualify. Further the tariff act stipulated musical instruments need to be at least 130 years old, and rugs and carpets need to be 230 years old. Even the measurement of 100 years might be excessive according to the *Antiques Dictionary* of Ethel Doan written in 1949. "Surely much of the glass we now search for and prize is not anywhere near the hundred mark in age," said Doan. The writer added that some prefer to classify an antique as something which is outmoded or that which is no longer manufactured.

Antique gold (color): Listed in 1927 as a deep orange yellow by the Sears and Roebuck catalog.

Antique ivory (color): Very deep cream, pale yellow as noted in the Sears and Roebuck catalogs of the 1920s.

Antique Spanish brass (color): Described as deep golden orange in the Sears and Roebuck catalog of the 1920s.

Antique verdigris (color): Noted in the 1920s era Sears catalog as a greenish bronze.

Anti-Saloon League: Federation of organizations promoting early twentieth century prohibition of liquor traffic.

Antwerp blue (color): According to the Sears and Roebuck catalog of 1927, a dark blue.

Apothecary: Term for bottles or jars specifically used by pharmacists for storage and dispensing medicinal product.

Appenzell: Early form of handmade embroidery which had its origins in Switzerland. Typically it involved the use of a very light blue thread on very white linen. In the nineteenth century it was exported to the United States in significant quantities and used in a wide range of items from baby clothing to women's fashions. Later a machine-made version of the Appenzell was instituted, which involved white rather than blue embroidering thread.

Apple corers: Truly outstanding small silver accessories of this type were part of elegant tableware towards the latter part of the eighteenth century in America. Generally in the same design as larger pieces.

Apple green (color): Basically a light green according to Sears and Roebuck in the 1920s.

Apple Man moving toy: Mechanical toy presented in 1911 and described as "cloth dressed Negro sitting in apple cart with painted apples." When wound the toy ran backwards with man moving his feet.

Apple shovel: Fully wooden shovel used for scooping apples when apple cider was a very popular family drink. Cider makers felt only wood, treenware, avoided altering the flavor of the harvested fruit.

Appleton, George: Ca. 1850s silversmith located in Salem, Massachusetts.

Appleton, Tracy & Co.: (see American Watch Co.)

Appleton, William: Cabinetmaker of late eighteenth and early nineteenth centuries in Salem, Massachusetts.

Apple wood: Exceptional fruit wood which was sometimes used in crafting fine furniture during some of the seventeenth century and much of the eighteenth century. Apple wood being a soft wood, in contrast to the hard woods of oak and maple, was often painted rather than being finished in the natural glowing color of other woods. It was used from time to time both in England and America.

Appliqué: Term for candle bracket when attached to the wall.

Appliqué patchwork: Regarding early quilt making, the term means the applying of colored materials at intervals for the pattern to be silhouetted on the quilt background.

Appointment clock: Unusual late nineteenth century slot machine device. A time or appointment was written on an ivorine table. At the appointed hour an alarm rang and the tablet was ejected.

Apron (clothing): Early twentieth century variety stores offered a range of aprons from lace trimmed to so-called lawn tea types. All were 10¢ each.

Apron (furniture): When used in regard to furniture of the past, the apron was that horizontal piece of wood placed directly beneath a table or chair seat. Usually it extended between the legs.

Armoire in Louis XVI style, carved panel doors. (Skinner Inc.)

Arranbee Doll Company's My Dream Baby, ca. 1924.

Art nouveau lamp with naturalistic leaves, early 1900s.
(Harris Auction Center)

Classic art nouveau lamp, early 1900s. (Harris Auction Center)

Such an apron, sometimes called a skirt, might have a lower edge that was shaped or straight depending upon the overall design of the piece.

Aquamanile: Early term for a metal jug which held perfumed water, and was passed around between courses of the main meal.

Arabesque: During the Tudor reign in England, this type of ornamentation was used to adorn flat surfaces of furniture. Derived from the Moors in Spain, it was sometimes carved in low relief, inlaid, or simply painted onto the design.

Arcade: Early furniture term dealing with the curved decoration representing a series of arches. Most often seen on British and French-made chairs.

Arcade card: For over half of the twentieth century arcade cards could be found in special sections of amusement parks in major cities and in the traveling carnivals that visited America's small towns. These graphic cards featuring an assortment of personalities from movie stars to sports legends were one of the few lasting items dispensed in the busy penny arcades themselves. Usually about postcard sized, they were typically printed in black and white but were sometimes tinted in bright colors. Major manufacturers included the Mutoscope Reel Company and the Exhibit Supply Company of Chicago. Exhibit became so dominate with their sports cards that by the 1920s they were sometimes all referred to as simply exhibit cards.

Arcade lawn mower (toy): Toy lawn mowers were made by Arcade in the late 1920s. Made of cast iron and enameled they came in three different sizes. The Clipper Lawn Mower was 36" long and had 4" wheels.

Arcade Manufacturing Company: Extensive producer of quality toy vehicles, farm toys, and other related toys in the 1920s and 1930s. Advertised "they look real," headquartered at Freeport, Illinois.

Arch (clock): Upper part of a circle on early clocks. The arch topped cases and dials.

Arched Queen Anne mirror: Tall and narrow framed mirror usually with balancing curves and slight central peak. Typically fancy grained walnut veneer. Ca. 1710 to 1730s.

Archer, Dr. Junius: Owner of the Bellona Arsenal foundry which produced Confederate cannon, including the Columbiads. Located in Chesterfield County, Virginia.

Archie, John: Silversmith operating in New York City, 1760s.

Architectural blocks: Sets of wooden blocks sold for children's entertainment in the late nineteenth century. Large sets contained over 100 blocks plus wagon and wheel shapes.

Architrave: Reference to the molded or flat beam resting on and extending between columns in post-and-beam construction.

Arctic Circle Enterprises: A latter twentieth century publisher of regional postcards, based in Anchorage, Alaska.

Areo-Speeders: Spring action mechanical toy with two revolving metal airplanes. Brightly lithographed item made by Marx in the 1930s.

Argand lamp: Nifty forerunner of the kerosene lamp developed in Switzerland during the 1780s. The lamp was the work of Aime Argand who spent considerable time refining burners and lamp wicks. Argand's insight produced a tubular necked burner on a lamp which allowed the air to circulate inside the flame. Given a woven wick and an accompanying metal tube connected with an oil reservoir, it produced a bright light with little smoke. Later the principle was further enhanced on American kerosene lamps of the nineteenth and early twentieth centuries.

Argus (glass): Thumbprint-like pattern on early pressed glass. It involved a series of regularly spaced indentations.

Arita: Area in Japan which produced an early form of richly decorated porcelain. Arita wares were emblazoned with red, blue, and gold.

Arkitoy: Construction toy set offered in the late 1920s by Sears, Roebuck Company and others. Boasted 50 to 398 pieces of hardwood, wheels, pulleys, nuts, and bolts.

Armchair: It would be difficult to determine the fairest armchair in all of American history. There were so many styles with so many origins. Toward the middle of the eighteenth century colonial America was enriched with beautifully crafted armchairs following highly admired Queen Anne and Chippendale styles. The most costly of these were made of cherry, mahogany, and walnut.

Arm lantern: Popular lighting device of the mid to late nineteenth century for use on railroads and in similar capacities. It allowed for the arm to be inserted into a tin ware band for portability without hand carrying.

Armoire: An old but continuing French term for a particular cupboard or clothing chest. Initially the chest was literally a place for storing a full suit of armor and accessories. Eventually armor was no longer fashionable but the armoire gradually became a place to store clothing instead.

Armorial form: This is primarily the use of the coat-of-arms or similar crests and heraldry in overall designs.

Armour and Company: Early 1900s publisher of American Girl postcard series.

Arm pad: Reference to a stuffed or upholstered pad attached to the arm of an early American chair.

Arms, T. N.: Silversmith in Albany, New York, ca. 1850.

Armstrong, John: Philadelphia based silversmith, ca. 1810 – 1815.

Arm support (furniture): An early reference to the upright attachment supporting the front end of a chair arm. Term was used for either the extended fore leg, or a separate member from the seat rail.

Army drab (color): Known as a medium shade of tan with a greenish cast in 1920s mail order catalogs.

Arnold, Jared: Clockmaker located in Amber, New York, ca. 1820s – 1840s.

Arnold Print Works: Products included cloth dolls in late nineteenth century and early twentieth century, North Adams, Massachusetts.

Arnoux, Anthony: Contracted with the Federal government in 1861 to make 15,000 Army uniforms. Located in New York City.

Arranbee Doll Company: Used the initials R and B in marking dolls made during the first half of the twentieth century in New York City.

Arrandale & Co.: Makers of "New Army Watches" under Federal contract during the Civil War. Located in New York City.

Arris (furniture): In connection with early furniture this was the sharp edge formed by two intersecting plain

Auburn Rubber Company red race car.

Audubon illustration of geese from 1860s re-issue of artist's works. (Skinner Inc.)

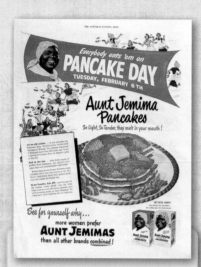

Aunt Jemima in Saturday Evening Post *advertisement, 1951.*

Autograph album from 1896.

surfaces. This corner or angle was sometimes prone to wear or damage.

Arrow back chair: In the nineteenth century this basic chair was a product of numerous factories in Connecticut. Using readily available hardwoods, workers processed entire sets of chairs for use in America's kitchens. Typically the arrow back chair was both painted and stenciled. The arrow term related to the fact that each chair had four to five spindles which provided an arrow shape to the overall chair. Some chair lines bore arms and some did not. For a limited time there was also a line of arrow back rockers in production.

Arsenal Pottery: A subsidiary of the Mayer Pottery Manufacturing Company. Considered in the early 1900s to be one of the few operations in the United States then producing majolica ware. Some of the finest efforts were Toby pitchers or jugs.

Art Fabric Mills: A producer of cloth or rag dolls between 1905 and 1910. Issues included a sateen French doll, Uncle, Baby, Billy, and Newly Wed Kid.

Art glass: Term for glass of remarkable quality produced during the latter part of the nineteenth century mostly in the United States. It marked a golden era of techniques and elements put to ultimate effect for remarkable coloring.

Articulation (doll): Reference to the jointing characteristics of particular types of dolls.

Articulus toys: Produced from the middle of the nineteenth century to the end of the nineteenth century, these were paper toys given movement by warm air. Through a series of wire connected parts and flywheels, these toys would display movement when placed over a warm-air register or near

a stovepipe. Most were illustrated with scenes of domestic activity, sports, or various crafts.

Artino Company: (see Branning, E. F.)

Art Nouveau: This rich decorative style flourished in Europe as the twentieth century approached, and eventually reached into the fashionable households of America. Basically it relied on the flowing vines and winding flowers of nature. It was sometimes combined with the straight-edged geometric look of colored glass. It was a look that encompassed everything from jewelry to fine furniture in what some called a renewal of Europe's artistic ideals.

Art pottery (ceramic): Generally applied to much decorative ware of the twentieth century. Originally meant to denote work of studio potters in limited numbers.

Arts and Crafts: Reference to a movement in the late nineteenth century and early twentieth century by various groups first in England and later in the United States. Basically an effort to return to hand craftsmanship and thus improve industrial art design and quality. It is perhaps best exemplified by Roycrofters in East Aurora, New York, and Rookwood Pottery in Cincinnati, Ohio.

A. Schoenhut Company: (see Schoenhut Company [toys])

Ashby, James: A Colonial period clockmaker operating in 1770s, Boston, Massachusetts.

Ashes of roses (color): Considered a soft shade of medium rose in Sears and Roebuck catalogs of the 1920s.

Ashfield Pottery: Relatively obscure ware produced during the middle of the nineteenth century in Massachusetts. Using about a half dozen workers, the pottery produced household stoneware including jugs, jars, crocks, and churns. It operated from around 1850 to 1857.

Ash, Gilbert: The first of three generations of cabinetmakers in New York City. Noted for Windsor chairs and succeeded by son Thomas Ash in the latter eighteenth century.

Ash glaze (ceramic): Reference to the use of wood ash to form lye in pottery making. The lye is then combined with other materials to produce a particular fired finish.

Ashmead, James: As of 1785, a silversmith in Philadelphia, Pennsylvania.

Ashold, Abel: Granted Civil War era patent for military camp stools, located in Garrettsville, Ohio.

Ashville Postcard Co.: Middle twentieth century publisher of regional postcards, based in Asheville, North Carolina.

Ash wood: Remarkably durable and hard wood which is cream white in color. Early cabinetmakers selected the relatively small tree for sturdy furniture including the top rails of Windsor chairs. A fairly bendable wood with a long and fibrous grain.

Astbury ware: A distinguished raised floral decoration stoneware named for English developer John Astbury. Such stoneware was produced early in the eighteenth century in the Staffordshire region of England. Around 1720 the innovative Astbury created a formula which introduced flint in the body of his Astbury ware, thus allowing for greater hardness in the firing process.

Aster carving: Theme used on chests in early Connecticut in which a three-flower or carved sunflower design was applied to the central panel.

Astragal design: Term used to define a small convex, beaded molding which was usually placed at the junction of a pair of doors on early cabinets, cupboards, secretaries, and bookcases.

Astral lamp: Notable lighting device created by Benjamin Thompson of Woburn, Massachusetts, in the nineteenth century. Ironically, however, the lamp was known as the Count Rumford astral lamp, based on an honorary title awarded to Thompson some years earlier in Bavaria. It was considered a significant improvement over the earlier Argand lamps because of a lessening of the shadow cast.

Astronomical clock: Remarkable early clocks which were elaborate and detailed enough to provide sunrise, sunset, moon phases, and even the movement of the tides. With all the extras, their price at the time was considered relatively astronomical, too.

Athenia (color): Classified in the Sears and Roebuck catalogs of the 1920s as a medium to dark old rose.

Athletic baby: Doll offered in 1911 by Sears, Roebuck and Company. Composition head, "modeled from life," and sold in two different sizes.

Athletic Girl Series: Set of postcards offered in 1913 variety stores featuring females rowing, swimming, and playing basketball. Price for five was 5¢.

Athol furniture: Name given to a wide range of furniture produced during the 1830s in Athol, Massachusetts.

Atkinson, Isaac: Philadelphia silversmith, ca. 1820s.

Atkinson, James: Doing business as a clockmaker in 1750s Boston, Massachusetts.

Atlantes (furniture): Decorative use of male figures, often grotesque, instead of columns or pedestals in early furniture.

Atlas trimmers: Brand of scissors offered in the notions department of S.S. Kresge Co. in the early 1900s.

Automobilia in the form of a 1950s General Motors polishing cloth tin.

Automobilia, Standard Oil Company road map of Illinois, 1936.

Gene Autry signed photo-graph, ca. 1938.

Gene Autry souvenir pro-gram, 1957.

Atlee, Charles: A silversmith in 1840s, Philadelphia, Pennsylvania.

Atmosphere (color): Regarded in the 1920s as a very light tan, lighter even than champagne.

Atwater, J. H. and Co.: Provider of military camp kettles and mess pans for Federal troops during the Civil War, located in New York City.

Atwood, Wm. H.: (see Columbia Daumon Victoria)

Auburn Post Card Manufacturing Co.: Prolific publisher of early twentieth century patriotic postcards, based in Auburn, Indiana.

Auburn Rubber Company: Maker of quality rubber toys starting in the 1930s. Originally based in Auburn, Indiana. The operation produced toy automobiles, race cars, farm tractors, and sports figures. Relocated to Mexico in the early 1960s and closed the same decade.

Aubusson carpet: Finely woven carpet produced starting in the seventeenth century in Aubusson, France. Originally such carpets were handwoven and attained worldwide appreciation for their craftsmanship. Later Aubusson carpets and other tapestries were mass produced by mechanical means and lacked the esteemed quality of the prior era.

Aubusson upholstering: Rich textile used to adorn chairs and sofas during the reign of Louis XIV. Various designs were incorporated with silk brocade and the image of colored flowers.

Auction card game: Offered as a "social game" for children and adults of the 1880s. Boxed Game of Auction was priced at 25¢ in The Youth's Companion.

Audubon, John James: Noted early nineteenth century ornithologist who gained attention in the United States for watercolor drawings of American birds. Contributed illustrations to The *Birds of America* by Robert Havell, Jr. published in installment during the 1820s and 1830s. Some 435 Audubon prints were produced. Various prints were later reproduced.

Augusta Arsenal: Supplier of military items including 12-pound Napoleon cannons for Confederate forces during the Civil War. Located in Augusta, Georgia.

Aunt Jemima: Fictional character based on the emergence of the late nineteenth century Aunt Jemima Mills Company. By the early twentieth century customers of the pancake mix firm were offered a whole family of cloth cut-and-sew advertising dolls. Buckwheat Flour also offered the dolls.

Aurene glass: Late nineteenth century and early twentieth century product of the Steuben Glass Works. A very striking iridescent glass which was sometimes compared to immortal Tiffany glass. Later produced at the Corning Glass Factory in Corning, New York.

Aurora Tool Co.: Also Aurora Independent Machine Tool Company, located in early twentieth century Aurora, Illinois. Makers of the Thor motorcycle from 1903 to 1920.

Austin, Benjamin: Silversmith based in Portsmouth, New Hampshire, ca. 1775.

Austin, Isaac: Philadelphia clockmaker, ca. 1780 to 1800.

Austin, John: Active from 1810 to 1820 as a silversmith in Charleston, South Carolina.

Austin, Richard: Crafting pewter in 1790s and early 1800s, Boston, Massachusetts.

Authors card game: Advertised in the *Youth's Companion* as early as the 1880s, a card game with a sketch of the authors and names of principle characters in their books. Initially sold for 25¢.

Autobus toy: Identified in 1911 catalogs as Lehman's Autobus, it was made of sheet metal. It offered a spiral stairway in the rear, and overall vehicle movement was keywound.

Autocar: Both two passenger and four passenger cars were manufactured in the early 1900s by the Autocar Company in Ardmore, Pennsylvania.

Auto dump wagon (toy): Late 1920s toy vehicle which came with a pull lever to actually dump the hopper of the truck. It was painted red and gold.

Auto fire engine (toy): Item produced by Arcade Manufacturing in the late 1920s. Made of cast iron, it was finished in red enamel and came with a driver and a rear tank.

Auto Garage (toy): Heavy cardboard item offered in 1911 Sears, Roebuck and Company catalog. Painted letters identified it as Auto Garage with stalls both for touring car and racing car.

Autograph albums: During the Victorian era and even through the early 1920s, autograph albums for children and young adults were quite popular. Covers were often embellished with elaborate and colorful decorations while pages were filled with the hand-written messages of classmates and friends.

Automata doll: One of the great mechanical accomplishments of the nineteenth century was the automata doll. Such dolls with their remarkable movement were firmly established in the marketplace of the 1870s. Combining earlier Swiss-made musical movements with the finest bisque dolls, French makers also spared no expense in dressing the automata dolls with the finest costumes and adding the most detailed accessories.

Automatic Toys Works: (see Creeping Baby)

Automobilia: Vast area of collectibles dating actually from the 1890s. Early in the twentieth century American consumers chose from over 1,500 different makes of automobile. Spin offs included advertisements, products, license plates, signs, manuals, postcards, and road maps.

Autry, Gene: Orvon Gene Autry became one of the twentieth century's most famous singing cowboy movie stars. Starred in film, sang Rudolph the Red-Nosed Reindeer, endorsed products from bedspreads to toy pistols.

Autumn brown (color): According to Sears and Roebuck in the 1920s.

A.V.C: Initials found on buttons on buckles of some Confederate soldiers during the Civil War. Stood for Alabama Volunteer Corps.

Aventurine: Term used to describe the application of tiny clippings of gold wire to the surface of early lacquered furniture.

Averill, Georgene: One of the pioneers in the creation of "baby" type dolls which revolutionized the doll market during the first quarter of the twentieth century. Averill and husband James also launched the Averill Manufacturing Company and Georgene Novelties Inc.

Avery, John and Robert: Father and son silversmith operation in Preston, Connecticut which operated from late eighteenth century to early nineteenth century.

Avery tractor (toy): Cast iron toy tractor made in the late 1920s by Arcade Manufacturing and in the 1930s by Hubley Toys. It was 4½" to 5" long and was painted green with red wheels. It bore the name Avery in raised letters.

Aviation collectible advertisement depicting Amelia Earhart, 1928.

Aviation collectible, framed vintage photograph of Charles Lindbergh.

Baby Snooks doll by Ideal Toy Company, ca. 1930s.

Band collectible, band member in uniform, dated 1953.

Aviation collectibles: The world of aviation collectibles is as old as Wilbur and Orville Wright and just as far reaching as any airlines in the world. As with many other collecting areas, items of aviation that seemed insignificant a few years ago are now sought out. Historic aviation personalities such as Charles Lindbergh and Amelia Earhart are major, but interest also extends to discarded flight schedules and outdated airline schedules.

Avis Lee: Maker of hand-carved wooden dolls in the 1940s. They were sold at Marshall Field's in Chicago, Illinois.

Avodire: Light colored African wood imported to America and used on occasion in Colonial cabinetmaking.

Avon Pottery: The small firm enjoyed a brief nineteenth century existence in Cincinnati, Ohio. Its wares were said to somewhat resemble the efforts of early Rockwood pottery. Reportedly it produced wares with gradual shadings of brown, pink, and light brown in the form of vases and figural images.

Ayers, Samuel: Listed as a leading clockmaker in early 1800s, Lexington, Kentucky.

Ayres, Martha Oathout: A distinguished American artist who lent her talents on occasion to the design of fine china head dolls.

Azure blue (color): Judged a light blue or sky blue in the Sears catalogs of the 1920s.

Babbier, Peter: Silversmith active in Philadelphia, Pennsylvania, during the 1820s.

Babbitt & Crossman: Operation of pewter craftsmen in 1820s, Taunton, Massachusetts.

Babcock, Samuel: Early eighteenth century silversmith based in Saybrook, Connecticut.

Baby Alive (doll): Doll that really eats and drinks. Advertised on TV and sold in 1973 Montgomery Ward catalog for $9.88.

Baby Beans (doll): Bean bag doll which talked in a lisping baby voice. Listed at $5.77 in the 1973 Montgomery Ward catalog.

Baby blue (color): A very light blue according to a 1920s Sears catalog.

Baby Delight: A soft body doll that walked and talked in the early 1930s. Price in the Montgomery Ward catalog was $3.33.

Baby pink (color): Very light pink, according to the 1927 Sears and Roebuck catalog

Baby shawl: Dime store bestseller in 1900s, the 25" square flannel item was 10¢.

Baby Snooks: Fictional radio child of comedy portrayed by Fannie Brice in the 1930s and 1940s. Character was depicted in a creative composition doll from Ideal Toy and Novelty Company, on a tin pail, and a few other items.

Baby Tenderlove: Made by Mattel and heavily marketed on 1970s television. The vinyl-foam doll spoke baby-talk phrases. A "newborn" Baby Tenderlove doll was smaller and did not speak.

Baby Wendy (doll): Infant-type vinyl dolls sold by Montgomery Ward in the early 1970s. The 18" doll drank, wet, and could be given a real bath. Ward's price was $9.49.

Bachmann Bros.: (see Plasticville, U.S.A.)

Back-Firing Ford: Toy vehicle in the image of a 1917 Model T Ford. Squeezing a trigger caused the plastic car to bang and bounce. Made by Precision Specialties in the early 1950s.

Back friend: Common early colonial term for chair at a time when stools were frequently more common than seating with a supportive back.

Bacon Mfg. Co.: Listed as a maker of Navy cartridge revolver, patented in 1864. Located in Norwich, Connecticut.

Badder, Isaac: Noted clockmaker in the 1830s, Dayton, Ohio.

Badger, Thomas: Noted pewterer doing business in late eighteenth century and early nineteenth century, Boston, Massachusetts.

Badman clock: Tall cased clocks made around 1780s by Joseph Badman of Colebrookdale, Pennsylvania.

Baecher, Anthony: Potter working in redware in 1870s and 1880s, Winchester, Virginia.

Baggott, Joseph: (see Gilliland's Brooklyn Glass Works)

Bagnell: Prominent clockmaker in early eighteenth century Boston who specialized in Queen Anne style tall case clocks. Mahogany or maple cases housed brass or wooden works.

Bag table (furniture): Basically a term for a late eighteenth or early nineteenth century work table which bore a fabric bag beneath it.

Baguette (furniture): Decorative application to early furniture usually in the form of delicate bead molding.

Bail: A handle consisting of a simple metal hoop.

Bailey and Brothers: Clockmakers located in 1840s, Utica, New York.

Bailey and Co.: Supplier of swords and sabers to U.S. government during the Civil War, located in Philadelphia, Pennsylvania.

Bailey, B. M.: Silversmith doing business in late nineteenth century, Ludlow, Vermont.

Bailey's tires: Early automobile tire made by C. J. Bailey in Boston, Massachusetts. They promised "perfect control of the car on all conditions."

Bailey, William: Listed as an active clockmaker in 1820s and 1830s, Philadelphia, Pennsylvania.

Baise: Term used for coarse material reportedly used to clothe both slaves and servants in early America. A newspaper advertised such material in the latter eighteenth century.

Baker coupe: Automobile produced in the early twentieth century as a luxury vehicle. It was manufactured by the Baker Motor Vehicle Company in Cleveland, Ohio.

Baker, George: Listed in the silversmith trade around 1825 in Providence, Rhode Island.

Baker, George: Noted clockmaker in 1820s, Providence, Rhode Island.

Baker, John: Bowie knife maker for Confederate troops during the Civil War. Located in Georgia

Baker, L. S.: Produced cap boxes and infantry cartridge boxes for Federal troops during the Civil War. Located in New York City.

Baker, M. A.: Provided rifled muskets to Confederate military during the Civil War. Located in Fayetteville, North Carolina.

Bakewell, Pears and Company: Considered one of the first successful flint glass factories in the United States, after its founding at Pittsburgh in 1808 by Benjamin Page. In 1814 it was reported the factory had two "houses" in operation and were also active at "glass-cutting." Production evolved to include bottles, decanters, drinking glasses, flasks, and pitchers.

Balance wheel: Term regarding toy vehicles, particularly horse-drawn types. The wheel, usually turning, helped move the toy across the floor.

Balch and Fryer: Silversmith operation around 1785 in Albany, New York.

Band collectible, postcard of regional band, dated 1912.

Band boxes, also called Hannah Davis boxes, all nineteenth century. (Skinner Inc.)

Carved and painted banister-back chair, late eighteenth century New England. (Skinner Inc.)

Inlaid mahogany banjo clock in Federal style, ca. 1815. (Skinner Inc.)

Balch, C. L. & Co.: Maker of cavalry and artillery badges during the Civil War, based in New York City.

Baldwin and Johnson: Provider of military canteens and kettles to Federal troops during the Civil War, located in New York City.

Baldwin, Anthony: A clockmaker in 1820s, Lancaster, Pennsylvania.

Baldwin, Ebenezer: Early nineteenth century silversmith doing business in Hartford, Connecticut.

Baldwin, H. E. & Co.: Noted source of military buttons for Confederate troops, based in New Orleans, Louisiana.

Baldwin, William: New York City maker of equipment for Federal troops during the Civil War.

Baleen: Substance used for carving of buttons, buckles, and various small ornaments by sailors. Initially it was harvested from the mouths of whales and was nearly as workable as whalebone.

Balky Mule: Key-wound children's toy sold in the early 1900s by Sears, Roebuck and Company. Both the driver and the mule moved in "realistic" fashion. Price was 29¢.

Ball, Albert: Supplier of .50 caliber carbines to Federal forces in 1863, located in Worcester, Massachusetts.

Ball and claw: Favored ending for cabriole chair leg in the eighteenth century, especially used by British designer Thomas Chippendale.

Ball and socket joint: Term for a joint where a spherical object is placed within the socket made to fit.

Ballard, C. H.: Supplier of .54 caliber carbines to state militia units and Federal forces in 1861.

Ball, Black and Co.: Maker of sabers and swords for U.S. troops during the Civil War, located in New York City.

Ball foot: Term for the rounded foot found on seventeenth century chests and other furniture crafted in America. It was in use as late as the early nineteenth century.

Ball-joint (doll): Term for the use of balls of wood or other material to provide joints for the limbs of dolls. Such joints provided a wide range of movement in early dolls.

Ball leg tip: A term for a small brass ball-shaped foot accompanied with a cup above it. The tip was fitted over the end of the chair leg or the table leg.

Balloon back (furniture): Reference to a balloon-shape of the back on an early chair. A splat would run across the back with the top rail rounded.

Balloon clock: Reference to the 1760s appearance of clocks with balloon-like shapes.

Balloon frame: Constructing a building based on a basket-like frame. Basically two-by-four studs were nailed together in that manner starting in the foundation and continuing in the rafters of the structure. In use during the middle of the nineteenth century.

Ball, True: Noted silversmith during the mid-nineteenth century in Boston, Massachusetts.

Balmoral boots: High-stepping boots worn both by fashionable women and men during the Victorian era. Such boots laced up from the front and were the 1860s choice of both Queen Victoria and Prince Albert.

Baltimore Glass Works: Starting in 1790, the factory in Baltimore, Maryland, produced quality bottles and flasks in clear and colored glass. Other names for the operation included Federal Hill Glass Works, Hughes Street Works, and Patapsco River Glass Works.

Baluster back: Furniture term describing the square or flat column supporting a rail. Typically a small, slender member with a square base.

Baluster-stemmed glass: Early drinking glasses with stems similar to the stair and furniture supports of the same name.

Balustrade (furniture): Denotes a row of balusters (slender turned members) or turned pillars supporting a railing in early furniture.

Bambi: Heart-tugging star of the Walt Disney cartoon film of the same name in the early 1940s. Adorable deer creature was eventually depicted on a range of items from books to wristwatches.

Bamboo (color): A medium tan in 1920s America.

Bamboo Windsor chair: A chair with spindles turned to represent bamboo sticks. An application of the late eighteenth century and early nineteenth century.

Bancker, Adrian: New York City silversmith during the eighteenth century.

Bandbox: Ladies once used such lightweight pasteboard or very thin wood boxes to store bonnets, capes, hats, lace, and similar finery garments.

Band collectibles: What followed the popularity and membership in high school and college bands of the twentieth century. Uniforms, photographs, plume hats, and related memorabilia are included.

Banderole: Ribbon-like decoration applied to early furniture in a carved or painted form.

Banding: Basically a decorative inlay, strip, or band of veneer providing contrast, by color or just in grain, between the strip and the decorated surface.

Band wagon (toy): Fisher-Price musical toy of the 1940s with a picture of a calliope-playing clown. Pair of horses and wagon made entirely of wood.

Bandy leg: Another early American furniture term for the curved cabriole leg. It was often typified by the then popular Queen Anne style.

Bangor Stoneware Co.: Firm doing business in stoneware starting in 1890s, Bangor, Maine.

Bangs, John T.: Noted silversmith operating around 1825 in Cincinnati, Ohio.

Banister-back: Used to describe eighteenth century chair which incorporated four or five spindles similar in design to the vertical uprights of a stairway. Banister chairs, an American original, were made both with and without arms, and with either rush or splint seating.

Banjo clock: Extraordinary clock given the name because hanging on the wall it resembled the musical instrument of the same name. Initially designed and crafted by Simon Willard of Roxbury, Massachusetts, in the very early 1800s.

Bank kiln: Rather basic baking oven built into the slope of a hill and used without the benefit of a chimney. Such kilns were used for firing small items of pottery.

Banks, Edward: Noted clockmaker operating in 1830s, Portland, Maine.

Bank (toy): Long an instrument to promote the value of savings to children, the toy bank was extremely popular in the latter nineteenth century and the early twentieth century. In the 1920s Butler Brothers catalogs offered a vast array of dozens of both iron still banks and "mechanical action" banks. Additionally there were combination safe toy banks, tin book banks, and pocket coin holders of both tin and nickel.

Banner Plastics: (see, Carnival Caravan and Junior Stewardess)

Still bank in the form of a building, by A. C. Williams Company, ca. 1930s. (Skinner Inc.)

Still bank in the form of a soldier, by A.C. Williams Company, ca. 1930s.

Boxed examples of Barbie, Midge, and Little Sister Skipper. (Harris Auction Center)

Walk America Barbie for March of Dimes.

Banquette: Originally a French term which referred to an upholstered bench.

Bantam work: Term used to define specialized lacquering applied to furniture for the British and Dutch trades of the late seventeenth century. Site of the process was Bantam, Dutch Java.

Bar back (furniture): Specifically the square back on an early side or armchair. Usually came with carved and reeded spindles as well as turned and reeded supports. Craftwork of Ephraim Haines and Henry Connelly in early nineteenth century Philadelphia.

Barbara doll: (see Madame Hendren)

Barbie: World's largest selling doll of the twentieth century and equally compelling name in advertising dolls. The 1959 brainchild of Ruth Handler and a goldmine for toy maker Mattel. Boyfriend Ken, friend Midge, sister Skipper, and an array of toys and other products.

Barbotine ware: Porcelain decorated with a kaolin clay thinly mixed and molded separately and attached to the surface of individual items.

Barclay Manufacturing Company: A major producer of toy soldiers during the 1930s and early 1940s. Based in New Jersey. Ceased operation in the early 1970s.

Barlett, P. S.: (see American Watch Co.)

Barley twist (clock): Reference to the twist decoration form on early clocks. Suggests twisted sticks of barley sugar in appearance.

Barnes, Timothy: A Colonial era clockmaker located in 1790s, Litchfield, Connecticut.

Barnet and Doolittle: One of the very early American lithographic firms, located in early 1820s, New York City.

Barney Google: Comic strip character, song subject, cartoon star, and the star of a few very fine wind-up toys during the 1920s. Along with horse companion Spark Plug, the character was seen in print or film for many decades.

Barns, B.: Noted pewter designer in early 1800s, Philadelphia, Pennsylvania. Often marked works with B. B. initials in oval held by an eagle.

Barnum, Charles: Under contract with the Federal government to make uniforms and overcoats during the Civil War. Located in New York City.

Baron, Louis: Participating in the silversmith trade in 1860s and 1870s, Rochester, New York.

Baroque: Decorative touch added to furniture starting in seventeenth century Europe. Initially a classical architectural style, but gradually all the curves and scrolls were considered perhaps too ornamental.

Bar pin: Stylish and decorative jewelry for the ladies. S.S. Kresge Co. offered long, thin rectangular versions for 10¢ each in 1913. Sometimes called veil pins.

Barred door: First introduced during the Chippendale and Sheraton periods, it relates to a framed-up door with traced patterns made up with moldings and splats called bars.

Barrel chair: Simply an upholstered chair shaped indeed like the upper half of a barrel.

Barrett, A. R. & Co.: Supplier of firearms to the Confederate forces during the Civil War. Located in Wytheville, Virginia.

Barringer and Morton: Supplier of gun carriages for Confederate troops during the Civil War. Located in Columbus, Georgia.

Barrows, James: Listed as a clockmaker in 1830s, Tolland, Connecticut.

Barry: A nineteenth century term for

petticoat, slip, or underskirt. Sometimes spelled barrie as well.

Bart & Hickox: Supplier of India-rubber goods during the Civil War, located in Cincinnati, Ohio.

Bartenstein (doll): Term for an early German made doll with revolving head. One side was a bonnet clad day face, on the other was a bonnet clad night face.

Bartholomae, Charles: Granted a patent in 1861 for a type of military canteen, located in New York City.

Bartholomew Company: Advertised the seven-passenger Glide Special automobile in 1910 for $2,500. Company was based in Peoria, Illinois.

Bartlett, E.: Maker of equipment and ornaments for Federal troops during the Civil War. Based in 1860s, New York City.

Bartlett, Edward: Listed as active silversmith in 1835, Philadelphia, Pennsylvania.

Barton, Benjamin: Noted clockmaker in 1830s, Alexandria, Virginia.

Barwell, Bartholomew: Listed as active clockmaker in 1750s, New York City.

Baryta (ceramic): Basically a barium sulphate used in jasperware and other early ceramic wares.

Basalt: Solidly black or very dark brown dense textured rock, sometimes referred to as traprock.

Basalt ware: Remarkable stoneware first developed in England by Josiah Wedgwood. Produced in the Black Works of the Wedgwood factory, it was a very hard ware sometimes known as Egyptian. This sturdy and unglazed material was named for, but not actually made of, the basalt rock. Used for urns, statues, and flowerpots.

Basin stand: Simple table used to support a wash basin and pitcher in the eighteenth and nineteenth century households without indoor plumbing.

Basket (aviation): Reference to the car suspended from a balloon, for passengers or ballast.

Basket chair: Unusual chair for a child made in the Windsor style but fitted with a side basket for holding books and slates in the 1840s and 1850s. Most were fitted with the seat mounted on a single iron support.

Basket stand (furniture): Basically a early work stand but with two tiers. The tiers were surrounded by galleries comprised of spindles or turnings.

Basket top (clock): A reference to the metal open-work at the top of an early clock case. Two tiers were sometimes known as a double basket top. Term bell top was also used.

Bas-relief: Basically a very shallow decorative sculpture or carving.

Basset, Frederick: Known pewter craftsman in 1790s, New York City.

Bassett and Warford: Two silversmiths at work in 1805, Albany, New York.

Basswood: Rather light and straight-grained softwood. Said to have acquired a brownish-yellow tone with aging. Cabinetmakers of the eighteenth century used it for the interiors of pieces such as drawer bottoms. However some chests, desks, and highboys were occasionally made entirely of basswood. Basswood bark was sometimes used for rushes in the seating of chairs.

Bateman, Hester: Silversmith of note during the latter eighteenth century in London, England. Reportedly also trained her sons and daughter in the art of fine silver making during that period.

Bath, Barten: Active clockmaker operating in 1840s, New York City.

Barney Google and Sparkplug by Schoenhut, painted wood, original clothing. (Harris Auction Center)

Batman Batmobile scale model hobby kit by Aurora, 1966.

Beadle's Dime Novel featuring Esther: A Story of the Oregon Trial, 1862.

Classic Beatles bobbin' head dolls made in Japan, ca. 1964.

Batman: Undoubtedly one of the most enduring characters who never lived. Introduced in an issue of Detective Comics in 1939, the Caped Crusader and Boy Wonder, companion Robin, have been fighting crime and maintaining celebrity ever since. Entire generations have grown up with Batman-related toys, drinking glasses, puzzles, buttons, watches, and even yo-yos. Television and Hollywood have kept Batman's career nearly timeless.

Batman (military): A World War I army term for an orderly in charge of a pack horse.

Bat printing: Process to enable transfer printing on china and other pottery in the nineteenth century. The name was devised from the bats of gelatin and glue used to extract the pattern from the copper plate onto the ceramic surface of an object.

Batsto ironware: Named for an operation in late eighteenth century, west New Jersey. Factory's furnace produced quality pots, skillets, and Dutch ovens.

Battens (furniture): Term for sections of wood which were attached by nail or screw across the grain of planks. The battens prevented cure warping by holding several planks together.

Battersea: Quite attractive enameled ware first developed in the 1750s. It was named for the town of Battersea near London, England. Stephen Jansson, using the enamel over a copper foundation, created numerous items from buttons to small jewelry boxes. Battersea was once a favored collectible of former First Lady Nancy Reagan.

Battledore: Wooden paddle used for flattening base of hot glass vessel.

Battleship gray (color): Considered to be a medium gray in early twentieth century catalogs.

Battleship tray: During the 1890s pressed-glass covered trays or boxes depicting ships of the United States Navy were sold in retail stores on the wave of patriotism following the outbreak of the Spanish-American War.

Bat wing (furniture): Reference to the brass handle plates and escutcheons on early furniture which resembled the outstretched wings of a bat. An early American term.

Bauer & Company: Producers of redware, stoneware, and yellow ware in early twentieth century, Los Angles, California.

Bauhaus design: Marked development in art and architecture which incorporated terms of modem materials and certain industrial methods. Originated in early twentieth century Germany.

Baum, J. H.: Pottery maker of note doing business in 1890s, Wellsville, Ohio.

Baxter, John: Maker of equipment for Federal troops in the 1860s including hatchets, mess pans, and kettles. Located in New York City.

Bayberry candle: In early New England the berries from that native bush were used to prepare a Colonial version of a scented candle. Greenish in color, they were said to be quite aromatic around the home.

Baylan, James B.: Issued a contract with the Federal government to make military clothing during the Civil War.

Baylor, John R.: Maker of smooth bore breach-loading cannon used by Confederate forces during the Civil War.

Baynes, Robert: Silversmith active in 1840s, Nantucket, Massachusetts.

Bayser, Stebbins and Co.: Contracted with the Confederate government during the Civil War to produce military bayonets. Located in Columbia, South Carolina.

Bay State Glass Company: Rather productive nineteenth century glasshouse located in Cambridge, Massachusetts. Roughly from the 1850s into the 1870s, it created an array of blown and pressed flint glass.

Bay wood: Another name for a type of mahogany which came from Central America in general and Honduras in particular during the eighteenth century. It was lighter and softer than mahogany taken from Cuba and the West Indies.

Beach, E. P.: Maker of rings for returning Civil War soldiers, each had enameled design of each division. Located in New York City.

Beach, Ralph: Potter doing business in 1840s, Philadelphia, Pennsylvania.

Beadle and Adams: Leading publisher of so-called dime novel adventure magazines during the late nineteenth century and early twentieth century. Titles included *Beadle's Dime Novels, Beadle's Half Dime Library, Beadle's New York Dime Library,* and *Beadle's Pocket Novels.*

Beaker: Drinking device which historically preceded both the cup and the stein. Often fashioned from pewter or silver, the beaker was without handles but bore straight sides and modestly flared top. Those used for religious ceremonies were sometimes engraved.

Beals, Fordyce: Contracted with the federal government to provide procession revolvers during the Civil War. Located in Ilion, New York.

Beal, William: Provided drums to Federal troops during the Civil War, located in 1860s, Lowell, Massachusetts.

Beard, Duncan: Clockmaker in 1780s, Appoquinemonk, Delaware.

Beard, Duncan: Silversmith operating in 1765, Wilmington, Delaware.

Bearing cloth: Term for a christening blanket, sometimes used in more rural regions of England and colonial America.

Beatles: Major musical singing group of the 1960s who came from England and changed the entertainment culture in America. Albums, record cases, pillows, jewelry, dolls, posters, and related memorabilia still delight fans.

Beau Brummell: Colonial term for a gentleman's dressing table. Typically it included a mirror, fitted drawers, and a fold-back top. Sometimes the name was also used for chests with fitted drawers also exclusively for a gentleman's use.

Beaufait: Early French word meaning buffet, suggesting a serving table in a formal dining room. Typically the buffet had several drawers and four or more legs. Sometimes spelled as beauffet, or beaufet.

Beauvais, Reno: Listed as a silversmith in 1850s, St. Louis, Missouri.

Beaver (color): An early 1920s version of brownish gray.

Beaver Falls Art Tile Company: Established in 1886, the firm initially crafted enamel, embossed, and intaglio tiles. Later the Beaver Falls, Pennsylvania, factory expanded to artistic design tiles for bathrooms, dining rooms, and libraries.

Bebe (doll): French term for dolls in the image of small children from infant to around seven years of age.

Beck, Charles A.: Early twentieth century publisher of holiday and patriotic postcards.

Becker, Philip: Colonial silversmith operating in 1765, Lancaster, Pennsylvania.

Becket: Woven rope handle used for sea chests. Sailors were known to have

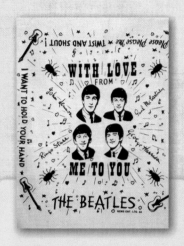

Beatles scarf from Nems Enterprises, ca 1964.

Bebe Jumeau packaging, late nineteenth century. (Harris Auction Center)

Biedermeier parcel-gilt walnut settee. (Skinner Inc.)

sometimes woven intricate patterns into the handles adding to their strength and design.

Beckwith organ: Major brand of parlor organs sold during the 1920s by Sears, Roebuck and Company. Shipped from a factory in Kentucky, they weighed 350 to 400 pounds and were 82" tall. Prices varied from $99 to $149. Beckwith play pianos were also sold at the same time by Sears.

Bedpost clock: Term for a brass-case clock which was designed in Colonial times for hanging on the wall between two posts.

Beebe, Stanton: A silversmith doing business in 1825, Providence, Rhode Island.

Beecher (doll): Cloth dolls crafted from silk lingerie by women of the Park Church of Elmira, New York. The operation began in the 1890s and included relatives of Harriet Beecher Stowe the author of *Uncle Tom's Cabin*. Each doll carried a letter to Mamma and had yellow worsted hair.

Beech wood: Distinguished hardwood used for seventeenth century chairs in England, and for some Windsor chairs in America. While the color of the wood varied from white to pale brown, it was frequently painted or gilded by colonial cabinetmakers.

Beehive: (see Crystal Glass Company)

Beehive (ceramic): Early nineteenth century symbol for industrial activity. Used on ceramic ware and glass at factories in Bohemia and Germany.

Beehive clock: Term for a mid-nineteenth century shelf clock made in Connecticut. Such small clocks were sometimes called flatiron clocks because they were shaped in the angular form of both objects.

Beeman's Gum: Early twentieth century pepsin chewing gum named for Dr. E. E. Beeman. It was marketed by the American Chicle Company.

Beerbower and Company: Pottery firm established by L. B. Beerbower in 1816, Elizabeth, New Jersey.

Beerbower and Griffen: Potters in operation in 1870s, Phoenixville, Pennsylvania.

Beer tray: Term for a round or oval tray with a stand-up rim used for carrying glasses of beer during the eighteenth and nineteenth centuries and later used as background decoration.

Begonia (color): Medium yellow or rust color, 1920s, U.S.A.

Beige (color): A light tan according to the 1927 Sears and Roebuck catalog.

Belber: Brand name for early twentieth century suitcases of traveling goods. Offered in 16 styles from $7.50 to $12. Marketed by Belber Trunk and Bag Co., of Philadelphia, Pennsylvania.

Bell and Davis: Granted a contract in 1861 to provide Bowie knives for Confederate military. Located in Atlanta, Georgia.

Bellarmine: German-made salt-glaze jug said to depict the image of Cardinal Bellarmine, but debated. Initially made in the sixteenth century and eventually made by various European potters in various sizes.

Belleek: Ivory colored china of a delicate nature first produced during the late 1850s in Donegal, Ireland. Much of the seashell-like ware was imported into the American market.

Bellenot and Ulrich: Suppliers of Confederate troop military buttons during the Civil War, based in New Orleans, Louisiana.

Bell flower: Once popular design or motif of a simple flower appearing on everything from pattern glass to painted furniture.

Belliard, Francois: Listed as a silversmith operating in 1820s, New Orleans, Louisiana.

Bell, James: Noted clockmaker active in early 1800s, New York City.

Bell, Joseph: New York City silversmith at the craft from 1815 to 1825.

Bell, J. T.: New York City maker of small cartridge boxes for 1860s Federal troops.

Bellmark Pottery Company: Pottery operation doing business in 1890s, Trenton, New Jersey.

Bell metal: Exceptional grade of bronze balanced with amounts of copper and tin to ultimately offer resounding tone when stuck.

Bellona Arsenal: (see Archer, Dr. Junius)

Bellow flask: Glass quart flask made in the shape of a bellows, eighteenth century. Later similar "violin" and Jenny Lind flasks were produced using similar forms.

Bellows: Air pumping device used to stimulate the dying embers of a fireplace. Typically the two wooden sides were decorated with carving or painting and joined together with strips of leather. Ending nozzle made of brass or other metal.

Bellows, Martin: Under contract with the Federal government during the Civil War to make 5,000 bootees. Located in Philadelphia, Pennsylvania.

Bell, Peter: Maryland resident who joined Samuel Bell and Solomon Bell to produce Shenandoah Pottery. This redware and stoneware was crafted from the 1820s into the 1880s.

Bell Pottery Company: Makers of pottery related items. Established in late nineteenth century, Findlay, Ohio.

Bell Telephone truck (toy): During the 1930 a cast-iron Bell Telephone truck was made in four different sizes by Hubley Toys. They varied from 5½" in length to 8½". All were olive green and bore the Bell Telephone name in raised letters on the side. The larger models came with ladders and digging tools.

Bell, Thomas M.: Granted a contract in 1861 for 15,000 cloth covered military canteens, doing business in New York City.

Bell top (clock): Generally the bell-like top appearing on an early clock case. Some had an ordinary curve and some had a concave curve.

Belmont Tonic Herb Bitters: Bottled "cure" sold by Benjamin Labe and Co. in nineteenth century, Philadelphia, Pennsylvania.

Belter, John H.: Highly acclaimed American cabinetmaker credited with excellent run of Victorian furniture. Belter, who was German born, began operations around 1840 in New York City and prospered with his pierced carved leaf designs on mahogany and rosewood. Highly decorative upholstering was the final touch.

Belton (doll): Misnomer for nineteenth century dolls incorporating one to three stringing holes in the pate. While an M. Belton was active in the Jumeau era, the specific Belton mark was not used.

Beltzhoover and Wendt Company: A small glass factory which began operation in 1813 at Birmingham, Pennsylvania.

Bench: A Colonial furniture term which referred to basically any extended stool used for seating at a table. The same

Biedermeier mahogany and maple fall-front secretaire.
(Skinner Inc.)

Biedermeier walnut fall-front secretaire.

Big Boy doll figures, molded vinyl.

item was sometimes known as a "form" in England.

Bench end (furniture): An early reference to the upright end of a church pew.

Benedict and Burnham Company: Clock making firm located in 1850s Waterbury, Connecticut.

Bennett & Brothers: Pottery producing with Rockingham and yellow ware during the 1830s and 1840s in East Liverpool, Ohio.

Bennett, James: Skilled nineteenth century potter who came to America from England in the 1830s and operated potteries in New Jersey, Indiana, and Ohio.

Bennett Pottery Company: English potter Edwin Bennett established the pottery in 1846 at Baltimore, Maryland. Early products were Rockingham ware and various yellow, sage, and blue wares. In 1869 production of white ware began, followed by a decorating department. The factory achieved fame with the Rebekah teapot and was thus renamed in 1890.

Bennington pottery: Unique source of both brown mottled Rockingham ware and fine porcelain Parian ware. Founded by ex-Revolutionary soldier Captain John Norton. Starting in the 1790s, the remarkable factory in the Vermont community of the same name was prolific in the production of pottery from bowls and crocks to jugs and plates. Operation ceased in the late 1850s.

Bennington Power Co.: Supplier of gunpowder to Federal troops during the Civil War, located in Bennington, Vermont.

Bent limb (doll): Term for curved limbs on dolls with five-piece bodies. Generally produced in the early twentieth century.

Bentson, Peter: Active silversmith in 1720s, Philadelphia, Pennsylvania.

Bentwood (furniture): Wooden furniture with sweeping curves formed through steam and pressure. Developed in 1830s in Germany by cabinetmaker Michael Thonet. Manufactured in 1840s in Austria. Imported and incorporated into American furniture making by the mid-nineteenth century.

Bergere: Late eighteenth century French term for upholstered armchair with closed sides.

Bergmann & Company: Noted maker of tinplate toys in the United States during the latter nineteenth century. Bell toys, clockwork toys, dollhouse furniture, banks, and similar items. Based in New York.

Berkshire Bitters: Pig-shaped bottle of mostly alcohol, manufactured in 1850s, Cincinnati, Ohio.

Berlin ware: Tin ware produced for more than 100 years, during the eighteenth and nineteenth centuries, in Berlin, Connecticut.

Bermuda chest (furniture): Decorative chest noted for ornamental use of dovetails. Crafted during the late seventeenth century and early eighteenth century in Bermuda.

Berrian Ware: Selection of copper, tin, japanned, willow, and wooden wares sold in the 1850s and 1860s by New York merchant William Berrian. Imported from other countries the ware was sold wholesale to retailers in many parts of the United States.

Berriman's Special: Selection of 25 Havana cigars sold in a round tin can during the 1920s. Sears and Roebuck Company price was $1.25.

Berry, William: Maker of Bowie knives for the Confederate army during the Civil War. Located in Georgia.

Berwick Doll Company: Doll makers in 1920s, New York City.

Bespoke: Colonial term suggesting an item would be made to order and not from current stock or inventory. Furniture, clothing, and other personal items were crafted on this basis at a higher cost to the customer.

Best room: Early term for the finest furnished bedroom in the home or rental room in an inn in colonial era. Later it was modified to guest room or simply spare room.

Betts, E. & A.: Supplier of tent tripods for Federal government during the Civil War. Located in Wilmington, Delaware.

Betty doll: (see Madame Hendren)

Betty lamp: Very basic metal tray device with a slightly turned-up edge. A hooked or curved handle allowed the lamp to hang from a mantel or suitable chair in seventeenth century colonial America. Crudely fashioned with a cloth wick and kitchen grease, the result was unpleasant. Later animal fat fuel was replaced with most any inflammable oil.

Bevel: In regard to early furniture, the plain chamfer or cut grove where two plain surfaces met.

Bezel: A term for the metal ring surrounding an early clock face. It was usually hinged.

B. F. Goodrich Rubber Co.: (See Silvertown Balloons)

Bibelot: French term for a small but interesting art object. Decorative and finely made.

Bible box: Sturdy wooden box which protected the family Bible. Some such boxes came with lock and key. Many were hinged; however some were assembled to allow the top portion to simply slide open. Still others had school desk-like slanted tops. Nineteenth century.

Bible flask: (see Book flask)

Bicknell, Francis: Doing business as a silversmith in 1820s, Rome, New York.

Biddle, Owen: Active Colonial clockmaker in 1770s, Philadelphia, Pennsylvania.

Biedermeier doll: Typically a chinahead doll crafted in Germany between 1815 and 1850. Such dolls had smooth heads with a black spot for attaching a wig and were identified with the particular era of German art and furniture.

Biedermeir furniture (also spelled Biedermeier): Most distinctive nineteenth century German furniture. Initially made for the middle class during the first half of that century. This French Empire-based design was named for Papa Biedermeir a German newspaper comic character.

Bien, Julius: Noted publisher of holiday, comic, and political postcards early in the twentieth century.

Biershing, Henry: Active silversmith in 1815, Hagerstown, Maryland.

Big Bang (toy): Both tank and field cannon offered in the 1940s. Cannon offered a big bang with a non-inflammable gas.

Big Boy: Icon of the fast-food chain which really took root in the 1950s. The image eventually appeared as a bank, figural ashtray, bobbing-head doll, and even salt and pepper set in the 1960s and 1970s.

Bigelow, Charles D.: Contracted with the Federal government during to the Civil War to make bootees, shirts, and socks. Located in New York City.

Bigelow, John: Noted silversmith in 1830s, Boston, Massachusetts.

Gunpowder company billhead, 1890s.

Tanning company billhead, 1890s.

Wrigley Gum company billhead, early twentieth century.

Nevin paint company billhead, 1890s.

Bigger, Gilbert: An early 1800s clockmaker operating in Baltimore, Maryland.

Big Jim (doll): A G. I. Joe-type of action figure from Mattel. Early in the 1970s Big Jim appeared in both black and white models. A bearded companion was Big Josh. The 9½" dolls had three sets of "action" outfits.

Big Josh: (See Big Jim)

Big Wheel: Popular sidewalk bike of the 1970s made by Marx. Molded plastic construction in bright day-glow colors. Large front wheels varied from 14" to 16". Prices were $8.88 to $10.98 from Montgomery Ward.

Bilbo mirror: Named after a Spanish city which exported their form. Usually with a marble or wood frame, accompanied with a classical marble veneer.

Bilhartz, Hall and Co.: Produced carbines for Confederate forces during the Civil War. Located in Danville, Virginia.

Billhead: Sometimes colorful and distinguished invoice on company letterhead which has evolved since the American Revolutionary War. They grew more decorative in the nineteenth century and became fully artistic in the early twentieth century.

Billiken (doll): Unique unbreakable animal manikin type of doll made in the early 1900s by Hoffman's American Doll and Toy Company. Later the firm was known as Aetna.

Billings News, Inc.: Publisher of twentieth century regional postcards, based in Billings, Montana.

Billups and Hassell: Provided rifles to Mississippi military during the Civil War. Located in Pentitude, Texas.

Billy and Ruth: Two idealized and fictional children who starred in toy industry and companion catalogs of the 1930s through the early 1950s. Their catalogs

were filled with the choicest of toys from Fisher-Price, Lionel, Mattel, Hubley, Gilbert, Structo, and Wolverine

Billy Batson: (See Captain Marvel)

Bilsted (wood): Term for the wood of the North American sweetgum tree or liquidambar. During the later eighteenth century it was sometimes used in American furniture in place of mahogany.

Binche lace: Fine and delicate lace which was said to have originated in the French province of Hainaut. Initially it contained highly intricate patterns difficult to duplicate elsewhere.

Birch, Thomas: Philadelphia artist noted for naval pictures of the War of 1812, and for combined efforts with his father William Birch.

Birch, William: Skilled engraver who came to America from England and worked in Philadelphia. William and son Thomas also produced Views of Philadelphia in 1800, and later a series of country home illustrations.

Birch wood: Highly patterned grain hardwood finished in tones ranging from amber to light brown. Popular choice for cabinetmakers from 1750s to early 1800s for chairs, four-poster beds, and tables. Considered denser and heavier than maple which was also abundant at the time in New England.

Bird box: Name given to certain Battersea enamel boxes involving a sitting bird. Lifting the bird revealed a small opening for storage of pins or similar items. Same name was sometimes also given to Chinese porcelain boxes with bird shapes.

Bird cage clock: Not a cage at all, but an early brass clock made in England during the latter 1650s. Sometimes called lantern clocks, such devices were expensive and available only to the wealthy classes. Typically they could be carried about by a handle, simply hung on a wall, or set upon a shelf.

Bird cage (furniture): A reference to the use of double block construction in the early tilt-top table. The method resembled a bird cage and allowed to the top to both rotate and tilt.

Bird candelabra: Victorian term given to candle structure using a design of bird figures.

Bird, James: Pewter producer doing business in 1820s, New York City.

Bird's beak lock: Reference to the bird's beak of a thrust-out bolt used in early cylinder tables and tambour tables made in America and England.

Birdsey, E. C. and Company: A 1830s clock making operation in Meriden, Connecticut.

Birge, Mallory, and Company: Active clock making operation in 1830s, Bristol, Connecticut.

Biscuit: A technical term for a piece of porcelain fired once but essentially left unglazed. After the so-called biscuit stage came the coloring, glazing, and necessary second firing.

Bisque: Common word once used expressly to describe unglazed ceramic material with texture left in a rough and granular state. Many consider the term an incorrect dissection of the porcelain reference to biscuit.

Bitter, Henry: New York City supplier of knapsacks and other equipment to Federal troops in the 1860s.

Bixler, Christian: Silversmith and cabinetmaker operating around 1785 in Easton, Pennsylvania.

Blackamoor: Fashionable figures of the Victorian era depicting black people. Often these were carvings of wood which sat in homes as table pedestals.

Others were plaster molds that were displayed in entrance halls and sometimes in parlors.

Black Gasoline Carriage: An 1890s creation of Charles Black in Indianapolis, Indiana. This self-propelled gasoline vehicle used a basic buggy body combined with a kerosene torch for ignition.

Blacking: An early reference to shoe polish.

Blake, W. S.: (see Kew-Blas)

Blanchard, Leonard: Awarded a Federal government contract during the Civil War to make 4,000 cavalry boots. Based in East Abington, Massachusetts.

Blanche (color): As noted in the 1920s Sears catalog, a basic white.

Blank, August: Stoneware potter doing business in 1890s and early 1900, California, Missouri.

Blanket chest: Generous term applied to many variations of a low or medium-height chest with a hinged lid top. Name was used both for chests with or without bottom drawers.

Blimp: Popular early twentieth century term for a non-rigid dirigible balloon.

Blind tiger: Prohibition era term for a secret or unlicensed place for the sale of liquor.

Blinking-eye clock: Such novelty items were made in America in the nineteenth century, but were mostly the work of German clockmakers of the eighteenth century and earlier. In full operation the "eyes" functioned as a part of the clock's wheelwork movement.

Bliss Manufacturing Company: Latter nineteenth century maker of wooden toys often incorporating lithographed paper. Produced toy tools, building blocks, trains, and boats. Based

Birch tall chest, red washed. ca. 1816. (Skinner Inc.)

in Pawtucket, Rhode Island. Despite change in ownership the firm produced wooden toys as late as the 1930s.

Block foot: Name accorded to the plain untapered end of a square chair leg. Probably most notable in classic Chippendale furniture design.

Bombe chest of drawers in Dutch rococo-style. (Skinner Inc.)

Block front: Method applied to early American furniture, and elsewhere, regarding three front vertical panels. The center panel was curved outward whereas the remaining two panels were straight or curved inward. Some attributed the baroque influence to this style on some desks, chests, and secretaries during the second half of the eighteenth century. Much of the innovation is credited to cabinetmaker John Goddard of Newport, Rhode Island, in the 1760s and 1770s.

Block (glass): Tool used in glassmaking in the form of a wooden one-handled mold, used to shape blown glass.

Blonde lace: French-made fabric of the 1750s using unbleached Chinese silk. When completed, the lace bore an ivory or blonde color instead of the white color derived from cotton thread. Moreover, the silk strands provided a special shine to the lace. Eventually fashion dictated the seemingly blonde lace be dyed black, however the name remained the same.

Blondell, Anthony: Noted silversmith of 1790s in Philadelphia, Pennsylvania.

Blondie and Dagwood: Enduring comic strip couple first appearing in U.S. newspapers in the early 1930s. Their domestic adventures eventually included Baby Dumpling, Cookie, Alexander, and dog Daisy. Spin-offs included books, card games, buttons, toys, movies, and television shows.

Blond satin (color): A medium light tan according to 1920s catalogs.

Blown glass: A nearly lost art of using a hollow tube to blow air into glass while it is in a liquid state. The blower's air in turn expands and shapes the mass of glass at the end of the tube or blowpipe. In the 1820s machines were devised for pressing glass, thus slowly replacing centuries of blowing glass by mouth.

Blue-banded (ceramic): Term for porcelain decorated with a blue band at the rim, usually imported from Asian countries.

Blue Belle: Brand of collar supports sold in S.S. Kresge Co. stores in 1913. Price for a card of four was 5¢.

Blue Boy: (see Jordan Motor Car Co.)

Blue gray (color): Noted in the 1920s Sears catalogs as medium gray with a bluish cast.

Blue heather (color): A heather or evergreen mixture with blue predominating.

Blue iridescent (color): A rainbow blue according to the 1920s Sears catalogs.

Blume, Fred: Maker of musical instruments and patriotic song books for Federal troops during the Civil War, located in 1860s, New York City.

Blunt arrow (furniture): Term for the ball-like termination in the leg of a Windsor chair. It was said to resemble the blunt end of a practice arrow.

Blunt, Orison: Listed as a maker of Enfield type rifled muskets in the 1860s, located in New York City.

Blush pink (color): An interesting flesh color with pink tint.

Boardman and Company: Leading producer of pewter wares from 1820s to 1840s in New York City and Philadelphia, Pennsylvania. Known for using name enclosed with an eagle. Later Boardman and Hart.

Boardman, Chauncey: Noted clockmaker located in Bristol, Connecticut, in 1815.

Boardman, Henry S.: Doing business as a pewter craftsman in 1840s, Hartford, Connecticut.

Boardman, Thomas D.: An active pewtersmith in 1820s and beyond, in Hartford, Connecticut.

Boat bed: Reference to American made beds in the Empire style which were similar to the sleigh bed or scroll bed. A very heavy design.

Bobeche: Reference to a disk used to catch the drippings of a candle. Usually made of glass and typically placed on the candle socket of a candlestick, chandelier, or sconce.

Boch & Brothers: Porcelain firm operated by William Boch in mid-nineteenth century, Greenpoint, New York.

Body (ceramic): A ceramic term relating to the basic clay from which the overall piece was created.

Bodying in (furniture): Related to a French term for polishing. Specifically it meant filling in the grain of the wood.

Bog oak: During the Tudor period in England (mostly the 1500s) a very dark oak from a peat bog was used for furniture.

Bohemian (glass): Term for eighteenth and nineteenth century glass stylishly decorated with flashed overlay or luster-enameled ruby cut through to clear glass. Applied to both enameled cut and engraved glass.

Bois de rose (color): Term in the 1920s for a dark rose color.

Boker, H. and Company: Contracted with the U.S. government to provide cavalry sabers in 1861, possibly imported from Europe. Located in New York City.

Bombe: (see Kettle base)

Bombe front: Originally from the French term for bulging or jetting outward. It referred to the rounded kettle-shape expansion on the lower portions of desk, secretaries, and sometimes other early furniture.

Bond, William: Listed as an active clockmaker in early 1800s, Boston, Massachusetts.

Bone china: In the twentieth century it was considered a "modern" term used by china manufacturers in England to suggest color. Neither excessively hard or excessively soft paste, the formula sought to produce somewhat of a moderation between the two.

Bonfanti, Joseph: Listed as an active clockmaker in 1820s, New York City.

Bonjean, James: Silversmith located in New Orleans, Louisiana, during the 1820s.

Bonnet doll: Particular dolls of the nineteenth century with decorated bisque hats. Often the bows or flowers of the hat were actually part of the bisque head mold of the doll. Some wax dolls were also rendered in the bonnet style.

Bonnetiere (furniture): French term for a tall, narrow cabinet used for storage of women's hats.

Bonnet top: A bonnet-like decoration thought fashionable for a time on the headpiece of highboys, secretaries, and some early American chests.

Bonnin and Morris china: Productive pottery operation briefly established in Philadelphia to produce porcelain wares that would rival English made Bow china. Most distinguished effort was a white glazed earthenware decorated in blue. Some pieces were marked with a capital P.

Book flask: Book-shaped pottery flask sometimes irreverently called a Bible

Chippendale bombe chest-on-chest, ca. 1760 – 1780.
(Skinner Inc.)

Bombe commode, eighteenth century. (Skinner Inc.)

flask. In Rockingham ware the result was a brown and white mottled earthenware version. Some examples even included book-like covers and edges.

Bootee: A nineteenth century term for a type of boot with a warm lining for cold weather. Sometimes considered a half or short boot.

Booth, Ezra: Active silversmith in mid-nineteenth century, Rochester, New York.

Bootjack: Device made either of iron or wood to assist in the removal of a gentleman's boot. Most had a v-shaped opening cut to fit the heel of the boot. One forcefully stepped on one end of the jack to hold it firmly to the floor, while lifting a remaining boot off. Bootjacks varied from plain designs to creative animal shapes.

Borden's truck (toy): Borden's Milk Truck, a cast-iron toy truck, was made by Hubley Toys of Lancaster, Pennsylvania, during the 1930s. It was painted white and bore the scripted Borden's on the side with milk and cream printed immediately below. There were two slightly different sizes.

Borgfeldt, George: Founder of the George Borgfeldt and Company, doll distributors in late nineteenth century, New York City.

Boss and Peterman: Pair of 1840s clock makers doing business in Rochester, New York.

Boss (furniture): Early furniture term for an ornamented circular or oval protuberance at the intersection of moldings.

Boston bag: Quality 14" long leather bag offered by Sears in the 1920s for men, women, and schoolchildren. Price was $1.59.

Boston Crown Glass Company: Glass production began in this New England operation in the eighteenth century. By the early 1790s the name of this firm had changed to Essex Glass and they excelled in crafting fine window glass. By 1809 the company was known as Boston Crown Glass, the crown term meaning window glass. Boston Crown closed during the middle 1820s.

Boston Earthenware Manufacturing Company: Source of brown-mottled yellow ware during the 1850s in East Boston, Massachusetts. It held a direct connection to the pottery operations of Frederick Mear in Burslem, England.

Boston Junior: Chair made in a smaller version of the Boston rocker, typically without arms. Sometimes referred to as nursing rocker.

Boston rocker: Classic high-backed rocking chair of the early to middle nineteenth century. Most Boston rockers were painted with a stencil design on the crown piece. The top rail was scrolled and the seat curved upward at the back. Usually the chair had no arms, but came with tapered spindles up the back.

Botany wool: A nineteenth century term for a very high grade of wool from Botany Bay, Australia. Gradually the term evolved to most any quality wool used for crafting garments.

Bottle collector: Term once used to describe junk dealers who rounded up old bottles to be recycled to early glass factories. Junk dealers sometimes simply sold the used bottles as new to vendors who filled them with most any product including so-called remedy cures. By the 1890s federal law prohibited reuse of spirit and wine bottles.

Bottle opener: A conventional means of opening individual bottles since the early 1900s. Basic hand-held helpers gave way to figural designs and a corresponding host of advertisers, some of which can be highly collectible.

Boudo, Heloise: Noted as a silversmith in 1830s and 1840s, Charleston, South Carolina.

Boudoir clock: Style of English clock dating from the middle of the nineteenth century. Such clocks were housed in brass cases which had lavish gilt and engraving. Dials were often silver with blue steel hands. Name was more for decoration than household location.

Bouillotte candelabrum: Basically a table lamp with a dish-shaped base. Supported by the base were mountings for two to three candle brackets and a metal shade. Named for bouillotte, the French card game.

Boulle: Very fancy inlay used on fine furniture in the latter seventeenth and early eighteenth centuries. Sometimes incorporating the use of brass and tortoise shell, the process was named for designer/inventor Andre Charles Boulle of France. The boulle process, sometimes spelled buhl, was quite fashionable with European cabinetmakers for a time.

Bouvier, Daniel: Listed as a silversmith doing business in 1815, Putnam, Ohio.

Bow-backed Windsor: An especially popular type of Windsor chair which centered around a bow-shaped wooden center section. The piece which held upright spindles in place was formed by injection in a special steaming tube which bent the solid wood section. A comb piece was sometimes added to the lady's version of the bow-backed Windsor just at the top of the bow section.

Bow china: Quality soft-paste porcelain made in the Stratford-le-Bow in East London, England. At one time called the New Canton Works, the factory first opened in the 1740s. By the late 1750s it advertised a wide assortment of wares. Initially the ware was decorated in an Oriental style, however later Dresden and Sevres patterns were favored by the makers.

Bowen, E. R.: Provided military goods including Henry rifles to federal troops during the Civil War. Located in Chicago, Illinois.

Bower, Michael: Colonial period clockmaker in 1795, Philadelphia, Pennsylvania.

Bowles, Samuel and Co.: Supplier of photograph albums to Federal soldiers during the Civil War, located in Springfield, Massachusetts in the 1860s.

Bowman, Elias: Silversmith operating in 1830s, Rochester, New York.

Bow top (furniture): In early furniture a reference to the chair's top rail flowing in a single low, unbroken curve across its entire width.

Boxwood: Described as having a fine uniform grain for early furniture. The West India imported yellowish-orange wood was reportedly used mainly for inlay details and marquetry. It was sometimes dyed green to offer distinctive inlay contrast.

Boyd and Sons: Makers of belt buckles for Federal troops during the Civil War, based in Boston, Massachusetts.

Boyd bed: Product of a prolific factory which employed as many as 20 people during the 1850s in Cincinnati, Ohio. Operation was founded and directed by Henry Boyd.

Boyd, J. & Sons: Maker of cartridge boxes during the Civil War for Federal troops. Based in Boston, Massachusetts.

Amber collectible bottle from chemical supply company.

Classic Pepsi-Cola bottle from the 1950s.

Apple cider vinegar bottle with paper label.

Boyd, John: Listed as a clockmaker in 1740s and 1750s, Sadsbury, Pennsylvania.

Boyd, Parkes: Noted pewter producer active in early 1800s, Philadelphia, Pennsylvania. Pieces often marked with name, eagle, and 15 stars.

Boyd, Thomas: Granted a patent for military tents in 1861. Located in Boston, Massachusetts.

Boyle and Gamble: Supplier of bayonets, and saber bayonet adapters for Confederate forces during the Civil War. Located in Richmond, Virginia.

Boyle, Robert: Pewterer doing business in mid-eighteenth century, New York City.

Boy Scout bicycle: Offered in U.S. catalogs around 1917 as the "best hard tire bicycle made for children from five to ten years" available. It came boxed and sold for $9.75.

Brabant, Isaac: Colonial silversmith in 1750s, Savannah, Georgia.

Bracket clock: Small clock for use on brackets or on small shelves in England.

Bracket foot: An eighteenth century furniture characteristic regarding the base of desks and chests. The simple bracket extended in two directions from the corner. Eventually some cabinetmakers in England and Colonial America added ornamentation to the previously plain furniture foot bracket.

Bradbury and Brothers: A 1810 silversmith operation in Newburyport, Massachusetts.

Bradford, William: Operating in the pewter craft in 1770s, Philadelphia, Pennsylvania.

Brad (furniture): Term for a very small slender nail used in cabinet making. The nail had little or no head and ranged from ¼" to 1" in length.

Bradley, Nelson: A noted clockmaker in 1840s, Plymouth, Connecticut.

Bradshaw China Company: Doing business as a maker of pottery ware starting in late nineteenth century, Niles, Ohio.

Brain pills: Early in the 1900s Sears, Roebuck and Company sold Dr. Hammond's Nerve and Brain Pills billing them as "a boon for weak men." The price was 60¢ per box or six boxes for $3.

Brands & Korner: During the Civil War a provider of drums, fifes, and other items to Confederate forces. Located in Columbus, Georgia.

Branning, E. F.: Noted publisher of private mailing card views with patriotic themes and Sunbonnet Babies series. Operated Artino Company based in New York City.

Brannon, Daniel: A latter nineteenth century potter working with Rockingham and yellow ware in East Oakland, California. Operated as Pioneer Pottery.

Bras de lumiere: French term denoting the art of a candelabrum.

Brasher and Company: New York City silversmith firm operating in the 1790s.

Brastow, Addison: Doing clockmaking business as Addison Brastow and Company in 1830s, Lowell, Massachusetts.

Braun, Charles W.: Stoneware potter doing business in latter nineteenth century, Buffalo, New York.

Brazelton, Isaac P.: Stoneware potter active in 1840s and 1850s, Milwaukee, Wisconsin.

Breakfast ale: Hearty beverage consumed from pewter mugs in England and the American colonies during much of the early seventeenth century. Colonists had no taste for hot beverages and preferred the room temperature mild ale instead. Later the East India Trading Company and others converted breakfast beverage fashion to tea and other heated liquids.

Breakfast table: Originally credited to Thomas Chippendale in eighteenth century England as a term for a small table suitable for one or two people. It had hinged side leaves, four legs, occasionally a small drawer.

Break front: Reference regarding the bookcase or cabinet with a center section not in full flow of the entire pieces. The section may be projecting outward or recessing inward between the remaining sections.

Brennan, T. N. & Co.: Supplier of six-pound and 12-pound cannons for Confederate troops during the Civil War. Located in Nashville, Tennessee.

Brewer and Company: Firm of silversmiths doing business in 1810, Middletown, Connecticut.

Brewster, Abel: Colonial silversmith doing business in 1795, Norwalk, Connecticut.

Brewster chair: Term used to describe a very sturdy New England chair of the early 1600s.

Brewster, G.: A clockmaker in 1850s, Portsmouth, New Hampshire.

Brewster limousine: A striking motor car crafted in 1911 by Brewster and Company, distinguished horse-drawn vehicle makers, in New York City. The interior was literally made to fit the size of the individual chauffeur and passenger.

Briar rose (color): According to the 1927 Sears catalog, a very bright rose hue.

Brick dust (color): A color considered slightly lighter than red-brown brick during the 1920s.

Bridgeton, New Jersey: Site of continuing glassworks starting with Stratton, Buck and Company in 1837. Later operations included Joel Bodine and Sons, Potter and Bodine, and eventually Cohansey Glass Manufacturing Company. At one

point aquamarine flasks were made with the Washington design.

Brigden, Timothy: Active silversmith in early 1800s, Albany, New York.

Bright cut: Reference to sparkling surface given engravings in the late eighteenth and early nineteenth century. Metal was altered by a form of bevel cutting.

Brindsmaid, Abraham: Silversmith, ca. 1815 in Burlington, Vermont.

Brinkop: (see Decoy [metal])

Brins: The sticks of elaborate hand-held fans. The brins or sticks might have been made of various materials including ivory, sandalwood, papier-mâché, or precious metal. In turn they held the fancy sections of paper, lace, silk, or velvet of the stylish fan.

Brisco Motor Corporation: Makers of the $625 automobile "with the half million dollar motor" in 1917. Based in Jackson, Michigan.

Brise-soleil: Architectural term for a shade providing grill or sun shield.

Bristol brown (color): Reference in 1920s Sears catalogs to a dark copper color.

Bristol China: English made porcelain purchased by Americans for household use, particularly tableware. The soft-paste pieces were made in the 1770s and early 1780s in Bristol under the direction of Richard Champion. Some figurines were of high quality, but other items sometimes suffered from production difficulties.

Bristol (doll): Composition head doll, about 20" long, with painted blue eyes. Credited to Emma Bristol of Providence, Rhode Island, in the late 1880s. Some bore a label saying, Bristol's Unbreakable Doll.

Bristol slip (ceramic): Reference to adding zinc oxide to white coating clay for an opaque effect.

Black figural bottle opener with banjo.

All metal Pepsi Cola bottle opener and key chain.

Cast iron alligator bottle opener.

Britains: Prolific maker of toy soldiers during the first half of the twentieth century. Based in England, the firm also made farm animals, zoo sets, and dollhouse furniture. Toy soldiers were of metal with hollow cast. Company switched to plastic soldiers in the 1960s.

Britannia: A brightly colored pewter-like metal produced under a single brand or trade name in 1750 England. There were various grades and different formulas for the application of copper, tin, lead, and other materials.

British gill: (see Noggin)

Britten and Rey: Most noted for lithographed scenes of the California Gold Rush in the mid-nineteenth century. Firm located in San Francisco and in operation into the 1880s.

Broad ax: Popular early American tool with a chisel-edge. Used for hewing round longs into square beams. Very large ax head typically with short bend handle.

Broadside: Poster-like newsprint announcing a single, urgent event. Printed on just one side, they were designed to be both distributed by hand and posted in public places.

Brockman Pottery Company: Enterprise of pottery making starting in the 1860s at Cincinnati, Ohio.

Broderick and Bascom Rope Co.: (see Powersteel Autolock)

Brogan: Nineteenth century term for a heavy and coarse work shoe. Some had cleats or studded nails.

Bronson, I. W.: Active clockmaker in1830s, Buffalo, New York.

Bronze (color): Noted in mail order catalogs of the 1920s as simply the color of bronze.

Brooch: Best known perhaps as a central object of Victorian jewelry. Worn by fashionable women in the nineteenth and even early twentieth centuries, their origins can be traced to their earlier use by men to keep fir and skin clothing in tact.

Brooks, B. F.: Noted as a clockmaker in1850s, Utica, New York.

Brooks, David S.: Pewter craftsman doing business in 1820s, Hartford, Connecticut.

Brooks, D. B. & Brothers: Provided patent writing and toilet case for Federal soldiers and sailors. Located in Salem, Massachusetts.

Brooks, E. A.: Civil War era maker of military uniforms and overcoats. Located in New York City.

Broome, Isaac: Granted a contract in 1861 to produce 1,000 lances for the Federal government. No location listed.

Broome, Isaac: Known to be a potter in 1880s, Trenton, New Jersey.

Brown and Company (toys): Noted maker of clockwork toys in the nineteenth century. Founded by George W. Brown and based in Forestville, Connecticut. Mechanical toys included bell toys, vehicles, and dancing figures.

Brown and Tetley: Civil War supplier of military knives to the U.S. Army, located in Pittsburgh, Pennsylvania.

Brown, B. F. & Co.: Army and navy supplier of blacking (shoe polish) during the Civil War, based in Boston, Massachusetts.

Brown, David: Early nineteenth century clockmaker operating in Providence, Rhode Island. Crafted mostly smaller clocks and unique wall clocks.

Brown, Ebenezer: A silversmith in 1795, Boston, Massachusetts.

Browner, E. H.: Granted a Federal government contract during the Civil War to supply 50,000 bootees. Located in Syracuse, New York.

Brown, Gawen: An eighteenth century clockmaker who came to America from England and made long-case clocks and watches out of a shop in Boston, Massachusetts.

Brown heather (color): Heather or evergreen mixture with brown predominating.

Brownie doll: (see Cocheco Manufacturing Company)

Brown, Laurent: Active as an early American clockmaker doing business in Rochester, New York.

Brown, Robert: Known as active silversmith in 1815, Boston, Massachusetts.

Brown's Beery Bitters: Sold sometimes as Dr. Brown's Berry Bitters. Mostly a concoction of alcohol and herbs, manufactured in 1890s, St. Louis, Missouri.

Brown's Celebrated Indian Herb Bitters: Contained in a bottle shaped like an Indian woman, and patented in 1868. Mostly rye whiskey in bottles of various colors.

Brown's Foundry: Provided military cannons for Confederate forces during the Civil War. Located in Columbus, Georgia.

Brown sugar (color): During the 1920s, a material the color of brown sugar.

Brownsville, Pennsylvania: There were "four or five glass-works" operating in Brownsville during the early 1830s according to a memorial sent to Congress.

Brown, William Henry: Adept maker of silhouettes or profiles in middle nineteenth century America. Operating out of South Carolina he sometimes made full-length profiles of prominent residents and families. Additionally Brown also did profiles of railroad engines and steamships, and in 1846 published Portrait Gallery of Distinguished American Citizens.

Bru doll: Exquisite nineteenth century dolls manufactured in France. Second in quality only to French maker Jumeau, the Bru dolls were usually marked on the lower left back side of the bust with the vertical letters B R U. Bru dolls for all their elegance typically had heavier features and darker coloring than did Jumeau dolls.

Brunette (color): Term for a dark cream in the 1927 Sears and Roebuck catalog.

Brunswick Stew: Grocery item in the 1890s which sold for 35¢ a can. Mixture sold by the Cold Spring Packing Company of Atlanta, Georgia.

Brussels lace: Remarkable vintage lace first made in Brussels, Belgium. Initially patterns were outlined on a pillow with needle and thread and then background was added onto the design. In later years old patterns were reproduced by machine rather than created by hand.

Bryant, George: Under Federal government contract to make 7,000 military bootees during the Civil War. Located in East Bridgewater, Massachusetts.

Buck, Azariah: Silversmith of the 1850s in Rochester, New York.

Buckfield Mills: Provider of gunpowder to Federal forces during the Civil War, located in Paris, Maine.

Buckinghamshire lace: Simple but elegant lace crafted in England at a school of the same name during the late 1600s. Young girls living in poverty were given training using coarse thread on narrow strips of cloth. Background and design were crafted into the bottom lace at virtually the same time.

Bucklen and Co.: (see Electric Bitters)

Buckles, Colonial: Colonialists took a fancy to both the ornamental shoe and knee buckle in the eighteenth century

Breakfast table with inlaid mahogany, ca. 1790s. (Skinner Inc.)

Brooch, gold and enamel with rose-cut diamond. (Skinner Inc.)

after they became highly fashionable in England. At one point in the 1700s thousands of pairs were being imported to America. Most were made of pewter, however others were bejeweled with silver or gold applications.

Buck Rogers: Science fiction spaceman who grabbed national attention in the 1930s as a comic strip, radio show, and movie serial. Most famous related artifact was probably the rocket pistol and holster from Daisy in 1934, although there were many other treasures from buttons to wind-up toys.

Buck saw: Early sawing tool with a wooden bow frame. Heavy stationary blade used to "buck" logs by cutting them in proper lengths. Often the buck saw included a centered winding stick.

Buckwheat Flour: (See Aunt Jemima)

Bucranium: Basically the design of an ornament in the shape of an ox head or ox skull.

Buddy, Daniel: Practicing silversmith in 1770, Philadelphia, Pennsylvania.

Buddy L: (see Moline Pressed Steel)

Buffalo Electric Vehicle Co.: Maker of Buffalo Electric automobiles early in the twentieth century. The automobile maker was located in Buffalo, New York.

Buff (color): In a 1920s reference, a medium tan with a yellow cast.

Buffet: Term for American sideboard or dining room dresser.

Buick sedan (toy): Special Buick sedan made by Arcade Manufacturing in Freeport, Illinois. Issued in 1927, the model was made of cast iron and finished in green paint. The Buick name appeared on the radiator and on the tire carrier.

Bull, G. W.: Noted silversmith in 1840s, East Hartford, Connecticut.

Bull's-eye mirror: Product of the American Federal period both in convex and concave mirror forms, usually in a round gold frame.

Bultos: Carved religious figures of the Christian faith appearing in eighteenth and nineteenth century Southwestern portions of the United States and Mexico. Early examples were often carved from cottonwood root. Some were clothed.

Buly, John: Listed as a silversmith in 1780, Philadelphia, Pennsylvania.

Bun foot: British version of ball foot used on early furniture. The English ball foot was somewhat flatter and less cylindrical in design.

Burdick Sewing Machine: Sold by Sears, Roebuck and Company in the early 1900s. Models varied from three to seven drawers, and came with or without attachments. Woodwork came in oak or walnut.

Burdick, William: Active silversmith in 1810, New Haven, Connecticut.

Bureau: Late eighteenth century designer Thomas Sheraton suggested they were common desks with drawers. The term transcended to mean more of a bedroom chest.

Burford Brothers Pottery Company: Small pottery-making firm in 1890s, East Liverpool, Ohio.

Burger & Son: Pottery doing business in nineteenth century, Rochester, New York.

Burger, David: A noted silversmith doing business in 1805, New York City.

Burkmar, Thomas: A Colonial era clockmaker located in Boston, Massachusetts in the 1770s.

Burl: Malfunction of the grain of certain very hard woods when cut crosswise. The result for cabinetmakers was a mottled or speckled design within the wood. Sections of large sized burls were used in making veneers or for other decoration. Smaller burls were sometimes applied to chopping bowls and other tableware.

Burley & Lyford: One of the most industrious makers of cottage furniture in the Midwest during the middle nineteenth century. Cincinnati firm offered landscaped furniture, Grecian style beds, veneered grains, ornamental accessories, and even furniture for American steamboats of the 1840s and 1850s.

Burling, Thomas: An accomplished cabinetmaker operating in New York during the late eighteenth century. Burling sometimes labeled his furniture and is credited with crafting a writing desk for George Washington in 1795.

Burlington pottery: Initially a pottery operation established in early 1800 by Norman Judd in Burlington, Vermont. Most popular for brown and yellow ware crafted of the same name.

Burl panel: Use of a thin section of tree burl to form a thin portion of veneer.

Burmese glass: Very striking glass produced first in the late 1880s by the Mt. Washington Glass Company in New Bedford, Massachusetts. Ultimately it was offered in a wide variety of lovely hues ranging from deep pink to yellow. Some delicate shades of Burmese glass had a dull acid-treated satin surface texture, while other items had a quite shiny surface. Operations lasted little more than five years, but decorative pieces of Burmese glass proved to be exceptional.

Burnet, Samuel: Distinguished silversmith operating in 1795, Newark, New Jersey.

Burnett, Enoch: Stoneware potter active in 1850s and 1860s, Washington, D.C.

Burnside, A. E.: Supplier of .54 caliber

carbines to the U.S. Army during the 1860s, located in Providence, Rhode Island.

Burnt brass (color): Used to describe a dull unpolished brass finish early in the twentieth century.

Burnt orange (color): Noted as a natural orange with a reddish cast in the 1927 Sears catalog.

Burnt sienna (color): Considered to be a rich reddish brown in Sears catalogs of the 1920s.

Burnt umber (color): The 1920s catalog term for a dark brown.

Burot, Andrew: Silversmith known to be active in 1820s, Baltimore, Maryland.

Burr elm: (see Elm)

Burr, Cornelius: Early to middle nineteenth century silversmith located in Rochester, New York.

Burr, Ezekiel: Doing business as a clockmaker with William Burr in 1790s, Providence, Rhode Island.

Burroughs & Mountford Company: A pottery operation doing business in 1880s, Trenton, New Jersey.

Burslem: Center of pottery production in seventeenth century England. Home to numerous pottery factories.

Burt, Addison: Contracted to provide rifled muskets to the U.S. government during the Civil War, located in New York City.

Bush, George: Listed as an active clockmaker in 1820s and 1830s, Easton, Pennsylvania.

Bushnell, Phineas: Silversmith located in 1760s, Guilford, Connecticut.

Buster Brown: A fictional character first created by artist R. F. Outcault in the early 1900s as a comic strip. Buster and dog Tige went on to star on a leading brand of shoes and became a premium for other products as well. Buster also

Advertisement for Buck Rogers rocket pistol in 1934.

Butternut and cherry Shaker sewing case, ca. 1840. (Skinner Inc.)

delighted children on Saturday morning radio in the 1940s and early 1950s.

Buswell, Jason: Recorded as a silversmith in 1840s, Portsmouth, New Hampshire.

Butler, Aaron: Head of an established nineteenth century family of tinsmiths in East Greenville, New York. Butler's daughters who participated in the operation included Ann, Minerva, and Marilla.

Butler, Henry: Successful silversmith operating in 1835 Philadelphia, Pennsylvania.

Butter cupboard: Similar to the traditional pie safe but much smaller, it had pierced doors to allow for circulating air. Used for storage of butter, cheese, and similar goods, they were handmade and sometimes given fancy decoration in the eighteenth century. During the nineteenth century butter cupboards were sometimes manufactured and sold commercially.

Butterfield, Jesse: Listed as a maker of Army percussion revolver, patented in 1855. Located in Philadelphia, Pennsylvania.

Butterfly hinge: Decorative butterfly-shaped iron hinge used on Colonial furniture of the early 1700s.

Butterfly table: Small table of American origin which offered drop leaves on either side of a solid center piece. Swinging wooden brackets held the leaves in place. Such tables were crafted as early as 1670 in Connecticut.

Butterfly wedge: Reference to a butterfly-shaped wedge of wood used to join two additional pieces of wood. Wedge could also be metal.

Butter molds: Most extensively used from the 1750s to the 1880s in America to design small pats of butter. Usually of wood, but also of pottery and tin ware, they provided a 3" to 5" image when turned with a wooden handle. Images included hearts, tulips, cows, and various other patterns.

Butternut wood: This hardwood saw some use in the eighteenth century in Queen Anne highboys, and during the early nineteenth century in middle America for a variety of furniture from chests to tables. Close-grained wood could be polished into a very light brown tone. Sometimes mistakenly called white walnut.

Butterscotch Beaver: (see Dairy Queen)

Butterworth, James: A noted nineteenth century artist of marine scenes whose works were eventually lithographed by the prolific Currier and Ives firm during the second half of that century.

Butt joint: Cabinetmaker's term describing the joining at the grain ends of two plain squared surfaces of wood.

Byam, C. C.: Noted clockmaker located in 1860s, Amesbury, Massachusetts.

Bybee Pottery: Art pottery and stoneware producers doing business in 1930s, Madison County, Kentucky.

Bye-Lo Baby (doll): (see Putnam, Grace Story)

Byrne Stomach Bitters: Mixture of alcohol and other ingredients in a fancy amber bottle of the 1870s. Credited to Professor George Byrne, New York.

Byrne, George: (see Byrne Stomach Bitters)

Byrne, George C.: Listed as producer of military equipment for Federal troops during the Civil War. Based in 1860s, New York City.

Cabinet: Term used to designate a form of cupboard used for the display or storage of china or plates. Previously it had also described a small, private consulting room.

Cable, Stephen: Active as a clockmaker, 1840s to 1860s in New York City.

Cabochon: Early furniture reference to a plain or round surface surrounded with ornamentation and extending inward or outward.

Cabriole: Colonial furniture term to describe the curved leg of some pieces. Typically such a leg curved outward at the top and then curved inward below.

Cacolet: Term for a mule-drawn litter or chair-like devise used to transport injured during the Civil War.

Caddy box: Simply another early name for the tea caddy.

Caddy spoon: Functional spoon used to dip into the tea caddy for a small amount of tea leaves to be placed in the teapot. Early caddy spoons were usually silver and highly ornate.

Cadet blue (color): Described as a medium grayish blue.

Cadillac Tonneau: Excellently constructed vehicle in 1903 based on the design by Henry M. Leland. A large rear body was detachable, while the front seated two passengers. The model featured a one-cylinder five horsepower engine.

Cady, Samuel: New York City silversmith of the 1790s.

Café au lait (color): A rich coffee cream color in 1920s mail order terms.

Caire and Company: Stoneware firm operated by John B. Caire in 1840s and 1850s, Poughkeepsie, New York.

Cairns, John: Spirited silversmith located in 1825, Rochester, New York.

Calder, William: Noted pewtersmith during the 1820s in Providence, Rhode Island. Wares often marked with name and eagle logo.

Calendar aperture (clock): Dial of a clock where it is possible to view the date and the month.

Calliope Clown: A jolly, bouncing clown playing the keyboard of a calliope wagon as offered in the 1952 Billy and Ruth catalog. The pull toy was made by Mattel and was 8" tall.

Calyo, Nicolino: Italian-born artist best known for tonal etchings of the 1835 Great Fire of New York. Calyo also sketched other New York street scenes of that period.

Calyx (clock): Reference to an elaborate clock decoration involving a whorl of leaves. On early clocks it usually included a flower bud within the leaves.

Camber: Describes the upward curving of the surface or arch of crafted furniture in the colonial era.

Cambric cloth: Originally a finely woven cloth produced in Cambric, France, and imported to America. Later a similar cotton-based cloth as made in the industrial United States, and for a time the term was used for any white or colored lightweight cotton cloth.

Cambric tea: Strictly a non-tea served to children and elderly people who were considered unsuitable for true tea. Cambric tea, composed mostly of hot water, sugar, and milk was named for the white Cambric cloth its color resembled.

Cambridge Art Pottery: A maker of quality pottery ware. Established in late nineteenth century, Cambridge, Ohio.

Camden Mills: Provider of gunpowder to Federal troops during the Civil War, located in Camden, Maine.

Camel back: The double curved crest rail of some late eighteenth century George Hepplewhite chair backs. The outline of such chairs suggested the humped back of a camel. Later the term was also used in connection with a style of trunks

Camel (color): Medium tan according to Sears in the 1920s, as in the color of the animal with the same name.

Campbell's Soup logo on ceramic mug.

legendary included the photomatic decoder badge and the mirro-flash code-o-graph.

Carcase: Term in early furniture referring to a box-like piece with doors or fittings, but without any ornamentation.

Carcel lamp: Early lamp with a clockwork pump providing oil from a reservoir at the base. A variation of the Argand lamp, sometimes called a mechanized lamp.

Cardinal (color): Considered a bright red in the Sears and Roebuck catalog in the 1920s.

Cargill Company: Early twentieth century publisher of women's suffrage postcards, based in Grand Rapids, Michigan.

Carhart steam wagon: Brainchild of Dr. W. W. Carhart operating in 1870s, Racine, Wisconsin. Complete with short smokestack it operated on 20 gallons of water and used buggy wheels.

Carmine (color): Very brilliant red in 1920s terms.

Carner, S. A.: Granted Civil War era patent for military camp chest, based in Brooklyn, New York.

Carnival Caravan: Boxed selection of carnival vehicles and games as featured in the 1952 Billy and Ruth Catalog. Games included Ticket Seller and Trip to the Moon. Made by Banner Plastics, it sold for $1.98.

Carnival glass: A relatively inexpensive iridescent glass made in the late nineteenth century and early twentieth century. Sometimes called taffeta glass, was said to be an attempt to imitate Tiffany's Favrille glass.

Carpathian Herb Bitters: Bottled mixture of alcohol and herbs, sold by the Hollander Drug Company,

in nineteenth century Braddock, Pennsylvania.

Carpenter celluloid doll: Early in the 1880s W. B. Carpenter was granted a patent for a celluloid doll with moveable neck and real hair. They were produced by the Celluloid Manufacturing Company in Newark, New Jersey.

Carpenter, Charles: Silversmith doing business in 1805, Boston, Massachusetts.

Carpenter, Frederick: Early nineteenth century stoneware potter doing business in Boston, Massachusetts.

Carpenter gothic: Transition of Gothic Revival design from stone to wood. At its height it involved such offerings as gingerbread trim. The trim was elaborately given jig-sawed cusps and trefoils.

Carrell, Daniel: Philadelphia silversmith operating in late 1700s and early 1800s.

Carrington, William: Inventive silversmith of record in 1830, Charleston, South Carolina.

Carrol, James: Listed as a silversmith in 1835, Albany, New York.

Carrollton China Company: Early 1900s producers of whiteware in Salineville, Ohio.

Carrot (color): Basically a light orange according to early Sears and Roebuck.

Carr, Thomas: Cannon rifling machine maker for Confederate forces during the Civil War. Located in Portsmouth, Virginia.

Cartlidge & Company: Porcelain firm headed by Charles Cartlidge in 1840s and 1850s, Greenpoint, New York.

Cartouche: Decorative furniture reference regarding the ornamental form of scrolling or shield-shape design painted or inscribed on an otherwise plain surface.

Silver-plate caster set complete with cruets.

Cartwright Brothers: A small producer of pottery ware in 1880s, East Liverpool, Ohio.

Cartwright, John: English-born engraver who sketched acid treated tonal views of American scenes during the very early 1800s.

Carver chair: Described as a side chair in the seventeenth century, named for the governor of Massachusetts. Typically it was a heavy chair made entirely from turnings fitted into each other horizontally and vertically.

Caryatid and/or Caryatide: (clock): Decoration on early clocks where female figures were used instead of regular columns. Also used in other forms of architecture.

Cary, James: Active clockmaker in 1830s and 1840s, Brunswick, Maine.

Case automobile: Made by J. I. Case Company located in Racine, Wisconsin. In 1922 they advertised the Case Model X available as a touring car or sedan.

Case, Dyer, Wadsworth and Company: Group of clockmakers operating in 1830s, Augusta, Georgia.

Case, Erastus: Noted clockmaker working in 1830s, Bristol, Connecticut.

Case, John: Granted a patent on a military type canteen in 1861, located in Philadelphia, Pennsylvania.

Casement window: Term for a framed window which could swing in or out because it was hinged at the side.

Casey, Samuel: Noted eighteenth century silversmith located in Newport, Rhode Island.

Cassin's Grape Brandy Bitters: Bottled liquor sold as medication, ca. 1900 to 1910, maker unknown.

Caster (furniture): Term for a small roller attached to the base of a furniture piece to make for easier moving.

Caster set: Victorian term for assembly of glass bottles, sometimes metal encased, and cruets holding condiments for elaborate table servings. The bottles contained salt, pepper, vinegar, and other seasonings which were then "cast" upon the servings upon the plate. The decorative metal used ranged from pewter to silver plate.

Castleman, E.: Provided swords and sabers to military forces during the Civil War, located in Alexandria, Virginia.

Caswell, H. A.: Supplier of playing cards for Federal troops during the Civil War, based in New York City.

Catlin, George: Famous for drawings and illustrations of western America during the middle of the nineteenth century, particularly life among the Indians. Catlin created the lithographs for the North American Indian Portfolio published in England in 1844.

Catmallison: Furniture term for a cupboard placed in or about a chimney to preserve dried and smoked meats.

Cato, J. R.: Produced six-pound cannon carriages and caissons for Confederate military. Located in Richmond, Virginia.

Cat whisker (radio): A fine spring wire of early radio resting lightly on the crystal of a detector.

Caughley (ceramic): Porcelain factory active in latter eighteenth century, Shropshire, England. Major production involved a soft-paste porcelain.

Cauldron: Grand cooking pot, also sometimes known as a kettle, used for all boiled foods in early America and elsewhere. Most were made of iron, although some cauldrons could be made of brass or copper. They were constantly in use at a time when most all food preparation involved a boiling pot.

Cauliflower ware: Glazed earthenware of green and yellow colors typically in

Shirley Temple celebrity doll by Ideal.

the form of cauliflower or pineapple. Credited to the Whieldon-Wedgwood partnership of the latter part of the eighteenth century.

Cavetto: Early furniture term relating to a hollow, round, concave molding application.

C. C. Thompson Pottery Company: Maker of pottery and other items in late 1860s, East Liverpool, Ohio.

Cedar wood: Pleasant scented wood in colors of red or white. It was sometimes used in furniture, but most often used to line chests, drawers, and eventually closets.

Celebrity doll: A doll created basically in the likeness of a well-known personality. Usually marketed based on the popularity of that particular personality.

Celestial blue (color): Sears in 1927 suggested it was simply a very light blue.

Cellaret: Seen in the early sideboard, a deep drawer or tray for bottles.

Celluloid Manufacturing Co.: (see Carpenter celluloid doll)

Century Doll Company: Noted doll maker in early 1900s, New York City.

Ceramic Art Company: Factory noted for its exceptional Beleek ware founded in 1889, Trenton, New Jersey.

Cerise (color): Early Sears catalogs considered it light red with a purple cast. Later definitions compared it to ripe cherries.

Certosina (clock): Term for the geometrical design of inlay on early clocks and other pieces. Very small pieces were used in the overall design.

Chad Valley Company: British doll maker found in 1920s, Birmingham, England.

Chadwick, Joseph: Listed as an active clockmaker in 1820s, Boscowen, New Hampshire.

Chafing dish: Term used to cover many forms of a dish used for heating foods directly at the serving table. Some silver examples were quite elegant; others were crafted of lesser metals. Most provided a heavy handle and a burner base for charcoal.

Chainless Wolverine: (see Reid Manufacturing Company)

Chaise watch: A popular eighteenth century time keeping device fitted into the pocket of a horse-drawn carriage. Usually in pocketwatch style, but 3 to 4" in diameter.

Chalkware: A type of plaster ware produced in middle to latter nineteenth century in various parts of the country. Various pewter, tin, and wax molds were used to produce images of birds, dogs, farm animals, and other figures. Vendors still offered it into the 1890s.

Challinor, Taylor and Company: Firm noted for its quality of milk glass and slag glass during the 1870s and 1880s in Tarentum, Pennsylvania.

Chalmers-Detroit coupe: Stylish motor car produced in 1910 by former cash register manufacturer Hugh Chalmers. Reported to be one of the best designed and sturdiest built automobiles of that era.

Chamber clock: Prior to the introduction of the pendulum, this was a reference to iron lantern clocks.

Chamberlin, William: Noted clockmaker operating in 1840s and 1850s, Towanda, Pennsylvania.

Chamfer: Term for the beveled cutting away of a corner or molding. Typically applied to smooth corners on early chests and other case furniture. Chamfered corners varied in width and were sometimes in reed form or fluted.

Champagne (color): According to Sears in 1927, a light creamy tan.

Champion: Brand name of wooden handled fly swatter sold in early 1900s S.S. Kresge Co. stores.

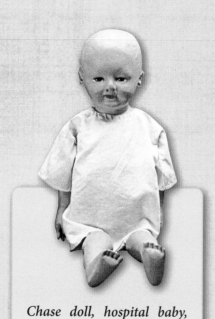

Chase doll, hospital baby, designed by Martha Chase during the 1920s for health care training. (Skinner Inc.)

Chandler Six automobile: Early twentieth century motor vehicle which was a product of the Chandler Motor Car Company in Cleveland, Ohio. In 1916 the Chandler Six sold for $1,295.

Chandler, Stephen: Silversmith doing business in 1810, New York City.

Chanel red (color): A dark red or garnet.

Chantilly (ceramic): Term for eighteenth century French made soft-paste porcelain.

Chapbook: Name given to the eighteenth century equivalent of the nineteenth/early twentieth century dime novel. The inexpensive chapbook often contained songs, poems, and brief stories and were typically sold by passing peddlers.

Chapin, George: Supplier of various military tent poles for the Federal government during the Civil War.

Chapman, C.: Supplier of Model 1841 rifles to the Confederate military during the Civil War.

Charger: Term for a large, round pewter or silver plate used to serve meat. Some sources define three or more sizes. The Webster's dictionary of 1867 however defines charger as simply a large dish.

Chase doll: Originally designed in the late nineteenth century by Martha Chase of Pawtucket, Rhode Island. Chase Stockinet Dolls were popular cloth dolls with a round baby face trademark. Other Chase dolls were designed for training in hospitals.

Chase, Martha Jenks: (see Chase doll)

Chase, Timothy: Clockmaker in 1830s and 1840s, Belfast, Maine.

Chase, Wesley: Provider of military camp chests to Federal forces during the Civil War, located in Buffalo, New York.

Chasing: Decorative indentations applied to metal surfaces by a blunt instrument.

Chasing hammer: Reference to a special tool for metal surfaces. Specifically it was used for adding relief decoration.

Chat, Easton: Operating as a silversmith in 1795, Philadelphia, Pennsylvania.

Chatelaine: Elegant brooch, usually of gold or silver, with small chains that carried other attachments. The attachments could range from thimble cases to miniature scissors. More elaborate chatelaine pieces were decorated with precious stones and gold inlay.

Chauncey souvenir spoon: Issued during the 1890s in honor of Chauncey Depew, "the silver-tongued orator of America." Silver spoons, bowls, and even knives carried the image of Depew and other famous persons.

Checker Cab (toy): Late 1920s item from Arcade Manufacturing in Freeport, Illinois. Firm also produced special finish cabs and Yellow Cab vehicles of cast iron in the same period.

Chein and Company: Early twentieth century toy firm based in New York City. Enchanted the public with lithographed tinplate toys and later steel toys. Colorfully illustrated and well marked, the toys included banks, drums, tops, and tea sets. Also incorporated images of Mickey Mouse, Donald Duck, and Popeye.

Chelmsford Glass Company: Makers of glass plates, glassware, and window glass in Pembroke, New Hampshire. The company was incorporated in July of 1839. Earlier the works had been located in Chelmsford, Mass.

Chelsea (ceramic): Reference to an eighteenth century factory in England which produced soft-paste porcelain. Figurines and decorated china pieces bore various marks including triangle and anchor. Early nineteenth century product was Chelsea-Derby ware.

Chein and Company metal clown bank, late 1930s.

Cherry wood dressing table in Queen Anne style, ca. 1770s. (Skinner Inc.)

Chelsea China Company: Undertaking of pottery making, established in 1888, New Cumberland, West Virginia.

Chelsea Keramic: Pottery making firm operating in late 1860s, Chelsea, Massachusetts.

Chenango China Company: Producers of whiteware pottery in early 1900s, New Castle, Pennsylvania.

Cheney, Benjamin: Noted clockmaker working in 1780s, Manchester, Connecticut.

Chequer: In effect a checker-board type of furniture decoration involving squares which are colored alternately or shaded differently.

Cherb: An angelic winged child-like celestial creature.

Cherry bloom (color): A bright rose pink in mail-order terms early in the twentieth century.

Cherry (color): A fairly bright red as defined by Sears in the 1920s.

Cherry wood: Exceptionally hard and close-grained wood used in early American furniture. Reddish-brown color was somewhat similar to mahogany. It took a good polish and colored well with age. Favored by some eighteenth century colonial cabinetmakers for butterfly tables and other pieces. Early in the nineteenth century, cherry was also sometimes used for bed posts and tall case clocks.

Chesapeake Pottery: Noted for excellent design and decoration of wares in early 1880s, Baltimore, Maryland. Founded by D. F. Haynes and Company, it crafted grayish-olive Severn ware as well as fine semi-porcelain Parian ware during that decade.

Cheshire Clock Company: Clockmaking operation of the 1880s in Cheshire, Connecticut.

Cheshire Crown Glass Works: Factory producing window glass starting around 1812 and continuing to 1852 in Cheshire, Massachusetts. Later the company began producing plate glass in Brooklyn, New York.

Chesterfield: Furniture term designating an overstuffed double-ended couch.

Chester Glass Company: Small glass factory which began making window glass in 1812 at Chester, Massachusetts. The company was incorporated in 1814 and was successful using "local" sand in its operation.

Chester Pottery Company: Doing business in 1890s, Phoenixville, Pennsylvania.

Chestnut wood: Considered a medium-hard wood by early cabinetmakers. Distinctive grain pattern sometimes compared to oak. Finished color was judged to be a brownish yellow. Chestnut was used in the eighteenth century for large chests, and combined with other woods in beds and tables. Chestnut was sometimes a substitute for a similar grained satinwood.

Cheval glass: Large glass or mirror swinging in two framed supports.

Chevalier, John D.: Listed as a provider of military knives during the Civil War, located in New York City.

Chevreuse (color): A French term, considered a dark old rose color by early Sears catalogs.

Chevrolet coupe (toy): Arcade produced a complete set of miniature Chevrolet automobiles in the late 1920s. Included were the sedan, touring car, roadster, and utility express truck. Most were about 7" long.

Chevron: Reference to the V-shaped inlaid design or other decoration. Also used as a military insignia for rank.

Chicago Colortype Co.: Noted as printer and engraver for some government postal cards of the late 1890s.

Chief: Name of brass plated padlock offered by S.S. Kresge Co. stores in 1913.

Child, Pratt and Fox: Makers of military trousers, overcoats, and jackets for Federal troops during the Civil War. Located in St. Louis, Missouri.

Children's bread and milk sets: Distinguished cut glass serving sets for children produced in the 1890s by C. Dorflinger and Sons of New York. The boxed sets included jug, bowl, plate, and started at $5.

Child, True W.: Active clockmaker in 1820s, Boston, Massachusetts.

China: Once widely used as a term in ceramics as a reference to all types of porcelain. Originally it was an English designation dealing with tableware actually imported from China. Eventually it became standard for all similar glazed ware.

China head doll: Generally quite durable nineteenth century dolls with heads made of white clay. The doll heads could be tinted, fired, and dipped in glaze before refiring.

Chin chin blue (color): In the 1920s, Sears defined it as a light Copenhagen blue.

Chinese red (color): According to the Sears catalog a very bright red.

Chintz: Defined in the mid-nineteenth century as a cotton cloth, printed with colors and flowers.

Chip carving (furniture): A reference to the use of flat chisels and semi-circular gouges to provide simple carving of furniture in low relief.

Chippendale, Thomas: Legendary English cabinetmaker and designer of the eighteenth century and author of the 1754 book, *The Gentleman and Cabinet Maker's Directory.* After much success a third and enlarged edition of the book was issued in parts from 1759 to 1762. Chippendale's style was often imitated in Colonial America.

Chisholm Brothers: Early twentieth century publishers of regional and exposition postcards, based in Portland, Maine.

Chittenango Pottery Company: Producer of pottery in late nineteenth century Chittenango, New York.

Chittenden bed: Sturdy cast iron beds produced by Samuel Chittenden in 1850s, New York City.

Chivalry board game: Popular game of skill that came boxed with a lithographed folding board in the 1890s. The game of chance with 40 pieces was manufactured by George S. Parker and Company in Salem, Massachusetts.

Chocolate: First introduced as a drink in the seventeenth century, by 1678 it was being sold in Boston as chuchalette. An early favorite in New York, it later became trendy in Pennsylvania.

Chocolate pot: Such pots were similar to early coffee pots, however their form included a sliding cover or detachable piece which concealed a small hole. The hole provided room for a small stick used to stir the chocolate liquid.

Chopping bowl: Basically a wooden bowl used to chop food in during earlier times. Such bowls were said to have been originally crafted from tree trunks.

Christening blanket: (see Bearing cloth)

Christmas box: Webster's in 1867 defined it as a box in which presents are placed at Christmas.

Christmas collectibles: Clearly a leading seasonal area of collecting. Interest extends from early ornaments and Santa figures to early 1900s postcards and even metallic Christmas trees.

Blonde china head doll, nineteenth century Germany.

Christ, Rudolph: Potter crafting redware and stoneware in early nineteenth century, Salem, North Carolina.

Christy bread knife: Bestselling knife made by the Christy Knife Company in 1890s, Fremont, Ohio. Their three-knife set included one of paring, one for cake, and one for bread.

Christy, Peter: Accomplished silversmith from 1815 to 1825 in New York City.

Chrome era: Postcard term which suggests the glossy surface period related to Kodachrome film. Infrequently seen in the 1940s, but a dominate process in late decades.

Chrome green (color): Defined in the early 1920s as having mixed shades of green.

Chrome lemon (color): Having mixed shades of yellow according to Sears in 1927.

Chrome orange (color): Offering mixed shades of orange during the 1920s.

Chromo picture: Trendy latter nineteenth century procedure where oil paintings were commercially reproduced on fabric and sold to an admiring public. Chromolithographic suggested use of full color.

Chubb The Fishing Rod Manufacturer: Noted 1890s fishing rod maker Thomas H. Chubb who advertised in *Harper's*. In 1890 their new eight-strip split bamboo offer was billed as the King of all fishing rods for $4. Readers could write Chubb at Post Mills, Vermont.

Chuck muck: Not the poor fellow a year behind you in high school, rather an early term for the tinderbox which assisted in lighting fires.

Church and Rogers: Silversmiths in 1820s, Hartford, Connecticut.

Churchill and Treadwell: Boston silversmiths of note in the early 1800s.

Churchill, L. & H.: Contracted with the Federal government during the Civil War to provide 5,000 military bootees. Located in Rochester, New York.

Churchwell, Charles: Practicing Colonial silversmith in 1780, Philadelphia, Pennsylvania.

Cigarette card: Cardboard pictures of baseball players, boxers, and stage stars used in the 1880s and into the early 1900s by cigarette companies to protect packages and encourage sales.

Cinched waist (doll): (see Wasp waist)

Cincinnati Art Pottery Company: Highly regarded factory first started in 1880 by T. J. Wheatley and Company. Noted early for under-glaze work, and later for remarkable ivory-covered faience decorated with gold scroll work and in flowers with natural colors.

Circa: Meaning around or about that specific date, also used as ca. Example ca. 1840.

Cisco Kid: Originally a short story character of the 1900s, but best known for television's depictions in the 1950s. Cisco rode to black and white fame with partner Pancho and also spanned numerous related premiums for Tip-Top Bread and others.

City Pottery Company: Firm established in 1859, Trenton, New Jersey.

Claggett, William: Noted clockmaker active in 1730s and 1740s, Newport, Rhode Island.

Claiborne Machine Works: During the Civil War this firm produced six- and 12-pound cannons for the Confederate military. Located in Nashville, Tennessee.

Clapboard: Basically a type of pine timber used for paneling in early American homes and imported from Europe.

Claret wine (color): Early Sears catalogs

Large china head doll with sculptured black hair.

considered it a medium wine color. Later defined as a dark purplish color.

Clark and Lambe: Listed as providers of sharpshooters' rifles to the Confederate military during the Civil War. Located at Deep River, North Carolina.

Clark, Curtis: New York City silversmith active in 1825.

Clark, Daniel: Cabinetmaker trained in Boston who established a successful business in Salem, Massachusetts. Clark specialized in household furniture at the end of the eighteenth century and well into the nineteenth century.

Clark, Daniel: Listed as a clockmaker in 1840s, Waterbury, Connecticut.

Clarke, Ephraim: Colonial era clockmaker working in 1790s, Philadelphia, Pennsylvania.

Clark, Joseph: Silversmith known to be doing business in Danbury, Connecticut from 1790 to 1820.

Clark, Lewis: Noted silversmith in 1835 Utica, New York.

Clark, Lucius: Active as a clockmaker in 1840s, Winstead, Connecticut.

Clark's Glass Works: Little known glass factory operating in 1830s, Washington, D.C.

Clarkson and Co.: Supplier of knives to Confederate military during the Civil War. Located in Richmond, Virginia.

Clarkson, Crolius: Active stoneware potter in early nineteenth century, New York City. Later joined by Crolius Clarkson Jr.

Clasp knife: A nineteenth century term for a large knife in which the blade shuts into the handle. Basically another term for pocket knife.

Claudette (doll head): Sold in the Montgomery Ward catalog of 1973, the Claudette doll head and base came with washable nylon-rooted hair. Hair could be set in "the latest styles" and

even be cut. Complete with plastic rollers, the full price was $7.99.

Clauss shears: Brand of shears and scissors manufactured by the use of natural gas in the 1890s. A product of Clauss in Fremont, Ohio.

Claw and ball: Generally suggesting the foot of a piece of furniture in the image of the claw of a bird clasped around a ball.

Clawson & Mudge: Prosperous furniture making firm in 1850s, Cincinnati, Ohio. A workforce of 130 produced more than 100 bedsteads each day. Using various hardwoods their products sold from under $2 to $75 each.

Cleat (furniture): Term used by cabinetmakers to describe a strip of wood typically fastened across the grain of boards to prevent warping later.

Clements, Moses: Listed as a clockmaker in 1750s, New York City.

Cleveland, Aaron: An 1820s silversmith located in Norwich, Connecticut.

Clifton Art Pottery: Doing business in early twentieth century, Clifton, New Jersey.

Clincher Tire: (see Morgan & Wright)

Clockwork: Mechanism for early toys involving interlocking gears powered by an unwinding spring. The device in turn would provide movement for the toy.

Club foot: Furniture foot used as a straight alternative or contrasting design to the curved or cabriole leg. Frequently used in Chippendale and early Queen Anne pieces. Also called pad foot.

Cluster, Isaac: Midwestern silversmith doing business in 1850s, St. Louis, Missouri.

Coal hod: (see Pipkin)

Cobalt blue: Remarkable hard blue opaque ware of china-like weight.

Cobbie Corn: (see Del Monte Corporation)

Christmas light bulb in the form of snowman, milk glass, ca. 1920s.

Santa Claus figural light bulb, made in Japan, ca. 1920s.

Raggedy Ann's Christmas Surprise book, 1952.

Coca-Cola: A product which predates the twentieth century and overshadows most other brand-related collectibles. More than a century of Coke images from calendars to wall signs have been produced.

Cocheco Manufacturing Company: Maker of cloth dolls in the 1890s, which were sold in dry goods stores around the country. Choices included the darky doll, white doll baby, Brownie doll, Japanese doll, and baby elephant.

Coead, Upton: Noted silversmith in 1840s, New York City.

Coffee mill: A small mill for grinding coffee.

Coffee mill (toy): Various types made by Arcade Manufacturing Co. One marked Juvenile and other marked Little Tot. Both had hardwood boxes, iron parts, and turning crank. Circa 1920s.

Coffee pot: Relatively tall pot, sometimes with straight sides, first used during the latter seventeenth century in England. In the nineteenth century it was described in the U.S. as simply a covered pot in which coffee is boiled.

Coffer: Early term for a six-board chest used to store valuables as well as for sitting. An attached handle at either end made for easy carrying, or for storage on ship or stagecoach. Some were covered with leather and constructed with metal bands.

Coggle wheel (ceramic): Term for a pottery wheel used to make decorations into soft clay. Usually wooden or metal with a handle.

Cogswell, Henry: Silversmith of 1840s and 1850s, Boston, Massachusetts.

Cohansy Glass Co.: (see Bridgeton, New Jersey)

Cohen, Thomas: Established Midwestern silversmith in 1810, Chillicothe, Ohio.

Coin silver: High quality silver used to mint coins in America, and also melted down in making silverware during the Victorian era. Eventually the practice of using coin silver in tableware was banned by law.

Coit and Mansfield: Silversmiths doing business between 1815 and early 1820s in Norwich, Connecticut.

Colburn, C. and Co.: Makers of cavalry boots for Federal troops during the Civil War. Located in Boston, Massachusetts.

Cold Spring Packing Company: (see Brunswick Stew)

Coldwell, George: Doing business as a pewter craftsman in 1790s, New York City.

Cole, Albert: Diligent silversmith active in 1844, New York City.

Cole Eight automobile: A product of the Cole Motor Car Company of Indianapolis, Indiana, in the early twentieth century. In 1917 the seven passenger Cole Eight touring car sold for $1,595.

Coleman doll: In 1917 Harry H. Coleman was granted a patent for a doll that walked. The procedure worked by lifting the doll's hand and moving it slightly to the side. Through the early 1920s they were produced as Dolly Walker dolls in three different sizes.

Colgate's cold cream: Brand of cold cream sold by S.S. Kresge Co. stores in 1913. Price per tube was 10¢.

Collared toe: A reference to that ornamental band placed at the base of a chair leg or table leg in early colonial furniture.

Collette, Lambert: Active silversmith during the 1830s and 1840s in Buffalo, New York.

Collins, Timothy: Accomplished craftsman of the nineteenth century at the New England Glass Works in Sandwich, Massachusetts.

Colonial Georgian: Used to describe a style of furniture and decoration based upon the work of eighteenth century English cabinetmakers who had relocated to the United States.

Colonial Revival: Reference to revival in architecture and furniture in the late nineteenth century of previous American Colonial style. Such a revival, particularly of furniture, continued into the twentieth century.

Colonnade: A row of columns with entablatures or decorative space horizontally above any two columns.

Colors, colonial interior: During the eighteenth century colonial homes were often decorated in pale and medium hues of blue, green, red, and yellow. Also favored were ocher and coffee, and occasionally partial gilding.

Colt pistol: Remarkable revolver created by Samuel Colt in latter 1830s and early 1840s in Patterson, New Jersey. After a round of bankruptcy, Colt returned to manufacturing in Hartford, Connecticutt in 1847.

Columbia Daumon Victoria: Produced by the Columbia Electric Vehicle Company in 1897 based on the design of William H. Atwood. With a Victorian carriage and boxes of batteries the vehicle could reportedly attain speeds of up to 30 miles per hour.

Columbiads: (see Archer, Dr. Junius)

Columbian (doll): A cloth doll with painted features first created for the Chicago World's Fair of 1893. Handcrafted by Mariatta and Emma Adams of Oswego, New York, they were later made by their married sister, Marie Ruttan. Each doll's muslin body was stuffed with excelsior and marked with a rubber stamp.

Columbia Electric Runabout: (see Electric Vehicle Company)

Columbia tricycle: Very popular three-wheeled vehicles for "ladies and gentlemen" during the 1880s. Complete with "power gear" for added leverage on steep grades they were priced at $180 by the Pope Manufacturing Company of Boston.

Columbo Peptic Bitters: Bottled mixture of herbs and mostly alcohol, ca.1860s, produced by L. E. Jung, New Orleans, Louisiana.

Columbus Arsenal: Provider of infantry accouterments and harness to the Confederate cause during the Civil War. Located in Columbus, Georgia.

Columbus Iron Works: Supplier of brass field pieces for the Confederate military during the Civil War. Located in Columbus, Georgia.

Columbus Motor Vehicle Co.: Makers of early 1900s automobiles including the Santos Dumont advertised as the Flying Automobile. The Santos had 20 horsepower and sold for $2,000. The company was located in Columbus, Ohio.

Colwell and Lawrence: Silversmiths during the 1850s in Albany, New York.

Comet: (see Horn of plenty [glass])

Comfort Bag (military): A World War I term for a small individual bag containing articles useful to a soldier in the field.

Comic strip: A selection of panels relating a comic story appearing in newspapers and in magazine form.

Comic supplement: American newspapers began offering comic strip sections in 1900 and continuously in black and white or color since that time. By the 1940s the most popular strips in the supplements were Barney Google, Blondie (and Dagwood), Buster Brown, the Gumps, Little Abner, and Mutt and Jeff.

Cisco Kid and Poncho on puzzle from Saafield, published in 1951.

Commander Sedan: (see Studebaker Manufacturing Company)

Commeraw Pottery: Producer of hard earthenware and salt-glazed stoneware in 1780s, Corlears Hook, New York.

Commode: Term used to describe a small cabinet or pedestal for bedroom use. Later used to include a chest of drawers. The most decorated of these in the mid-eighteenth century included inlaid, painted, and japanned examples.

Common Sense chair: Brand of chairs, tables, settees, and rockers sold in the late 1880s by F. A. Sinclair of Mottville, New York. "No light trashy stuff, but good, honest home comfort," noted advertisements. Price of a maple frame rocking chair was $2.75.

Compo: A representation of the word composition. In early furniture the term suggested it was a combination of glue, resin, and plaster mixed with water and used as a substitute for wood. Such work was also sometimes identified as stucco.

Composition doll: Initially this included a combination of wood, flour, starch, and rosin mixed with water. Early in the twentieth century they were made in Germany, and later in the United States up until about the 1940s.

Compote: Term for basic ceramic or glass bowl on a pedestal foot or stem.

Compton and Co.: British provider of pewter medical canteens to Federal troops in the 1860s.

Comstock, J. S. and Co.: Under contract with the Federal government during the Civil War to provide military boots and shoes. Located in St. Louis, Missouri.

Conch (furniture): Shell-like ornamentation typically seen on furniture of the Federal style. Sometimes inlaid and sometimes painted.

Condict, J. E.: Cavalry cartridge box and cap box maker for Federal troops during the Civil War. Based in New York City.

Condict, Wooley & Co.: Chicago based maker of horse equipment including saddles for Federal troops during the 1860s.

Coney, John: Highly regarded Colonial silversmith and noted engraver located in Boston. Coney made plates for Colonial paper money in 1690, among many other accomplishments.

Confederate Naval Works: Provided military cannon for the Confederate Army during the Civil War. Located in Columbus, Georgia.

Confederate States Armory: Supplier of bayonets, lances, buttons, swords, and other military equipment to Confederate forces during the Civil War. Located in Kenansville, North Carolina.

Confidante: In terms of early furniture it was a reference, to a sofa with seats at each end.

Conley camera: Exclusive Sears and Roebuck early 1900s brand of folding camera which used roll film. Conley Junior and Conley De Luxe both came with carrying case. Prices varied from $9.85 to over $43.

Connecticut chest (furniture): An early term used to describe specialized chests highlighted with three carved panels. Usually crafted in New England, they were also sometimes called Connecticut dower chests or New England chests.

Connelly, Henry: Cabinetmaker working in Sheraton and Empire styles during the early 1800s in Philadelphia.

Conning, J.: Silversmith doing business in 1840s, Mobile, Alabama.

Console: Early term for a table having only front legs and consequently attached

Coca-Cola serving tray from 1926.

in bracket-like fashion to the wall. The term derives from the French word for bracket.

Contemporaneous: Reference to something occurring in the same time period. A diary kept during the Civil War for example.

Continental size: Reference to postcards larger than normal, usually extending to 4" x 6".

Converse & Son (toys): The company of Morton Converse and Son produced large numbers of toys early in the twentieth century. Drums, rocking horses, and doll trunks were part of their specialty based in Winchendon, Massachusetts.

Convert Motor Vehicle Co.: Early 1900s maker of town and country automobiles. Located at Lockport, New York.

Conyers, Richard: Identified as a silversmith operating in 1690s, Boston, Massachusetts.

Cook & Brother: Tent and playhouse sellers headed by E. C. Book in the late 1880s. Tents were marketed to boys and playhouses marketed to girls. Also sold other sporting goods.

Cook, Benjamin F.: Awarded a Federal government contract during the Civil War to supply "Negro" brogans (heavy and coarse work shoe).

Cook, Erastus: Active silversmith from 1825 to 1865 in Rochester, New York.

Cook Pottery Company: Pottery firm crafting porcelain and whiteware in early twentieth century, Tenton, New Jersey.

Cook, Zenas: Leading clockmaker in 1815, Waterbury, Connecticut.

Cooley, J. G.: Maker of a type of portable printing press for the use of Army and Navy during the Civil War. Marked Cooley's Cabinet Printing Office. Operation in 1860s, New York City.

Cooley, Oliver: Noted silversmith doing business in 1830, Utica, New York.

Cooper and Bogue: Silversmiths known to be doing business in 1850s, Columbia, South Carolina.

Cooper & Son: New York City based maker of military equipment including pans and kettles for Federal troops during the Civil War.

Co-Operative Manufacturing Company: Doing business as a doll maker in 1870s, Springfield, Vermont.

Cooper, James M.: Listed as maker of Navy percussion revolvers, patented in 1851. Located in Pittsburgh, Pennsylvania.

Coors Pottery: Maker of porcelain and whiteware in early twentieth century, Golden, Colorado.

Copeland Steam Tricycle: Steam-driven vehicle devised by Lucius Copeland in late 1880s, Phoenix, Arizona. Basically a bicycle with a small steam engine, it was later modified to become a tricycle.

Copper (color): Simply the color of copper in 1920s Sears catalogs.

Copper green (color): Considered to be a natural copper background, with green sheen and red and green decorations.

Copperleaf (color): Defined by early Sears as similar in color to a new copper penny.

Copper luster: A hue from certain china used in the nineteenth century and early twentieth century on various bowls, mugs, pitchers, and plates. The copper tint on dark backgrounds is credited by some to early Spanish methods.

Copp, Nathaniel: Doing business as a successful silversmith in 1835, Albany, New York.

Coral (color): A deep rose pink or the color of coral itself as presented in the 1920s.

Coca-Cola calendar from the summer of 1942.

Coca-Cola case trunk, ca. 1950s.

Coralene: Victorian era decoration applied to colored glass and credited to the Sandwich Glass Company. Craftsmen reportedly attached the lemon-yellow coralene in a vine or running stem pattern which reflected light in a fascinating manner.

Corbel bracket (clock): Basically a bracket which jutted out from the wall to hold a clock. Most references suggested the clock may have been built into the wall.

Corbet, H. A.: Cap box manufacturer for Federal troops during the Civil War, based in St. Louis, Missouri.

Cordovan (color): Dark reddish brown, later considered the color of tanned leather.

Corliss, James: Maker of clocks during the early 1800s in Weare, New Hampshire.

Corliss, John: Redware potter doing business in nineteenth century, Woolrich, Maine.

Corn (color): Like the color of the vegetable itself, a light yellow.

Cornelison Pottery: Stoneware pottery first operating in nineteenth century, Bybee, Kentucky.

Cornelius and Baker Lamps: One of the first mass producers of assorted lamps during the 1820s in Philadelphia.

Corner block (furniture): Term for a triangular block set in early furniture, particularly chairs, to reinforce the overall structure.

Corner chair: A chair with a diagonal seat designed to specifically fit into the corner of a room. Such chairs were also known as roundabout chairs.

Corner cupboard: Basically a triangular shaped cupboard constructed to fit into a corner. Considered a standard of eighteenth century American households, and still popular in the early decades of the nineteenth century.

Corner table (furniture): Defines an early table crafted to fit into a corner. Decorated in the Federal period with lacquer work or marquetry, and usually fitted with a marble top. Often made in pairs. Sometimes called a encoignure.

Cornice: Considered the top piece of wood on a cupboard or other early furniture. Sometimes considered a term for the upright column on any finished top molding.

Corning Glass Works: Very noted glass firm first organized as the Union Glass Works in Somerville, Massachusetts. Amory Houghton started in the operation in 1852 and sold out to purchase the South Ferry Glass Works in Brooklyn, New York, in 1864. The operation was moved in 1868 to Corning, New York, and was eventually reorganized to become the Corning Glass Works.

Corn, Samuel: Supplier of army clothing via Federal government contract during the Civil War. Located in New York City.

Cornucopia: Sometimes a reference to the horn of plenty in the nineteenth century. Typically the image of a container pouring forth fruits, vegetables, and flowers. Once popular as a decorative device of American glassware, later incorporated into seasonal designs and decorations.

Cornwell, Nathan: Established clockmaker doing business in 1820, Darien, Georgia.

Coromandel wood: A light-colored type of ebony with striped markings. Found on the southeastern coast of India's peninsula, it was sometimes called zebra wood.

Cotrall, J. G. & Son.: Supplier of military uniforms and caps under Federal government contract during the Civil War. Located in Albany, New York.

Cottage clock: Term for a miniature bracket style clock dating from the late eighteenth and early nineteenth centuries. Usually about 7" or 8" tall and about 2" deep.

Cottrell, S. S. & Co.: Supplier of Confederate infantry accouterments during the Civil War. Located in Richmond, Virginia.

Couglan, Langley, Boice and Co.: Granted a contract by the Federal government for military clothing during the Civil War. Doing business in New York City.

Count Rumford: (see Astral lamp)

Court cupboard: Basically a recessed cupboard sitting above a chest on legs. Most likely seen in the late 1500s and early 1600s.

Courting mirror: Basically a small 10" by 12" mirror with box-like frame that hung on the wall of colonial homes in New England. Although the mirrors were usually plain they were sometimes decorated with painted or enameled glass on the outside.

Courtney and Tennent: Provider of military buttons to Confederate forces during the Civil War, based in Charleston, South Carolina.

Cove molding (furniture): Term for a large hollow molding or recess applied to early furniture, generally acting as a cornice. Typically a hand-tooled method usually not seen after 1850s steam powered manufacturing.

Coventry Glass Works: Organized around 1813 in Coventry, Connecticut. The firm made hollow ware, decanters, and tumblers before later producing flasks, snuff jars, and inkstands. Notable flasks created at that location include those honoring General Lafayette and DeWitt Clinton, and the 1825 opening of the Erie Canal.

Cowan, William: Active clockmaker in 1820s, Richmond, Virginia.

Cowen & Wilcox: Pottery firm crafting stoneware in nineteenth century, Harrisburg, Pennsylvania. Also operating under the name Harrisburg Stoneware Company.

Cowles, Ralph: Craftsman doing silversmith work in 1850s, Cleveland, Ohio.

Cowperthwaite, John K.: Noted chair maker from 1800 to 1835 at Chatham Square in New York City.

Coxon and Company: Doing business as whiteware potters in latter nineteenth century, Trenton, New Jersey.

Crab apple (color): A reddish orange according to Sears in 1927, the average color of a ripe fruit.

Cracker Jack: Colorfully illustrated wax-package of peanuts and popcorn made even more famous by 1908 song, *Take Me Out to the Ballgame*. Each box contained a small prize, and ensuing years saw early baseball cards, tin toys, plastic figures, and paper whistles.

Crackleware: Term for the striking effect on glass items of various colors. Black pigment was sometimes rubbed into the surface of the cracks to give emphasis to the pattern. The cracks were created when pieces were heated and then plunged into cold water, causing a certain rate of expansion and contraction. The procedure was reportedly first accomplished in ancient China.

Cradle: In Colonial America, two types of cradles were dominant. One was designed to swing between uprights. A second had a hood and was mounted on short rockers. Some Pennsylvania Germans fully decorated cradles in the eighteenth century.

Craftsman (furniture): Term for a Mission style furniture crafted in early 1900s America by Gustav Stickley.

Coca-Cola wooden menu board, ca. 1940s. (Harris Auction Center)

Crafts Pottery: Family of nineteenth century potters who produced assorted stoneware at locations including Maine, Massachusetts, and New Hampshire.

Craft, Stephen: Distinguished silversmith active in 1810, New York City.

Cranberry (color): Suggested in the 1920s to be a rich dark red, the color of cranberries.

Cranberry glass: During the second half of the nineteenth century this purple-toned gold and ruby glass was popular in America and England.

Crandall's donkey and rider: Mechanical toy made of wood involving Barnum's Tricky Mule and the Dusky Rider. Offered in retail stores and by mail order in 1879. Price was 50¢ or 70¢ by mail.

Crane, S. G.: Provider of military camp chairs for Federal troops during the Civil War, located in Rochester, New York.

Crane, Theodore: Civil War maker of military equipment for Federal troops, based in New York City.

Craven, Dorris J.: Stoneware potter active in latter nineteenth century, Seagrove, North Carolina.

Craven, J. H. and Son: Pottery operation doing business in late nineteenth century, Mossy Creek, Georgia.

Crazing: Flaws presented as fine lines on various ceramic works, usually caused by drawing the piece from the hot kiln before it was properly cooled. Such crazing defects were also sometimes caused by other misadventures in the firing process.

Cream (color): Not surprisingly, the color of cream as listed in Sears and Roebuck.

Original comic strip of The Born Loser, 1970s.

Original comic strip of Frank and Ernest, 1970s.

Creamer: Term which covers the evolvement of the American cream pitcher from the relatively early eighteenth century's pear-shape to the more elaborate three-legged scroll-handled examples. Later inverted pear-shapes appeared. Covers also varied from domed to helmet-shaped.

Cream ware: Term for that cream-colored earthenware first introduced in 1750s England. Eventually it was produced by Wedgwood and a host of other accomplished potters. It remained popular well into the nineteenth century.

Cream white (color): Noted in the Sears catalog as white with a yellow cast.

Credence: Term for a side table in the Gothic style, usually made of oak. Later it made reference to the sideboard used for serving. At some point it went from simple to more elaborate, adding a backboard and cupboards below.

Credenda bicycle: Brand name of one of the better bicycles of the 1890s, produced by A. G. Spalding and Brothers, which sold for $115 each in 1893.

Credenza: An evolved piece of furniture which began in Italy simply as a low sideboard with doors and drawers. Later it was adopted in other parts of Europe and America where it was somewhat more decorative and was used as a serving table as well as a place for storage for silverware and other valuables.

Creeping Baby: A popular wind-up doll of the 1880s which made a "creeping" movement when wound, moving hands and feet. Price from Automatic Toys Works was $5.

Cremnitz white (color): Considered by Sears of 1927 to be a pure white, later described as a lead white.

Crescent Pottery Company: Whiteware and yellow ware pottery active in 1880s and 1890s, Trenton, New Jersey.

Cresting: Early furniture term making reference to the carved decoration on the top most point of chairs, daybeds, and mirrors of the Colonial era.

Crest Manufacturing Company: Makers of the Crestmobile in the early 1900s. In 1904 "the simplest car made" sold for $750. The company was located in Cambridge, Massachusetts.

Crestmobile: (see Crest Manufacturing Company)

Crewel (textile): Term for variety of stitches involving embroidery on linen. Chiefly two-stranded twisted wool popular during the seventeenth and eighteenth centuries in England and America.

Cries of Paris: (see Acier)

Crimson lake (color): According to the Sears catalog of the 1920s, a deep transparent red.

Crinoline: Defined in middle nineteenth century America as a lady's skirt expanded by hoops or being made of haircloth.

Crissy (doll): Popular doll sold in the early 1970s with wide variety of outfits and hair styles. Basic doll from Ideal was $5.77 and her five-outfit wardrobe was $6.66.

Cristallo (glass): Term for an early Venetian type of glass later popular in many parts of Europe. Overall it was thin and brittle, often gray in color.

Crocket (furniture): Reference to a rather elaborate ornament which amounted to a spire-like projection. Sometimes further detailed with carved foliage. Used to decorate furniture in Gothic and Gothic Revival styles.

Crockett: Curved foliage-like ornamentation attached to a gable or spire.

Croft: Term given for a small, late eighteenth century filing cabinet with a writing top and drawers. It was designed to be readily moved about a library.

Crone, Henry: Midwestern silversmith located in 1825, Cleveland, Ohio.

Cronin, Huxthal & Sears: Supplier of military blankets to Federal troops during the Civil War, based in New York City.

Crooksville China Company: Doing business as a maker of pottery ware in late nineteenth century, Crooksville, Ohio.

Croquet: In 1867 it was described as an open-air game played with wooden balls and long-handled mallets.

Crossman, E. A.: Firm making cavalry cartridge boxes for Federal troops during the Civil War, based in Newark, New Jersey.

Crossman, West & Leonard: Listed as pewter and Britannia ware craftsmen in 1820s, Taunton, Massachusetts.

Cross rail: Term used by early cabinetmakers to designate the horizontal piece of wood used on the back of a chair.

Crotch mahogany: Selective term used to describe wood taken from the crotch of mighty trees where the most beautiful grain was believed to be located. Such highly regarded wood was used sparingly by early cabinetmakers only for veneer and not entire furniture structures. The term was also applied to other quality hardwoods.

Crouch ware: A seventeenth and early eighteenth century English-made salt-glaze ware incorporating white clay. It represented a transition of sorts between brown earthenware and grayish-white ware.

Crow, John: A Colonial era clockmaker in 1790s, Wilmington, Delaware.

Crow, McCreary & Co.: Civil War era supplier of blankets to Federal troops, based in St. Louis, Missouri.

Crown glass: Simply an early term for window glass manufactured in the

Walnut corner cupboard with hand-chamfered doors.
(Harris Auction Center)

United States. Webster's in the 1860s asserted it was "the finest sort" of window glass.

Crown Greetings: Middle twentieth century postcard publisher of regional views, based in Cleveland, Ohio.

Crown Milano (glass): Distinctive white opal art glass given raised enamel decoration.

Crown opening (doll): Term for the cutaway portion on the head of a doll. Typically the doll head was left open to allow space for eye mechanisms. In other cases the hollow crown opening meant less weight and lower shipping costs.

Crown Pottery Company: Doing business as a maker of pottery ware in 1890s, Evansville, Indiana.

Cruet: Mentioned in 1860s America as a small glass bottle for vinegar or oil.

Crushing and Mack: Supplier of stoves and stove pipes for Federal troops during the Civil War, located in Lowell, Massachusetts.

Crystal glass: Originally a term used to denote an exceptionally clear and colorless glass.

Crystal Glass Company: Maker of household glass with the trademark beehive, in Pittsburgh, Pennsylvania. The company made bread trays with sheaves of wheat, and in the 1880s they issued butter plates with portraits of James A. Garfield and Winfield S. Hancock.

Crystalline form: (see Feldspar)

Crystal white (color): Basically a transparent white according to the Sears catalog of the 1920s.

C.S.A.: Confederate States of America. See also Minchemer, Frances.

Cullet (glass): Reference to glasshouse fragments once cleaned and recycled into new glass.

Cummins, William: Established clock maker from 1790s to 1830 in Roxbury, Massachusetts.

Cupboard: Historically the cupboard was but a single shelf or board which was used to store cups. Later more shelves were added to the piece and a door or doors were added in an effort to keep out dust and dirt. Glass doors were sometimes a further evolvement of the basic cupboard, as the contents became more elaborate and worthy of display.

Cupboard cloth: An innovation of the colonial era in America, and in England, involving cloth covering the top of the cupboard. Generally it was thought the cloth protected the typical display of china, glass, or pewter.

Cup caster (furniture): Reference to a brass furniture roller with a cup-like form fitted over the end of the table leg or chair leg.

Cupid's bow: A reference to the top rails of chairs designed by Chippendale in which a compound or serpentine curve was applied. Such top rails typically had a double curve said to resemble the outline of a cupid's bow.

Cupola: Described in the nineteenth century as a spherical vault on the top of an edifice.

Cup plate: Term designating a small glass or china plate, usually only 3" or 4" in diameter and used to hold the cup after hot tea had been poured in a saucer for cooling. In early Victorian days hot tea was served in handle-less cup, thus sometimes difficult to hold. As a result the hot tea was poured in an accompanying saucer to cool and a small plate was then used to rest the empty cup. At one point such plates were quite fashionable and glasshouses produced them in highly decorative styles.

Currier and Ives print titled Jane, 1870s.

Cure, Lewis: Brooklyn, New York, clock-maker doing business in the early 1830s.

Cure, William: Doing business in the clock making trade in 1830s, New York City.

Curly maple: Largely an American usage of a brown variety of maple in less formal latter eighteenth century furniture. It was widely used for a time, although sometimes known as rock maple. The wavy or curly grain is much admired in highboys, slant-front desks, and some tables.

Currier and Ives: Very prolific American company responsible for thousands of fascinating lithographs in the nineteenth century starting with Currier alone in 1835, New York. The vast parade of prints were earlier in black and white and later in color.

Currier, Edmund: Listed as an active silversmith in 1830, Salem, Massachusetts.

Currier, Nathaniel: Talented lithographic artist first founded the firm that would be known worldwide as Currier and Ives. Some 7,000 scenes documented circus, sports, hunting, farming, and various other aspects of mid-nineteenth century American life.

Curtis, Joel: Colonial silversmith doing business in 1785, Wolcott, Connecticut.

Curtiss, Candee, and Styles: Operation of silversmiths located in 1830s, Woodbury, Connecticut.

Curt Teich Co.: A major producer of postcards in America during the first two thirds of the twentieth century. Usually clearly marked linen-type postcards.

Curule chair: In Roman times it was considered the chair of high office. Eventually the term evolved to suggest a folding chair with curved legs. In the latter eighteenth century the curved legs were replaced by two curving segments which met the base at a single point.

Cushman, Paul: Stoneware potter active in the trade in early nineteenth century, Albany, New York.

Cushman's Foundary: Supplier of Confederate smooth bore cannon during the Civil War. Located in Houston, Texas.

Cutie Pie: A finger puppet-like doll sold in the 1950s via Billy and Ruth Catalog. It was made of vinyl material by National Mask and Puppet. Complete with blanket it sold for $1.95.

Cutlass: Noted in a mid-nineteenth century reference as a broad, curving sword.

Cutler: Described in Webster's 1867 dictionary as one who deals in knives or cutting instruments.

Cutler, Abner: Noted maker of various household furniture in 1830s, Buffalo, New York.

Cutler, William: Noted silversmith of the 1830s operating in Portland, Maine.

Cut nail machine: A patent for the first cut-nail machine in America was granted in 1786 to Ezekiel Reed of Bridgewater, Massachusetts. The innovative device could now produce so-called "cold nails" at a fraction of the cost of hand forged nails. Gradually similar machines replaced the old-fashioned and much slower method of heating iron and shaping each single nail. Generally, with some isolated exceptions, most all nineteenth century American nails were machine made.

Cutting, James: (see Ambrotype)

Cybis Porcelains: Figural porcelain operation which began in 1940s, Trenton, New Jersey.

Cylinder (furniture): Early reference to

Currier and Ives print titled American Homestead Autumn, ca. 1860s.

Daguerreotype of young man with harness making device, leather case. (Harris Auction Center)

the opening of a writing table in the shape of a quadrant or arc of a circle.

Cyma curve (furniture): Cabinetmaker's term in reference to a wave curve or double curve in furniture making. Based on the Greek word meaning wave form.

Cyma recta (furniture): Denotes a double-curved style in an elongated S-shape. The upper section is concave or curved outward, the lower section is convex or curved inward. Seen on Victorian era drawer fronts and other furniture.

Cypress wood: Perhaps the most durable of woods used by early American cabinetmakers. It was generally reddish in color and very fine grained. A pale to dark brown version was used in the country's southern states mostly for drawers and linings.

Czar bank: Combination bank made during the 1920s by Arcade Manufacturing in Freeport, Illinois. Made of steel, front nickel plated. About 3" tall.

Dado: Term for that horizontal border of wood extending around the lower part of a room's wall. Early American homes used wood above the dado strip, but later plaster walls were in vogue.

Dagswain: Early term for colonial bed covering or table covering. This coarse and thick cloth was also sometimes used as a floor covering in cold weather.

Daguerreotype: Type of early photograph of the 1840s and beyond. Such pictures, fixed on chemically treated copper plate, were framed in velvet-lined cases of hard rubber or gutta percha. The procedure was credited to Louis Jacques Mande Daguerre.

Dahlia (color): Classified as dark orchid during the 1920s.

Daily Dozen: A fitness program of phonographs and pictorial charts featuring Yale football coach Walter

Camp. Complete with portable phonograph the outfit sold for $18.25 early in the 1920s.

Dairy Queen: Ice cream-themed franchise that offered plush dolls in the 1980s including Butterscotch Beaver and Flavor Friends.

Daisy air rifle: Famous brand of toy pistol and air rifles in the twentieth century. Most notable products included the Buck Rogers Rocket Pistol and the Red Ryder Cowboy Carbine.

Daisy Texas Ranger Set (toy): A 1973 commemorative set marking the 150th anniversary of the Texas Rangers. Set included a Western carbine, leather holster, two cap pistols, red cotton bandana, belt, and three-bullet keeper. Price was $5.99.

Dale, T. N. & Co.: A principal manufacturer of U.S. buttons during the Civil War, located in New York City.

Dally and Halsey: Firm of silversmiths doing business in 1780s, New York City.

Damascus table (furniture): Moorish style of small side table, frequently inlaid.

Dame: Initially an honored term for the English wife of a knight or baronet. Later in America it denoted a school mistress or schoolteacher. Casual usage in the twentieth century made it less distinguished.

Damiana Bitters: A nineteenth century bottled medicinal product manufactured by Lewis Hess, in Baja, California.

Dana, George: Clockmaker operating in 1805, Providence, Rhode Island.

Dana, Payton: Early nineteenth century silversmith located in Providence, Rhode Island.

Dancing Betty: Mechanical toy of the 1920s which danced and shimmied "in a comical manner" when wound by a key.

Danforth, I. Thomas: Pewter craftsman of early eighteenth century Connecticut. First in long line of family pewter makers.

Danforth, Samuel: Early nineteenth century pewtersmith active in Hartford, Connecticut. Hallmarks included initials and eagle.

Daniel Boone (television): A fictionalized depiction of frontier legend was presented on CBS television in the 1960s. The series fostered numerous items including coonskin caps, card games, pin-back buttons, and plastic wallets.

Daniel, Charles: Practicing silversmith in 1835, Troy, New York.

Dan Patch toy auto: Noted brand of toy automobiles sold in the 1920s and based on the name of a popular trotting race horse. Butler Brothers catalogs offered eight different varieties.

Dan Patch wagon: Popular selling children's wagon with the name of a famous race horse. Sold by Sears, Roebuck and Co. in the 1920s.

Danziger Magen Bitters: Milk glass bottles of liquor and various other additives made in the latter nineteenth century by Rheinstrom Brothers of Cincinnati, Ohio.

Dapper Dan: A 1920s update of Coon Jigger toy, danced when wound and bore lithographed hotel and baggage labels.

Darby and Joan settee: Sort of sweetheart seat of its time, which held two people and seemed romantic.

Darcy (doll): Unique jointed wooden dolls produced early in the twentieth century by Ruth Williams.

Daredevil Flyer (toy): Featuring a plane that rose on its own power to "loop the loop" around a building. Lithographed metal with 10" tower sold for 89¢ in 1930.

Dargee, John: Listed as an enterprising silversmith in 1810, New York City.

Darky doll: (see Cocheco Manufacturing Company)

Darly, Mathis: Noted eighteenth century engraver and designer who contributed to Thomas Chippendale's Directory and a number of other furniture publications.

Darrow, Elijah: Listed in the clock making trade in 1820s, Bristol, Connecticut.

Darrow, John: Silversmith in 1820, Catskill, New York.

Darrow Manufacturing Co.: Produced dolls in 1860s and 1870s, Bristol, Connecticut.

Daunce, Simon: Early 1800 silversmith located in Philadelphia, Pennsylvania.

Daus, Felix: (see Eclipse umbrella)

Davenport: Early term for a small writing desk which later evolved into defining an upholstered sofa.

Davenport bed-sofa: Sofa by day and bed by night offered by Sears and Roebuck during the 1920s. The golden oak model sold for $29.95.

Davenport, Samuel: Silversmith of the 1740s in Milton, Massachusetts.

Davenport ware: Quality earthenware created by John Davenport in 1790s, Staffordshire, England. The factory, known for rich decorations and apple-green coloring, operated into the 1880s.

David Bradley: Brand name for farming equipment sold in the 1920s by Sears, Roebuck and Company. Available were Bradley walking plows, riding plows, tractor disc harrow, corn planter, cultivator, grain grinder, corn sheller, and cob crusher

David Maydole Hammer: David Maydole's nail hammers were sold by Sears,

Postcard of David Bradley factory serving Sears and Roebuck Company, early 1900s.

Classic Mallard duck decoy, early twentieth century. (Harris Auction Center)

Roebuck and Company in 1902. They had hickory handles and varied in size.

Davidson, Barizillai: Active as a clockmaker in 1820s, New Haven, Connecticut.

Davidson, Charles: Known to be active in the silversmith trade from 1805 to 1835 in Norwich, Connecticut.

Davis, A. A.: Founder of toy company in 1860s, Nashua, New Hampshire. Specialized in combining lithographed paper and wood for animals and figures, including General U.S. Grant.

Davis, Alexander Jackson: A nineteenth century architect noted for drawings of colleges, homes, and towns which later became engravings.

Davis, John: Noted joiner and cabinetmaker located in early 1700s, Lynn, Massachusetts.

Davis, S. M.: Granted a patent for military type tents in 1861. Located in Lawrence, Massachusetts.

Davy Crocket (television): Fictionalized account of historic frontier fighter appeared on CBS television during the 1950s. Wide array of items resulted including coonskin cap, pin-back buttons, trading cards, pocketknife, playsuit, and cookie jar.

Davy, Joseph: Maker of cap boxes for Federal troops during the Civil War, based in Newark, New Jersey.

Dawkins, Henry: Noted 1750s engraver who specialized in billheads and maps, but noted for Princeton's View of Nassau-Hall published in the 1760s.

Dawley's Ten Cent Novels: Early dime novels published by T. R. Dawley and Company of Boston in the 1860s. Sometimes known as Camp and Fireside Library.

Dawson, William: Colonial era silversmith active in 1765, Philadelphia, Pennsylvania.

Day bed: Typically daytime furniture adjustable for night time sleeping in use as early as the 1600s in England. Initially oak with cane seating, later various materials.

Day, Benjamin: Noted pewter craftsman in eighteenth century, Newport, Rhode Island.

Day, Horace: Designer of a military shelter tent made of gutta percha cloth for the Federal government during the Civil War.

Dayton Friction Toy Company: Producer of heavy gauge steel friction toys in the latter 1920s. Selections include the speed wagon, freight engine, roadster, and Victoria coupe.

Dayton Motor Company: (see Stoddard-Dayton limo)

Dead grass (color): According Sears in the 1920s, a greenish brown.

Dead leaf brown (color): Basically a medium to dark brown used on eighteenth century Chinese porcelain.

Dead Shot: Name for toy pistol made of iron sold in stores and catalogs of the 1890s. Billed as the "best selling" of toy pistols, price was 10¢.

Deadwood Dick: Star of a series of over 120 stories written by Edward Wheeler for dime novels including Beadle's Half Dime Library in the 1890s and early 1900s.

Deal: Not an agreement but simply an English cabinetmaker's term for pine imported from Scotland. Apparently it was little used in America.

Deane, F. B. & Sons: Maker of 12-pound howitzer cannons for Confederate forces during Civil War. Located in Houston, Texas.

Dean's Rag Book Co.: Cloth doll maker since early 1900s in London, England.

Debbie (doll): Life-size walker doll, Debbie was three feet tall in nylon jumper dress. In 1965 the doll was available in white or "colored" models for $9.97 each.

Decalomania: Early nineteenth century term describing the practice of transferring pictures from paper to furniture or other surfaces. Method used by clockmakers for decorating glass door of a clock case.

Decanter: Fashionable glass container in eighteenth century England, typically with globular body and ring neck and then called a bottle. Stoppers were also decorative. Decanters of the nineteenth century were also made of elegant glass, body shapes varied but rings persisted.

Decker, James: Enterprising silversmith located in 1830s, Troy, New York.

Decoder badge: (see Captain Midnight)

Decolorizing: Glassmaking term involving the use of oxide of manganese to remove impurities which caused unwanted green or brown hues.

Decor bois: Unusual decoration dating from the 1770s involving imitation wood grain and the image of curled parchment paper.

Decoy (folk art): Art of carving duck decoys and other wildfowl was popular American folk art from the colonial period in the latter 1700s through the Civil War in the middle 1800s. Typically bodies were carved from solid blocks of wood and heads were done separately. Makers added paint and glass eyes.

Decoy (metal): Metal decoys were sold in large numbers during the 1890s. Brinktop Metal Duck decoys had a single metal body with detachable thin sheet metal head.

Dedham Pottery Company: A pottery operation in 1870s, Dedham, Massachusetts.

Deer Foot: Name of a popular selling hunting knife with deer's foot handle. Complete with leather sheath, they sold for $1.85 each in the 1894 Sears, Roebuck and Co. catalog.

De Forest and Company: Silversmith firm operating in 1820s, New York City.

Deham Pottery: Art pottery maker during the first half of the twentieth century in East Dedham, Massachusetts.

DeLaroux, John: Active silversmith in 1820s, New Orleans, Louisiana.

Delaware Pottery Company: A pottery operation doing business in 1890s, Trenton, New Jersey.

Delftware: Noted pottery first made in early seventeenth century, Delft, Holland. Initially this ware was given a blue design on white ground. Later polychrome coloring allowed variations. It was eventually produced by many potteries in England.

Delmar spy glass: Sold by Sears, Roebuck and Company in 1902. The Delmar Spy glasses or telescopes came in four sizes and were made of lacquered brass and black morocco leather. Prices ranged from $1.45 to $3.25.

Del Monte Corporation: Noted canned goods company promoted with plush dolls of Country Yumkin series during the 1980s. Included were Brawyn Bear, Cobbie Corn, Cocky Crow, and Sweetie Pea.

Delta: Brand of wrought steel padlock sold by Kresge's Five and Ten Cent Stores early in the twentieth century. Price was 10¢.

Deltiology: Technical term for the postcard hobby or business.

Demilune table: Term for one of a pair of half-moon tables. Typically drop-leaf in design, the pair would fit together smoothly or could become part of an extending dining facility.

Dennis the Menace vinyl doll with cloth outfit, 1958.

Demorest Fashion & Sewing Machine Co.: Noted New York City company of the 1880s which also published the *Madam Demorest Illustrated Fashion Journal.*

DeMorgan, William F.: Latter nineteenth century craftsman initially worked with stained glass and later with lustre painting on English pottery.

Demorsy, Jean: Noted silversmith operating in 1820s, New Orleans, Louisana.

Dendritic: Pottery term suggesting tree or branch-like markings.

Denim Kid: Name used to promote cowboy play outfit marketed in 1973 Montgomery Ward catalog. Included two cap pistols, vest, double holsters, saddle bag, hat, neckerchief, and Centennial rifle. Price $11.99.

Dennis, Ebenezer: Recorded as a silversmith in 1755, Hartford, Connecticut.

Dennis the Menace: Comic strip character of the 1950s. Later a television series and movies. Generated dolls, books, and other memorabilia.

Dennis, Thomas: Noted maker of chairs, chests, and other furniture during the late 1600s in Ipswich, Massachusetts.

Denny and Beelen: Glassworks operation in 1800, Pittsburgh, Pennsylvania. Later they established a small glassworks in northern Ohio.

Dent Hardware Company: Original firm of Henry Dent based in Fullerton, Pennsylvania. Starting with cast iron toys and still banks in the 1890s, the firm went on produce large numbers of toys. By the 1930s many of their toy cars, planes, tractors, and other toys were being made of cast iron.

Dentil: Type of early molding decoration involving the use of oblong or rectangular blocks, usually with intervening spaces. Typically seen as ornamentation over fireplaces.

Denver China & Pottery Co.: Noted as a producer of art pottery briefly in the early 1900s. Located in Denver, Colorado.

Denver (clock): Offered in oak or walnut by the Waterbury Clock Company, this shelf clock was priced at $6.25 in the 1890s.

Department Store game: Popular children's game featured in the 1905 holiday catalog of John Wanamaker.

DePauw, W. C.: (see New Albany Glass Works)

DePeyster, William: Listed as a silversmith doing business in 1735, New York City.

Derby porcelain: Fine quality ware first produced in 1770s, Derbyshire, England under the direction of William Duesbury. It was noted for its design and coloring throughout remainder of the eighteenth century. Later the firm was closed and ultimately formed with Royal Crown Derby porcelain.

Derby Silver Company: Maker of silver-handled nail files, button hooks, mirrors, combs, and puff boxes in the 1920s.

DeRemier and Mead: Partnership of silversmiths in 1830s, Ithaca, New York.

Derringer: Name for a short-barrel pistol popular in the nineteenth century, and named for its inventor.

Derry China Company: Small pottery firm operating in 1890s, Derry Station, Pennsylvania.

Deruta ware: Term for an early type of majolica and named for a particular town in Italy.

Detroit Publishing Company postcard with view of State Street in Chicago, Ill., early 1900s.

Desk: Originally little more than a box with a slated top in England. During the seventeenth century the box and table were combined into a single piece. Afterwards the desk evolved into a full furniture item complete with drawers or even a secret drawer.

DeSoto Six automobile: In 1924 this vehicle retailed for $845. It was produced by the DeSoto Motor Company, a division of Chrysler Corporation, in Detroit, Michigan.

Dessert service: An early nineteenth century term referring to a set of plates and dishes with silver gilt bordering corresponding white dinner service.

Detecto: American maker of "personal" oven baked white enamel bathroom scales, ca. 1928.

Detroit Jewel gas range: National advertised gas range of the 1890s. A product of the Detroit Stove Works in Detroit, Michigan.

Detroit Publishing Company: Leading publisher of American postcards during the first few decades of the twentieth century. Topics ranged from cartoons to steamships and involved leading artists.

Detroit Stove Works: (see Detroit Jewel gas range)

Deutsch and Company: Fashionable Fifth Avenue store in 1890s, New York City. Specialized in riding habits, coats, capes, gowns, hats, bonnets, and fur garments. Also "carriage, street and evening wear ready made."

Deutsche blumen: An eighteenth century process involving painting flowers on porcelain in natural colors. Initially begun in Meissen, Germany.

Develin, Hudson & Co.: Maker of military overcoats for the U.S. Army, and uniforms for New York regiments during the Civil War. Located in New York City.

Devil Dogs (military): A World War I term originally used by German soldiers in reference to fighting U.S. Marines.

Dewey girdle: Patriotic item for "girls of America" supporting the nation in 1898. The sash-like belt included an embossed medallion buckle. It also included a red, white, and blue ribbon on white metal. It sold for 20¢.

Dewey's Manila Bitters: Unique marketing of low-grade curative concoction featuring portrait of Admiral Dewey and battleship on bottle's label. Ca. 1890s.

Dewing, Francis: Boston engraver and printer most noted for Bonner Map of 1722 Boston. Map was reprinted several times in the eighteenth century.

DeWitt, John: Operated a firm specializing in Windsor chair making in 1790s, New York City.

DeWitt, Robert M.: Publisher of mid-nineteenth century dime novels in New York. Titles included Champion Novels and DeWitt's Ten Cent Romances. In the 1870s Robert was succeeded by Clinton DeWitt.

DeWitt's Stomach Bitters: Amber liquid in rectangular bottle produced during the second half of the nineteenth century in Chicago.

Dexter, John: Practicing the silversmith trade in 1755, Marlboro, Massachusetts.

Dexter, Joseph: A noted clockmaker in 1820s, Providence, Rhode Island.

Dexter Shoe Company: Specialized in ladies' patent leather tip shoes and French kid button boot for $2 a pair in the 1890s.

DeYoung, Michael: Baltimore, Maryland, clockmaker during the 1830s.

Diamond Brand Orange Bitters: Offered in crockery jug containers during the

Dick Tracy Target game, ca. 1930s.

Dick Tracy Detective Game, 1937, by Whitman Publishing.

Dick Tracy Secret Patrol badges, radio premiums from the 1930s.

Dick Tracy lunch box from Aladdin.

mid-nineteenth century by Diamond Wine Company of Sandusky, Ohio.

Diamond-daisy: Term describing the American design on glass of a daisy-like flower with a square diamond. Credited to eighteenth century, finely etched Stiegel glass.

Diamond Dick Jr. Weekly: Title of a series of dime novels published in the 1890s and 1900s by Street and Smith of New York.

Diamond harness: Diamond heavy truck harness sold during the 1920s. Diamond bridles, lines, traces, and breeching were also offered for work horses.

Dibble: Term for a small pewter plate.

Dickerson, John: Listed as a silversmith in 1780, Morristown, Massachusetts.

Dickey seat: An 1890s innovation which amounted to an extra passenger seat in the rear "when baby number two arrives" in the family. Seat could also be used as a detachable carriage basket, from Rattan Manufacturing Company, New Haven, Connecticut.

Dick Tracy: Twice-lived comic strip character who first rose to fame and public favor in the 1930s and 1940s and again in the 1990s as a Hollywood movie. Decades of related memorabilia has ranged from toy badges and books, to Crime Stoppers kits and action figures.

Diecast: Basically an object cast from a metal mold.

Dillon & Company: Stoneware operation led by Charles Dillon in 1830s, Albany, New York.

Dilution Separator: Name for popular cream separator sold by Sears and Roebuck during the 1920s. It worked in three to four hours, the 14-gallon model was $4.60.

Dime bank: Cylindrical, metal coin

holders sold by S.S. Kresge Co. stores early in the twentieth century for 10¢ each.

Dime registering bank: Novelty toy which registered dimes and opened automatically when amount reached $10. Several variations were offered around 1917 including the Uncle Sam Dime Registering bank.

Dinah-Mite (doll): Barbie-like fashion doll sold in the 1970s. Dinah's accessories included stylish outfits, carrying case, beach house, and boyfriend Don.

Dingee, H. A.: Produced cartridge boxes and military belt buckles for Federal troops during the Civil War, based in New York City.

Dingen's Napoleon Cocktail Bitters: Bottled liquor disguised as medication marketed by brothers John and C. Bertrand Dingen from the 1830s to the 1870s in Buffalo, New York.

Dinner service: During the eighteenth century elaborate silver dinner services included matching plates, dishes, tureens, and related items. Gradually rim designs became more complex and sometimes included the family coat of arms.

Dionne Quints: Born in 1934, the Dionne quintuplets arrived at a time when multiple births of five were stunning. The Canadian females were used to promote numerous products from bread to soap.

Directoire: Based on the period of classical furniture which was crafted in the 1790s. Originally a French term, for furniture of that era, but probably best portrayed by the work of English designer Thomas Sheraton.

Dirigible: Early twentieth century reference to a self-propelled balloon which could be steered. Usually an indication of a cigar-shaped airship.

Dirigible (toy): One of four toy "sensations" offered in 1929 by Sears, Roebuck and Co. Cost of the 28" all-steel, three-wheeled vehicle was $1.

Disbrowe, Nicholas: Pioneering maker of furniture in seventeenth century America, born in England and based in Hartford, Connecticut.

Dished (furniture): Dished corner made reference to the concave corners of eighteenth century gaming tables. Dished top was a term for the thick surface of tilt-top tables also of the eighteenth century.

Dish (pewter): Term used in pewter making for larger plates up to 12" in size.

Dish rings: Late eighteenth century stands, usually made of silver, put to use in fashionable American homes to protect elegant tables from hot dishes. Possibly of Irish origin.

Disney: Empire of delight founded by Walt Disney initially through animated films of the 1930s and 1940s. The legion of related characters from Bambi to Zorro in turn created a multitude of memorabilia. Later came the nations of Disneyland and Disney World.

District Messenger Boy: Boxed game with metal figures issued by McLoughlin Brothers in the 1890s. Successful player attained presidency, highest office in telegraphic service.

Divan: Term for a low sofa or upholstered seat. Initially simply a rug-covered cushion in Turkey which evolved into the wooded framed version of eighteenth century England.

Divided back: Landmark reference to early twentieth century American postcards. Until 1907 only an address was permitted on the back, no message. The divided line then allowed for both.

Dixie (brand): Brand name for a series of health products offered by Sears and Roebuck during the 1920s. Items include corn plaster and foot tablets.

Dixon (clock): An 1890s shelf clock in walnut case manufactured by the Waterbury Clock Company.

Dixon, Wm. T. and Brother: Contracted to make "Negro" brogans (work shoes) for the Federal government during the Civil War. Located in Philadelphia, Pennsylvania.

Doan, Ethel: (see Antique)

Doccia porcelain: Fine grade of porcelain first produced in 1730s, Doccia, Italy. Hard white paste was used to create artfully decorated assorted candlesticks, clock cases, figurines, vases, and other items.

Doctor Pierce's Medical Discovery: Patent medicine offer for a cure of everything from consumption to constipation during the 1870s. Price was $1 per bottle.

Doctor's car: (see Prescott automobile)

Document box: Originally a term for a small wooden box with sliding lid. Pennsylvania-German folk artists sometimes painted and elaborately decorated such boxes with dates, flowers, and names.

Dodge, Benjamin: Active silversmith in 1835, Boston, Massachusetts.

Dodge, Nehemiah: Listed as an active clockmaker in early 1800s, Providence, Rhode Island.

Dodge pedal car: Toy automobile offered by Sears, Roebuck and Company in the 1920s based on the brand name of the bestselling real car. The steel construction, wood trim vehicle sold for $9.98.

Dodge, Simon F.: Bowie knife supplier for the Confederate military during the Civil War. Located in Winchester, Virginia.

Walt Disney's Donald Duck Duet, a tin windup by Marx, ca. 1946. (Harris Auction Center)

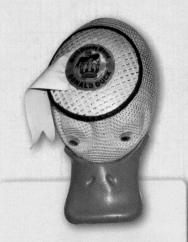

Disney World souvenir Donald Duck hat, made in USA.

Walt Disney Productions composition Pinocchio, from Crown Toy Manufacturing Co., ca. 1940s.

Domino's Pizza advertising doll Noid, Acme label, 1988.

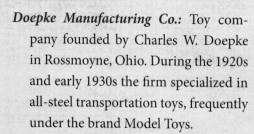

Doepke Manufacturing Co.: Toy company founded by Charles W. Doepke in Rossmoyne, Ohio. During the 1920s and early 1930s the firm specialized in all-steel transportation toys, frequently under the brand Model Toys.

Dog collar: Stylish dogs in nineteenth century England sometimes wore elaborate silver collars provided by wealthy owners.

Dog ear: Largely a latter eighteenth century term for a projecting rectangular ornament at the head of paneling or of a door frame.

Dogwood: Very hard wood from a relatively small bush or shrub sometimes used for furniture inlay as late as the eighteenth century. Most was bright yellow in color in the outline of darker colors.

Dolby, L. M.: Provider of military tent poles and tripods to Federal government during the Civil War. Located in Philadelphia, Pennsylvania.

Dole cupboard: (see Almery)

Doll: Term used for child-like toy starting in the eighteenth century in Europe and around the middle of the eighteenth century in America. Prior to that time such playthings were often referred to as simply baby, or later baby doll.

Doll-E-Nurser: A 21-piece set for little girls to prepare baby feedings just like Mom does. In 1952 the outfit sold in the Billy and Ruth catalog included a cooker for sterilizing the bottles. Other Doll-E items included a high chair, formula feeder, bath, and dish washing set.

Doll's Toy Parlor Set: Nine-piece set advertised in *Youth's Companion* during the 1880s. Included actual marble top table, sofa, six chairs, and a bureau.

Dolly Dimple: Name of a doll offered in the 1890s as a premium for subscribing to a leading magazine. Dolly Dimple was a 5½" doll with bisque head. She came with a "trunk of treasures" which included mirror, brush, extra dress, and underwear.

Dolly Drake: Name of a novelty, dressed doll offered by Sears, Roebuck and Company in 1911. Came with composition head and removable head in two sizes. Companion doll was Bobby Blake.

Dolly Sunshine: A line of dolls offered by Sears, Roebuck and Company in the late 1920s. Dolls had sleep eyes, composition head, and real-silk bonnet and dress. Some said ma-ma.

Dolly Walker (doll): (see Coleman doll)

Dolphin candlestick: Once popular dolphin-image candlestick made by Sandwich Glass Company. Forms appeared in clear, vaseline, white, and other colors.

Dolphin hinge (furniture): Early furniture term, in reference to the contour shape of a hinge used in connection with quadrant stays of secretary construction.

Domestic: Name of a popular brand of sewing machine in the 1870s. Advertised as "light running."

Domino's Pizza: Nationwide franchise which featured red stuffed Noid dolls of various sizes during the 1980s.

Donaghho, A. P.: Listed as a stoneware craftsman in late nineteenth and early twentieth century Parkersburg, West Virginia.

Donald Duck: Loveable rascal of a duck first starred in comic strips and cartoons in the 1930s. Later as one of Disney's elite, Donald went on to everything from comic books and pull toys to grocery products and wrist watches.

Donnell's Indian Root Bitters: Bottled liquor and other elements labeled with image of Indians, made by Donnell Manufacturing Company, St. Louis, Missouri.

Doolittle, Amos: Engraver noted for 1775 views of the Battles of Lexington and Concord and later Federal Hall in New York. Based in New Haven, Connecticut.

Doolittle, Isaac: A Colonial era clock-maker doing business in 1790s, New Haven, Connecticut.

Door of Hope: Mission which crafted dolls in early twentieth century Shang-hai, China.

Door stop (glass): During the nineteenth century some British glassmakers used green bottle glass for making door stops of the shape of beehives. Some designs enclosed plant and bubble forms within them.

Doran, John: Midwestern silversmith located in 1825, Cincinnati, Ohio.

Dorchester Pottery Works: Ambitious stoneware operation from 1900s to 1970s in Dorchester, Massachusetts.

Dorflein, Philip: Noted glassmaker in lat-ter nineteenth century Philadelphia. Made molds for glassware and bot-tles, some of which depicted famous Americans.

Dorflinger glass: First established by Christopher Dorflinger in 1850s Brooklyn, New York. After early flint glass efforts, the company established a cut glass operation at Long Island's Greenpoint.

Doris side saddle: Popular-selling leather saddle for women sold in the 1920s by Sears and Roebuck. Retail price was $14.85.

Dorsey, Joshua: Known to be a practicing silversmith from 1795 to 1805 in Phila-delphia, Pennsylvania.

Dot (clock): Small clock of the late nine-teenth century offered with or without large alarm bell by the Waterbury Clock Company.

Dotter (doll): China head dolls patented and produced by Charles T. Dotter in 1880s, Brooklyn, New York. Cloth bodies had corsets printed on fabric, china heads imported from Germany were patented and dated on back shoulder.

Doty, John: Noted clockmaker of the 1815 period, located in Albany, New York.

Double multiplying reel: Popular fishing reel sold during the 1920s by Sears and Roebuck. Made of nickel-plated brass, it came with two screw-off oil caps and sold for 90¢.

Doughboy (military): World War I slang term for American infantryman.

Dough tray: A nineteenth century term for a rectangular box used for mixing bread. Typically the box was dovetailed, had sides sloping outward, and had a lid. Most were plain and unadorned, sometimes with legs or handles.

Douglas, James: Colonial silversmith doing business in 1790s, Philadelphia, Pennsylvania.

Douglas Shoes: Gentleman's shoe com-pany operated by W. L. Douglas in 1890s. Based in Brockton, Massachu-setts, Douglas sold "the best $3 shoe in the world."

Douglass, M. B.: Awarded a contract from the Federal government to supply military bootees during the Civil War. Located in Newark, New Jersey.

Doulton ware: Notable stoneware begin-ning in 1870s, Lambeth, England. Initially a salt glaze ware which was later jugs and pots decorated with hand-painted designs.

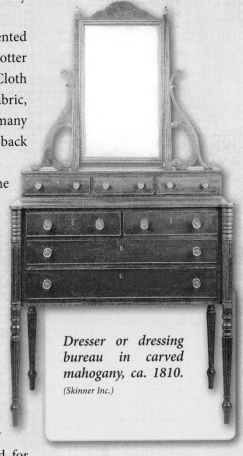

Dresser or dressing bureau in carved mahogany, ca. 1810.

(Skinner Inc.)

Dressing glass, early nine-teenth century, mahogany and walnut Federal inlaid.
(Skinner Inc.)

Dove gray (color): Considered to be gray with rose tint, one shade lighter than shadow.

Dovetailing: Particular cabinet-making method of joining pieces of wood to resemble a dove's tail. Basically this involved the interlocking of tenons (projecting parts) especially on drawer cases. Later drawer cases were nailed, glued, or even stapled together.

Dowel: Term for the wooden pin which was used to fasten two pieces of wood together in furniture making. Early dowels were handmade and consequently shaped unevenly. Later dowels were machine made and more exacting.

Dower chest: Special chest made for the young woman to be filled with linen and other household necessities for her eventually marriage. German-American dower chests in Pennsylvania were first given the term. Later they were sometimes defined as hope chests.

Dowler, Wm. H.: British supplier of military uniform buttons for Confederate forces, located in Birmingham, England.

Downs, H. S.: Cavalry boot maker for Federal troops during the Civil War. Located in Boston, Massachusetts.

Dowst (toy maker): Two brothers, Charles and Samuel, organized the original Dowst Brothers Company which developed into a maker of toy cars, trains, and planes early in the twentieth century. In the 1920s their diecast toys were named Tootsietoy after a grand-daughter.

Doyle's Hop Bitters: Brand name for variation of bottled brews sold for medical cures in the 1870s. Some bottles listed Asa Soule of Rochester, New York, as the proprietor.

Drab (color): A dark shade of grayish brown according to early twentieth century catalogs.

Dragon's claw foot: Early cabinet-making term for the fashionable claw-and-ball foot of furniture.

Drake foot: Term used to described rare use of webbed-like three-toed furniture foot in eighteenth century America and England.

Drake's Plantation Bitters: Liquor and other ingredients offered in a log-cabin-shaped bottle during the 1860s, credited to S. T. Drake.

Dralle's Illusion: Brand of fancy imported perfume sold in the 1920s. Each bottle was sold in a polished wood box at a pricey 79¢ each.

Draper, Joseph: Silversmith active from 1815 to 1830 in Wilmington, Delaware.

Drawing book (furniture): Descriptive term used in connection with an early American chair back. Selected from Thomas Sheraton's *The Cabinet-Maker and Upholsterer's Drawing-Book* by American cabinetmakers.

Drawknife: Early American tool with blade in the center between two handles. Cutting was done by drawing the blade toward the operator. Used for tapering and trimming, it was sometimes called a snitzel knife or drawing knife.

Draw table: Early form of extending table. Designed to allow leaves beneath the main top to rise and fit evenly using a series of tapered bearers.

Dreadnaught Racer: A popular sled of the early 1930s which featured a box of elm wood and parts of steel. It was 49" in length and retailed at $2.75.

Dresden china: Originally a hard paste porcelain made in 1700s, Dresden, Germany. Later it was used to describe

Meissen ware, and still later, other wares.

Dresden head: Term used to describe some glazed china doll heads which bore the crossed-swords mark of the factories in Dresden, Germany. The mark generally was located under the glaze on the back of the left shoulder. Certain unglazed Parian dolls were also called Dresden.

Dresser (furniture): Based on the French word dressoir used to describe a simple set of shelves that served for displaying china or pewter. By the eighteenth century, especially in America, dresser came to mean a regular piece of furniture with drawers. Ultimately it extended to include most any bureau or chest of drawers.

Dressing glass: Another early term for mirror. In America it related to a mirror attached to a dressing table.

Dressing table (furniture): Reference to small table or stand with a mirror attached.

Drey, John: A potter in early 1800s, Easton, Pennsylvania.

Dr. Hammond: (see Brain pills)

Dr. Hood's Plain Talks: Massive book sold by Sears, Roebuck and Company in the early 1900s dealing with sexual matters, birth control, prostitution, and the duties of married life. It was supplemented by a 32 page illustrated pamphlet.

Drissell, John: A folk artist operating in 1790s, Pennsylvania. Crafted document boxes, salt boxes, and other small wood objects. Markings were added in English and German, and usually signed by Drissell.

Drive Game: Battery-operated, Japanese-made device allowing participants to "get behind the wheel" and compete. Steering wheel, 60-second timer, and

dash board included in 1970s version. Price in the 1973 Montgomery Ward catalog was $11.44.

Drive wheel: For toys this is basically a powered piston rod moving a wheel, as with a toy locomotive.

Drop handle: Early furniture term depicting a drawer pull made of brass or iron, and elongated to the shape of a pendant. Also sometimes called a pendant drop.

Drop leaf: Term for a table with one or two hinged leaves which can be raised into place. Variations include Pembroke, gate-leg, and butterfly table.

Drowne & Moore: Supplier of military badges and veteran pins during the 1860s, based in New York City.

Drowne, Benjamin: Silversmith listed as doing business in late eighteenth century, Portsmouth, New York.

Drowsy (doll): Talking doll of mid-1960s from Mattel. Cuddly stuffed body with 11 "sleepy time" sayings retailed for $5.66.

Dr. Scott: (see Electric corset)

Druggist (clock): Clock with a large illustration of a druggist filling the entire face. Made of nickel it was priced at $2.10 in 1893.

Drum head clock: Latter nineteenth century circular clock with a distinguished base. Popular in banks and other offices.

Drum table: Term for the Federal era (1780s to early 1800s) table with the drum-shaped top, usually containing one or two drawers.

Dublin glass: Term for quality glass produced in early eighteenth century, Dublin, Ireland. Wide variety of glassware was made there including

Dressing table, carved walnut in Queen Anne style. (Skinner Inc.)

Drop-leaf table of carved mahogany, credited to Thomas Seymour, ca. 1820. (Skinner Inc.)

chandeliers. Later cut glass became a specialty. Operations continued into the 1890s.

Dublin pottery: Tin-glazed earthenware produced during various times of the eighteenth century in Dublin, Ireland. Some latter century ware was said to be blue or purple with Chinese scenes or landscapes.

Dubois, Philo: During the 1840s and 1850s an active silversmith in Buffalo, New York.

Duche, Andrew: Credited with early work in American porcelain in the latter eighteenth century. Also worked a fine clay in Savannah, Georgia, which was exported to the Bow factory in England.

Duchesse: Early term for two or three-sectioned long chair or chase lounge.

Duchess phonograph: Popular Silvertone phonograph sold by Sears, Roebuck and Company in the 1920s. Available in mahogany, walnut, or oak, it came with 30 Columbia records and sold for $129.

Duck foot (furniture): Reference to the eighteenth century ending of a cabriole leg. Typically a circular flat foot furniture design. See also Drake foot.

Dudgeon steam wagon: Early steam-powered vehicle developed by Richard Dudgeon in 1850s, New York. Believed to be coal burning and capable of achieving speeds up to 10 miles an hour.

Dudgeon (wood): An element of burl wood taken from the boxwood tree or boxwood root, generally considered rare.

Dudley, Benjamin: Active clockmaker in 1840s, Newport, Rhode Island.

Dueber watch case: Quality "silverine" pocket watch cases made by Dueber Watch Case Manufacturing Company

in the 1890s. More elaborate case illustrations included deer and locomotive.

Duffle, James: Active silversmith in early 1800, Georgetown, South Carolina.

Duke (watch): Pocket watch offered in gilt or nickel by Waterbury Watch Company in 1893. Also a companion Duchess model.

Dulciana (clock): Mahogany case mantel clock marketed in the late 1920s by E. Ingraham Company of Bristol, Connecticut.

Dulcimer: Musical instrument in which metal strings were stretched across a sounding board. Sound resonated from the hammers striking the chords. Originally a Jewish instrument, but popular in nineteenth century America.

Dumbbell plan: Architectural term for a ground plan in the shape of a dumbbell. Two large areas would be connected by a narrow straight element.

Dummer, George and P. C.: Founders of flint glassworks in 1820s, Jersey City, New Jersey. Operations continued there until the early 1860s.

Dummer, Jeremiah: A silversmith apprentice at age 14, became a notable early silver craftsman in America during the late seventeenth and early eighteenth centuries.

Dunbar and Merriam: Firm of clockmakers located in early nineteenth century, Bristol, Connecticut.

Dunbar, Benjamin: A noted clockmaker operating in 1830s, Bristol, Connecticut.

Dunham, Rufus: Mid-nineteenth century pewter craftsman operating in New England.

Dunlap Detachable Tire: Product of the Hartford Rubber Works in early 1900s, Hartford, Connecticut.

Dunlap, Samuel, Jr.: Leading cabinetmaker in late eighteenth and early

Queen Anne drop-leaf dining table, ca. 1750. (Skinner Inc.)

American Sheraton drop-leaf breakfast table, ca. 1800.

nineteenth century, Concord, New Hampshire. Noted for fretwork and large shell motifs.

Duplicate whist: Popular card game sold in stores and by catalog in the 1890s. Playing cards, score cards, rule books, and other material sold in boxes sets. A leading seller of sets was Ihling Brothers and Everard of Kalamazoo, Michigan.

DuPont Powder Mills: Gun powder provider to Federal troops during the Civil War, doing business in Wilmington, Delaware.

Dupruy, Odram: Clockmaker known to be doing business in 1730s, Philadelphia, Pennsylvania.

Dupuy, Bernard: Accomplished silversmith of the 1830s and 1840s in Raleigh, North Carolina.

Durand, Asher Brown: Portrait and subject engraver who also did bank notes in the 1820s. Also noted as a landscape painter in the 1830s.

Durand glass: Name for early twentieth century iridescent art glass produced in Vineland, New Jersey.

Durant Four automobile: Product of Durant Motors, Inc. located in New York City. In 1924 the Durant Four Touring automobile was available for $890. Numerous other sedans and coupes were also advertised.

Durgin, William: Noted 1850s silversmith located in Concord, New Hampshire.

Durrie, George H.: Noted mid-nineteenth century artist who contributed farm winter scenes for prolific publisher Currier and Ives.

Dusenberg Straight automobile: Product of the Dusenberg Automobile and Motors Company in Indianapolis, Indiana. Dusenberg Straight 8 was billed as the "world's champion automobile" in 1922 advertising.

Dust board: A horizontal division between drawers of a chest or dresser. Initially used to prevent dust and also prevent tampering with contents. Also sometimes called a dust bottom.

Dusting cap: Two types of head gear were offered for ladies in S.S. Kresge Co. stores early in the 1900s. Both were 10¢ each.

Dutch Boy Paints: Famed paint brand featured various cloth advertising dolls during the 1950s, fabric bodies with some vinyl parts.

Dutch cupboard: Term for a buffet or cabinet with open shelves which in turn were used to display china dishes or pewter plates and other ware.

Dutch foot (furniture): A reference to the early use of a thickened disc attached, to the cabriole leg. When attached, it gives the appearance of turning outward toward the corner of the piece it supported.

Dutch Kids: Series of "comical" postcards sold by S.S. Kresge Co. stores in 1913. Cards sold six for 5¢.

Dutchman (furniture): Early furniture-making term in reference to the double dovetail used to hold two pieces of wood together.

Duval, Peter S.: Leading Philadelphia lithographer during the mid-nineteenth century. Also noted for railroad prints.

Dwarf (clock): An 1890s alarm clock in onyx case with porcelain dial. Catalog price was $3.50.

Dwight, Timothy: Boston silversmith doing business in the 1670s and 1680s.

Dyar, Warren: Active as a clockmaker in 1830s, Lowell, Massachusetts.

Dy-Dee: A 1940s doll billed as "almost human" including drinking, wetting, and blowing bubbles. Ears and body were of rubber, sizes varied from 11" to 20".

Drowsy talking doll from Mattel, 1962.

American silver tankard hallmarked by Jeremiah Dummer, early eighteenth century.

Gilded and molded copper eagle, a nineteenth century architectural element, wing spread 55". (Skinner Inc.)

Rare eagle mark on deep pewter dish by Thomas Danforth III, ca. 1790. (Skinner Inc.)

Dyke's Beard Elixir: Sold in the 1880s to grow "massive whiskers, and hair on bald heads" for 25¢ per package. Smith Mfg. Company, Palatine, Illinois.

Dyottville Glass Works: Dr. Thomas W. Dyott purchased existing Kensington Glass Works during the early 1830s in Kensington, Pennsylvania. The factory had produced bottles and flasks since the 1770s and continued under Dyott's direction. Dyott also manufactured bottles for his patent medicine products.

Eagle bank (toy): Among the legendary mechanical banks of the 1890s. Putting a coin in the bird's beak and pressing a lever caused eaglets to rise from the nest.

Eagle Cut Glass Co.: Early 1900s firm based in Minneapolis, Minnesota.

Eagle design: The American eagle appeared as a major emblem early in the country's history. It appeared on painted china, engraved silver, and on molded glass. It was also a theme on brass buttons, fans, ribbons, laces, tavern signs, and even weathervanes.

Eagle head foot (furniture): Term for the carved eagle head shape of the terminal leg of furniture. Federal period ornamentation applied to tables, sofas, and other pieces.

Eagle hut (military): World War I term for a hut or place of entertainment offered by the Y.M.C.A. for American soldiers and sailors.

Eagle Manufacturing: Producer of glass items in the 1890s as Eagle Glass and Manufacturing, and early 1900s as Eagle Manufacturing Co. in Wellsburg, West Virginia.

Eagle Manufacturing Co.: Supplied 5,400 rifled muskets to the U.S. Army during the Civil War, located in Mansfield, Connecticut.

Eagle Pencil Company: Prolific maker of pencils, pencil boxes, and crayons in 1930s, New York City. Desk companion sets included pencils, crayons, compass, ruler, and bank.

Eagle Pottery: Stoneware pottery operated by James Hamilton from 1850s to 1890s in Greensboro, Pennsylvania.

Eagle Pottery Co.: Latter nineteenth stoneware pottery located in Macomb, Illinois.

Eagle range (toy): Hubley Toys made a number of toy ranges in the 1930s. Both gas ranges and coal ranges were produced. All were cast iron and usually bore the Eagle name in raised letters on the front.

Eagle's claw: Sold as a device for catching fish in the 1880s. Pulling a lever triggered a cluster of hooks, "the fish catch themselves."

Eagle watch: $1 watch sold in the 1890s by the J.A. Foster Company of Providence, Rhode Island.

Eames, Joshua: Silversmith operating in 1830s, Boston, Massachusetts.

Ear (furniture): Term for ear-shaped end pieces on cresting of chairs in the Chippendale style.

Earl, Ralph: Noted portrait painter during in latter 1700s, America. Earl's 1775 drawings of the Battles of Lexington and Concord were later engraved by Amos Doolittle.

Early Winter: Title of a noted Currier and Ives 14" by 20" print of the nineteenth century.

Earthenware: Basically most any pottery made of clay and baked. Some consider it involving a glazed surface accompanied by a permeable body.

East End Pottery: Porcelain and whiteware crafters operating in nineteenth century, East Liverpool, Ohio.

Easter gifts: Specialized sterling silver items marketed for the 1890s Easter seasons by J. H. Johnston and Company of New York. Items included Easter key ring, Easter lily tie-holder, and Christopher Columbus stamp box.

East India Trading Co.: Group of seventeenth century companies based in England, France, and Holland organized to trade with China, Japan, and India. American colonies were forced by law to purchase wares (and tea) only from this organization.

Eastlake, Charles: Noted English architect credited with the introduction of refined Victorian type of medieval Gothic furniture in both England and the United States during the 1870s.

East Lake Glass Works: Late nineteenth century glass firm located in East Bridgeton, New Jersey.

East Liverpool Glass Co.: Glassmaking company in early 1880s, East Liverpool, Ohio. Later relocated to Jeannette, Pennsylvania.

East Liverpool Pottery Company: Pottery-making firm established in 1890s, East Liverpool, Ohio.

Eastman, Robert: A noted clockmaker in early 1800s, Brunswick, Maine.

Eastman, Seth: Established silversmith operating in 1820s, Concord, New Hampshire.

Eastman's Yellow Dock: Bottled bitters bearing the name of Dr. E. P. Eastman, ca. 1870s, Lynn, Massachusetts.

East Middlebury Glass Co.: Maker of window glass in early 1800s, East Middlebury, Vermont. Later absorbed by the Vermont Glass Factory.

East Morrison China Works: Manufacturer of china and other items in 1880s, New York City, New York.

Easton and Sanford: During business as silversmiths in 1830s and 1840s, Nantucket, Massachusetts.

East Palestine Pottery Company: Manufacturer of pottery ware. Operation started in late nineteenth century, East Palestine, Ohio.

East Trenton Pottery Company: Active pottery firm in 1890s, Trenton, New Jersey.

Easy chair: Described by designer Thomas Sheraton in early 1800 as a stuffed chair "both easy and warm" for comfort.

Easy Money: Board game offered by Billy and Ruth catalog of 1952. Made by Milton Bradley, $1.98.

Easy Riders: Series of molded plastic riding toys offered in the 1970s. Included Cootie, Mr. Potato Head, and Inchworm.

Eaton, Elon: Doing business as a clockmaker in 1860s, Grand Rapids, Michigan.

Eaton Hall chair: British design of the 1860s by A. Waterhouse. Padded rails and arms, circular seat, short turned legs.

Eaton, W. & O.: Operators of the Lincoln Pottery located in 1880s and 1890s, Lincoln, Nebraska. The specialized in redware and stoneware.

Ebenezer Cut Glass Co.: Operation manufacturing glass items during the first half of the twentieth century in Ebenezer, New York.

Eberly, Jacob: From 1880s to 1900s crafted redware in Strasburg, Virginia.

Eberman, John: Listed as an active clockmaker in 1780s, Lancaster, Pennsylvania. Later joined by John Eberman Jr. in the trade.

Ebonized: Attempt with black staining and high gloss treatment to imitate the appearance of true ebony. Frequently seen in America during the Empire furniture period.

Memorial Civil War quilt with eagle symbol in the center, ca. 1863. (Skinner Inc.)

Eastlake chest with drop-lid desk. (Harris Auction Center)

Eastlake style furniture including rocker, sofa, and side chairs. *(Harris Auction Center)*

Postcard of Economy gasoline engine inventory of Sears and Roebuck Company, early 1900s.

Ebony: High quality wood, very close grain, and exceptionally heavy. Imported from Africa and tropical countries by cabinetmakers especially during the Empire period. Also sometimes used by piano makers in the United States.

Ebony black (color): Basically a deep dull black.

Ebony (color): Listed in the 1927 Sears catalog a simply black.

Ebony knife: Ebony handle corn knife, 4", sold by S.S. Kresge Co. for 10¢ in 1913.

Echshrank: A Pennsylvania-German term for the basic corner cupboard.

Eckardt Toy Company: Maker of dolls, stuffed animals, and other novelty toys in 1930s and 1940s, New York City.

Eckha: Advertised in the late 1880s as "the leading society game" from Milton Bradley. Described as a game of skill, elegantly boxed for $1.

Eclat: Popular Bond Street brand fedora-style men's hat offered in the 1920s by Sears, Roebuck and Company.

Eclipse forge: Quality forge and blower sold in the 1920s to "meet requirements of ordinary shop" for $16.40.

Eclipse Tumbler Co.: Maker of glass items in early 1900s, Lansing, Michigan. Later part of the Findlay Glass Company in Findlay, Ohio.

Eclipse umbrella: Quality umbrella made of silk in the 1880s. Priced at $4 each by Felix F. Daus, New York, manufacturer of umbrellas and parasols.

Eclipse wagon: Sold by Sears, Roebuck and Company for children via catalog in 1902. This tricycle self-propelling item came with a body made of sheet steel and tinned steel wheels. Price was $2.99.

Economy Gasoline Engine: Brand name for bestselling engines from Sears, Roebuck and Company during the first quarter of the twentieth century. Offerings ranged from boat engines to factory-sized pumps.

Economy King: Brand name for range of cream separators sold by Sears, Roebuck and Company during the 1920s. Their best model could skim about 200 quarts of milk per hour. Price was $70 for the separator with stand.

Ecran: French term for early fireplace screen.

Ecru (color): A light tan, considered slightly lighter than beige.

Ecuelle: A French term for a domed two-handled vessel similar to the English porringer, and popular in the eighteenth century. Typically made of silver, but also crafted from pewter.

Eddystone clock: Reference to a type of alarm clock designed in the 1820s by Simon Willard. The tapered wooden base resembled a lighthouse. A glass case above held a bell and alarm dial.

Edgell, Simon: Noted pewter craftsmen working in early eighteenth century, Philadelphia.

Edison Talking Doll: An 1890s version fully advertised by the Edison Phonograph Toy Manufacturing Company of New York.

Edmands & Company: Stoneware operation in nineteenth century and very early twentieth century, Strasburg, Virginia.

Edson electric garter: Offered in the 1880s to end "ill-shapen and dwarfed limbs" and prevent pain. Sold by London Electric Fabric Company, New York.

Edson, Jonah: Listed as clockmaker in 1820s, Bridgewater, Massachusetts.

Edwards, Abraham: Colonial silversmith doing business in 1765, Ashby, Massachusetts.

Edwards, Abraham: Maker of tall clocks in 1790s and early 1800s at Ashby, Massachusetts. Early clocks had wooden works, and later brass works.

Edwards, Samuel: Active clockmaker doing business in 1820s, Gorham, Maine.

Edwards, Samuel: Noted silversmith in latter eighteenth century, Natick, Massachusetts.

Edwin, David: Engraver noted for portraits of American leaders and generals, active in late eighteenth and early nineteenth century, Philadelphia.

Effanbee Dolls: Highly prolific doll-making company which began operation in 1910, New York City. The odd name represented a merger of Fleischaker and Baum.

Egerton, Matthew: Cabinetmaker doing business in eighteenth century, Brunswick, New Jersey.

Egg and dart: Term for a style of molding carved with egg-shaped pieces and pointed darts. Seen from time to time on carved furniture and some interior work.

Egg cup: Ca. 1850s and later creations of silver frames issued in sets which included spoons. More elaborate egg boiler cups held water and allowed for heating beneath the frame.

Egg poacher: Easy egg poacher, in "Maryland pattern" cooking three eggs at once. Offered by S.S. Kresge Co. for 10¢ in 1913.

Egg rattle: Egg-shaped rattle, made of celluloid, from 1913 S.S. Kresge Co. Colors were pink and white or blue and white.

Egg shell porcelain: Term for very thin fifteenth century porcelain made in China. Later certain nineteenth century British factories used the term for their ware.

Egyptian style: Early nineteenth century fashion based in part on Napoleon's success in Egypt and the appeal of rediscovered art and artifacts there. A trend followed in Europe featuring the sphinx, Egyptian headdress, exotic animals, and lotus buds all in carved wood, gilded bronze, or similar composition images.

Egyptian ware: (see Basalt ware)

Ehren: Popular model of shelf clock manufactured by the Waterbury Clock Company during the 1890s. Came with enameled iron gilt ornaments.

Eicke, Edward: Supplier of military goods to the U.S. government during the Civil War, located in New York City.

Eight-legged table: Basically an eighteenth century British form of the gate leg table.

Eisenbrant, E.: Maker of large fife musical instruments for Federal government during the Civil War, located in 1860s, Philadelphia, Pennsylvania.

Eisenhower watch: Pocket watch with the image of "Ike, the Hero" in deep relief on the case. Face with American flag and eagle. Price was $57.50 in the 1973 Montgomery Ward catalog.

Elastic Tip Company: Maker of rifle which fired rubber tipped arrows in the early 1890s. Also offered a projectile firing pistol as the world's lawn and parlor game.

Elba: Fancy enameled clock made by Waterbury with bronze columns and

Effanbee's Patsy Ruth doll.

Effanbee doll designed by Dewees Cochran, ca. 1936.

Effanbee baby doll, ca. 1940s.

Patsyette doll by Effanbee, ca. 1928.

Sweetie Pie doll from Effanbee.

gilt base. Various face styles in 1893 ranged from $15 to $16.50 retail.

Elderkin and Staniford: Silversmiths doing business in 1790s, Windom, Connecticut.

Electrical Glass Co.: Maker of glass insulators for telegraph poles and glass for electrical devices in late 1880s, Sandwich, Massachusetts.

Electrical Supply Co.: Providers of electric light, telephone, and telegraph supplies in 1880s, New York City.

Electric Bitters: Ca. 1870s product of H. E. Bucklen and Company, Chicago, Illinois. "Positively cures all diseases of the stomach, liver and kidneys," according to paper label.

Electric brougham: (see Woods Motor Vehicle Company)

Electric corset: Product advertised in the 1880s to promote "vigorous health and a graceful figure." Sold for $3 each by Dr. Scott's Electric Hair and Flesh Brushes.

Electric football: Game sanctioned by the National Football League in the 1970s. Montgomery Ward catalog version, with automatic timer, was $19.99.

Electric Game Company: Noted maker of a long line of so-called electric sports games during the 1930s and 1940s in Holyoke, Massachusetts. Graduated to further batter-operated quiz games in the 1950s.

Electric Motor (toy): Offered as a toy for children in 1905. Standard motor was $1, however larger sizes were priced at $3, $5, and $10.

Electric Push-M-Up: Pinball game offering light-up plastic domes from Northwestern Products in the early 1950s.

Electric Thriller (toy): This 1917 toy produced a "slight or severe shock" just by turning the crank. Price was 95¢.

Electric Vehicle Company: Makers of Columbia automobiles in 1904, including the Columbia Electric Runabout and the gasoline powered Tonneau. Company located in Hartford, Connecticut.

Electro magnetic brush: A flesh brush offered in the 1880s to prevent "softening of the brain" and other ailments. Sold by Electro-Magnetic Brush Co. of Cincinnati, Ohio.

Electro-Magnetic Crane (toy): Early 1940s offering by Lionel. Remote control lifting of metal scrap as an adjunct to toy railroad.

Electroplate: Process first commercially developed in the early 1840s. Basically involved adding a thin layer of silver or other metal to an object by using electricity. It was eventually perfected in the latter nineteenth century to allow plating of most any metal including silver, gold, and nickel.

Electrotype: Basically the reproduction of certain metals on a plaster mold that has been covered with a coating of electricity conducting lead. Late in the nineteenth century and early in the twentieth century it was sometimes used to imitate more valuable pieces.

El Escorto cigars: Unique brand of cigars offered in stores and mail-order catalogs of the 1920s. Pocket packages included tobacco from Wisconsin and Pennsylvania with wrappers from Connecticut. Can of ten was 50¢.

Elfe, Thomas: Noted cabinetmaker in mid-1700s, Charleston, South Carolina. Regarded for elaborately carved case pieces.

Elf Land Railroad: Boxed set of picture blocks sold by Marshall Field and Company in the 1890s. Made by McLoughlin Brothers, it featured the view of an immense train serving elves.

Elgin bicycle: Popular brand of bicycle sold by Sears, Roebuck and Company in the early 1920s. Selections include boys, girls, and women's models. The line also included motor bikes.

Elgin Bluebird: Advertised as the bike of the century in 1935. It retailed via Sears, Roebuck and Company for the then monumental price of $44.95. A companion Sears Elgin Blackhawk sold for $33.95.

Elgin street sweeper (toy): Hubley made a cast-iron Elgin pickup street sweeper during the 1930s. It was marked "The Elgin" in raised letters on the front. The model was 8½" in length and had a releasing dump lever

Elgin watch: During the 1920s Sears, Roebuck and Company offered a series of Elgin pocket watches both open face and hunting case style. Prices ranged from $12 to $41.

Elisabetta: Name for doll offered in Montgomery Ward catalog in the early 1970s. Vinyl and velvet figure retailed at $17.

Elizabethan: General reference to period during the reign of Queen Elizabeth in England from the late 1500s to the early 1600s. In terms of furniture it usually involved massive oak pieces and elaborate carvings.

Elkloid Company: Firm specializing in dominoes, dice, poker chips, and related games in 1930s and 1940s, Providence, Rhode Island.

Ellenville Glass Works: Operation of glassmakers in early 1830s, Ellenville, New York. Maker of bottles and related items up until the middle of the nineteenth century.

Ellenville Wood Novelty: Company producing wooden toys and related items in 1930s and 1940s, Ellenville, New York.

Ellery, William: (see American Watch Co.)

Ellicott, Joseph: Noted clockmaker in eighteenth century, Philadelphia. Also crafted famous mahogany-cased musical clock in 1769.

Elliott, George: Active silversmith located in 1835, Wilmington, Delaware.

Elliott, James: Known as a silversmith in early 1800s, Winnsboro, South Carolina.

Elliott, John: Specialized in looking glass pieces as a cabinetmaker in 1770s and 1780s, Philadelphia.

Elliott, Joseph: Silversmith of note in 1770s, New Castle, Delaware.

Elliott, Thomes & Talbot: Boston-based publishers of dime novels, including Ten Cent Novelettes, during the second half of the nineteenth century.

Ellis & Company: Provided six pound cannons to Confederate military during the Civil War. Located in Nashville, Tennessee.

Ellis, Britton & Easton: Firm making wooden carts, dolls, sleds, wagons, and related toys during the second half of the nineteenth century in Springfield, Vermont. Best known for Ellis Wooden Doll of the 1870s. The multi-talented Joel Ellis also directed toy-making projects Vermont Novelty Works and the Cooperative Manufacturing Company.

Elsie the Cow with vinyl head and plush body, ca. 1977.

Empire rolled-arm sofa. (Harris Auction Center)

Empire sofa with original finish. (Harris Auction Center)

Energizer Bunny, 18" plush figure, 1995.

Ellis, Joel: (see Vermont Toy Works)

Ellsworth, William J.: Accomplished in pewter work in 1780s and 1790s, New York.

Elm: Very hard but flexible wood used frequently in early furniture. Later burr elm was sometimes used as veneer.

Elmira Window Glass Co.: Maker of window glass and other items during the early 1900s in Elmira, New York.

Elmore automobile: Produced in the early 1900s by the Elmore Manufacturing Company in Clyde, Ohio. The two-cycle Elmore was listed at $1,750 in 1907.

Elsie the cow: Major advertising figure for Borden company mostly late 1930s through late 1950s. Image appeared as doll, mugs, cookie jar, and other items.

Elsinore Pottery Co.: Whiteware pottery doing business in early 1900s, Elsinore, California.

Elsmore: Name given to Honor-Bilt "already cut" home in special Sears, Roebuck and Company catalog of 1926. Price for the five-room boxed and shipped bungalow was $2,391.

Elsworth, William I.: Known as a pewter craftsman in 1790s, New York City.

Eltonhead, Thomas: Colonial silversmith doing business in 1835, Baltimore, Maryland.

Ely's Cream Balm: Sold as a treatment for headache and deafness, "contains no cocaine or mercury." Retail price for circular container 50¢.

Embossed markings (doll): Reference to those raised letters and numbers used by doll makers. Usually they appeared on the back of the doll's head or shoulder plate. However they could also appear elsewhere.

Embossed postcards: Embossed birthday postcards sold by S.S. Kresge Co. stores in 1913, six for 5¢ in 100 different designs.

Embossing (metal): Practice of producing raised or projecting figures or designs in relief on the surface of metalwork.

Embrasure: Term for window recess in brick houses mostly in the eighteenth century. Typically the recess was upholstered in velvet or silk to correspond with the window's curtains, and served as a window seat.

Embroidery: Basically the art of producing ornamental patterns by needlework on any workable fabric. Principally used fabrics include linen, silks, flannels, satin, and velvet.

Emenee Industries: Noted maker of plastic musical instruments and toys including Gene Autry guitar and Arthur Godfrey ukulele in the 1950s. Player snapped on the instrument to make playing easier.

Emerald green (color): According to early twentieth century catalogs, a bright green.

Emerson and Silver: A supplier of swords and sabers during the Civil War, located in Trenton, New Jersey.

Emery stone: Extremely hard stone used for cutting and engraving some pottery and porcelain, and also for some metalworking and statuary.

Emery, Thomas: Operating as a silversmith from the 1780s into the early 1800s in Boston, Massachusetts.

Emmert-Hammes Company: Maker of toy aluminum planes, boats, and related items in 1930s, Warren, Michigan.

Emmet, Fisher and Flowers: Glassmaking firm in early 1800s, East Cambridge, Massachusetts. Later the small operation was acquired by the New England Glass Company.

Emons and Marshall: Listed as suppliers

of swords and sabers to Federal forces during the Civil War. Located in Philadelphia, Pennsylvania.

Empire (furniture): Style of heavy and extremely ornate furniture most notable in the early nineteenth century. Often centered on mahogany with flares of rosewood and ebony. Most credit French emperor Napoleon with the style, although it was originally based on designs of ancient Greece and Rome.

Empire bed: Term for an early nineteenth century French bed set low against a wall or slight alcove and only one side open. Other relative and evolving structures were said to include the boat bed, gondola bed, and ultimately the American-designed sleigh bed.

Empire City: Brand of fishing gear sold by S.S. Kresge Co. in 1913.

Empire Clock Company: Noted clock making operation in 1850s, Bristol, Connecticut.

Empire green (color): Presented as a medium light green by Sears.

Empire Pottery Company: Pottery-making firm doing business in 1860s, Trenton, New Jersey.

Empire Powder Mills: Gun powder supplier for the U.S. government during the Civil War. Operations in Kingston, New York, and Sangerties, New York.

Empire State Glass Works: Maker of flint glass and other items in latter nineteenth century, Brooklyn, New York. Later part of Thill and Sons Company.

Empire Troll Spoon: Empire City Trolling Spoon offered by S.S. Kresge Co. in 1913. Price for the fluted, nickel-plated fishing device was 10¢.

Empire wreath: An addition to the Empire style of decoration as advertised in the 1890s. Wreath design was offered by silversmith Daniel Low on brooches,

scarf pins, cuff links, and even toothbrush cases.

Empress belt: Metallic belt for women and children sold by Empress Metallic Belt Company during the 1870s. Combined silvered gilt with jet and sold for $1.

Empress embroiderer: Device sold in the 1880s by the Empress Embroiderer Company as an adapter to sewing machines. Price was $2.

Enameled pottery: Basically a coarse ware covered with heavy white enamel, originally known by the Latin word for tin.

Enamel (furniture): As a decorative touch on early furniture a finish was prepared by coating the wood with whiting and a kind of weak glue known as size. The level was then rubbed down and finally finished off with a French polish.

Enamel kettle: S.S. Kresge Co. offered a "heavy gray enamel" preserving kettle for 10¢ in 1913 catalog.

Enamelware: Wide variety offered by S.S. Kresge Co. in 1913. Listings include baking pan, bread pan, strainer, fry pan, German stew cup, covered bucket, and wash basin.

En cage box: Dainty cosmetic box of eighteenth century France, often included miniature paintings under glass and gold bordering.

En case (furniture): Basically a term used during the first half of the eighteenth century in France for a small marble-topped table. Typically the piece housed a small drawer and cupboard below.

Encaustic tile: Use of a colored clay different than the basic tile body, thus providing an inlaying design of contrast.

Encoignure: During the eighteenth century this was a generally accepted French term for the corner cupboard.

Hobnail pattern epergne by Fenton glass.

Clear glass epergne.

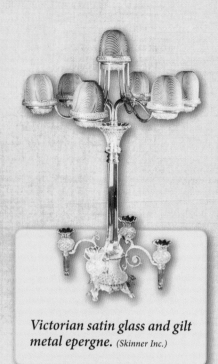

Victorian satin glass and gilt metal epergne. (Skinner Inc.)

Stylish majolica epergne.

Enders, William & Co.: Under Federal contract to supply military uniforms during the Civil War. Located in Boston, Massachusetts.

Endive scroll: Term for a carved ornament applied to Chippendale style furniture.

End of day (glass): Term for small decorative glass objects reportedly made near the end of work period or at odd times. Usually in limited supply and not of regular production line. Sometimes called off-hand glass.

Energex sweeper: Modernistic electric vacuum cleaner offered in the early 1920s. Customers could "sweep and sew the electric way" for $29.85.

Energizer Bunny: Pink and white plush figure issued in various sizes up to 18" in the 1990s by the Eveready Battery Company. Smaller vinyl figures were also offered.

Enfield rifle: Weapon featured as "now used by English Volunteer Corps" in the 1864 military goods catalog issued by Schuyler, Hartley & Graham.

Engine house (toy): Essential piece of late nineteenth century toys depicting fire-fighters and their equipment. Cast-iron engine house with 1882 patent date.

England, George: New York City silversmith active in the early 1800s.

English Duplex: (see Norton, Charles P. and Co.)

English Female Bitters: Bottled product of the 1880s, Louisville, Kentucky.

English oak (color): During the 1920s, a reddish medium brown.

English teapot: English pottery tea ball teapot offered by Manning-Bowman during the 1920s. The English pot was black with royal blue band and nickel plated mountings.

Engraving (furniture): Reference in furniture making applied to the decoration of marquetry. A relief effect was produced by engraving fine lines on the veneers. Afterwards the lines were rubbed in with a colored composition to further enhance them.

Engraving (glass): Process of decoration accomplished with use of various copper wheels.

Engraving (metal): Silversmiths in the colonial era used an ornament to cut lines in silver. Often initials were engraved to establish ownership. In the 1700s guidebooks were sometimes used to aid silversmiths and goldsmiths.

Engraving (pottery): Typically involved use of an abrasive wheel to instill patterns or other facets. Some stoneware was engraved in this manner late in the nineteenth century.

Entablature: That space horizontally above and between two columns.

Entenmann dolls: Pastry brand's series of Beanbag Sweeties plush dolls from 1998 including Chip Cookie, Richie Donut, and Sprinkles Cupcake.

Enterprise Glass Company: Late nineteenth century glass factory in Honesdale, Pennsylvania. Later the Enterprise Cut Glass Company located in Elmira Heights, New York.

Enterprise Manufacturing Co.: Makers of the Enterprise Meat Chopper in the late 1880s. The hand-cranked device was advertised as "unexcelled" for chopping sausage meat, codfish, hamburger steak, and hog's head cheese.

Enterprise Pottery: A small pottery firm operating in 1880s, Trenton, New Jersey.

Entree dish: Term for a dining dish of the latter eighteenth century often covered and sometimes provided with a ring handle. Some later entree dishes came with compartments to hold water, and stands for heating.

Envelope table: Latter eighteenth century square-topped table with envelope-like flaps. When flipped back the flaps provided more table surface. A forerunner to some card tables and the triangular handkerchief table.

Epergne: Originally from France, the epergne amounted to a fancy table decoration with several glass containers grouped around a center stem. Frequently they appeared as flower-like vases or glass baskets.

Erector outfit (toy): Gilbert's Erector outfits were a popular toy as early as 1916. Each outfit had hundreds of steel parts and often a motor for elaborate construction from bridges to sewing machines.

Erector tool chest (toy): Full 23-piece tool chest from Erector for children in the 1920s. Saw, hammer, brace, level, and manual included.

Erickson Glass: Small glassmaking operation in 1940s and 1950s, Bremen, Ohio. Making mostly lead glass under the direction of Carl Erickson.

Ermine cloak (ceramic): Term for decorated wear with a motif in blue similar to the ceremonial garment worn by medieval royalty. The ware usually bore a shield containing a monogram, crest, or even a floral design.

Erskine Six automobile: A 1920s product of the Studebaker Manufacturing Company in South Bend, Indiana.

E. R. Thomas Motor Co.: Makers of the Thomas Flyer automobile in early 1900, United States. Based in Buffalo, New York. Their four cylinder 1905 model was priced at $3,000.

Ertl Company: Noted firm founded in the latter 1940s in Dubuque, Iowa, and later relocated to Dyersville,

Iowa. Extensive maker of toy metal farm equipment, vehicles, and related items.

Erwin, Andrew: Listed as a silversmith in 1840s, Philadelphia, Pennsylvania.

Escabelle (furniture): A seventeenth century version of a small chair with a framework of underlying supports.

Escallop shell (furniture): Term for a carved ornament on eighteenth century English furniture. It gave the appearance of a marine shell and was said to represent the emblem used on the shields of the Crusaders.

Escritoire: Originally a French term, but used in other countries to describe a lady's rather delicate and refined desk.

Escutcheon: Initially a crest or shield carved ornament on furniture. Term also applied to a keyhole's brass fitting.

Eskay's Albumenized Food: Brand of 1890s food supplement for infants and invalids. Product of Smith, Kline & French Co. of Philadelphia, Pennsylvania.

Eskimo lamp: Artic region lamp constructed of stone or clay which burned seal and whale oil, frequently used by Eskimo tribes. Often native clay was shaped and dried to form these lamps.

Eskimo Pie doll: Variations of the Eskimo Pie boy in cloth dolls starting in the 1970s from Eskimo Pie Corporation.

Essex Glass Works: Factory established around 1787 by Robert Hewes and Charles Kupfer in Boston. Produced window glass and in 1809 was renamed the Boston Glass Manufactory. Later relocated in South Boston.

Esso bank: Figural bank of Little Oil Drop issued by oil company in the 1950s. Hard red plastic.

Estelle Toy Company: Ambitious firm known for children's outfits depicting

The "New" Erector set from 1927 Sears, Roebuck and Company.

Erector set instruction booklet from A.C. Gilbert Co., 1939.

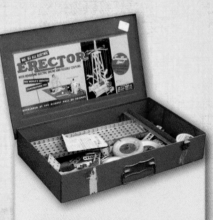

All electric erector set, 1954.

Pawnee Bill circus wagon by Ertl.

Country doctor by Ertl.

Eskimo Pie Corporation cloth doll, the Eskimo Pie Boy, ca. 1970s.

cowboys and Indians during the 1950s and 1960s. Based in Honeoye Falls, New York.

Estes: Name of standard bungalow provided by Sears, Roebuck and Company, boxed and ready to assemble in 1926. Price "cut and fitted" was $672.

Estey Organ Company: A leading seller of music organs for the home in the latter nineteenth century. The firm relied heavily on print advertising in magazines and on colorful trade cards. In the 1930s they provided similar products for children.

E. T.: Initials for extra-terrestrial in the famed 1982 movie *E. T.* The fictional character was represented on lunch boxes, trading cards, clocks, phones, and other novelty items.

Étagère: Originally a French term, but commonly used during the nineteenth century in England and the U.S., describing a group of small display shelves, sometimes known as a what-not shelves, with ornate scrolled design. Some had marble shelves.

Etched glass: Glassmakers used corrosive acid applied to unprotected glass surfaces to achieve lettering and image.

Etowah Iron Works: Supplied knives to the Confederate military during the Civil War. Located in Etowah, Georgia.

Etruria Pottery: American pottery factory based in Trenton, New Jersey. Under the direction of Ott and Brewer, the firm produced Belleek-like china from American materials. Later the firm also produced granite ware and hand-painted software china.

Etruscan ware: Originally a 1770s ware credited to the work of Josiah Wedgwood of England. A highly ornamented ware with gold trim and other coloring reminiscent of ancient earthenware.

Ettenger and Edmond: Under contract with the Confederate States of America to produce cannon carriers and caissons. Located in Richmond, Virginia.

Etui: Term for a lady's small box with fitted compartments containing scissors and other personal objects. Often crafted of porcelain or silver.

Eureka steam cooker: Available in seven sizes during the 1890s from Eureka Steam Cooker Company in Chicago. Priced from $1.75 to $10.

Euro Disney dolls: Euro Disney was featured with two Barbie dolls in the 1990s, Weekend Barbie and Fun Barbie. Both were boxed and marketed by Mattel.

European Timekeeper: (see Norton, Charles P. and Co.)

Evans and Hassal: Noted as providing swords and sabers to U.S. government in the 1860s. Located in Philadelphia, Pennsylvania.

Evans, D.: Maker of U.S. military buttons during the Civil War, located in Attleboro, Massachusetts.

Evans, G. G.: Specialized in photograph card pictures and albums during the Civil War, located in 1860s, Philadelphia, Pennsylvania.

Evansville Toy: Maker of garden sets, shovels, and related metal items for children in 1930s, Cleveland, Ohio. A division of American Fork and Hoe Company.

Everet, James: Doing business as a pewter artisan in early 1700s, Philadelphia, Pennsylvania.

Everlast Toy Company: Maker of wood toys and furniture for children in 1930s and 1940s, Tacoma, Washington.

Eves, William: Listed as an active clockmaker in 1830s, Cincinnati, Ohio.

Ewan, William: A silversmith in 1850s and 1860s, Charleston, South Carolina.

Ewer: Basically a one-handled jug or vessel for carrying water and a spout for pouring. Mainly used for hand washing at the table, ewers varied in material including china, glass, and metal.

Ewery cupboard: Term for a low cupboard with toilet accessories located below the basin and ewer container.

Excel Manufacturing: Toy appliance maker including toasters in 1930s, Muncie, Indiana.

Excelsior: In reference to toys, this was basically shredded wood used for stuffing dolls and such. The material was also used for packing crates.

Excelsior Aromatic Bitters: A nineteenth century bottled product bearing the name of Dr. D.S. Perry and Company, New York.

Excelsior Glass Company: Glassmaking firm operating around 1860 in Martin's Ferry, Virginia.

Excelsior Glass Works: Glassmaking operation active in 1840s and 1850s Camden, New Jersey. Later it was re-established under various names.

Excelsior Lawn Mower: Advertised in the 1870s as the largest selling mower in the world. Four sizes for hand power and four sizes for horse power, $15 to $200.

Excelsior Manufacturing: Manufacturer of bicycles and exercise equipment in 1930s and 1940s, Michigan City, Indiana.

Excelsior motorcycle: The Excelsior Motor Company started making single cylinder motorcycles in 1907. The operation was purchased by Ignaz Schwin in 1917. In 1925 the Excelsior-Henderson Company produced the Super-x model motorcycle. Ultimately the company failed during the Great Depression of the 1930s.

Excelsior scale: S.S. Kresge Co. catalog of 1913 offered Excelsior improved kitchen scale. Heavy ring and hook, brass face for 10¢.

Exfoliate: Act of removing the surface in thin layers or thin pieces. A peeling off process.

Exhibit Supply Co.: (see Arcade card)

Exide: Brand name of batteries made for electric vehicles early in the twentieth century. Producer of the Exide was the Electric Storage Battery Company of Philadelphia, Pennsylvania.

Expanded ribbing (glass): Method of imposing ribbing on hot glass by use of a topless mold with corrugated walls. Once dipped, the glass is withdrawn and blown, allowing for ribs to become thinner but wider.

Express Freight (toy): One of the premier o-gauge Lionel electric trains of the early 1940s. Came with an electro-magnet crane and remote control couplers.

Express Train: Highly regarded nineteenth century railroad print by Currier and Ives.

Express Wagon: Toy wagon made of steel sold during the early 1900s by Sears, Roebuck and Company. Both bed sizes and wheel sizes varied. Starting in the 1890s a frequent term for various toy vehicles in the image of contemporary horse-drawn freight delivery wagons.

Extension table: Made famous in early nineteenth century America by Duncan Phyfe, but known earlier in England. Top separated in the center to allow for an additional leaf in the open space.

Extinguisher: Typically a silver cone-shaped device used to extinguish the flame of a candle. Usually they were the quality of accompanying silver candlesticks.

Estey Organ Company trade card, ca. 1880s.

Estey Organ depicted on 1880s trade card.

E.T. collector card dated 1982.

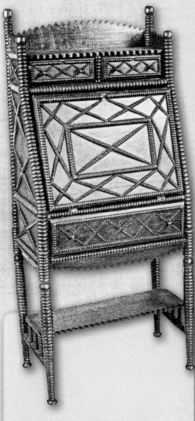

Fall front lady's desk, stained pine, ca. 1900. (Skinner Inc.)

Eyland, James: James Eyland and Company operated a silversmith trade in 1820s and 1830s, Charleston, South Carolina.

Ezeout: Brand of cake pans and pie plates offered by S.S. Kresge Co. stores in 1913.

Faber, A. W.: Late nineteenth century maker of drawing pencils, calculating rules, and similar items. Located in New York City.

Faber, William: Diligent silversmith active in 1835, Philadelphia, Pennsylvania.

Fabric doll: Term applied to all manner of cloth dolls including felt, rag, and cotton sheets. Some of the earliest advertising dolls were made of fabric which bore the name of the company and sometimes a commercial message. Extends to Lenci felt dolls and Kathe Kruse cloth dolls. Also sometimes a reference to cotton sheets with doll image prints issued as advertisements or promotions.

Face painting: Another term for individual portraits accomplished by traveling artists in early America. Sometimes the surrounding images were prepared previously so only the facial details were added.

Faden, William: British map publisher who produced the 1776 North American Atlas and the 1793 Battles of the American Revolution.

Faience: Term for decorative enameled earthenware distinct from tableware. Typically with polychrome decorations. Originally derived from Faenza, Italy.

Faience Manufacturing Co.: Maker of pottery tiles in 1880s and 1890s, Greenpoint, New York.

Fainting couch: (see Recamier [furniture])

Fairchild, Joseph: Silversmith of note in 1825, New Haven, Connecticut.

Fairy lamp: Term for a late nineteenth century night lamp made of glass and lighted with a candle. An early patent for fairy lamps was granted to the British firm of Clarke and Company.

Faldstool: Term for an early American folding stool used in taverns and other public places. Like modern folding chairs, the stools could be stored when not needed.

Fales, G. S.: Clockmaker working in 1830s, New Bedford, Massachusetts.

Fales, James: Noted as a clockmaker in 1815, New Bedford, Massachusetts.

Falk, J. (toys): Late nineteenth and early twentieth century toy maker based in Nuremberg, Germany. Noted for steam-operated boats, various toy model steam engines, and optical projectors.

Fall-front desk: Another term for the drop-front or slant-front desk. Basically the front was designed to "fall" when the desk was opened.

Fall-leaf table: Used as an alternative term for drop-leaf table.

Fallows and Company: The Philadelphia firm founded by James Fallows noted for tin ware toys of the latter nineteenth century including boats, trains, and horse-drawn vehicles. It became Fallows and Sons in the early 1890s and still later Frederick & Henry Fallows Toys.

Family Soap: Box of 100 bars of Family Laundry Soap sold in the 1902 Sears, Roebuck and Company catalog. Price for the full wooden box was $2.95.

Fanback: Distinguished fanlike flare shape of spindles in the Windsor chair style.

Fancy furniture: Early and middle nineteenth century term for delicate pieces mainly intended for ornamental usage, and fancy painted furniture. Decorations were often stenciled.

Fan light: Half-round or elliptic window over a door. Light was filtered through the radiating designs of vertical leading.

Farm bell: In their 1902 catalog Sears, Roebuck, and Company offered farm bells of various sizes from 15" in diameter at the mouth to 20". They also sold large bells for church, factory, and schoolhouse use.

Farmer's Glass Company: Relatively obscure glassmaking factory located in Clarksburg, Massachusetts. It was incorporated in 1814.

Farmer's Home (print): Title of four different distinguished Currier and Ives prints issued in the nineteenth century including autumn, harvest, summer, and winter. Most scarce, winter scene.

Farm Knowledge: A two-volume set offering "reliable and authoritative" information for the farm family in the 1920s. Sears and Roebuck sold the sets for $4.95.

Farnham, S. S.: Active clockmaker in 1840s, Oxford, New York.

Farnum, Henry & Rufus: Partners in clockmaking operation of 1780s, Boston, Massachusetts.

Farrar, C. D.: Maker of long-case clocks with carved hoods and broken pediments in 1760s and 1770s, Lampeter, Pennsylvania.

Farrar, Wm. H.: Founder of the Southern Porcelain Manufacturing Company in Kaolin, South Carolina. Specialized in porcelain and whiteware during the 1860s and 1870s.

Farr, John C.: Noted silversmith and clockmaker operating in 1830s and 1840s, Philadelphia, Pennsylvania.

Farthingale chair: Fashionable chair for women of the early 1600s. It allowed room of the abundantly full dresses of that era, which were called farthingale dresses. Typically a high back chair with no arms, and an upholstered seat.

Fasbender, J. H.: Doing business as a clockmaker in 1770s and 1780s in Charleston, South Carolina.

Fashionable Turnout (print): Fully titled, Fashionable Turnouts in Central Park, highly prized print by Courier and Ives. The nineteenth century original edition was large at 18x28".

Fashion doll: Reference to stylishly dressed adult dolls wearing the elegant clothing of their particular era. French fashion dolls of the late nineteenth and early twentieth centuries were particularly indicative of the highest fashion.

Faun (furniture): Used as a decorative device on eighteenth century furniture, particular of English designer Robert Adams. The faun itself was a legendary ancient deity represented as half man and half goat, complete with pointed ears.

Fauteuil (furniture): Early term for a French armchair with fully upholstered seat and back. The open arms were also upholstered. Popular in the eighteenth and early nineteenth centuries.

Favorite Mill: Top brand of coffee mill sold in early 1900s by Sears, Roebuck and Company. Included a raised hopper mill, hinged cover, and hardwood box. Prices varied from 18¢ to 31¢.

Favrille (glass): Describes striking iridescent cased glass which was the hallmark of Aurene, Durand, and Tiffany.

Fawn (color): Generally a light tan, the color of its namesake animal.

Fay Manufacturing Co.: Maker of chairs for invalids and tricycles "for cripples" during the 1890s. Located at 21 Pine Street in Elyria, Ohio.

Fay, Theodore Sedgwick: Editor of the

Federal bow front bureau, ca. 1810. (Skinner Inc.)

1830s *Views in New York and its Environs* published by Peabody & Company of New York. The work was published in eight parts which included text, map, and various engraved scenes.

Feather edge: Term for beveled edge of panel board.

Feather veneering: Reference to feather-like or plume-like appearance of cut and applied veneers or sometimes marquetry banding.

Federal Hill: (see Baltimore Glass Works)

Federal period: Era which began with the end of the American Revolution in the 1780s and continued generally until 1810. Patriotic motifs were frequently seen in furniture renderings including cannon, eagles, and swords. Much of the classic style was credited to Robert Adam.

Feekhart, August: Active silversmith in 1850s, Rochester, New York.

Feldspar: Group of minerals in crystalline form. Colors can vary from white, blue, and green.

Felix the Cat: Animated character featured in early comic strips and cartoons. Numerous twentieth century toys, including games, dolls, and pin-back buttons paid tribute to Felix.

Fell and Thropp Company: Noted as a pottery operation in late nineteenth century, Trenton, New Jersey.

Fellows, Abraham: Silversmith active in 1820, Newport, Rhode Island.

Fellows, August: Silversmith in 1850s, Rochester, New York.

Fellows, James: Listed as an active clockmaker in 1830s, Lowell, Massachusetts.

Fellows, Read, and Olcott: New York City clockmakers during the 1830s.

Fender: Term for ornamental guard used in the early fireplace. Usually made of brass.

Fisher-Price fire truck #200, Winkey-Blinky, 1950s.

Fenestra: Brand of steel windows produced early in the twentieth century by Detroit Steel Products Company.

Fenno and Hale: Operation of silversmiths in 1840s, Bangor, Maine.

Fenton, Christopher Webber: Noted nineteenth century potter especially known for porcelain and flint enamel pottery. Vermont native with ties to the Bennington Pottery in the 1840s and 1850s.

Ferris, Tiba: Doing business as a clockmaker in 1840s, Wilmington, Delaware.

Ferris, Ziba: Silversmith in business during the first half of the nineteenth century in Wilmington, Delaware.

Ferrotype: Term for an early photograph which incorporated use of a thin piece of metal or tin. A chemical process fixed the image on the metal surface. Sometimes called a tintype.

Fessenden, John: Listed as silversmith in 1845, Newport, Rhode Island.

Fessler, John: Noted clockmaker active in 1790s and early 1800s, Frederickstown, Maryland.

Festoon: Wreath or garland of flowers and leaves as presented in carved or inlaid design on early furniture.

Fibula: Term for a brooch-like pin once used as both a decorative device and as a practical means of holding clothing together.

Fiddle back: Reference to the violin-shaped back splat of an early chair. Typically fancy grained wood veneer or painted.

Fiddle-back grain: Reference to a high-quality figured veneer resembling the finely marked sycamore once used in violin backs.

Fiddle bottle: (see Violin bottle)

Fido bank: A particular cast iron bank in the image of a dog was produced by

Hubley Toys in the 1930s. The animal bore a collar with the name Fido and was copyrighted.

Field bed: Basically a four-poster canopy type bed used in the late eighteenth and early nineteenth centuries. For high ranking military officers.

Field, Brother & Co.: Provided blankets for Federal troops during the Civil War, based in St. Louis, Missouri.

Fielding, George: New York City silversmith operating in the 1730s.

Fields, Philip: Listed as a pewterer active in 1799, New York City.

Fields, Samuel: Active silversmith in 1815, Philadelphia, Pennsylvania.

Filber, John: A Colonial era clockmaker in 1790s and 1800s, York, Pennsylvania.

Filch, Allen: Colonial silversmith operating in 1785, New Haven, Connecticut.

Filet: References to a fine lace, usually with a square mesh background and design which is darned. Applied to both French and Irish lace, but based on the French word for net.

Filigree: Ornamental work of pierced metal or wire. Traditionally done in gold or silver.

Filley, Giles F.: A supplier of stoves, camp kettles, and military mess pans to Federal troops during the Civil War, located in St. Louis, Missouri.

Findlay Iron Works: Supplier of 12-pound Napoleon cannons to the Confederate military during the Civil War. Located in Macon, Georgia.

Finger-roll carving: A term for scroll-like carvings which appeared on chairs, sofas, and other elaborate furniture of the Victorian era.

Finger vase (ceramic): Unique five-fingered vase crafted by Delft and in other ceramic centers. Each "finger" was a specific flower holder.

Finial: Carved ornamental device to decorate eighteenth century furniture. Shapes included acorn, pineapple, and flame. Typically attached to the terminal of a column or post.

Fire back: Term for the cast iron back wall in the early American fireplace. Used to protect bricks and to radiate heat. Often the fronts of such devices were decorated with initials or coat of arms. Some were even dated.

Fire (color): According to 1920s catalogs, simply the color of fire.

Fire dogs: Term for fireplace andirons based on their animal-like appearance. Early American reference but of English origin.

Firefly (color): Listed by Sears and Roebuck as a deep bright pink.

Fire mark: (see Fire plate)

Fire pan: (see Fire paw)

Fire paw: Early American term for metal container used to bear burning embers from the fireplace to another room or another house for kindling purposes. Sometimes called a fire pan.

Fire plate: Term for a cast iron plate attached to the outside of an eighteenth century and early nineteenth century American house to denote an insurance company. In case of fire, specific fire-fighters would respond to properly marked and insured dwellings only. Sometimes called a fire mark.

Fire sack: Early American term for canvas or linen bag used to carry family valuables in the event of fire. Typically marked on the outside with family name or symbol.

Fire screen: Device for protection from excessive fireplace heat. Often decorated in early American homes, sometimes with painted scenes, and mounted on pedestal with tripod feet. Some screens were embroidered. Later screens were made of glass.

Flash Gordon Air-Ray gun, red metal, ca. 1940s. (Skinner Inc.)

Flash Gordon coloring book, 1979, Rand McNally Co.

Firing glass: Reference to small wine glass popular in late eighteenth century England. About 4½" in height, each came with a heavy base. Individuals used the base to rap on a wood table as a positive response, and produce a gunshot "firing" sound.

Firmin and Sons: British source of military uniform buttons for some Confederate forces, located in London, England.

Fischer and Company (toys): Early twentieth century toy maker based in Germany. Noted for series of comic character toys and tin action figures. Some were distributed by George Borgfeldt of New York City.

Fisher-Price (toys): American toy making firm founded in the 1930s and highly successful with early toys of colorful lithographed paper and wood. Later the company replaced wood design with plastic. Many items were Disney-related characters. Sold in 1969 to Quaker Oats Company.

Fish, Isaac: Noted clockmaker in 1840s, Utica, New York.

Fish skin (decoration): Dressed and dyed fish skin was used by early craftsmen for covering clock cases. It was often featured with a combination of silver mounts and fittings.

Fish slice (silver): Flat shaped silver server. Typically pierced and engraved piece on a wooden handle. Later called a pie knife.

Fisk's Burial Casket: (see Raymond, W. M. and Co.)

Fisler and Beckett Company (glass): Glassworks established by Jacob Fisler and Benjamin Beckett in 1850, Fislerville, New Jersey. Later the firm became the Fisler and Bacon Glass Company, and still later the Moore Brothers Glass Company. In the 1860s the town's name was changed to Clayton.

Fitch, Dennis: Established silversmith active in 1830s, Troy, New York.

Fitment: An early nineteenth century term for specially built bookcase, fireplace, panel, or other unique feature in a household room. More elaborate homes had a greater number of fitments. Probably of English origin.

Fitzhugh (ceramic): Reference to the border of stylized bees and pomegranates on eighteenth century ware exported from Asian countries.

Five back: Term to describe a chair with five horizontal slats as a back. A rural New England reference to a slat-backed chair.

Fix, Joseph: Active as working clockmaker in 1830s, Reading, Pennsylvania.

Flag: Lesser used word for the rush material used in weaving a chair seat. Marsh and swap lands were prime growing places for flag or rush.

Flagg and Homan: Noted crafters of pewter in 1840s and 1850s, Cincinnati, Ohio.

Flagg, Josiah: Silversmith in 1760s, Boston, Massachusetts. Later joined in the business by his son Josiah Jr. who continued into the early 1800s.

Flagon: Drinking device made of pewter or similar metal, and used to hold liquor. Some included handles and spouts. Some flagons held communion wine for church services in Colonial America.

Flag seat (furniture): Use of a woven rush-type material on early American furniture.

Flagship (toy): Wooden pull-toy airplane offered by Sears, Roebuck and Company in 1942. The model of an American Airlines twin-motor plane had a wingspan of 20".

Flake white (color): A very pure white according to an early mail-order catalog.

Flame (color): Considered a bright orange, the actual color of a burning flame.

Flamingo Ukelele: Toy musical instrument sold with Arthur Godfrey uke player in the early 1950s. Player snapped on the instrument to make playing easier. Made by Emenee Industries, priced at $4.98.

Flare (furniture): In cabinetmaking a reference to a chair seat or other piece that was wider at the front than at the back.

Flashed (glass): Describes that thin layer of contrasting color added to an item of glass by dipping or "flashing" into a different colored hot glass.

Flash Gordon: Imaginary science fiction character was a major attraction in 1930s comic strips and later movies. Character was revised for 1950s television. Flash Gordon Click Ray Pistol was marketed in the early 1950s. Other memorabilia ranged from books and buttons to board games and puzzles.

Flatiron clock: (see Beehive clock)

Flax wheel: Device used for converting long stems of flax into linen thread, involving a relatively small spinning wheel and foot treadle. Used in America during the eighteenth and early nineteenth centuries.

Fleischaker & Baum: (see Effanbee doll)

Fleming, Joseph Adam: Acclaimed maker of musical harpsichords in New York City during the late 1700s.

Flemish (furniture): Flemish furniture emerged from a similarity to Dutch furniture in the middle of the seventeenth century to a more distinctive style. It adhered to extensive use of oak and very elaborate carving. The result was heavy and bulky furniture was remarkable decoration. One of the most noted was the Flemish scroll.

Flemish scroll (furniture): Decorative application on latter seventeenth century American and European furniture involving a hollowed out reverse spiral. Original curve broken by an angle came from Flemish influences.

Flesh (color): Simply a pale pink or a skin color.

Fletcher, Charles: Doing business as a clockmaker in 1830s, Philadelphia, Pennsylvania.

Flight and Barr: Known as late eighteenth and early nineteenth century makers of quality Worcester porcelain.

Flint enamel (ceramic): Late 1840s improvement in the brown Rockingham glaze patented by Lyman, Fenton and Company of Bennington, Vermont. Potters used metallic powder to dust on the glaze which produced flecks or streaks of color.

Flint glass: Starting in the late seventeenth century, a term for a particular type of glass which sand was heavily incorporated in the process. Selected sand included a large proportion of flint and the resulting glass, originally made in England, had a definitive ring when struck. Lesser lime-type glass of the nineteenth century lacked that telling sound.

Flintlock: Early nineteenth century firing device for guns. Basically it involved the use of a percussion cap which fired a flint and in turn ignited a pan of gunpowder.

Flintstones: Initially a television cartoon from Hanna-Barbera in 1960. Later the pre-historic gang of Fred, Wilma, Pebbles, and others were featured on Marx toys and other memorabilia. Characters also were used in product promotion from cereal to vitamins.

Flip glass: Drinking glass of the eighteenth and early nineteenth century made for consumption of spiced brew known

Fred Flintstone doll, ca. 1962, made in Japan, vinyl head. (Skinner Inc.)

Flintsone plastic car by Play-skool, ca. 1976.

as flip. More elaborate styles included paneling and copper engraving. The flaring tumbler-shaped glasses varied in size up to one quart.

Flip-top table: Term for the double top of a gaming table which, when not in use, could be turned over for a standard console appearance.

Flirting-eye doll: Reference to nineteenth century German dolls whose eyes moved from side to side and not up and down. Typically bisque or papier-mache.

Flivver: Slang term for the early twentieth century low-grade automobile.

Flobert Target Rifle: Breech-loading rifle imported from Belgium and sold in the United States during the 1880s and early 1890s. It fired .22 caliber cartridges and came with a painted iron flying-bird target.

Flood gate hammer: A 25 pound grist mill tool used for moving the gate there.

Floor runner (toy): Regarding toys this was a model designed to run on a flat surface, usually with flat wheels or runners.

Florentine Pottery Company: Enterprise of pottery making starting in 1890s, Chillicothe, Ohio.

Florida water: Brand of toilet water sold in bottles by S.S. Kresge Co. stores early in the twentieth century.

Flossie Flirt (doll): Flossie Flirt was a very popular doll of the 1920s. Eyes moved from side to side and the doll made the "ma ma" sound. Clothed in a party dress, they varied in size from 14" to 20". Similar dolls advertised as Flossy Flirt. Flossy series via Sears and Roebuck also included Vanity Flossy and Happy Flossy.

Flott, Lewis: East coast silversmith doing business in 1815, Baltimore, Maryland.

Flower van (toy): Hubley Cast Iron Toys produced the Indian Flower Van during the 1930s. The motor was marked Indian. The side of the vehicle said, "Say it With Flowers." It was over 10" long.

Flow Blue (ceramic): Initially an 1840s transfer-decorated white earthenware. Of British manufacture, its designed allowed for the pattern to flow into the glaze.

Fluting: Early American term dealing with semi-round channels cut into aprons, legs, and other extensions. The channels ran parallel to each other with flat areas between the flutes known as fillet.

Flux: Ceramic term used to describe material involved in the fusion of over glaze colors onto a surface. Feldspar, borax, and bismuth are mineral examples of flux.

Flyer, Orasmus: Doing business as a clockmaker in 1830s, Burke, Vermont.

Flying-machine: Broad term used in the early twentieth century for most any vehicle or apparatus which achieved in-air flight.

Flying Merkel: (see Merkel motorcycle)

Flying Roadster: A four cylinder automobile produced in the early 1900s by Olds Motor Works in Lansing, Michigan. Price in 1908 was $2,750.

Flying shuttle (sewing): Device used on a loom which could be cast from side to side.

Fly-leg (furniture): Term for an early type of drop-leaf table. In this design the leaves were supported by legs which would swing out or fly out from the base of the table. The number of legs could vary from four to eight.

Fly rail (furniture): A specific term for the side rail of an early flap table, the rail opened to support the accompanying flap.

Flywheel (toy): (see Friction wheel)

Foliated (furniture): Extensive use of leaves and related foliage on any wood carved surface. Often the curled-up leaf tip of the acanthus plant.

Folio: Reference to the size of standard paper once folded to make into a folio. Early books and engravings were printed in this folio size which was somewhat similar in dimensions to single newspaper page.

Folsom, Charles: Listed as a supplier of military goods to the U.S. Army during the 1860s, located in New York City.

Folsom, John: Practicing silversmith in 1780s, Albany, New York.

Folson, Henry and Company: Listed as providing military swords and sabers to U.S. Army during the Civil War. Located in St. Louis, Missouri.

Folwell, John: Noted early American cabinetmaker based in Philadelphia, Pennsylvania. Credited with crafting a case for an early mechanical planetarium device.

Folwell, Samuel: American profile artist who excelled at making a likeness in black mounted on a white background. Late eighteenth and early nineteenth centuries.

Food cupboard: (see Pie safe)

Foote, William: Colonial silversmith practicing the trade in 1795, East Haddam, Connecticut.

Foot warmer: Portable sheet metal device for maintaining and carrying hot coals. Container was usually held inside a wooden frame complete with bail handle for transportation to various locations.

Forbes, Garret: New York City silversmith active from 1810 to 1835.

Ford China Company: A pottery operation active in late nineteenth century, Ford City, Pennsylvania.

Ford, J. B.: (see Louisville Glass Works)

Ford, Samuel: Colonial era silversmith active in 1795, Philadelphia, Pennsylvania.

Fordson Tractor (toy): Models of the famous Fordson tractor were made by Arcade Manufacturing in Freeport, Illinois. Made of cast iron, the iron driver was removable. Featured item in 1927.

Ford (toy): Arcade Manufacturing made cast iron examples the Ford Tudor sedan, Fordor sedan, Ford coupe, Ford (pick-up) truck, and Ford Touring car during the late 1920s. Some also produced in the form of banks.

Forest green (color): In the catalog world of the 1920s, a medium green.

Forestville Manufacturing Co.: Active clock manufacturing operation in 1820s, Bristol, Connecticut.

Form seat: (see Bench)

Forst, Mann and Company: Under federal contract to provide foot artillery swords in 1861. No location listed.

Forty-wink chair: (see Wing chair)

Foster Company: (see Eagle watch)

Foster, H. L.: Calvary jacket manufacturer under Federal contract during the Civil War era.

Foster, John: A noted clockmaker active in 1830s, Portland, Maine.

Foster, John: Massachusetts native who became one of the first printers in Boston. Foster engraved the first American map which appeared in the 1677, *A Narrative of the Troubles with Indians in New England.*

Fountain clock: Remarkable nineteenth century clocks of French design. Rotating spiral glass gave the impression of moving water. Usually fitted with an eight-day movement, however the so-called fountains required winding usually every four hours.

Four o'clock stove: Early American stove

Franklin Automobile advertisement from 1904.

with a small box for use in the bedroom. Named for the regular 4 p.m. lighting to warm the room by bedtime.

Four-poster bed: Term for more elaborate bed with posts or corners extending upward a distance above the head boards and foot boards. Typically they supported a canopy or tester.

Four-Wheel Drive Wagon Company: (see Mogul)

Fowler, Gilbert: New York City silversmith doing business in the 1820s.

Fox & Polhemus: Supplier of military tents and tripods in the Federal government during the Civil War.

Fox, Charles: Supplier of military caps under Federal contract during the Civil War era. Located in New York City.

Fractur: Reference to the hand-lettered illuminated manuscripts and decorative drawings by Pennsylvania Germans. Originally the work of clergymen and schoolmasters, and gradually the artistic renderings of all walks of life. A shorting of the word frakturschrift the practice included birth certificates, baptismal documents, bookplates, rewards of merit, and other pen and brush documents.

Frame (furniture): Early American estates frequently indicated an inventory of separate four-legged frames to support varying pieces of furniture when needed.

Franciscus, George: Colonial era silversmith doing business in 1775, Baltimore, Maryland. Franciscus was joined by George Franciscus Jr. who continued the trade into the 1820s.

Franklin Auto Co.: (see Airman Limited)

Franklin automobile: Manufactured during the early 1900s by the H. H. Franklin Company in Syracuse, New York. A bestseller was their 24-horse power touring car.

Franklin Automobile advertisement from 1907.

Franklin clock: Quality shelf clock of the 1820s and 1830s with wooden movement. So named by maker Silas Hoadley of Plymouth, Connecticut.

Franklin stove: Attributed to American inventor and statesman Benjamin Franklin in the 1750s. Made of cast iron it stood away from the wall providing better radiating heat than a traditional fireplace. The open grate could burn coal or wood.

Frankoma Pottery: Producers of highly regarded art pottery starting in late 1940s, Sapulpa, Oklahoma.

Franks, William: Doing business as silversmith in 1840s, Philadelphia, Pennsylvania.

Fraser, Charles: Leading producer of portrait miniatures in nineteenth century Charleston, South Carolina. Over 300 Fraser works were exhibited in 1857 at Charleston.

Freed bridle (clock): Term for connection from battery to earth in electrical timepieces.

Freedom box: Silver box typically engraved with the arms of a city or other honoring agency and presented to a worthy citizen. Most were in the size of a tobacco box.

Freedom quilt: Attributed to the eighteenth century products of young men serving apprenticeships and seeking freedom to find other work and marry. Later it was simply prepared by family members for a young man to offer his bride-to-be.

Freeman, Austin: Listed as a maker of Army percussion revolvers, patented 1862. Located in Binghamton, New York.

French bed: Term for a bed in the French Empire style of rolled-out ends rather than posts. Also applied to nineteenth century scrolled and sleigh beds popular in America.

Frit

French beige (color): Considered to be a medium pinkish tan.

French bisque: Used at one time to denote blonde bisque doll heads made in France. Mainly a reference to the highly regarded Jumeau factory.

French blond (color): A medium shade of tan, according to Sears in the 1920s.

French blue (color): According to the 1927 Sears catalog a medium blue.

French China Company: Enterprise of pottery making established in late nineteenth century, Sebring, Ohio.

French, Daniel Chester: Noted American bronze sculptor of the early twentieth century who was a student of William Rimmer. French died in 1931.

French fashion doll: Highly regarded late nineteenth century dolls crafted in France by superior makers including Jumeau and Bru. The dolls were dressed in the latest and most elegant fashions and available only to children of the very wealthy.

French foot (furniture): A cabinetmaking term for a combined decorative skirt and a slightly out sweeping bracket foot.

French (furniture): Initially in the sixteenth century French furniture was solid and mostly made of walnut. It was elaborately carved but not distinguished until it became more fanciful in the late seventeenth and early eighteenth century. Like early American furniture, local woods were more in use and creations were much more stylish. Some credit French designs of that era with influencing noted British designers including Thomas Chippendale and Thomas Sheraton.

French gray (color): Simply a medium gray in 1920s catalogs.

French nude (color): Oddly listed as a shade darker than flesh.

French polish: Very high gloss furniture finish credited to French cabinetmakers. It was credited to the use of shellac and various spirits combined with a special pan and applied vigorously.

French tan (color): According to Sears during the 1920s a dark tan.

French, Thomas: An early nineteenth century American gunsmith doing business in Canton, Massachusetts.

Fresco: Term referring to the light colored painting applied to walls of plaster. Typically water was mixed with the selected paint to modify the shade.

Fretwork: Use of thin wooden strips cut into lacy-like patterns for decorative panels or other attachments. Often incorporating the use of a fret saw with a very fine blade. Also applied to geometric latticework. Initially a decorative form in China, later in Europe including the highly regarded work of Thomas Chippendale. Sometimes simply called fret.

Friction match: Advanced technology from the late 1820s in the form of combustible chemicals and phosphorous combined to cover the tip of a small extension of wood. The friction caused by scraping the tip of the wooden match against a rough surface created a flame.

Friction wheel (toy): On a friction toy an inert wheel rotates a shaft which in turn moves lesser wheels once friction movement is applied. Sometimes called a flywheel.

Frieze: Plain or ornamental part of entryway arch in classical architecture. Uppermost decorative panel or relief.

Frieze drawer (furniture): A reference to the overhanging top drawer in a chest of drawers. Typically supported by columns or pillars.

Frit (ceramics): A reference to the material

Finely attired French Fashion doll.

Fruitwood Louis XV Provincial armoire, late eighteenth or early nineteenth century.
(Skinner Inc.)

used for glazing china. Typically it was a mixture which involved borax, lime, silica, and other minerals.

Frog mug: When drained of its contents the mug contained the image of a tiny frog at the bottom or on the lower sides. The ceramic illusion amused some and distracted others. It was made in many America potteries.

Frontier Mills: Producer of gunpowder during the Civil War for the U.S. government, located in Xenia, Ohio.

Frontier rifle: Manufactured by Hubley and sold in the 1952 Billy and Ruth catalog. The toy weapon used roll-type caps and was 35" long. Price was $3.98.

Frontier Town: Complete "Wild West of yesteryear" set sold by Montgomery Ward in the early 1970s. The 170-piece set included jail, general store, and Dodge City Bank. Including 23 horses, cows, and dogs the price was $8.99.

Frost and Munford: Silversmiths and clockmakers doing business in early 1800s, Providence, Rhode Island.

Frosting (glass): Process involving potassium fluoride and hydrofluoric acid to render a gray-like finish on glass. Some glass surfaces can be protected from the frosting by use of an additional resisting chemical.

Frost, Oliver: Enterprising maker of clocks in early 1800, Providence, Rhode Island.

Frothingham, Benjamin: Boston-born cabinetmaker ultimately noted for mahogany block-front furniture in the distinguished styles of Chippendale and Hepplewhite. Served with General George Washington during the American Revolution before returning to his craft in the 1780s.

Frozen Charlotte (doll): Dolls linked to the dark tale of a nineteenth century girl named Charlotte who allegedly perished in freezing weather. The small dolls made of bisque or china had no joints or moving parts.

Frozen Dainties: Cookbook of the 1890s regarding frozen creams, ices, sherbets, and fruits. A free promotion of the White Mountain Freezer company located in Nashua, New Hampshsire.

Fruit wood: Any fruit-bearing wood used by early American cabinetmakers for solid pieces or veneer work. Mainly apple, cherry, and pear woods.

Fryer, John: Noted Colonial era silversmith operating in 1785, Albany, New York.

Fuchsia (color): A stylish maroon tinged with purple.

Fuller, Alexander: Silversmith doing business in 1810, New York City.

Fullerton: Name for "already cut" and fitted six-room home sold by Sears and Roebuck during the 1920s. The two-story residence including roofing and siding sold for $2,294 unassembled.

Fulper Pottery Co.: A noted producer of art pottery and other pottery from 1800s to 1920s in Flemington, New Jersey.

Fulton American washer: A bestselling washing machine sold by Sears, Roebuck and Company in the early twentieth century. It had a removable tub and an iron enameled pinwheel. It was guaranteed to wash "five shirts at a time, clean without the use of a washboard." Price was $4.44.

Fulton hatchet: A brand of high grade hatchet sold in the 1920s by Sears, Roebuck and Company. Also sold were Fulton work benches, nail hammers, rules, levels, and measuring tapes.

Funeral pie: A pie baked for presentation during mourning in early Pennsylvania and elsewhere.

Fursdon, Roger: A Colonial era silversmith active in 1780s, Charleston, South Carolina.

Fustic (wood): Yellow appearing wood used during the eighteenth century for veneering. Apparently the wood did not hold its color over time and went into disuse. Briefly imported from Central American and also the West Indies.

Fyler, Orasmus: An 1830s clockmaker in Burke, Vermont.

Gabriel Industries: (see Hubley Manufacturing)

Gabriel, Sam: Early twentieth century publisher of distinguished holiday postcards.

Gadroon (furniture): Term for early carving on edges and borders of furniture. An eighteenth century signature of Thomas Chippendale and others, it appeared as ruffles or in the form of an inward curving flute.

Gaines, John: Noted clockmaker operating in early 1800s, Portsmouth, New Hampshire.

Galbraith, Patrick: Colonial era clockmaker, 1790 to 1810, in Philadelphia, Pennsylvania.

Gale, John: New York City silversmith of note active in the 1820s.

Gallager, M. J.: Supplier of .54 caliber carbines during the 1860s, located in Savannah, Georgia.

Galle (glass): A noted French glass manufacturer during the late nineteenth century. A distinguished maker of cameo glass.

Gallery (furniture): A term for a raised rim or railing of wood or metal surrounding an early table top. It could also apply to the top of a cabinet or sideboard.

Gallipot (ceramic): Round earthenware jar with spout and handle. Frequently with blue Delft decoration, and later known as apothecary jar.

Galt, Samuel: Colonial era silversmith doing business in 1750s, Williamsburg, Virginia.

Gamboge: Noted simply as yellow in the early Sears catalogs, later called a strong yellow pigment.

Garage: Automobile stable, storage, or repair place.

Gardiner, John: A noted clockmaker in 1850s, Ansonia, Connecticut.

Gardiner Stoneware Co.: Productive stoneware pottery operating in 1870s and 1880s, Gardiner, Maine.

Gardner, F. J.: Listed as a supplier of wooden canteens to Confederate troops during the Civil War.

Gardner, John: Midwestern silversmith established in 1825, Cincinnati, Ohio.

Garford Six automobile: An automobile priced at $2,750 in 1910. It was a product of the Garford Company of Elyria, Ohio.

Gargoyle: Originally an ornamental water spout on ancient buildings. Basically in the form of an ugly creature once favored in Gothic architecture and believed to ward off evil. Later used in American design on buildings and other structures including garden furniture.

Garland (furniture): Initially a wood carving in the form of fruit or flowers added as ornamentation for furniture.

Garnet: Considered a dark red in the 1927 Sears catalog.

Garnet (jewelry): Fashionable Victorian era gemstone dark red in color. It was used in the mid-nineteenth century for both men's rings and women's stickpins. At their fashion height they were sometimes identified as carbuncles.

Garratt and O'Hara: Under contract with the Confederate government to provide

Gong Bell Company's tin equestrian bell toy, late nineteenth century. (Skinner Inc.)

Vase marked Grueby Faience Company, early 1900s. (Skinner Inc.)

was highly ornamental and often involved a mirror in the overall design. Typically they were mounted on a wall and often provided a marble base. Silver or brass mountings were sometimes further enhanced with gilt wood.

Girard, Henry: Listed as a silversmith in 1805, New York City.

Gitter and Moss: Supplier of knives for the Confederate military during the Civil War. Located in Memphis, Tennessee.

Glasgow Pottery: Rockingham, whiteware, and yellow ware producer in latter nineteenth century, Trenton, New Jersey. Operated by John Moses and Sons.

Glaze (ceramic): Term for the application of clay, water, and other materials to a ceramic body before firing. After firing, the glaze forms a protective water-resistant covering.

Gleason, Roswell: Pewter craftsman of record in 1830s, Dorchester, Massachusetts. Often marked wares with last name in rectangle.

Glide Special automobile: (see Bartholomew Company)

Glitter Chest: Jewelry box complete with toy plastic jewelry in the 1952 Billy and Ruth Catalog. Inscribed Glitter Chest on the inside lid, it included 16 jewelry items and was priced at $1.69.

Globe Pottery Company: An undertaking of pottery making in 1880s, East Liverpool, Ohio.

Glory hole: Reference to the opening in the glass furnace especially for reheating glass while it is being worked.

Gloucester Porcelain Co.: Noted porcelain pottery during business in 1860s and 1870s, Gloucester, New Jersey.

Glover, William: Listed as an active clockmaker in 1820s, Boston, Massachusetts.

Gminder, Jacob: Noted as a source of military buttons for Confederate troops in the Civil War, based in Baltimore, Maryland.

G. N. Pierce Company: Maker of the Arrow Motor Car and the Stanhope Model automobile during the early 1900s. Based in Buffalo, New York.

Goddard (furniture): Highly acclaimed eighteenth century block-front furniture crafted by John Goddard of Newport, Rhode Island. Frequently added shell carvings to cabinets, chests, desks, and other pieces.

Goddard, John: (see Block front)

Godey doll: A distinguished china head doll with molded headdress of vertical and pointed curls. Both blonde and brunette dolls were produced.

Godey's Lady's Book: Noted fashion magazine of the nineteenth century. Published monthly in Philadelphia from the 1830s to the 1890s. In addition to the latest fashions for ladies, it also included fiction, poetry, advertisements, cooking recipes, patterns, and other timely information.

Godfrey, B. D.: Provided military boots and shoes under Federal governmental contract during the Civil War. Located in Guilford, Massachusetts.

Godwin, Joseph H.: Hatchet, kettle, and pan manufacturer for Federal troops during the Civil War, based in New York City.

Goffering iron: Reference to a cast-iron or cast-brass shoe used for heating other irons in a fire. Also a term for ironing ruffles.

Gold (color): In the early Sears catalogs explained simply as the color of gold, deep yellow.

Golden age: Regarding postcards, it generally covers the 1890s through the end of World War I in 1918. Considered an era of high postcard quality.

Golden amber (color): Presented as a golden yellow during the 1920s.

Golden and Dunlop: Supplier of military caps via Federal contract during the Civil War. Located in New York City.

Golden brown (color): Described by Sears in the 1920s as medium brown with a gold cast.

Golden (color): A light khaki according to the Sears catalog of 1927.

Golden iridescent (color): Simply described as a rainbow amber.

Golden rod (color): Classified as basically the color of the golden rod flower.

Golden tan (color): A Sears color described as a dark tan with a yellow cast.

Goldstein, B.: Listed as a supplier of U.S. Army clothing during the Civil War era. Located in New York City.

Goldthwaite, Joseph: Spirited and active silversmith doing business in 1750s and 1760s, Boston, Massachusetts.

Golf green: As listed in Sears catalogs of the 1920s, a very dark green.

Gombroon: Term for porcelain prior to the 1640s in England based on the similar name of a shipping port. Under the East India Trading Company later porcelain was known as chinaware in reference to is point of origin in China.

Gong Bell Manufacturing (toys): A noted bell making firm which also expanded to include toys in the late nineteenth and early twentieth centuries. Made a specialty of pull-type bell toys. Based in East Hampton, Connecticut.

Goodale & Stedman: Listed as stoneware potters operating in 1820s, Hartford, Connecticut.

Goodhue, John: Noted silversmith with established trade from 1820s to 1850s in Salem, Massachusetts.

Goodwin, Horace Jr.: Noted clockmaker in 1830s, Hartford, Connecticut.

Goodwin, Ralph: Established silversmith in 1830s, Hartford, Connecticut.

Goodyear Rubber doll: One of America's earliest advertising dolls, based on an 1865 patent obtained by Nelson Goodyear. The hard rubber doll's head was stamped on the back with the name.

Googly eyes (doll): Term for large eyes in proportion to the doll's face that "looked" to one side. Other terms included goo-goo and roughish.

Gooseberry green (color): According to mail-order firms early in the twentieth century, a light green.

Gooseneck (furniture): Reference to the double curved arch pediment of latter eighteenth century secretary furniture and similar items. Sometimes called swan neck.

Gordon, George: Enterprising silversmith doing business from 1800 to 1825 in Newburg, New York.

Gordon, Thomas: Doing business as a clockmaker in 1760s, Boston, Massachusetts.

Gorgas, Jacob: A noted clockmaker in 1770s, Lancaster County, Pennsylvania.

Gorham, Jabez: Established silversmith trade in 1815 in Providence, Rhode Island. In 1840 the operation became known as Jabez Gorham and Son.

Gorham Manufacturing Co.: (see Martele)

Gothic (furniture): Reference to furniture and other woodwork of the Middle Ages, the fourteenth, fifteenth, and sixteenth centuries.

Gould, John: Noted silversmith in 1840s, Philadelphia, Pennsylvania.

Gould's Coaster: Hardwood four wheeled wagon with metal disc wheels used for coasting down a slope or hill. Marked Toddler Toys and sold by Sears, Roebuck Company in the 1920s for $7.98.

Gouraud's Cream: Dr. T. Felix Gouraud's

Grueby pottery base with Tiffany dome shade lamp.
(Skinner Inc.)

Oriental Cream or Magical Beautifier was sold as a beauty cream in the 1890s. It claimed to remove tan, pimples, freckles, moth patches, and all blemishes.

Gourdin and Company: French source of military uniform buttons for some Confederate forces, located in Paris, France.

Gowdey, John: An established silversmith between 1750s and 1780s in Charleston, South Carolina.

Gowen, William: Colonial era silversmith operating in 1770s, Medford, Maine.

Gracklehead blue: A rich medium blue, darker than Copenhagen, yet lighter than navy.

Graham Chemical Pottery Works: Pottery making firm headed by Charles Graham in 1880s, Brooklyn, New York.

Graham, Daniel: Operating as a silversmith in 1790, Sheffield, Connecticut.

Grain: As the name implies, according to Sears, the color of ripened yellow grain.

Graining (furniture): Practice of painting inexpensive wood (usually pine) to give the grained effect of expensive wood (usually oak). Applied with varying degrees of success in the late nineteenth century to raise the appeal lesser pieces.

Grand-daughter clock: Term for a rather short long-case clock. Basically a three to four foot miniature of the grandfather clock.

Grandfather chair (furniture): Term for the upholstered wing chair which originated in England. Such large chairs bore stylish front legs with carving and fancy feet. The back legs meanwhile were usually plain.

Grandfather clock (furniture): Typical long case clock standing six feet tall. Such clocks might have brass or wooden workings with cases ranging from pine to mahogany. They were especially popular in American during the eighteenth and early nineteenth centuries.

Grandmother clock (furniture): Considerably shorter and scarcer than the taller grandfather clock, they were often more elaborate. Far fewer grandmother clocks were made compared to longer case examples.

Grand Rapids (furniture): Specifically applied to mid-nineteenth century furniture made in Grand Rapids, Michigan. However, it was also generally applied to similar furniture of quality mass produced in other parts of the United States.

Grant, Thomas: An eighteenth century silversmith doing business in 1755, Marblehead, Massachusetts.

Grass green: Suggested simply as the color of grass in the 1927 Sears catalog.

Graves, Henry: Listed as active in the pewter trade during 1840s in Middletown, Connecticut.

Graves, Thomas: Midwestern silversmith located in 1830, Cincinnati, Ohio.

Gray Iron (toys): Memorable manufacturer of toy soldiers made of metal during the first half of the twentieth century. Known for a wide variety of dimestore figures into the early 1950s. Based in Mount Joy, Pennsylvania.

Gray, John D.: Supplier of Bowie knives, pikes, Enfield rifles, carbines, sabers, and other military goods to Confederate troops. Locations in Graysville and Columbus, Georgia.

Gray, W. H.: Granted a U.S. patent in 1861 for military epaulettes. Located in Philadelphia, Pennsylvania.

Great Fire: (see Calyo Nicolino)

Greek chair: (see Klismos)

Greek key: Repeating pattern of interlocking geometric shapes sometimes used as a border. Originally said to represent love or friendship.

Greek Revival: Applied not only to furniture but architecture roughly from the 1820s into the 1850s. Seemingly a revival of the ancient Greek forms and use of ornamental details.

Green, Andrew: Doing business as a pewter craftsman in late 1700s, Boston, Massachusetts.

Greene, William: The William Greene Company was active in the silversmith trade in 1815, Providence, Rhode Island.

Green gold (color): A yellow green according to mail order catalogs of the 1920s.

Green, James: New York City silversmith active from 1805 to 1820.

Green, John: A Colonial era clockmaker active in 1790s, Philadelphia, Pennsylvania.

Green, Samuel: Active in the pewter trade from 1798 to 1825 in Boston, Massachusetts.

Greenwood and Gray: Rifle, carbine, and saber provider for the Confederate military during the Civil War.

Greenwood, Miles & Co.: Supplier of altered Austrian flintlock muskets to the U.S. Army in 1861. Located in Cincinnati, Ohio.

Greenwood Pottery: Porcelain and whiteware pottery operation from latter nineteenth century to the 1930s in Trenton, New Jersey.

Greeting card: In postcards the term for holiday or other special occasion postcard. Also reference to non-postcard single card and folded card greetings.

Gregg, William: Noted silversmith engaged in the trade in 1830s, Columbia, South Carolina.

Gregory, John: Redware potter doing business in early 1800s, Clinton, New Jersey.

Greiner doll: A nineteenth century manufactured doll with papier-mache head and cloth body. Such dolls were patented by Ludwig Greiner in 1858. One of the first manufactured and patented dolls in America, they were stamped on the back of the head with the Greiner name and patent number. Eyes varied from simple paint application to glass. Hands varied from leather-like material to wood.

Greyhound wagon: A 1950s red, white, and blue wagon made by Hamilton. The metal wagon came with chrome hub caps and nickel plated rails.

Gridiron: A reference to the heavy metal hearth object used as a surface for pots and kettles above the fire.

Griffen, Smith & Hill: Producers of majolica, whiteware, and yellow ware in 1880s and 1890s, Phoenixville, Pennsylvania.

Griffon (furniture): Figural image of mythological creature used by leading eighteenth century designers on some furniture. Typically a grotesque half-eagle and half-lion character also sometimes used to decorate other items.

Grignon, Rene: Listed as a silversmith, 1710 to 1715, in Norwich, Connecticut.

Grilley, Thomas: Noted as a pewter artisan in 1790s, Waterbury, Connecticut.

Griswold, William: Doing business as an enterprising silversmith in 1820s, Middletown, Connecticut.

Gruby, Edward: Listed as an active clockmaker in 1830s, Portland, Maine.

Grueby Pottery: Highly regarded art pottery and tile making operation in early 1900s, Boston, Massachusetts.

Gruff, J. C. and Company: Listed as a provider of cavalry sabers in 1861 federal government contract. No location listed.

Diana Ross doll made by Ideal, ca. 1970s.

Ideal's Wake-Up Thumbelina, ca. 1970s.

Ideal bride doll, ca. 1950s.

Inchworm: (see Easy Riders)

Incised lacquer (furniture): Reference to a form of decoration on furniture involving carving into several thick coats of previously applied lacquer.

Incised markings (doll): Markings made by doll makers which were pressed into the mold instead of being raised. The letters or numbers were usually related to production pieces.

Incised ornamentation (furniture): A very early form of furniture decoration where the ornamentation is cut in or engraved into the surface. Afterwards a colored composition was used to fill in the earlier incisions.

Incised ware (ceramic): Hand-drawn designs cut into china while the body of the ware is still soft and pliable.

Indiana pottery (ceramic): An ill-fated attempt by English potter James Clews in late 1830s, Troy, Indiana. Clews' efforts at blue and yellow ware were limited and eventually abandoned. Clews blamed the nature of regional clays and inability of American laborers for the failure.

Indian corn: A reference to the multicolored Native American plant, known also as maize.

Indian motorcycle: A product of the Indian Motor Cycle Company of Springfield, Massachusetts. Their first single-cylinder motorcycles were produced in 1903. In 1912 their twin-cylinder model sold nationally for $250. Sales dwindled following World War I and ultimately the firm closed in the 1950s.

Indian motorcycle (toy): A number of Indian brand toy motorcycles were made by Hubley during the 1930s. They included the Indian armored car, the Indian side car, the Indian crash car, Indian U.S. Mail truck, and Indian traffic car.

Indian red (color): Noted in 1920s Sears catalogs as a deep red.

India-Rubber Belt Co.: Supplier of India-rubber goods to the U.S. Army during the Civil War, located in New York City.

India shawl (textile): Originally a term for hand woven shawl from the Kashmir Valley of India. Such garments represented the finest cashmere wool used in the most skilled fashion. Sometimes they were referred to as pieced shawls because they were pieced together and woven on hand looms. Later machine-made paisley shawls were sometimes misnamed India shawls.

Indigo: A blue dye originally obtained from the indigo plant, later synthesized from coal tar.

Indigo (color): Simply dark blue, later defined as blue-violet.

Individual portraits: (see Face painting)

Ingersoll compressor (toy): Hubley Toys held exclusive rights to manufacture the Ingersoll-Rand toy compressor during the 1930s. The 8½" toy bore the Ingersoll-Rand name in raised letters across the tank.

Ingersoll, Daniel: Active as a clockmaker in early 1800s, Boston, Massachusetts.

Ingersoll, Henry: Cabinetmaker born in New York and doing business in 1850s, Indianapolis, Indiana.

Ingraham, Reuben: Clockmaker in early 1800s, Preston, Connecticut.

Ink pool: Term for a shallow basin filled with ink into which someone is made to gaze steadily in order to be hypnotized. Once prevalent among occultists and mystics of the Far East to read the present and the future.

Inkstand: Once popular ornament for housing pen or quill atop the desk. Some were made of silver, pewter, brass, or other materials including glass and china. Inkstands could be highly ornate and elaborate in design or relatively plain. Some sets also included sealing wax and other related materials.

Inlay (wood): Work involving pieces of wood usually of contrasting grain and color. The individual pieces were placed into wood surfaces in various patterns and design forms.

Inman, Benjamin: Silversmith doing business during the first half of the nineteenth century in Philadelphia, Pennsylvania.

Innis, John: Chair maker doing business in 1850s, Parke County, Indiana. Born in Pennsylvania.

Innovative furniture: Reference to machine-made nineteenth century furniture which incorporated technical advances, including mechanical devices for folding or reclining chairs, metal and tubular construction, and various laminations.

Insignia: Term for badges of honor or military office.

Intaglio eyes (doll): These were painted-on doll eyes with slight indentations of the pupils. They were in contrast to glass inset doll eyes.

Intarsia inlay: Term relating to exquisite inlay on woodwork dating back several centuries. Animals, flowers, fruits, and other scenes were achieved by gluing cut pieces of wood on a common ground. The thickness of pieces varied to create a relief image out of the overall inlaid wood. Typically the inlaying woods were of different colors and grains on a much darker wood background.

International Art Company: A leading postcard publisher of the early twentieth century. Noted for holiday postcards and stable of leading artists.

Interurban: Popular early twentieth century term for electric railroad cars. Also used for other city-to-city transportation including ferry boats.

In the white: Early cabinet making phrase indicating natural wood before it was filled, stained, or polished.

Irelan, Linna: Pottery maker who established operations in 1899 in San Francisco, California.

Iridescent blue (color): Considered by Sears to be a dark blue with bright luster.

Iridescent green (color): A dark green with a bright luster according to early Sears.

Iridescent purple (color): A bright luster on a dark purple in the 1927 Sears chart.

Iridescent white (color): Considered by early Sears catalogs to be white with an opal cast.

Irish, Charles: Listed as a clockmaker in 1815, New York City.

Irish, Charles: Louisiana-born cabinetmaker working in 1850s, Vigo County, Indiana.

Irish Chippendale (furniture): Sometimes used as a reference to a heavier form of furniture than the usual style of eighteenth century designer Thomas Chippendale. Mahogany was usually the wood of choice for Irish Chippendale.

Irish glass: Term for exceptional glass crafted in various parts of Ireland mainly in the nineteenth century. Such class was noted for it clarity of ringing tone and its bluish-gray color. Skilled glassmakers traveled from one plant to another refining patterns and production. Much of the quality glass was made for the American market.

Irish lace (textile): Distinguished trim for children's clothing and ladies' garments, made in Ireland for the American market. Initially the fine lace was crocheted

Indian Motorcycle advertisement from 1912.

Ives cast iron Presidential train from fictional Ives Railway Lines. (Skinner Inc.)

Early 1900s Ives Railway locomotive, as presented in the Ives catalog.

Electric locomotive as illustrated in the 1914 Ives catalog, list price $13.

Latter nineteenth century train engine from Ives company. (Skinner Inc.)

Jackson Automobile advertisement, early 1900s.

Jasper dip mantle plaque, late eighteenth century. (Skinner Inc.)

from native linen thread by hand. Later machines and cotton thread were used to imitate Irish lace in China.

Ironstone (ceramic): This particular earthenware was made in several early American potteries, but it origins date to 1790s, England. The first patent for the ware with heavy concentrations of flint and slag went to Charles Mason in the Staffordshire region. In early production the heavy ware was sometimes decorated in bold colors, and sometimes left in basic white.

Irwin, C. W.: Granted a U.S. patent in 1861 for a military camp chest. Located in St. Louis, Missouri.

Isaacs, Michael: Listed as an active silversmith in 1765, New York City.

Island Curio: Publisher of early twentieth century Hawaiian postcards, based in Honolulu, Hawaii.

Israel, Charles: German immigrant cabinetmaker active in the trade in 1850s, Lawrenceburg, Indiana.

Ives & Company (toys): Major maker of cast iron and tinplate toys including quality trains and accessories. Founded by E. R. Ives in late 1860s, Plymouth, Connecticut. Made both electric and wind-up trains early in the twentieth century. Operated by Lionel Manufacturing in the 1930s.

Ives, Chauncey: Enterprising clockmaker in 1830s, Bristol, Connecticut.

Ives, Lawson: A noted clockmaker operating in 1830s, Bristol, Connecticut.

Ivoride: An early reference to a variety of artificial ivory.

Ivory black (color): Defined in the 1927 Sears chart as a clear jet black.

Ivory (color): Briefly noted in Sears catalogs as a cream color.

Ivorytype: Term for a particular kind of early twentieth century photographic picture with an ivory-like surface.

Ivory white (color): Presented in the early 1900s as white with a slight cream or ivory cast.

Ivy green (color): A soft shade of medium green according to early Sears.

Izzard: An ancient term for the letter z.

Jackfield ware (ceramic): Highly decorative eighteenth century ware credited to the Jackfield Pottery in England. Basically a black ware made from red clay, it was highly glazed. Some pieces had gold banding and trimming, while others had colored decoration. Most intense production was in the 1760s and early 1770s.

Jacks, George Jr.: Clockmaker in 1800, Chester County, Pennsylvania.

Jacks, James: Colonial era silversmith active in 1785, Charleston, South Carolina.

Jackson, Andrew: Cabinetmaker born in Ohio and working in 1850s, Dearborn County, Indiana.

Jackson Automobile Company: Makers of Jackson cars early in the twentieth century and located in Jackson, Michigan. The 50 horsepower Model 52 was priced below $1,800 in 1913.

Jackson, Franklin: Native of Ohio who practiced the cabinetmaking trade in 1850s, Muncie, Indiana.

Jackson, Harvey: Chair maker born in North Carolina and working in 1850s, Hamilton County, Indiana.

Jackson, John: Listed as an active silversmith in 1730, New York City.

Jackson, John: Noted cabinetmaker active in 1840s, Franklin, Indiana.

Jackson, Joseph: Noted clockmaker in 1810, Philadelphia, Pennsylvania.

Jackson, William: Producer of redware pottery in early 1800s Lynn, Massachusetts.

Jackstones (toy): Nickel-plated jacks made by Arcade Manufacturing Company in the late 1920s. Full sets included the jacks and a ball packed in bags of assorted colors — red, white, or blue.

Jacobean (furniture): Considered to be that furniture crafted in England during the 1600s. Typically it involved native oak crafted into bulky and heavy tables and cupboards of various sizes. The furniture's name and the period were derived from Jacobus, the Latin name for James.

Jacquard loom: Major innovation for the weaving industry credited to Joseph Jacquard in 1806, Lyons, France. Basically the Jacquard invention was an attachment on traditional looms which allowed larger and more complex patterns to be produced. It was eventually adopted for all looms in Europe, the United States, and elsewhere.

Jade (color): Considered by Sears to be a bright medium green.

J. A. Foster Company: (see Eagle watch)

Jager, Joseph: (see Peoria Pottery Company)

Jagger, Daniel H.: Listed as active in the pewter trade of 1840s, Hartford, Connecticut.

Jagger, James H.: Doing business as a pewtersmith in 1830s, Hartford, Connecticut.

Jamb (architecture): Term for the upright surface which abounds an opening, such as the wood at the side of a fireplace or at the side of a door.

Jamison, Eli J.: Cabinetmaker born in Maryland and working in 1850s, Muncie, Indiana.

Jamison, Henry: Pennsylvania-born cabinetmaker doing business in 1850s, Terre Haute, Indiana.

Jane West: (see Johnny West)

Janvier, Louis: Noted silversmith in 1745, Charleston, South Carolina.

Japanella: Brand of cold cream sold in jars and other cosmetics sold by S.S. Kresge Co. stores early in the twentieth century. Price was 10¢.

Japanese red (color): A very bright red according to the 1927 Sears catalog.

Japanning: An enhanced lacquering process involving coating metal or wood with a type of varnish and then oven drying it. It had origins in the Far East centuries before it became popular in Europe.

Jardiniere (furniture): A term denoting a box or pedestal specially designed to hold flowers or plants.

Jasper: Name for a reddish brown, square-shaped mineral. Attributed to the quartz family.

Jasper dip (ceramic): Process of dipping certain clay vessels first attributed to Josiah Wedgwood in 1785 and practiced well into the nineteenth century.

Jasper ware (ceramic): Decorative process of the eighteenth century involving unglazed porcelain and the relief application of colored designs. Dominate colors were blue and green with further relief designs in white.

Jaspe taupe (color): Oddly considered a two-tone taupe or moderate charcoal. Jaspe was later considered the color of burnt sand.

Javain, Henry: Briefly noted as a silversmith from 1835 to 1840 in Charleston, South Carolina.

Jazz age: Period of the 1920s which gave birth to coonskin coats and crossword puzzles. Also featured the great Bambino Babe Ruth and English Channel swimmer Gertrude Ederle.

J. Chein and Company: (see Chein and Company)

Jasper dip vase and cover from Wedgwood. (Skinner Inc.)

Jasper dip oval plaque, eighteenth century. (Skinner Inc.)

Wedgwood plate blue jasper dip oval portrait medallion, ca. 1784. (Skinner Inc.)

Jasper two-handled vase and cover, ca. 1780. (Skinner Inc.)

Johnny West in original box, by Marx.

Johnny West and accessories by Marx.

Johnny West figure of turquoise color.

Jefferies, William: Supplied Confederate troops with cartridge boxes, belts, and harness during the Civil War. Located in Charlottesville, Georgia.

Jefferis, Emmer: Listed as an active silversmith, ca. 1850s in Wilmington, Delaware.

Jeffers & Company: Rockingham and yellow ware pottery headed by J. E. Jeffers in late nineteenth century, Philadelphia, Pennsylvania.

Jeffery automobile: Jeffery Four and Jeffery Six models were offered in 1916 in prices ranging from $1,000 to $1,465. They were produced by the Thomas B. Jeffery Company in Kenosha, Wisconsin.

Jeffery Company: (see Rambler delivery wagon)

Jeffords, David: Cabinetmaker born in Vermont and working in the trade in 1850s, De Kalb County, Indiana.

Jenkins, Ira: Enterprising clockmaker operating in 1815, Albany, New York.

Jenkins, John: Active silversmith in 1715, Philadelphia, Pennsylvania.

Jenkins, John L.: Listed as a cabinetmaker doing business in 1850s, Crawford County, Indiana.

Jenkinson's Pittsburg Stogies: Brand of nationally-advertised cigars sold in the 1890s. A box of 100 was $1.50. The R. & W. Jenkinson Company was located in Pittsburgh, Pennsylvania.

Jenks, Alfred & Son: Supplier of 98,000 rifled muskets to the Federal government during the Civil War, located in Philadelphia and Bridesburg, Pennsylvania.

Jenks, W. M.: Supplier of carbines used by U.S. Navy and cavalry units during the Civil War, located in Chicopee Falls, Massachusetts.

Jennens and Co.: A British source of military uniform buttons for some Confederate forces, located in London, England.

Jennings, David: Virginia-born cabinetmaker active in 1850s, Connersville, Indiana.

Jennings, Jacob: Colonial era silversmith doing business in 1780s, Norwalk, Connecticut.

Jennings, Marmaduke: Cabinetmaker from New Jersey who crafted coffins, bedsteads, stands, and tables in 1850s, Fountain County, Indiana.

Jerome Manufacturing Company: Clockmaking firm active in 1850s, New Haven, Connecticut.

Jersey City Pottery: Operation established in 1829 Jersey City, New Jersey. Also see D. & J. Henderson.

Jessops Wire Factory: Source of Confederate army military buckles during the Civil War. Located in Richmond, Virginia.

J. E. Stevens Company (toys): (see Stevens Company [Toys])

Jetmore, Nathan: Ohio born cabinetmaker doing business in 1850s, Wabash County, Indiana.

Jewell, P & Sons.: Contracted maker of cartridge boxes and gun slings for Federal troops during the Civil War, based in New York City.

Jewett, A. & Co.: Federal government supplier of military tents and camp kettles during the Civil War.

Job, Charles: Cabinetmaker from Kentucky working in 1850s, Morgan County, Indiana.

Jocelyn, Nathaniel: Colonial clockmaker in 1790s, New Haven, Connecticut.

Jockey red (color): Bright red as defined by the 1927 Sears catalog.

Joel Ellis doll: Name for a jointed wooden type of doll produced in Springfield, Vermont. The dolls had mortised and tenon (rectangular wood) joints.

Johnny West: Very popular action figure doll of the 1970s. Accessories included buckboard and horse Thunderbolt, Sheriff Garrett, Sam Cobra and Satan, Chief Geronimo and Morning Cloud, a Rocky Mountain gear box, Circle K Ranch building, and Jane West and Flame.

Johnson, Chauncey: Noted clockmaker in 1830s, Albany, New York.

Johnson, John: Listed as an active silversmith in 1815, Pittsburgh, Pennsylvania.

Johnson, Lorenzo: Listed as a potter working in redware in mid-nineteenth century, Newstead, New York.

Johnson, Peter: Active ship builder, cabinetmaker, and builder of other structures in 1830s, South Bend, Indiana.

Johnson, Samuel: New York City silversmith doing business there in the 1780s and 1790s.

Johnston and Co.: (see Easter gifts)

Johns, William: Granted a U.S. patent in 1861 for military cloak. Located in Georgetown, D.C.

Joice, Jacob: Chair maker born in Ohio and working in 1850s, Tippecanoe County, Indiana.

Jolier: Reference to a machine used for pressing clay into a plaster mold.

Jolliffe, William: Ohio-born cabinetmaker doing business in 1850s, Johnson County, Indiana.

Jones, Abner: Colonial period clockmaker in 1790s, Weare, New Hampshire.

Jones, Benjamin: Noted cabinetmaker in 1850s, Washington County, Indiana.

Jones, Frederick & Co.: Granted a Federal government contract during the Civil War for "Negro" brogans, cavalry boots, and bootees. Located in Boston, Massachusetts.

Jones Furniture Co.: Selling fine oak dining chairs for between $4.75 and $6.25 in the 1890s. Located in Syracuse, New York.

Jones, George: Doing business as a clockmaker in 1840s Wilmington, Delaware.

Jones, George: Noted as a silversmith doing business in 1840s Boston, Massachusetts.

Jones, J.: Designed a mule-drawn litter in 1862 for carrying two persons in connection with U.S. Army requests. Located in New York City.

Jones, J.: Well-established maker of Windsor chairs and other chairs and settees in late 1820s, Vincennes, Indiana.

Jones, John: Noted as a silversmith (possibly related to George) doing business in 1840s, Boston, Massachusetts.

Jones, Samuel: Active clockmaker in 1820s, Baltimore, Maryland.

Jones, Thomas: Operator of the Thomas Jones and Company chair factory in 1850s, Jennings County, Indiana. Four men were employed there.

Jones, William: Active as a silversmith in 1850s, Rochester, New York.

Jordan Motor Car Company: Makers of the Jordan Playboy and Jordan Blue Boy automobiles early in the 1920s. Company was located in Cleveland, Ohio.

Jordan, Peter: Listed as active in silversmith trade during the 1820s in Philadelphia, Pennsylvania.

Josephine bicycle: The 1902 ladies' model bicycle sold by Sears, Roebuck and Company. The drop curved frame came with dress and chain guards. A companion bicycle for gentlemen was the Napoleon. The Josephine, with Morgan and Wright tires, sold for $15.75.

Joseph, Isaac: Listed as a clockmaker in 1820s, Boston, Massachusetts.

Selection of Jumeau fashion dolls. (Harris Auction Center)

Jumeau Depose bebe doll.

A nineteenth century Portrait Jumeau doll.

Jumeau doll with original nineteenth century clothing.

Joslyn, Benjamin: Maker of thousands of carbines during the Civil War for use by the U.S. Army, located in Worchester, Massachusetts.

Josyln, B. F.: Contracted with the federal government to provide Army percussion revolvers in 1862. Located in Stonington, Connecticut.

Joslyn, James: Colonial era clockmaker operating in 1790s and early 1800s, New Haven, Connecticut.

Joyce, Thomas: An active clockmaker in 1820s, Philadelphia, Pennsylvania.

Judson, Hiram: Noted silversmith doing business from 1820s to the 1850s in Syracuse, New York.

Jugendstil (furniture): Highly decorative style of Art Nouveau furniture developed in Germany in the late 1890s and early 1900s. Stressed flowing leaves, flowers, and curving and twisting lines of design.

Jugtown Pottery: Doing business in art pottery starting in the 1920s at Seagrove, North Caroliana.

Jumeau doll: Quite possibly the finest doll ever made in the nineteenth century. These bisque dolls were crafted at the Jumeau factory in France from the 1860s through most of the 1890s. They had high quality blown-glass eyes and came in 14 sizes. Swivel necks and jointed wooden bodies were produced after 1869. Later makers used elastic to string composition bodies.

Jumper, Jacob: Cabinetmaker born in Ohio and doing business in 1850s, Vigo County, Indiana.

Jung, L. E.: (see Columbo Peptic Bitters)

Jungle green (color): Listed in the 1920s by Sears as a dark rich forest green.

Junior Stewardess: A 13-piece plastic dinner set in the Billy and Ruth Catalog of 1952. It was said to be "inspired" by United Airlines Mainliner dining service. Crafted by Banner Plastics, the boxed set sold for $1.98.

Justice, P. S.: Supplier of some 400 Enfield type rifled muskets to the U.S. Army in 1863, also contracted for 5,500 cavalry sabers and 4,000 rifled muskets in 1861. Located in Philadelphia, Pennsylvania.

Justis, William: Ohio-born cabinetmaker active in the trade in 1850s, Dearborn County, Indiana.

Juvenile: (see Coffee mill [toy])

Kaki: Japanese word describing the combination of persimmon yellow and a rust brown opaque. It was frequently used as a glaze on early china and often in the body of the design as well.

Kakiemon, Sakaida: Japanese pottery artist active in the seventeenth century and known for the use of colored enamel designs on porcelain.

Kaleidoscope: First patented in 1817 by Scots physicist David Brewster. Essentially a combination of loose particles of colored glass and reflecting mirror-like surfaces. Assembled in a tube-like container, the base was turned by hand to provide changing patterns as seen through the opposite end. The kaleidoscope became a popular toy in both the nineteenth and twentieth centuries.

Kalep, Elvy: (see Parachute doll)

Kamkins (dolls): (see Kampes, Louise)

Kampes, Louise: Noted maker of Kamkins dolls in 1920s, Atlantic City, New Jersey.

Kaolin (ceramic): Modification of a Chinese term for original china clay.

Kapok (toy): This mass of silky fibers from the seeds of the ceiba tree was often used in soft or stuffed toys.

Karsch, Adam: Cabinetmaker born in Germany and doing business in 1850s, Evansville, Indiana.

Karyn (doll): A 1970s battery-operated talking doll. Phrases included, "you're pretty." Came with vinyl head and sleeping eyes.

Kas: Reference to a Dutch cupboard. Such large, two part cupboards were seen in Colonial America and later. Typically the upper section offered two heavy doors and shelves. The bottom section offered a single drawer and a four-legged base. The word kasse was also sometimes used in describing them.

Kausler, Christian: German-born cabinetmaker working in 1850s, Evansville, Indiana.

Kawin and Company: Early twentieth century publisher of historic event postcards, based in Chicago, Illinois.

Kearn, Felix: Doing business as a clockmaker in 1850s, New Haven, Connecticut.

Kedzie, John: Silversmith doing business in 1850s, Rochester, New York.

Keeler: Colonial term among German settlers for shallow tub with handles to cool and transport milk taken from the cow and carried to the house.

Keeler, Thaddeus: New York City silversmith listed in 1805 as active in the trade.

Keen, Walker and Co.: Listed as a supplier of carbines to the Confederate military during the Civil War. Located in Danville, Virginia.

Keiper, Christian: Active cabinetmaker in 1840s, Rockville, Indiana.

Kelley, Henry: Listed as an active silversmith in 1850s, Nantucket, Massachusetts.

Kellogg prints: Lithographed work of Elijah Kellogg and his brother starting in 1835, Hartford, Connecticut. Their historical, sporting, comic, nautical, and religious prints were comparable to Currier and Ives, but despite their quality, never reached that level of popularity. Kellogg died in 1881.

Kellogg, P. V. and Co.: Supplier of military uniforms under Federal contract during the Civil War era. Located in Utica, New York.

Kelly, Allan: An enterprising clockmaker in 1820s, Sandwich, Massachusetts.

Kelly, Allen: Active silversmith in 1810, Providence, Rhode Island.

Kelly green (color): A bright green according to 1920s Sears catalogs.

Kelmo, Francis: A noted clockmaker operating in 1850s, Chelsea, Massachusetts.

Kemble, P.: Listed as a supplier of military camp kettles and mess pans during the Civil War, located in New York City.

Kendall, James: Colonial era silversmith operating in 1795, Wilmington, Delaware.

Kendall, Reuben: Cabinetmaker in 1840s, Rockville, Indiana. Later succeeded in business by sons William Kendall and Harry Kendall.

Kendrick, William: Enterprising silversmith in 1840s, Louisville, Kentucky.

Kennedy, James: Painter and chair maker working in 1820s, Washington County, Indiana.

Kennedy, Patrick: Noted Colonial clockmaker in 1790s, Philadelphia, Pennsylvania.

Kenner Products Company: Maker of cloth dolls and other toys beginning in late 1940s, Cincinnati, Ohio.

Kenny, Asa: Operating as a clockmaker in early 1800s, West Milbury, Massachusetts.

Kensington Glass Works: (see Dyottville Glass Works)

Kenton Hardware (toys): Also known as Kenton Toys and based in Kenton, Ohio. Produced a wide variety of metal toys starting in the early 1900s. Active toy making firm into the early 1950s.

Kent, Paine and Co.: Source of military buttons for Confederate forces

Kewpie-style dolls, Rosebud and Buddy from Lee Middleton Original Dolls.

Kewpie-style dolls, Breezy and Angelic, from Lee Middleton Original Dolls.

King Eight advertisement from the King Motor Car Company, 1917.

in the Civil War, based in Richmond, Virginia.

Kenwood Folding Camera: One of Sears' finest cameras. Sold in 1902. Materials included Honduran mahogany and Moroccan leather. Price of the larger 5x7 model was $7.90.

Kenyon & Ross: Undertakers and furniture makers doing business in 1850s, Montgomery County, Indiana.

Kepner, Barnett: Painter born in Pennsylvania and doing business in 1850s, New Albany, Indiana.

Kerr, John: Native of South Carolina, worked as an active cabinetmaker in 1850s, Fayette County, Indiana.

Kerson, William: Chair maker working in 1850s, Lafayette, Indiana with chair maker James Wallace.

Ketchum, Wm. F.: Granted a patent by the U.S. government in 1861 for a military grenade. Located in Buffalo, New York.

Kettell, Thomas: Colonial era silversmith in 1790s Charleston, Massachusetts.

Kettle: (see Cauldron)

Kettle base (furniture): A kettle-like outward swelling of the lower section of eighteenth century furniture. Sometimes called bombe.

Kettle front (furniture): Bulging or swelling front on drawer cases and chests of Dutch origin. Popular on English furniture of the eighteenth century, the kettle front was considered to provide a sharper curve than the existing bombe front.

Kew-Blas (glass): An 1890s iridescent glass similar to Tiffany glass and attributed to W. S. Blake at the Union Glass Works. Gold oxide was added to the glass to provide striking colors and a high retail cost. Blake scrambled the letters in his name to come up with Kew-Blas.

Kewpie (doll): Small and delicate elf-like features found on a type of doll. Usually all-bisque and credited to the images created by noted artist Rose O'Neill.

Kewpie Kamera: Oddly spelled trademark of Sears and Roebuck for selection of box-shaped cameras during the 1920s. No focus was necessary, just push the lever.

Keyes, John: Painter and chair maker doing business in 1820s, Salem, Indiana. Also advertised as sign painter.

Key pattern: Reference to a geometric band or border design based on ancient Greek design.

Keystone (furniture): Term for the centerpiece at the very top of the arch in early furniture.

Khaki (color): Regular army tan as presented by Sears.

Kidney table (furniture): Term for a fashionable oval-shaped table in eighteenth century England. Designed by Thomas Sheraton and others, these small tables were used for dressing and writing.

Kiln: Oven-like device used for firing decorated colors on china. Typically the kiln was smaller than the actual oven used for firing ware into its preliminary state.

Kiln-dried: Special drying treatment applied to lumber. The lumber was dried in an enclosed warming chamber, preventing weather extremes of conventional drying.

Kimball, Lewis: Documented in the silversmith trade in 1830s, Buffalo, New York.

Kimball, Robinson & Co.: Provided cavalry boots and shoes for Massachusetts troops during the Civil War era. Located in Boston, Massachusetts.

Kimberly, William: Active silversmith in 1790s, New York City.

Kimport (doll): Combination native

woods and composition dolls were made in the 1940s by the Kimport Doll Company of Independence, Missouri. The small firm made novelty portrait dolls and state commemorative types using mainly spruce and cedar woods.

King Eight automobile: An eight-cylinder motor vehicle produced by the King Motor Car Company in Detroit, Michigan. In 1917 the King Eight roadster was priced at $1,585.

King Horseless Carriage: An automobile crafted from what was originally a horse-drawn wagon in 1896. Its inventor was machine shop operator Charles King in Detroit, Michigan. His four-cylinder motor was unique at the time.

King, J. A.: Supplied brass framed tourniquet with screw to Confederate Army during the Civil War. Located in Mobile, Alabama.

King, Joseph: Noted silversmith doing business in 1775, Middletown, Connecticut.

King Motor Car Company: Makers of the King Eight Touring car and other automobiles during the early 1900s. Firm was located in Detroit, Michigan.

Kingston, John: Prominent New York City silversmith during 1770s.

King's yellow (color): Noted as a bright but medium yellow in the Sears catalog.

King, Thomas: Noted clockmaker in 1820s, Baltimore, Maryland.

Kinky: Described as a "pickaninny" baby doll in the 1931 Montgomery Ward catalog. Composition doll had three black pigtails and was 10" tall.

Kinney, Thomas: A Colonial era silversmith doing business in 1790s, Norwich, Connecticut.

Kinsey, David: Noted silversmith operating during the 1830s and 1840s in Cincinnati, Ohio.

Kinsey, W. & Co.: Maker of cap boxes and cavalry cartridge boxes for Federal troops during the Civil War, based in Newark, New Jersey.

Kinsley, Rhololphus: Granted a patent for cartridge making machine, 1862, Springfield, Massachusetts.

Kip, Benjamin: Doing business as a silversmith in 1700, New York City.

Kippen, George: Colonial era silversmith who practiced the trade in 1790s and early 1800s, Bridgeport, Connecticut.

Kirby, William: Noted pewtersmith active in 1780s and 1790s, New York City.

Kirk, Charles: An active clockmaker in 1820s, Bristol, Connecticut.

Kirk, Edward: Cabinetmaker born in Pennsylvania and working in 1850s, Porter County, Indiana.

Kirk Manufacturing Company: Located in Toledo, Ohio, and makers of the Yale Touring Car during the early 1900s. The car "with the jar and doubt left out" sold for $1,500.

Kirkpatrick, C. & W.: Stoneware pottery operation during the second half of the nineteenth century in Anna, Illinois. Also known as Anna Pottery.

Kirkpatrick, William: Listed as a chair maker born in South Carolina and active in 1850s, Shelby County, Indiana.

Kirk, Samuel: Active in the silversmith trade in 1850s, Baltimore, Maryland.

Kirk, Thomas: Pennsylvania-born cabinetmaker active in the trade in 1850s, Shelbyville, Indiana.

Kirkwood, Peter: Noted silversmith during the 1790s in Charleston, Maryland.

Kirtland, Joseph: Active silversmith during the 1770s and 1780s in Middletown, Connecticut.

Kitchen, Andrew: Doing business as a chair maker in 1850s, Rush County, Indiana.

World's Greatest kitchen cabinet as featured in 1923 Sears catalog.

Extra wide "Hoosier" kitchen cabinet in 1922 Montgomery Ward catalog.

Kitchen cabinet: In 1902 Sears, Roebuck and Company offered a variety of kitchen cabinets including "higher grades" from central Indiana. Their bestsellers had varied tops with panels or glass doors. Bottom cupboards were designed to hold baking powder, soda, and large boxes of salt and pepper. Better models sold for over $8 each.

Kit fox (color): Basically a Sears 1920s medium gray.

Kitson, Richard: Listed as a redware potter doing business in nineteenth century, North Bridgton, Maine.

Kittredge, B. and Co.: Noted manufacturer of the metal Bennett cartridge box for Federal forces during the Civil War, based in Cincinnati, Ohio.

Kitts, John: Silversmith active in 1840s, Louisville, Kentucky.

Kittysol: (see Quitasol)

Kline car: Product of the Kline Car Corporation in Richmond, Virginia. In 1922 the firm advertised roadster, sedan, coupe, and touring car selections.

Kline (furniture): Term for a sofa-like piece which served ancient Greeks as a couch and day bed. Typically with sweeping curved back.

Kline, John: Enterprising clockmaker doing business in 1830s, Reading, Pennsylvania.

Klismos (furniture): Reference to the Ancient Greek chair as depicted on vase paintings. During the Greek Revival of the first half of the nineteenth century, this design was incorporated into furniture.

Kneading table: Term for the basic bread trough which was used for kneading bread. The table or trough was typically mounted on legs.

Kneehole desk (furniture): Reference to a desk with a small open space immediately below the writing surface for the user's legs. Typically either side of the central space is lined with drawers. Usually with sweeping curved back.

Knife box: Case used during much of the latter eighteenth century for storing silverware including forks, spoons, and knives. Pairs of knife boxes were used on sideboards with one at each end. Usually made of mahogany, they often had a slanting cover allowing for the insertion of knives up to the handle.

Knight's Blacksmith Shop: Listed as a supplier of knives for Confederate troops during the Civil War. Located in Amelia, Virginia.

Knight, W. W.: Active pewter artisan in early 1800s, New York City.

Knives: The knife came into common use on the tables of Colonists and Europeans early in the eighteenth century. Most were made of steel with bone or ivory handles. Eventually porcelain, silver, and wooden handles were in use. Later some fancy tableware designs came with mother-of-pearl handles.

Knocker: Wrought iron door knockers were first used in the American colonies. After the S-shaped wrought iron devices in the early and middle eighteenth century came the brass knockers of the 1770s. Brass knockers, often decorated with patriotic symbols, were popular following the American Revolutionary War.

Knotty pine: A soft pine wood avoided by early cabinetmakers because of its frequent knots and gnarled texture. However in the twentieth century the yellowish-white wood was re-discovered and used, particularly for cabinets and paneling.

Knowles China Company: Well regarded producer of whiteware starting in the

1850s under the direction of Edwin M. Knowles.

Knowles, Taylor & Knowles: Prolific producer of various pottery wares including Rockingham. Operated from the 1870s to the 1920s in East Liverpool, Ohio.

Knox, George: Cabinetmaker and house builder active in early 1800s, Switzerland County, Indiana.

Knox Three-Wheeler: Iron framed three wheeled vehicle of the late 1890s based on a design by Harry A. Knox of Springfield, Massachusetts. It eventually led to the prolific Knox Company, one of the leading commercial auto producers of the early twentieth century.

Knuckle carving: Reference to furniture carving which resembled that of the human hand.

Koehler, Joseph: Noted publisher of early twentieth century postcards, particularly historical events. Based in New York City.

Kollinsky, Colomannus: Granted a patent for a type of military uniform cap in 1861. Located in Washington, D.C.

Kookie (doll): A cloth advertising doll promoting the Automatic Gas Range Company designed by Spence Wildey.

Koplin, Washington: Noted clockmaker operating in 1850s, Norristown, Pennsylvania.

Kranele & Gills: Cabinetmaking shop operated by Francis Kranele and Leonard Gillis in 1850s, Evansville, Indiana.

Krater: Term for a fashionable two-handle bowl in ancient Greece. Used for mixing wine and water.

Krause, John: Noted silversmith doing business in 1820s, Bethlehem, Pennsylvania.

Kreutner, Charles: Maker of Mississippi rifles during the Civil War. Located in Montgomery, Alabama.

Krider, J. H.: Listed as a maker of .58 caliber rifles in the 1860s, located in Philadelphia, Pennsylvania.

Krider, Peter: Enterprising silversmith active in 1850s, Philadelphia, Pennsylvania.

Kropp, E. C.: Prolific postcard publisher during the early twentieth century, particularly historical events and expositions.

Kruse, Kathe: Noted maker of cloth dolls and wife of well-known German sculptor. Kruse's child-like dolls first appeared during Christmas of 1910.

Kryptok: Brand for bifocal eyeglasses early in the twentieth century. Kryptok (pronounced crip-tock) glasses were marketed by the Kryptok Company in Boston, Massachusetts.

Kucher, Jacob: Listed as a silversmith in 1820s and 1830s, Philadelphia, Pennsylvania.

Kuchler, Otto: Documented as an active silversmith in 1850s, New Orleans, Louisiana.

Kuhlman, Peter: Listed as a cabinetmaker in 1850s, Evansville, Indiana. Born in 1820s Germany.

Kumes, Harry: Indiana born cabinetmaker working in 1850s, Lafayette, Indiana.

Kungle, Michael: German-born cabinetmaker listed as active in the trade in 1850s, Lawrenceburg, Indiana.

Kurtz, Jacob: Born in 1790s, Kentucky, and working as a cabinetmaker in 1850s, Putnam County, Indiana.

Kylix: Ancient Greek form of a shallow footed bowl. Used as a drinking vessel, it usually had two handles.

Labe, Benjamin: (see Belmont Tonic Herb Bitters)

La Belle Company: Glassmaking firm located in 1879, Bridgeport, Ohio.

LaBelle Wardrobe: Popular basswood wardrobe trunk offered by Sears and

Roebuck in 1923. Piece was 40" tall and priced at $25.

Laburnum (wood): Hardwood found in southern Europe with a yellow to reddish-brown hue. Used for inlays and veneering in the Queen Anne era, and highly polished.

Lacey, John: An active clockmaker in 1820s, Philadelphia, Pennsylvania.

Lacquer: Application of various coats of shiny substance on furniture and related items. Originally a delicate and time-consuming process developed in China, in the seventeenth and eighteenth centuries, it was also practiced in France, Italy, and other parts of Europe.

Lacy glass: Term for a particular type of pressed glass which bore a delicate lace-like appearance. Several glass factories offered lacy glass items early in the nineteenth century ranging from bowls to platters.

Lacy glass pieces from the mid-1800s. (Skinner Inc.)

Ladder-back (furniture): Denotes the ladder-like back of early American chairs. Typically they were composed of a varying number of horizontal slats, as few as two or as many as seven.

Ladd, William: Listed as New York City silversmith during the 1790s.

Lady Janis: Brand name for coconut oil shampoo, soap, and other products for women during the 1920s. Sold by Sears, Roebuck and Company.

Lafar, John: Active as a silversmith along with Peter Lafar in early 1800s, Charleston, South Carolina.

LaFayette automobile: Early 1920s product of the LaFayette Motors Company based in Indianapolis, Indiana.

Lafetra, Moses: Listed among pewter craftsmen active in early 1800s, New York City.

Lafever Pottery: Stoneware business in latter nineteenth century, Baxter, Tennessee.

Three pressed lacy glass items from the Sandwich Glass Co. (Skinner Inc.)

LaForme, Vincent: Silversmith also doing business as La Forme Brothers in 1850s, Boston, Massachusetts.

Lagynos: Reference to a Greek wine jug originally with a narrow neck, broad base, and loop handle.

Lamar, Benjamin: Noted silversmith active in 1790s, Philadelphia, Pennsylvania.

Lamar, Matheas: Colonial era silversmith active in 1780s and 1790s, Philadelphia, Pennsylvania.

Lamb and Brother: Confederate supplier of 1841 model rifles during the Civil War located in Jamestown, North Carolina.

Lambert Gasoline Buggy: An 1891 achievement by John Lambert in Ohio City, Ohio. It was one of the first fully gasoline-powered vehicles, and operated with three wheels.

Lambeth deft: A term applied to late seventeenth century English faience or delft which had a cream-colored glaze. Often plates bore portraits of royalty or religious subjects.

Lambrequin: Drapery which hung from a shelf, mantel, or window. Also a reference for valance frame for a window.

Lamerie, Paul: Noted silversmith and goldsmith based in England during the first half of the eighteenth century. His exceptional work from cups to punch bowls was often marked with an oblong shield, crown, and the initials P. L.

Lamothe, John: Recorded as enterprising silversmith in 1820s, New Orleans, Louisiana.

Lampadaire: Basically an early pedestal designed to hold a candlestick or more elaborate lamp.

Lamp black (color): A true black as noted by mail order catalogs of the 1920s.

Lampe, John: Silversmith of the Colonial period doing business in 1785, Baltimore, Maryland.

Lamson, Goodnow and Yale: Contracted with the Federal government to provide 50,000 rifled muskets during the Civil War, located in Windsor, Vermont.

Lancashire chair (furniture): British reference to a eighteenth century spindle-back chair. Typically the top rail was decorated with a shell-like ornament in the middle, and the seat was made of rush.

Lancet clock: Victorian era mantel clock with a pointed arch to lancet top. Typically mounted on two small feet.

Landaus auto: (see Woods Motor Vehicle Co.)

Lane, Aaron: Colonial era silversmith active in 1780, Elizabeth, New Jersey.

Lane, George C.: Granted a patent in 1861 for military camp chests, located in Buffalo, New York.

Lane, Mark: Doing business as a clockmaker in 1830s, Southington, Connecticut.

Lang, Edward: Practicing the silversmith trade with Richard Lang in 1750s, Salem, Massachusetts.

Lantern: Popular lighting device in Colonial America, sometimes called a lanthorn. Colonial lanterns could be carried about and then hung on a wall to light a room or stairway. Initially pierced metal was used, and later transparent horn, and finally various types of glass.

Lantern clock: A reference to a type of English shelf clock with extensive brass. First produced in the 1600s, they were eventually imported to America and sometimes called birdcage clocks.

Laperhouse, John: Listed as an active silversmith in 1830s, New Orleans, Louisiana.

Lashing, Peter: Noted silversmith doing business in 1805, New York City.

Latch: Early metal device, first of iron and later of brass, used to keep doors closed. Typically latches could be opened from either side of the door. Later householders tended to incorporate them with keys and locks, and ultimately simply locks.

Lathe-turned: A reference in toy making describing wood shaped by a chisel while being rotated on a lathe device.

Lathrop, Ralph P.: Contract holder for 5,000 military hatchets in 1861, located in Albany, New York.

Lattice (furniture): Term used to denote the carved crisscross pattern once used for furniture including many chairs.

Latticinio (glass): Stylish glass decoration involving delicate bandings of non-transparent and white glass. The bandings were crossed and interlaced to provide a pattern. Originating in Italy, it was later imitated over the centuries in France and other countries.

Latvuit, John: Active silversmith listed in 1830s, Washington, D.C.

Laughlin Company: Homer Laughlin Company specializing in porcelain and whiteware, began operations in 1870s, East Liverpool, Ohio.

Laurel (color): Considered to be a dark green shade.

Laurel leaf (furniture): During the eighteenth century the term made reference to the ornamental carving used on interior woodwork and on furniture. Application of the leaf decoration was sometimes referred to as laureling.

Laurel oak (color): According to Sears in 1927, a reddish brown.

Lava glass: Exceptional dark blue luster glass, often decorated in gold or silver by the renowned Tiffany.

Lavender (color): A light purple as noted in an early twentieth century catalog.

Lawn tea apron: Name for a variety of aprons offered by S.S. Kresge Co. stores

LaFayette automobile advertisement for company in Indianapolis, Indiana.

Lantern made by Dietz, ca. 1920s.

Early twentieth century Hot Blast tubular lantern.

in 1913. Complete with tie streamers, they were 10¢ each.

Lawrence, Bradley and Pardee: Granted a 1861 patent for a cacolet or mule-drawn litter for military use, located in New Haven, Connecticut.

Lawrence, George: Noted clock-maker located in 1830s, Lowell, Massachusetts.

Lawrence, Josiah: Doing business as a silversmith from 1815 to 1825 in Phila-delphia, Pennsylvania.

Lawrie, Robert: Listed in the 1840s as a silversmith in Philadelphia, Pennsylvania.

Lazy Baby (doll): Made of fuzzy baby-blanket material, with round face and yarn curls. Offered in the early 1940s in pink or blue for $1.25 each.

Lazy susan: Reference in the early nine-teenth century to a revolving tray in the center of the fashionable dining table. The device, ranging from simple wood to elegant silver, rotated to pro-vide a selection of condiments and seasonings.

Leach, Caleb: Colonial period clock-maker active in 1780s, Plymouth, Massachusetts.

Leaching tub: Frequently seen in nine-teenth century America, this hickory or oak tub was set upon a leaching stone which formed the bottom of the tub. Wood ashes were used with such tubs and water for the formation of potash or lye, used in soap making. Lower edges of such tubs were notched to allow the flow of the potash solution.

Leach, Nathaniel: Active in the silver-smith trade from 1790 to 1810 in Boston, Massachusetts.

Leacock, Stephen: Silversmith during the 1750s and 1760s in Philadelphia, Pennsylvania.

Lead glaze (ceramic): A form of powered lead or galena was used in the earliest application on chinaware. Typically the ware was dusted with this sulphide powder before being fired. During the 1750s a liquid involving white lead and ground flint came into use, allow-ing for a dipping rather than a dusting prior to firing.

Leaf brown (color): Simply a light golden brown.

Leaf green (color): Suggested as a light green in the Sears catalog of the 1920s

Leafwork (furniture): Reference to group-ings of carved leaves used to decorate cabinets and the legs of other furniture during the eighteenth century.

Leather tan (color): What the Sears cata-log considered to be a brownish tan.

Leavenworth, William: Active clockmaker in 1810, Waterbury, Connecticut.

Leavitt, Daniel: Listed as a manufacturer of percussion revolvers, patented in 1839. Located in Hartford, Connecticut.

Leddell, James: Pewter craftsman doing business in 1770s, Taunton, Massachusetts.

Leeds (ceramic): Initially the English fac-tory of the late eighteenth century and early nineteenth century which specialized in white earthenware and luster-decorated ware. In the nineteenth century, it came to be a general term for blue-bordered cream-colored earthen-ware made in Staffordshire, England.

Leeds Company: Produced brass breech-loaders, and 12-pound Napoleon cannons for the Confederate military during the Civil War. Located in New Orleans, Louisiana.

Lee, James: Supplier of .44 caliber car-bines during the Civil War, located in Milwaukee, Wisconsin.

Lee, Richard: Established in the pewter producing business in 1830s, Taunton, Massachusetts.

Lee, Samuel: An active silversmith starting in the 1820s and later in the 1850s with Samuel Lee Jr. in Rochester, New York.

Leigh, David: A noted clockmaker in 1850s, Pottstown, Pennsylvania.

Leighton, Wm.: (see Wheeling [glass])

Leland, Henry: (see Cadillac Tonneau)

Lemon (color): Simply yellow in the 1927 Sears catalog.

Lemonescent: (see Vaseline glass)

Lenci doll: Some of the twentieth century's most charming and elegant cloth dolls were crafted by Madame Lenci in Turin, Italy. During the 1920s the maker combined cloth and felt for beautifully costumed dolls.

Lenhart, George: Listed as an active silversmith operating in 1840s, Bowling Green, Kentucky.

Lenhart, Godfrey: Listed as an active clockmaker in 1790s, York, Pennsylvania.

Lenox, Inc.: Porcelain producer of note, starting in 1900s, Trenton, New Jersey.

Lenox Iron Company: The Lenox company operated an iron furnace at Lenox, Massachusetts. In the early 1850s they added a glassworks which operated off and on into the 1860s.

Leonard, Allen: During the 1830s and 1840s a participating silversmith in New York City.

Leonard, Reed & Barton: Group of pewter craftsmen doing business in middle nineteenth century New York City. Hallmark often included names in rectangle.

Leonard refrigerator (toy): A toy Leonard refrigerator model made by Arcade Manufacturing Co. in Freeport, Illinois. Just under 6" tall, it was made of cast iron and had a white lacquer finish. Featured in the 1927 company catalog.

Leon Rubay automobile: (see Rubay Company)

Leopard (color): The color of a leopard's fur, tawny yellow with black markings.

Le Raix, John: Noted as a silversmith specifically in 1725, New York City.

Lester, Robert: Doing business as a clockmaker in 1790s, Philadelphia, Pennsylvania.

Levick, Rasin & Co.: Supplier of cavalry boots under Federal contract during the Civil War. Located in Philadelphia, Pennsylvania.

Lewis, E. M.: Provider of military uniform buttons for Confederate troops during the Civil War, located in Richmond, Virginia.

Lewis, John: Listed as an active silversmith in 1810, Albany, New York.

Lewis, John W.: Under contract with the Federal government to provide military shirts and drawers during the Civil War. Located in New York City.

Lexington automobile: Originally produced in Lexington, Kentucky, during the early 1900s. Production was later moved to Connersville, Indiana. The Lexington Motor Company made both four and six cylinder automobiles. Their Minute Man Six sold for $1,585 in 1919.

Libbey (glass): Quality product produced during the latter nineteenth century at the Libbey Glass Company in Toledo, Ohio. Noted firm was originally operated as the New England Glass Works in Cambridge, Massachusetts.

Liberty Loan: Reference in World War I to five various war loans made by the United States.

Liberty's: Well known import shop operating in late nineteenth century London, England. Operated by Arthur Liberty and specializing in goods and wares from Asia.

Lidden, John: Silversmith in 1850s, St. Louis, Missouri.

Lindy Lockheed-Sirius toy airplane, ca. 1930s, made by Hubley.

Linen postcard of American Red Cross headquarters in Wilmington, Delaware.

Lionel Train catalog from 1953.

Light Manufacturing Co.: (see Merkel motorcycle)

Light Six (automobile): The Studebaker Manufacturing Company's finest brand of auto as nationally advertised in 1918. It seated five passengers. See Studebaker.

Light-up Box: Battery-operated vanity case complete with Mazda light. Priced at $3.25 in 1923 Sears and Roebuck catalog.

Lignum vitae (wood): Consider by earlier cabinetmakers to be nearly the most dense and hardest of woods. It was harvested in tropical locations of New Zealand and Australia.

Lilac (color): Considered by Sears in the 1920s to be a very light purple.

Limeburner, John: Colonial era clockmaker located in 1790s, Philadelphia, Pennsylvania.

Limed oak: Term for whitish-gray effect of basic oak treated with lime.

Lime (glass): Fine type of very clear glass incorporating lime, bicarbonate of soda, and other ingredients. Less expensive than earlier leaded glass but absent the distinctive ring. Credited to the efforts of William Leighton at the Hobbs Brockunier Company in 1860s, Wheeling, West Virginia.

Lime wood: Unique light colored, close-grained wood used for elaborate carving. Used in late seventeenth century England.

Limner (folk art): Term used to describe traveling artist who made portrait paintings of individuals, particularly in the nineteenth century. Portraits, usually done in oils, were often prepared in advance and only the final facial features were added while the client posed.

Limoges (ceramic): Generally a designation for fine china made in France.

Lionel Trains magazine advertisement from 1953.

Originally a reference to elegant china specifically produced in Limoges, France. The Haviland works began operations there in the 1870s.

Lincoln, A. L.: Listed as practicing the silversmith trade in 1850s, St. Louis, Missouri.

Lincoln Pottery: (see Eaton, W. & O.)

Lincoln rocker (furniture): Reference to the upholstered and high-backed rocker said to have been used by President Abraham Lincoln at the Ford Theatre on the night of his assassination. The rocker was described as having arms, upholstered in red velvet, and made of walnut. The furnishings of the presidential box at the theatre reportedly included the rocker, a matching straight high-backed chair with casters, and two sofas.

Linden, Clarence: Patented "airbed" for Federal troops during the 1860s in Eden Township, Illinois. Device folded into a knapsack-like form for soldiers.

Lindy airplane (toy): Hubley Toys manufactured various toy planes cashing in on the popularity of Charles A. Lindberg. The Lindy Airplane came in two sizes. Additionally there was the Lind Lockheed-Sirius and the Lindy Glider.

Linen era: Reference to the linen-like finish of certain postcards printed starting generally in the 1920s. Some of these quality cards were still in production during the 1950s.

Linen press: Originally an eighteenth century Dutch device in which linen textiles were pressed smooth. Generally the press involved the application of two screws to function.

Linsey-woolsey (textile): Cozy combination of linen warp and wool filling used for ladies' nineteenth century petticoats. The woven fabric was also used for linings of the undergarments.

Lion clock: Reference to a clock which employed the use of a bronze lion on a marble base. Popular in the middle in the eighteenth century, mostly in France.

Lionel Manufacturing (toys): A major maker of electric trains and related accessories during the first half of the twentieth century. Later known as Lionel Corp., it acquired rivals Ives and American Flyer before ending production in the late 1960s.

Lion head pull (furniture): Drawer pull in the form of a lion's head with a ring suspended from the mask. Usually brass or gilded bronze.

Lion paw foot (furniture): Furniture foot in the image of a lion's paw, mostly in the Empire period. Attached to chairs, sofas, and other pieces.

Lion period: Generally a two decade period, the 1720s and 1730s, when the image of the lion was popular and fashionable in English furniture. It could be seen on chairs and settees.

Liquidambar: (see Bilsted [wood])

Lithograph: Printing process first developed in Germany in the 1790s. Stone surfaces were treated experimentally with copper plates to enhance printed images. The art of lithography spread to the United States in the nineteenth century where it was practiced extensively by many printers, including the famed Currier and Ives.

Little Country Doctor Kit: Early in the 1950s Transogram made all-plastic Little Country Doctor and Little Play Nurse kits for children complete with simulated alligator carrying case.

Little Duke: Brand of toy playing cards sold by S.S. Kresge Co. stores in 1913.

Little Lori (doll): Doll in chubby toddler series of the early 1970s. Sold with six extra outfits for $6.99 in the Montgomery Ward catalog.

Little Oil Drop: (see Esso bank)

Little Tot: (see Coffee mill [toy])

Little, William: A Colonial era silversmith doing business in 1780s, Newburyport, Massachusetts.

Livermore Foundry: Listed as a supplier of cannons for the Confederate military. Located in Memphis, Tennessee.

Liverpool jug (ceramic): Simple jug or pitcher given extensive transfer designs incorporating noted people and famous ships. Typically a black on white background was used for eighteenth century production in Liverpool, England. Eventually American scenes were used on the cylindrical products and marketed in the America.

Liverpool ware (ceramic): Originally the term designated china subject to transfer printing in early nineteenth century Liverpool, England. Such transfer printing under the direction of John Sadler and others had advanced to the point where various colors could be used as well as black and brown. As the transfer process spread to other makers the Liverpool ware term was often applied to most any pottery which reflected its use.

Livery cupboard (furniture): Initially an English cupboard used to store clothing for those wearing uniforms as servants or in similar domestic service. Later the cupboards held rations or simple foods as well. Eventually the term livery stable designated a location for the caretaker of horses.

Livingston, Bell & Co.: Provided military uniforms boots, canteens, and knapsacks under Federal contract during the Civil War. Located in St. Louis, Missouri.

Lobby chest (furniture): Elaborate piece

Lithographed poster for Blue Soap, ca. 1880s.

Lithographed poster for magic act in 1890s Germany.

of early nineteenth century furniture involving a half chest of drawers and a pullout writing board. Used in England often as bedroom furniture or in other smaller rooms.

Locker (furniture): Early cabinetmaker's term for the central miniature cupboard within the interior of a desk or writing interior of a desk.

Lock, J. B.: Pewter artisan doing business in 1830s, New York City.

Lock, Joseph: (see Amberina glass)

Lockwood, James: Active silversmith from 1800 to 1825 in New York City.

Locomobile: Gasoline-powered automobile produced in the early 1900s by the Locomobile Company of America in Bridgeport, Connecticut. Prices were $2,000 and upward.

Logix computer: Working computer with 112 page programming manual allowing operator to play games. Operated on three C batteries. Sale price in 1973 was $23.95.

Lolling chair (furniture): Early armchair with tall upholstered back. Often serpentine arched with arms that were curved and open. Also called a Martha Washington chair.

Lombard, Benjamin: Doing business from 1830 to 1845 as a silversmith in Charleston, South Carolina.

London Electric Fabric Co.: (see Edson electric garter)

London hearing horn: Offered by Sears, Roebuck and Company in 1902. They were sold in two sizes, the largest being 4" in length. Price was $1.35.

Long alarm clock: A new item in the Sears, Roebuck and Company catalog of 1902. Clock's alarm ran from 20 to 30 minutes. Case finished in "superfine" oxidized copper. Price of the 10" clock was $2.50.

Long clock: Simply another term for grandfather's clock or tall clock.

Longhorn bike: Sidewalk bike for children ages four to eight. In the early 1970s it came with Longhorn-style handle bars and a banana shaped seat. Made mostly of molded plastic. Price complete with training wheels was $16.66.

Long, James & Family: Stoneware pottery operating in nineteenth century, Byram, Georgia.

Longley & Co.: Cartridge and cap box maker for Federal troops during the Civil War, based in Lewiston, Maine.

Lonhuda Pottery: Exceptional art pottery establishment in 1890s, Steubenville, Ohio.

Loom: Term for any machine used for weaving various types of yarn into fabric.

Loomis, George: Active silversmith operating as George Loomis and Company in 1850 and 1860, Erie, Pennsylvania.

Loop-back Windsor: Used as a term for early American Windsor chairs fashioned without arms and with a bow back.

Loop the Loop: Game made by Wolverine involving cars on a track operated by a key-wind motor. Early in the 1950s the 19" long game sold for $2.95.

Loo table: An early oval table made especially for the popular eighteenth century card game of loo.

Loper (furniture): In the early fall-front desk or secretary the loper was that device which supported the extended lid of the desk. Typically this sliding arm was concealed within a channel inside the desk.

Lord, Benjamin: A Colonial era silversmith working 1785 to 1795 in Pittsfield, Massachusetts.

Loring, Elijah: A silversmith from 1750s to 1780s in Barnstable, Massachusetts.

Lorton, William: Active clockmaker doing business in 1820s, New York City.

Loth stove (toy): Toy model of Loth stove made in the 1920s by Arcade Manufacturing Co. Marked Loth's Fuel-Saver on the front. Made of cast iron with white oven door that opened.

Lotz (glass): Reference to iridescent art glass produced by Johann Lotz in Austria. Richly done in Art Nouveau style.

Louisiana Pottery Works: (see Hernandez & Saley)

Louisville Glass Works: Glassmaking firm was located in Louisville, Kentucky, during the latter nineteenth century. The company produced whiskey flasks with American eagle designs under the direction of Captain J. B. Ford.

Louisville Pottery: (see Melcher, Henry)

Louis XIV (furniture): Reference to the period of major accomplishment in French furniture. Actual reign of Louis XIV was from 1643 to 1715. During much of that time, artists and craftsmen housed at the palace crafted lavish furniture. Gold gilding and tortoiseshell veneer were applied to structures of oak, mahogany, and walnut. Velvet and brocade fabrics provided a final touch.

Lounge (furniture): Furniture term for a type of nineteenth or twentieth century couch. Covered with leather or woolen cloth, early examples often had one high end to serve as a pillow for reclining.

Love chest (furniture): Still another term for the popular eighteenth and early nineteenth century dower chest said to originate in Pennsylvania.

Love seat (furniture): Term for a small upholstered settee or sofa designed to seat only two people.

Lovett, Robert: Active New York City silversmith from the 1820s to the 1840s.

Low Art Tile Works: Producer of quality tiles in 1890s and early 1900s, Chelsea, Massachusetts.

Low-back chair (furniture): Small side chair which represented a middle seventeenth century improvement over mere stools and benches.

Low, Daniel: (see Empire wreath)

Lowestoft (ceramic): Controversial pottery operation in late eighteenth century Lowestoft, England. The firm produced highly decorated soft-paste porcelain in Chinese patterns. The operation closed by 1803 but decades of early production was later disputed. Some sources insisted the ware was actually made in China for import to wealthy British households. Others insist it was all made in England including the underglaze painting.

Low, John: Participating silversmith during the 1820s and 1830s, in Salem, Massachusetts.

Lownes, Edward: Noted silversmith operating in 1820s and 1830s, Philadelphia, Pennsylvania.

Low tile (ceramic): Originally decorative tiles crafted by John C. Low in late 1870s, Chelsea, Massachusetts. Later similar, but less creative, tiles were produced in other factories and given the same general name.

Lozenge (furniture): Term for a diamond-shaped ornamental feature of eighteenth century overlays on some crafted furniture.

Lozier automobile: Relatively pricey motor vehicle priced at $4,750 in 1913. Based in Detroit, Michigan.

Lucifer match: Basically the wooden match ignited by friction. It involved

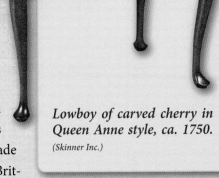

Lowboy of carved cherry in Queen Anne style, ca. 1750.
(Skinner Inc.)

potassium chlorate and other combustible materials collected on a stick and held with gum. Friction on the head caused combustion. By the 1840s the production of Lucifer or friction matches had replaced use of the earlier tinder box.

Luckes' Rolls: Nationally advertised brand of 1890s cigars. Produced by J.H. Lucked and Company of Cincinnati, Ohio.

Ludwig, John: A Colonial era clockmaker in 1790s, Philadelphia, Pennsylvania.

Lukens, Seneca: Listed as a clockmaker in 1830s, Horsham Meeting, Pennsylvania.

Lunette (furniture): Cabinetmaker's reference to the carved inlay image of a half moon or semi-circular decorative design.

Lupp, Henry: Active as a silversmith in 1785, New Brunswick, New Jersey.

Luster ware: Resulting iridescent decoration applied to the surface of ceramics. Basically the use of acid to dissolve oxides of metals such as copper, gold, or silver and provide a metallic over-glaze. The procedure dates back to ninth century Spain, but was made popular later by potters in England who refined the process and marketed it.

Lyman, Fenton & Co.: Rockingham, porcelain, and flint enamel producers in 1850s, Bennington, Vermont.

Lynn, Adam: Colonial era silversmith in the trade in 1780s and 1780s, Alexandria, Virginia.

Lyons Pottery: Stoneware pottery operation during business in nineteenth century, Lyons, New York.

Lyre back (furniture): One of the more prominent designs used by early American cabinetmakers including Duncan Phyfe for chair backs. It was considered a classical touch to provide the image of the ancient musical instrument on fashionable furniture. Usually wood and metal were involved in its application.

Lyre clock: First used in the eighteenth century for a lyre-shaped clock, resembling the musical instrument.

Lytle, Robert: Silversmith in 1830s and 1840s, Baltimore, Maryland.

Macomb Pottery Company: Noted stoneware pottery starting in 1880s, Macomb, Illinois.

Macon Arsenal: Supplied Confederate forces with canteens, knapsacks, and edged weapons. Located in Macon, Georgia.

Macrame: Originally an Arab term for ornamental fringe or edging, in later usage it came to mean the broader act of weaving pieces of string together in knots to form a decorative pattern.

Madame Hendren: Doll brand offered in early 1930s Montgomery Ward catalog. Betty and Barbara dolls were $5.25 for both.

Maddock & Sons: Pottery business headed by Thomas Maddock in 1860s, Trenton, New Jersey. Later known as John Maddock and Sons.

Magee and George: Cartridge box supplier for the Confederate cause, doing business in New Orleans, Louisiana.

Magenta (color): According to Sears, a dark purple red.

Magic lantern: Late nineteenth century and early twentieth century form of slide projector. Early examples used a candle or oil lamp to project light through a complex lens and magnify images on painted glass. Sometimes called a stereopticon.

Magic Skin (doll): Realistic latex bodied doll sold by mail-order catalog during the 1950s. Sizes varied from 13" to 20".

Lowboy of carved walnut in Queen Anne style. (Skinner Inc.)

Carved mahogany organ stool made in Austria. (Harris Auction Center)

Magnet and grape (glass): Term for use of grape and grape leaf designs in a particular pattern of pressed glass.

Magnolia (wood): Straw-colored native American wood used for light-colored veneers. Sometimes called the American tulip tree.

Mahogany brown (color): Sears listed it as a brown with a maroon cast.

Mahogany (color): A dark reddish brown as presented by Sears.

Mahogany (wood): One of the classic woods used in early American furniture. Early in the eighteenth century imported mahogany began to surpass walnut as the choice of cabinetmakers. By middle of the eighteenth century mahogany was being imported to the American colonies from Central America, San Domingo, and the West Indies. It remained the favored wood for fine furniture well into the nineteenth century in America.

Maize: (see Indian corn)

Maize (color): Light yellow as in the color of the vegetable corn itself.

Maize pearl (color): Sears considered this to be a light yellow shade of corn.

Majestic Doll: Highest grade doll sold in 1902 by Sears, Roebuck and Company. It provided a "human shape body" made of "indestructible" composition. It had ball joints and moving eyes. The doll came in three sizes, 18", 23½", and 25½".

Majolica (ceramic): Originally the term made reference to buff colored, enameled decorated ware crafted on the island of Majorca off the coast of Spain. Later it was applied generally to opaque pottery with a highly glazed decoration. Ultimately majolica was produced worldwide.

Makit (toy): Construction toy offered in the 1940s, similar to Tinker Toy.

Various Makit outfits came in tubes or a full chest of items.

Malabar (textile): A bandana-like handkerchief made in Malabar, India. Examples were brightly colored and made of cotton.

Malaga pottery (ceramic): Reference to a high quality golden lusterware made centuries ago in the south of Spain.

Malt-Nutrine: Nationally advertised tonic containing just under two percent alcohol. An early twentieth century product of Anheiser-Bush.

Mammy rocker: (see Rockee)

Manchet: Ultimate Colonial treat in the form of a loaf of freshly baked bread. The best of wheat grains were used in this offering for special occasions. The Old English recipe for Manchet called for fine flour, hard liquor, and honey. Daily bread for Colonials was typically a coarse corn bread.

Mandarin (color): In the 1927 Sears listing, just the single word orange.

Manhattan Fire Arms Co.: Listed as a manufacturer of percussion revolvers, patented 1859. Located at Newark, New Jersey.

Mann, Alexander: Doing business as a silversmith from 1775 to 1805 in Middletown, Connecticut.

Mannerback, William: Active in the silversmith trade in 1820s and 1830s, Reading, Pennsylvania.

Mann, Harvey Jr.: Axe supplier for Federal troops during the Civil War, located in Bellefonte, Pennsylvania.

Manning-Bowman: (see English teapot)

Manning, Richard: Noted clockmaker in 1750s, Ipswich, Massachusetts.

Manning, Thaddeus: Listed as active pewterer in 1840s, Middletown, Connecticut.

Mann, John: A potter of redware in nineteenth century, Rahway, New Jersey.

Mahogany carved side chair, ca. 1760. (Skinner Inc.)

Carved mahogany side chair, ca. 1750. (Skinner Inc.)

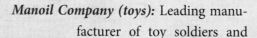

Block-front mahogany bureau table in Chippendale style. (Skinner Inc.)

Majolica figural as part of a larger vase.

Manoil Company (toys): Leading manufacturer of toy soldiers and other lead figures and accessories during the 1930s. Originally based in New York City and later relocated. During the 1940s composition replaced metal as the main ingredient of toy figures and toy vehicles. Later plastic was used. Manoil closed in the middle 1950s.

Mansfield, Elisha: Doing business as a silversmith from 1795 to 1815 in Norwich, Connecticut.

Mansfield, Lamb & Co.: Granted a contract for 10,000 cavalry sabers by the U.S. government in 1861. Located in Smithfield, Rhode Island.

Mansfield silver: Among the first silver to be manufactured in America. The pieces were the work of John Mansfield in 1630s, Boston. Most if not all of the Mansfield silver was believed unmarked.

Mantel (furniture): By the early nineteenth century the wooden shelf over the fireplace was considered a major feature of the parlor. Usually softwood was used for the lengthy piece. It was sometimes carved, and sometimes painted to match surrounding wood trim.

Maple (wood): Hard wood with a fine grain, could be polished to a high sheen. Popular with American cabinetmakers and extensively used during the Colonial period. For all of its qualities, it was brittle and was usually unsuitable for carving.

Marblehead Pottery: Art pottery and tile maker active from early 1900s into the 1930s at Marblehead, Massachusetts.

Marble, Simon: An accomplished silversmith in 1830s and 1840s, New Haven, Connecticut.

Marbling (furniture): Reference to efforts to paint columns, commode tops, tables, and other furniture to give the illusion of actual marble.

Marieburg Pottery: Name for a brightly colored enameled ware produced in eighteenth century Sweden. Later the firm also produced stylish figures and tableware.

Marine Clock Manufacturing Co.: Clockmaking firm in 1840s, New Haven, Connecticut.

Marion-Handley: Nationally advertised automobile of the early twentieth century. Their Six-Sixty model, made by Mutual Motors Company, sold for $1,650 in 1917.

Markle, Benjamin: Active as a silversmith in 1840s and 1850s, Albany, New York.

Marks, Isaac: Colonial era clockmaker in 1790s, Philadelphia, Pennsylvania.

Marlborough leg (furniture): Reference to a straight leg which was grooved and ended with a block foot. Stylish during the middle eighteenth century.

Marmon car: Automobile made by Nordyke and Marmon Company of Indianapolis, Indiana. In 1905 the four cylinder Marmon sold for $2,500.

Maroon (color): A dark red according the early Sears catalogs.

Marouflage (aviation): A reference to the wrapping of wooden parts in cloth.

Marquand, Frederick: A noted silversmith in 1820s and 1830s, New York City.

Marquetry (furniture): Method of using inlaid work for decoration on quality mahogany furniture. Typically the cabinetmaker relied on holly or satinwood for the actual inlay. In some cases ivory, shell, or mother-of-pearl was used.

Marquise chair: French reference to a late seventeenth century broad chair for two persons.

Marriage chest (furniture): Yet another term for the dower chest or hope chest of the bride-to-be.

Marseille, Armand: German doll making concern which patented some models in France. Dolls ranged from infant to adult. The zenith of their bisque head doll production was from the 1890s to the early 1900s. Manufacture ceased in 1927.

Marshall, Thomas: Active silversmith in 1840s and 1850s, Troy, New York.

Marsh, George: Clockmaker in 1830s, Torrington, Connecticut.

Marsh, Thomas: Noted silversmith doing business during the 1830s to the 1850s in Paris, Kentucky.

Marston, William: Manufacturer of firearms during the 1860s, provided rifled carbines to the U.S. Army. Located in New York City.

Martele (silverware): Trade name for quality line of Art Nouveau style silverware produced by Gorham Manufacturing Company.

Martha Washington chair: (see Lolling chair)

Martin, Peter: Silversmith of record from 1755 to 1765 in New York City.

Marver: Term for the ironwork table used to fashion molten glass in the early glass factories.

Mary Gregory (glass): Reference to a latter nineteenth century enameled glass decorated with human figures, usually children. It was produced in Sandwich, Massachusetts.

Maryland Glass Works: Glass firm founded by John Lee Chapman in 1850, Baltimore, Maryland.

Mary Muslin (doll): Name for a printed cloth doll of the early 1950s designed by Madame Alexander. It came in three different sizes with yarn hair.

Mase, Serephim: Little known silversmith operation in 1830s, Washington, D.C.

Mask motif (furniture): Elaborate carving on mahogany or walnut furniture of the full face of a creature, animal or human. Unusual, even grotesque, masks were frequently applied in early eighteenth Europe, however they were seldom used by American cabinetmakers.

Mason and Taylor: (see Witch doll)

Mason, George: Clockmaker in 1840s, Boston, Massachusetts.

Mason ware (ceramic): Heavy ware made by Miles Mason and others in early eighteenth century England. Initially enameled wares were made, sometimes with red and blue Asian designs. Later quantities of ironstone were also made.

Mason, William: Contracted with the Federal government to provide 30,000 rifled muskets during the Civil War, located in Taunton, Massachusetts.

Massachusetts Organ Co.: (see Webber singing doll)

Massachusetts Power Co.: Civil War supplier of gunpowder to Federal troops, located in Barre, Massachusetts.

Massachusetts shelf clock: Reference to Revolutionary War era clocks crafted by Massachusetts clockmakers. Usually they were brass and housed eight-day movements.

Masstricht: Name of a nineteenth century earthenware tableware made by potters in Holland and exported to the American market.

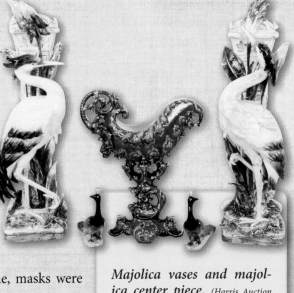

Majolica vases and majolica center piece. (Harris Auction Center)

Ornate majolica platter with handles.

Victorian era majolica vase of Herron with cattails.

Trio of Manoil toy soldiers.

Maton, Marcus: A pewter producer of note in 1820s, Hartford, Connecticut.

Matt Morgan Art Pottery Company: Pottery making firm established in 1883 at Cincinnati, Ohio.

Mauve (color): Considered to be a deep lilac, or a lavender.

Maxfer: An attachment to Ford automobiles which converted the vehicle into a one ton truck. The $350 Maxfer was marketed by the Maxfer Truck and Tractor Company in Chicago, Illinois.

Maxwell Mercury: Stream-lined automobile manufactured early in the twentieth century by the Maxwell-Brisco Motor Company of New York. In 1913 the Maxwell Mercury was priced at $1,150.

Mayer, Elias: A noted clockmaker in 1830s, Philadelphia, Pennsylvania.

Mayer Pottery Co.: Mainly whiteware producer from 1880s to 1900s in Beaver Falls, Pennsylvania. Also see Arsenal Pottery.

Mayflower stove: Brand of range complete with Sure Oven sold during the 1920s by Sears, Roebuck and Company. Shipped from factory they were nickel-plated and burned coal or wood.

Maynard, Edward: Patent granted to Maynard for cartridge loader in 1861, Washington, D.C. Supplier of more than 20,000 .58 caliber carbines to the U.S. Army during the 1860s.

Maynard rifle: Basically a lever-operated breech loading carbine used by both sides during the Civil War. It was the invention of Edward Maynard in the 1850s.

Tiger maple Federal era desk, ca. 1820. (Skinner Inc.)

Maytag washer (toy): In the 1930s Hubley Toys produced a Maytag toy washer complete with the popular brand name on the side. It included a workable wringer and removable gyrator.

McAboy, Mary: Crafter of Skookum dolls and other unique dolls, combining composition heads with cloth and wooden bodies. McAboy designed dolls starting in the 1920s in Missoula, Montana.

McClymon, William: An early 1800s silversmith located in Schenectady, New York.

McComb, Henry S.: Supplier of military tent poles and tripods during the Civil War in Wilmington, Delaware.

McConnell, Thomas: Active as a silversmith in early 1800s, Wilmington, Delaware.

McCormick, John: A silversmith in the 1840s in Schenectady, New York.

McCormick Thresher (toy): Produced by Arcade Manufacturing Company in the late 1920s. It was 12" long and made of cast iron.

McCormick Weber Wagon (toy): A miniature model of the McCormick-Deering Weber wagon complete with a team of horses was made by Arcade in the late 1920s. Including horses the cast iron piece was over 12" long.

McCoy Pottery Company: Fully known as Nelson McCoy Pottery and noted for high quality art pottery. Active from 1900s to 1960s in Roseville, Ohio.

McCrea, Robert: Doing business as a silversmith from 1785 to 1795 in Schenectady, New York.

McCully, William: Noted glassmaker who operated the Sligo Glass Works in 1828, Pennsylvania.

McDonnaugh, Patrick: Active silversmith from 1810 to 1825 in Philadelphia, Pennsylvania.

McDougall, Fenton & Co.: Contracted with the Federal government to provide military shirts and socks during the Civil War. Located in Syracuse, New York.

McDougall, William: Known as involved in the silversmith trade from 1825 to 1840 in Meredith, New Hampshire.

McFadden, John: Active as a silversmith from the 1840s to the 1860s in Pittsburgh, Pennsylvania.

McFee, John: Noted silversmith doing business from 1795 to 1810 in Philadelphia, Pennsylvania.

McGaw, Daniel: Listed as an active silversmith from 1770 to 1790 in Chester, Pennsylvania.

McGuffey Ana (doll): A 1940s doll inspired by the McGuffey Reader and sold individually or with an entire wardrobe and trunk. Models varied from 13" to 20".

McHary, Alexander: Doing business during the 1850s and 1860s as a silversmith in Albany, New York.

McIntire, Joseph: Active silversmith in 1840s and 1850s, Philadelphia, Pennsylvania.

McIntire, Samuel: Highly accomplished cabinetmaker and furniture designer active in late eighteenth century and early nineteenth century, Salem, Massachusetts. Noted for exquisite wood carving on furniture and mantelpieces.

McIntosh, John: Noted as a silversmith in 1760s, Fort Stanwix, Pennsylvania.

McKenzie, Duncan: Patent holder during the Civil War for military camp stoves, located in Brooklyn, New York.

McKinstry, Alexander: Listed as a maker of Bowie knives and Bowie-shaped pikes for Confederate forces during the Civil War.

McLaughlin, M. Louise: Pottery maker of note operating in 1870s, Cincinnati, Ohio.

McLoughlin (toys): Noted lithograph printer of children's books, board games, paper dolls, and puzzles in nineteenth century America. Eventually became McLoughlin Brothers and continued splendid color graphics into the 1920s.

McMurry, Vinkle, Meyer & Co.: Supplier of artillery ammunition to Federal troops in 1860s, St. Louis, Missouri.

McNeil, Edward: Listed in the 1840s as a silversmith in Troy, New York.

Meacham & Co.: Maker of maple wood fifes for Federal troops during the Civil War, located in 1860s Albany, New York.

Mead, Adriance: Doing business as Adriance Mead and Company clockmakers in 1830s, Ithaca, New York.

Mear, Frederick: (see Boston Earthenware Manufacturing Company)

Meccano (toys): Trade name of a British maker of construction toys. Founded by Frank Hornby in Liverpool, England. Also maker of Dinky Toys, some vehicles. Various twentieth century makings included Meccano, Hornby, and M. Ld. L.

Mechanical doll: Used to define dolls that can perform one or more various movements. Action varied from a single gesture to a sequence to movements. Typically the doll's framework held the necessary mechanisms.

Mechanical table (furniture): Basically operated by a concealed steel rod, movement of the rear legs allowed leaf brackets to move into a supporting position. Made in pairs, such tables could serve as console tables when not in extended use. Credited to Duncan Phyfe in the early nineteenth century.

One-drawer Shaker stand made of maple. (Skinner Inc.)

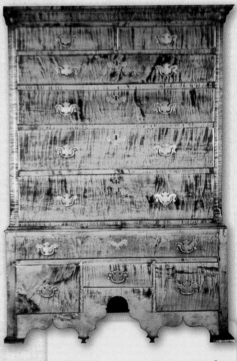

Queen Anne tiger maple high chest, mid-eighteenth century. (Skinner Inc.)

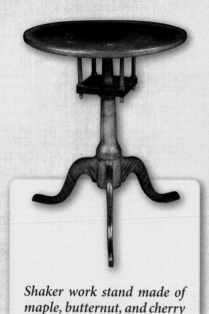

Shaker work stand made of maple, butternut, and cherry woods. (Skinner Inc.)

My Dream Baby produced by Armand Marseille, ca. 1920s.

Mechanized lamp: (see Carcel lamp)

Medallion back (furniture): Term for medallion or oval-shaped chair back or settee back.

Meeks, Edward Jr.: Active Colonial period clockmaker in 1790s, New York City.

Megascope: Another version of the late nineteenth century magic lantern. The primitive projecting device used light to magnify an image or picture on a white screen.

Megilp (color): Transparent and colorless according to Sears. Later described as a medium for oils paints involving linseed oil and varnish or turpentine.

Meissen ware (ceramic): Porcelain of remarkable quality produced in early eighteenth century, Saxony. The Meissen Porcelain Factory became renowned for delicate detail, robust colors, and brilliant glaze. Pieces were given a crossed-sword mark in blue on the back or bottom.

Meister, J. E.: Maker of enameled cloth for knapsacks for the Confederate military. Located in Columbia, South Carolina.

Melcher, Henry: Instrumental in stoneware pottery operating from the latter nineteenth century to the 1920s in Louisville, Kentucky. Also known as Louisville Pottery.

Mellor & Company: Pottery operation specializing in porcelain and whiteware from 1890s to the 1930s in Trenton, New Jersey. See also Cook Pottery Company.

Melodeon: Name for a relatively small, wind instrument popular in the middle of the nineteenth century. The instrument had keys similar to that of an organ, but was often portable with folding wooden legs.

Memorial picture: (see Mourning picture)

Memphis (color): A medium blue according to the 1927 Sears listings.

Mendenhall, Jones & Gardner: Suppliers of Mississippi rifles during the Civil War. Located in Jamestown, North Carolina.

Menner, John: Active potter in 1780s, Womelsdorf, Pennsylvania.

Mercer automobile: The Mercer, with the Mercer Motors Company brand, a product of Hare's Motors of New York City. In was advertised in 1920 as "built upon the sound principles for which that institution stands."

Mercer Pottery Company: A pottery operation established in 1868 at Trenton, New Jersey.

Mercury glass: A silvered glass produced during the nineteenth century which actually used mercury material between the inside and outside walls of a particular piece. Various mercury glass pieces were produced from bowls to vases by a variety of glass factories.

Meredith, John: Silversmith active from 1825 to 1845 in Baltimore, Maryland.

Merefield, Thomas: Doing business as a silversmith in 1840s and 1850s, Albany, New York.

Meridienne (furniture): French term for a day bed or small sofa. Usually with one arm lower than the other.

Merkel motorcycle: First produced in 1901 at Milwaukee, Wisconsin. Purchased in 1909 by Light Manufacturing and moved to Pittsburgh, Pennsylvania. The Merkel operation, including the Flying Merkel, was purchased by the Miami Cycle Manufacturing Company in 1911 and moved to Middletown, Ohio. The first self-starting Merkel was sold in 1913. Operation ceased in 1917.

Merkler, John: New York City silversmith shown as active in 1780.

Merrill, J. H.: Listed as a supplier of .54 caliber carbines to the U.S. Army during the 1860s, located in Baltimore, Maryland.

Merrill, L. T.: Military equipment maker including kettles and hatchets for Federal troops during the Civil War, based in New York City.

Merrimac Ceramic Company: Pottery making establishment in 1890s, Newburyport, Massachusetts.

Merriman, Samuel: Active silversmith from 1770 to 1805 in Litchfield, Connecticut.

Merriman, Silas: A noted clockmaker in 1770s, New Haven, Connecticut.

Metropolitan Arms Co.: Listed as a maker of percussion revolvers, model 1859. Located in New York City.

Mettam, Charles: Granted a patent in 1861 for military camp cots, located in New York City.

Metzger, E.: Maker of military cap boxes for Federal forces during the Civil War, based in Philadelphia, Pennsylvania.

M'Ewen and Son: Pewter business headed by Malcolm M'Ewen in 1790s, New York City.

Meyer and Sons: Operation headed by William Meyer producing redware and stoneware from 1880s to 1960s in Atacosa, Texas.

Meyer, Joseph: Noted silversmith in 1840s and 1850s, Canton, Ohio.

Mezzotint: Term for engraving that is wholly composed of light and dark areas rather than traditional lines.

Miami Cycle Manufacturing Co.: (see Merkel motorcycle)

Michigan Motor Car Co.: Makers of the Michigan automobile during the early twentieth century. Their Model 40 was priced at $1,585 in 1913. The company was based in Kalamazoo, Michigan.

Middle Lane Pottery: Enterprise of pottery making operating in 1890s, East Hampton, New York.

Milk cupboard: (see Pie safe)

Milk glass: Milk-colored opaque glass, also sometime in the past called opal or milk white. It was produced in great numbers both in the United States and Europe during the latter nineteenth century and early twentieth century.

Milk safe: (see Pie safe)

Millard, David J.: Under a federal government contract to supply 10,000 cavalry sabers in 1861. Located in Clayville, New York.

Millar, James: Active silversmith in 1830s, Boston, Massachusetts.

Millbury musket: (see Waters, A. H.)

Millefiori glass: Most frequently seen in paperweights, but the technique was also used in bottles, marbles, vases, and other quality glassware. The arrangement of rods of colored glass in bundles to form a pattern dates back several centuries. The rods of glass were then exposed to heat, cooled, sliced, and applied to other glassware before being reheated. Ultimately the process produced striking flower-like designs in the glass. This method was used extensively in the nineteenth century including at the New England Glass Works in America. True to its origin, the word itself is Italian meaning a thousand flowers.

Miller, Aaron: Doing business as a clockmaker in 1750s, Elizabethtown, North Carolina.

Miller, A. N.: A supplier of cannon and projectiles to the Confederate military during the Civil War. Located in Savannah, Georgia.

Miller and Company: Supplier of military goods to the U.S. Army during the 1860s, located in New York City.

Miller, Matthew: Enterprising silversmith in early 1800s, Charleston, South Carolina.

Meccano manual of instructions, 1916.

Boxed Meccano construction set, ca. 1930s.

Milk glass covered dish and milk glass Owl pitcher. *(Harris Auction Center)*

Milk glass Fox covered dish and milk glass Cat covered dish. *(Harris Auction Center)*

Milk glass Fish covered dish and Chick and Eggs covered dish. *(Harris Auction Center)*

Miller, William: Listed as an active silversmith in 1820s, Charleston, South Carolina.

Milne, Edmund: Doing business as a silversmith in 1790s, Philadelphia, Pennsylvania.

Milton Bradley Company: Legendary maker of educational toys. Established in 1860s, Springfield, Massachusetts. Line included building blocks, Game of Life, construction toys, puzzles, lithographed buildings, paint sets, and much more.

Minchemer, Frances: Under contract with the Confederate States of America to produce C.S.A. belt plates during the Civil War. Located in Atlanta, Georgia.

Minerva Dolls: Metal doll heads sold by Sears, Roebuck and Company in 1902. They had moving glass eyes and open lips. The heads were made of painted sheet brass and came in various sizes. A heart-shaped neck tag identified them as Minerva dolls.

Miniature portrait: Denotes the early American portrait of an individual painted in miniature. Some were rendered on ivory or porcelain and adorned a brooch or were set in a locket. Other miniatures were put in elaborate frames for table or wall display.

Mink brown (color): Described during the 1920s in Sears catalogs as a medium brown.

Mink (color): The color of mink fur, medium brown with darker markings.

Minnesota Machine: Very high grade sewing machine sold in 1902 by the Sears, Roebuck and Company. The machines, with Italian veneering oak cabinets, were shipped to customers direct from the factory in Dayton, Ohio. Price was $23.20.

Minnesota Stoneware Co.: Maker of quality stoneware products from 1880s to early 1900s in Red Wing, Minnesota.

Minton ware (ceramic): Production of pottery first begun by Thomas Minton in the 1790s, Stafford shire in England. Initially Minton produced earthenware but later provided a quality decorated porcelain in the early nineteenth century.

Mintzer, W. G.: A principal U.S. military button manufacturer during the Civil War, located in Philadelphia, Pennsylvania.

Minute Man Six: (see Lexington automobile)

Mirrors: The so-called looking glass was reflective of wealth in early America. Silvery surfaced mirrors imported from England were costly, affordable only to the most affluent. Early in the nineteenth century the household looking glass was seen somewhat more often in America, but remained an item of major expense.

Missal: Initially this term was a specific reference to the book which contained the Mass for the full year. However it later became a larger term for most any religious book of substance.

Miss Ducky (doll): Tru-Flesh (brand) rubber doll with realistic skin sold in the 1940s with or without her layette. Models varied from 11" to 16½".

Mission style (furniture): Reference to an early twentieth century style of furniture which emphasized oak used in very straight lines. It was also associated with some furnishings of Spanish missions in early California.

Mississippi Armory: Source of Maynard-type carbines for the Confederate military during the Civil War.

Mitchell automobile: Manufactured in the early 1900s by the Mitchell Motor

Car Company in Racine, Wisconsin. Advertised in 1907 as the "show me" car for $2,000.

Mitchell, George: Active clockmaker operating in 1830s, Bristol, Connecticut.

Mitchell Light Car: Early 1900s automobile priced at $700. Made by Mitchell Motor Car Company in Racine, Wisconsin.

Mitchell, William: Doing business as a silversmith in 1820s and 1830s, Richmond, Virginia.

Mitre joint: Widely practiced means of joining panels or wood into corners since the seventeenth century. Basically two sides are beveled at 45-degree angles to form a single 90-degree corner.

Mixing table (furniture): Originally a late eighteenth and early nineteenth century English table design to house bottles and glasses in a social setting. Typically made of mahogany with inlaid satinwood, they were a buffet-like supplement to the dining table.

Mix, James: Noted in 1815 as a silversmith active in Albany, New York.

Mobbs, William: Participating silversmith during the 1830s and 1840s in Buffalo, New York.

Mode (color): As presented by Sears in the 1920s, a medium shade of tan.

Model Toys: (see Doepke Manufacturing Co.)

Moffat, Charles: A New York City silversmith from 1830 to 1845.

Mogul: Automobile business wagon made for freight and delivery during the early 1900s. Manufactured by The Four-Wheel Drive Wagon Company of Milwaukee, Wisconsin.

Mohler, Jacob: Doing business as an accomplished silversmith in 1750s and 1760s, Baltimore, Maryland.

Molded glass: Combined the use of a three-section wooden mold and the skills of a glassblower. Such glass crafted in America was typically arched or patterned, geometric, or grand flowing baroque. Brilliant molded glass, when tapped, provided a long clear ring.

Mole Gray (color): Not surprisingly the color of mole fur, dark gray.

Moline Pressed Steel (toys): Noted twentieth century maker of steel cars, trucks, fire engines, and other toy vehicles. Based in East Moline, Illinois. Creator of the Buddy L brand. Buddy L was the name of founder Fred Lundahl's son.

Monarch tractor (toy): This cast iron toy tractor had a rocking motion when pulled. Raised Monarch letters were just below the engine. The red and black vehicle was made by Hubley Toys in the 1930s.

Money dish (furniture): A shallow or hollowed out space at the four corners of eighteenth century card or gaming tables. Such dishes served to hold counters for gambling, or in some cases actual money.

Monkey Orchestra: (see Acier)

Monkey skin (color): Offered by Sears as a light tan with a pinkish tint.

Monk, James: A Colonial era silversmith doing business from 1795 to 1810 in Charleston, South Carolina.

Monopodium (furniture): Reference to a single and continuing vegetable-like or animal-like axis used as a support furniture design.

Monross, Elisha: Clockmaker active in 1830s, Bristol, Connecticut.

Monteith, John: Known to practice the silversmith trade along with Robert Monteith in 1830s, Baltimore, Maryland.

Montgomery Arsenal: Provided leather goods to Confederate soldiers during the Civil War. Located in Montgomery, Alabama.

Baccarat quadrille paperweight with delicate Millefiori canes.

Uncle Wiggily Game from Milton Bradley Company, ca. 1918.

Wheel of Fortune Game, copyright 1975 by Milton Bradley Co.

Victorian era framed mirror.

Gilt wood and carved mirror, ca. 1750. (Skinner Inc.)

Chippendale style mirror, mid-eighteenth century. (Skinner Inc.)

154

Montgomery, J. A.: Granted a patent in 1861 for a military type canteen, during business in Williamsport, Pennsylvania.

Montgomery, Robert: A New York City clockmaker active in the 1780s.

Mont Storm, William: Maker of cartridges for the military in 1860s, New York City.

Mood, Joseph: Active as a silversmith starting in 1805, later joined by John Mood in Charleston, South Carolina.

Moon automobile: A product of the Moon Motor Car Company, built to luxury standards during the early 1900s. Company was located in St. Louis, Missouri. It closed in 1930. Price of the Six-43 touring car in 1917 was $1,395.

Mooney, James E.: Under contract to provide cartridge boxes for Federal troops during the Civil War, based in Indianapolis, Indiana.

Moore Brothers Glass: (see Fisler and Beckett Company)

Moore, Jared: Noted silversmith from 1825 to 1840 in New York City.

Moore, J. P.: Listed as a maker of Enfield type rifled muskets in the 1860s, located in New York City.

Moravian Pottery: Fully titled the Moravian Pottery and Tile Works. Produced art pottery and tiles from 1890s to the 1950s in Doylestown, Pennsylvania.

Moreen (textile): Term for a thick woolen upholstery material still in use in the nineteenth century. Typically it was filled with various selections of cotton and wool. In earlier centuries it was known as morine.

Morey and Ober: Engaged in pewter ware enterprise in early nineteenth century, Boston, Massachusetts.

Morgan & Wright: Chicago based makers of Clincher Tire for automobiles during the early 1900s.

Morgan, Elijah: A noted clockmaker in 1830s, Poughkeepsie, New York.

Morgan, Elijah: Listed as an active silversmith from 1805 to 1825 in Poughkeepsie, New York.

Morgan, Thomas: A Colonial era clockmaker in 1770s, Baltimore, Maryland.

Morganville Pottery: Specializing in redware, the pottery operated from the 1850s to 1900 in Morganville, New York.

Morine: (see Moreen)

Morning Glory: One of three patterns of "beautiful crockery" plates sold in 1913 by S.S. Kresge Co. for 10¢ each.

Morning glory (color): An iridescent silver according to Sears during the 1920s.

Morrel, Benjamin: Enterprising clockmaker in 1830s, Boscowen, New Hampshire.

Morris & Salom Electrobat: Basically an electric carriage perfected by Pedro Salom and Henry Morris in 1895. Batteries provided the power for motors attached to the front wheels, and the makers laid claim to speeds up to 25 miles per hour.

Morris chair (furniture): Reference to a late nineteenth century chair with an adjustable back. A horizontal bar held the back in position. Designed by William Morris, the upholstered chair also had back and seat cushions for added comfort.

Morrison, Murdoch: Supplier of Bowie knives and pistols to the Confederate military during the Civil War. Located in Rockingham County, North Carolina.

Morrison, S. G.: Provider of military canteens during the 1860s, located in Williamsport, Pennsylvania.

Morrison-Sturgis Electric: Primitive moving vehicle powered by storage batteries in 1890, Des Moines, Iowa. The carriage crafted by William Morrison and modified by Harold Sturgis could accommodate up to 12 passengers.

Morse, David: An early 1800s silversmith working in Boston, Massachusetts.

Morse, George W.: Supplier of breech-loading carbines to the Confederate military during the Civil War.

Morse, Henry: Active clockmaker in early 1800, Canton, Massachusetts.

Mortise joint (furniture): Fitting of a tongue-shaped tenon into slot-shaped hole in the board or timber of wooden furniture. Typically a signal of quality construction on early furniture.

Mosaic: A design of Italian origin incorporating glass, wood, or stone. A design or picture based on the inlaid arrangement of various pieces. Its uses have ranged from floors and walls to jewelry.

Mosaic blue (color): A medium blue, but darker than Copenhagen.

Mosaic Tile Company: Producers of quality art pottery and tiles from 1890s to 1960s in Zanesville, Ohio.

Moses and Sons: (see Glasgow Pottery)

Moses, Isaac: Doing business as a silversmith from 1780 to 1795 in Derby, Connecticut.

Moses, Jacob: Listed as a silversmith in 1830s, Birmingham, Alabama.

Moss green (color): According to Sears in that early twentieth century, a soft medium green.

Mother goose (color): Simply a medium tan according to the early Sears listings.

Motor Car Supply Co.: Early 1900s maker of items for the automobile including horns and bells. Located on Michigan Avenue in Chicago, Illinois.

Motor Corps of America: The volunteer organization of women serving as drivers of motor cars during W.W.I.

Mott, Jordan: Active in the silversmith trade 1790 to 1830 in New York City.

Moulton, Abel: Listed as a silversmith from 1815 to 1830 in Newburyport, Massachusetts.

Moulton, Enoch: An early 1800s silversmith located in Portland, Maine.

Moulton, Francis: A noted clockmaker in 1830s, Lowell, Massachusetts.

Mount and Robertson: Makers of office partitions, brokers' stock quotation boards, telegraph tables, book keepers' desks, and other office furniture during the 1890s. Located in New York City, New York.

Mourning picture: Usually a silk on satin embroidery or painting which depicted an urn, monument, or other stark object. Typically the object itself depicted bore the name of the departed. Most were framed and glass covered. Also called a memorial picture.

Mowry, J. D.: Contracted with the Federal government to supply 22,000 rifled muskets during the Civil War, located in Norwich, Connecticut.

Mrs. Beasley (doll): Remarkable character doll featured in a television show *Family Affair*. The doll was marketed in the late 1960s and early 1970s by Mattel. Mrs. Beasley, with a cotton body,

Mission style rocking arm chair designed by Gustav Stickley. (Skinner Inc.)

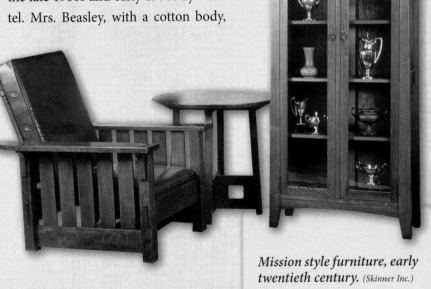
Mission style furniture, early twentieth century. (Skinner Inc.)

Murano vase by Benvenuto Barovier, ca. 1914. (Mint Museum)

Murano vases by Fulvio Vianconia, ca. 1950s. (Mint Museum)

spoke eight different phrases. Catalog price in 1973 was $7.99.

Mrs. Potts: Leading brand of sad irons sold in the 1902 Sears, Roebuck and Company catalog. They were sold in sets of three, one with rounded end and two with regular ends. Sets sold for 67¢. Sears offered them in polished finish and nickel finish with detachable handles.

Mrs. Winslow's Soothing Syrup: Nationally advertised product for children teething in the 1890s. Price was 25¢ a bottle.

Mueller Motor Carriage: Ambitious invention of Hieronymus Mueller in 1890s, Decatur, Illinois. Mueller designed several gasoline-powered vehicles using a series of gears and chains. The enterprising Mueller was killed when one of his experiments exploded in the early 1900s.

Muffin stand (furniture): An eighteenth century stand of English origin with a tier of round shelves to hold delicacies for serving with tea. Usually the muffin stand was equipped with a handle to allow carrying from one location to another. It had tripod feet for balanced sitting.

Muffle kiln: Special device used for low-temperature firing, helpful in fixing enamel colors and other tasks requiring less heat that the typical glass furnace.

Muir, William: Contracted with the Federal government to provide 30,000 rifled muskets during the Civil War, located in Windsor Locks, Connecticut.

Mulberry (color): Considered to be a reddish purple by Sears during the 1920s.

Mule spinner: Term for a late eighteenth century machine used for spinning fine thread into quality cotton. Englishman Samuel Crompton is credited with the invention which soon revolutionized the production of cotton spinning mills in that country.

Mulford, John: Doing business as a silversmith from 1835 to 1855 in Albany, New York.

Mulholland, James: Contracted with the Federal government to provide 5,500 rifled muskets during the Civil War, located in Reading, Pennsylvania.

Mullane, John: Produced six-pound rifled cannon for the Confederate cavalry. Located in Louisville, Kentucky.

Mulliken, Jonathan: Listed as an active clockmaker in 1770s, Newburyport, Massachusetts.

Mumford, Henry: Active silversmith in 1815, Providence, Rhode Island.

Muncie Clay Products: Art pottery operation in 1920s and 1930s, Muncie, Indiana.

Munger, A.: Doing business as a clockmaker in 1820s, Auburn, New York.

Munger, Asa: Listed as a silversmith from 1810 to 1820 in Herkimer, New York.

Munroe, Daniel: Operating as a clockmaker in early 1800, Concord, Massachusetts.

Munson, Amos: A Colonial era silversmith in 1770s, New Haven, Connecticut.

Munting (furniture): An early reference to the use of horizontal or vertical division bars for the framing of furniture, or of the same usage in doors or windows. Other spellings included muntin and mullion.

Murano (glass): A fine quality blown glass originating on the island of Murano near Italy. The beautiful and delicate work of the glassblowers there was the result of rigid recruitment of talented glassblowers and strict regulations of their labor. Considered one of the early glass centers of the world.

Murphy & Childs: Supplier of military uniform caps via Federal government contract during the Civil War. Located in New York City.

Murphy, James: Active silversmith located in 1815, Boston, Massachusetts.

Murray, John P.: Listed as a supplier of Mississippi rifles, muskets, 1855 carbines, and other armament to the Confederate military. Located in Columbus, Georgia.

Murray, Stevenson & Davis: Supplied artillery projectiles for the military, based in 1860s, Portsmouth, Ohio.

Muscogee Iron Works: Source of small arms and saddles for the Confederate military during the Civil War. Located in Columbus, Georgia.

Music Maker Man: Action toy made by Mattel in the early 1950s. Organ grinder moved his head as he turned a crank. Next, up jumps a bell-ringing monkey. About 11" tall.

Muslin (textile): Originally a reference to Moslem and fine gauze-like cotton fabric. Later it became a general reference to most any thin cotton cloth.

Mustache cup: Men's Victorian era drinking cup with a recessed level inside the cup. The design was used to protect the mustache from liquids. Typically such cups were gaily decorated on the outside.

Mutoscope Reel Co.: (see Arcade card)

Mutual Motors Co.: (see Marion-Handley)

Myers, John: A Colonial era silversmith doing business in 1780s and 1790s, Philadelphia, Pennsylvania.

Myers, Moses: Listed as an active clockmaker in 1840s, Poughkeepsie, New York.

Myers, S. A.: Listed as a supplier of military uniform buttons to Confederate troops during the Civil War, located in Richmond, Virginia.

Mygatt, Comfort: Doing business as a silversmith along with Ely Mygatt in late 1700s, Danbury, Connecticut.

Myrtle green (color): Basically a dark green according to Sears in 1927.

Nacre: Shiny iridescent material, mother-of-pearl.

Nadig Road Wagon: Gasoline-powered carriage built by Henry Nadig of Allentown, Pennsylvania. In 1891 the vehicle had a four-cycle engine weighing 300 pounds, and attained speeds up to 15 miles per hour.

Nagles, John: A noted silversmith working in 1750, Philadelphia, Pennsylvania.

Nailsea (glass): Reference to noted glass-producing area in eighteenth and nineteenth century, England. It featured exceptional bottle and plate glass. A distinctive latticinio type of glass was decorated with colored loops and threads. Resulting bands or stripes appeared in intense shades of pink, blue, red, and yellow. Nailsea also produced brightly colored hollow glass balls, sometimes know as witch balls, used in English homes to ward off evil witches or other unfriendly spirits.

Name dolls: Term for china head dolls manufactured in Germany starting in the late 1890s. Popular names for girls were embossed into the material and frequently painted gold. Among them Helen, Ethel, and Marie.

Nancy (glass): Highly regarded late nineteenth art glass factory in France. Most noted for distinguished cameo glass.

Nankeen (ceramic): Reference to late eighteenth century blue and white decorated ware produced in Asia and exported to Europe and America.

Naples yellow (color): A bright deep yellow in the 1920s catalogs.

Napoleon: (see Josephine bicycle)

Napoleon blue (color): According to early Sears entries, a very bright blue.

Thomas Nast full-figured Santa with children drawn in the 1880s.

Thomas Nast drawing of Santa at the piano, late nineteenth century.

Napoleon gun: A long range field gun used by both sides during the Civil War. Originally developed in France during the 1850s for Emperor Napoleon III.

Napp, August: German-born cabinetmaker working in 1850s, Noble County, Indiana.

Nappy: An early term for an uncovered serving dish, usually small and oval or rectangular in shape.

Nardin, Frederick: Native of France who practiced the cabinetmaking trade in 1850s, New Albany, Indiana.

Nase, John: Listed as a potter working in redware in 1830s and 1840s, Montgomery County, Pennsylvania.

Nash, John: Colonial era clockmaker in 1790s, Charleston, South Carolina.

Nast, Thomas: Famous newspaper cartoonist, book illustrator, and artist of the nineteenth century. Best known for his renderings of Santa Claus and Christmas in *Harper's Weekly*.

National blue (color): Presented simply as a dark blue.

National Call: Brand of footed alarm clock sold by Sears and Roebuck in the 1920s. Most were billed as automatic eight-day alarm clocks and retailed from $2.75 to $3.75.

National Flag Depot: Maker of flags, colors, and army unit flags in 1860s, New York City.

National Mask & Puppet: (see Cutie Pie)

National Motor Vehicles: Maker of gasoline powered and electric powered automobiles in early 1900s, Indianapolis, Indiana. A 1904 advertisement promised, "They go the route."

National red (color): In the 1927s Sears listing, a very bright red color.

National safe bank: A safe-like model of cast iron made by Arcade Manufacturing during the 1920s. Marked National Safe on the front, it had a combination lock and nickel plating.

Natural (color): Given a single word definition in the 1920s era, flesh.

Natural gray (color): Considered a dark cream with a gray cast.

Natural linen (color): Listed as tan, or the color of undyed linen.

Natural straw (color): Tan or the color of natural straw according to Sears.

Natural tan (color): Considered a light tan by Sears during the 1920s.

Natural tint (color): Somewhere halfway between black and white according to Sears.

Navajo gray (color): A light gray with Indian designs according to the catalogs.

Navy blue (color): Basically a dark blue as noted by Sears in 1927.

Neal, Daniel: Listed as an active clockmaker in 1820s, Philadelphia, Pennsylvania.

Neal, Israel: Chair maker from Ohio who apprenticed in Indiana and eventually operated the Neal and Burch cabinetmaking business in 1850s, Logansport, Indiana.

Neall, Daniel: Doing business as a silversmith in 1830s, Milford, Delaware.

Necking: In early American furniture any small band or molding near the top of a column, pillar, or shaft.

Needlepoint (textile): Term for fine embroidery done with silk or wool thread using a slanting diagonal stitch. Usually the stitches were even and across counted thread. More specifically petit point or gross point depending on the size of stitches.

Neihard, Moses: Born in Pennsylvania and mastered the cabinetmaking trade in Indianapolis. Listed as working in 1850s, Clinton County, Indiana.

Neiser, Augustine: A Colonial period

clockmaker active in 1770s, Germantown, Pennsylvania.

Nell rose (color): Not a proper name but a medium rose color instead.

Nelson, John: Occupied as a silversmith in 1780s, Portsmouth, New Hampshire.

Neo-classic (furniture): Term for eighteenth and early nineteenth century furniture designed to celebrate a revival of ancient classical designs. Additionally some Empire period furniture was called neo-classical.

Nesting tables (furniture): Used to describe a series of three or more tables in progressively smaller sizes. Such tables then could be placed beneath one another thus occupying just a single space.

Nettleton, W. K.: An active clockmaker in 1830s, Rochester, New York.

Neucomb, John T.: Originally from the District of Columbia, was active in the cabinetmaking trade in 1850s, Indianapolis, Indiana.

Nevill, Richard: Listed as a silversmith in 1765, Boston, Massachusetts.

New Albany Glass Works: Glassworks located in 1869, New Albany, Indiana. Firm was founded by Captain J. B. Ford (also of Louisville). After 1872 it was operated by W. C. DePauw.

New blue: During the 1920s it was considered a rich medium blue.

Newberry, Edwin: A noted silversmith operating in 1830s, Brooklyn, New York.

Newby, Thomas: Active cabinetmaker in 1850s, Washington County, Indiana.

New Canton Works: (see Bow china)

New Castle Pottery Company: Pottery operation based in late nineteenth century, New Castle, Pennsylvania.

Newcomb, Horace: Doing business as a silversmith in 1830s and 1840s, Watertown, New York.

Newcomb Pottery: Highly regarded art pottery operation doing business from 1890s to the 1950s in New Orleans, Louisiana.

Newel: Early term for the upright post at the foot of the staircase. It was used for the secondary upright post at the landing on the stairs.

Newell cloth doll: Cloth dolls with large printed features were patented and sold by E. G. Newell in early 1900, Glen Ridge, New Jersey. One popular type was Sweet Marie.

New England chest: (see Connecticut chest)

New England Company: A producer of gunpowder during the Civil War for Federal forces, located in Ware, Massachusetts.

New Haven Clock Company: Significant clock producing operation in 1850s, New Haven, Connecticut.

New, Heckman: Cabinetmaker who specialized in bureaus and tables in 1850s, Jennings County, Indiana.

Newkirk, Benjamin: An 1850s cabinetmaker in Lawrence County, Indiana. Eventually joined by a son, Benjamin Newkirk Jr.

Newland, James: Pennsylvania-born cabinetmaker who apprenticed in Kentucky and was working in 1820s Fayette County, Indiana.

Newly Wed Kid: (see Art Fabric Mills)

Newman, Timothy: Active silversmith in Groton, Massachusetts.

New Milford Pottery Company: Doing business in 1880s, New Milford, Connecticut.

New Queen: A leading brand of sewing machine sold in 1902 by Sears, Roebuck and Company. Price for the five-drawer drop head machine was $10.45.

New York City Pottery: Workplace

A 1860s style Santa drawn by Thomas Nast.

Child in top hat was 1880s Harper's Weekly *sketch by Thomas Nast.*

Northern Automobiles advertisement, early 1900s.

Wallace Nutting picture entitled The Guardian Mother.

(*Michael Ivankovich Antiques*)

producing pottery in 1850s, New York City, New York.

NFL Electric Football: Moving players on a metal football field complete with timer and speed control. Sold in floor model and table model sizes in the 1970s. Montgomery Ward catalog customers could order different professional football teams depending upon which city — Albany to St. Paul — the order was sent.

Niche: Term once used in cabinetmaking used to describe a depression or recess in a piece or in a wall to receive a bust, statuette, or other ornament.

Nicholette, Marie: Listed as a clockmaker along with Joseph Nicholette in 1790s, Philadelphia, Pennsylvania.

Nichols & Alford: Pottery making operation started in 1854, Burlington, Vermont.

Nichols, Basset: Identified as an active silversmith in 1815, Providence, Rhode Island.

Nichols, E. B.: Maker of cannon for Texas troops during the Civil War era. Located in Galveston, Texas.

Nickel gray (color): Noted by Sears as a medium light shade of gray.

Nickel plating: Term for coating cast iron or steel objects with molten nickel to prevent rusting and provide a shiny surface.

Niddy noddy: Oddly shaped wooden device for the winding of yarn into skeins as it was taken off of the spinning wheel.

Niello: Term for incised metal designs filled with a black metallic alloy.

Nile green (color): According to the Sears listings, just a light green.

Niloak Pottery: Producers of exceptional art pottery from 1900s to 1940s in Benton, Arkansas.

Nimbus: Term for a circle or disc in early illustrations or paintings of saints or sovereigns to indicate a radiant light. For a living person, a square nimbus was sometimes used for glorification.

Nimrod: Biblical term for mighty hunter. Applied in Colonial days to one who excelled at hunting, including exceptional ability with a gun upon encountering wild animals. Later was more generally used to describe an active and adventurous person.

Nixon, Joshua: Cabinetmaker born in Ohio and working in 1850s, Vermillion County, Indiana.

Noble Brothers: Listed as makers of cannon for the Confederate military during the Civil War. Located in Rome, Georgia.

Noble, Henry Clay: Undertaker and cabinetmaker working in 1850s, Centerville, Indiana. Later lived in Indianapolis, Indiana.

Noble, Joseph: Doing business in 1825 as a silversmith in Portland, Maine.

Noggin: Colonial term for a small cup or mug usually made of pewter or wood. Used for measurement in taverns serving ale. The noggin held a British gill or about four fluid ounces.

Noid doll: (see Domino's Pizza)

Non-flint (glass): Term used to describe glass which did not contain lead. Usually meaning glass produced prior to the early 1860s.

Nordyke and Marmon Co.: (see Marmon car)

Norris and Clement: Suppliers of 3,000 rifled muskets in 1863 to the State of Massachusetts, located in Springfield, Massachusetts.

Norris, Westley: Cabinetmaker born in Ohio and doing business in 1850s, Howard County, Indiana.

Northern Manufacturing Co.: Maker of Northern Automobiles including the $750 Northern Runabout and the $1,500 Northern Touring Car in 1904. Firm was located in Detroit, Michigan.

Northern Runabout: (see Northern Manufacturing Co.)

North, Norris: A noted clockmaker doing business in 1820s, Wolcottville, Connecticut.

North Star Stoneware: Pottery company doing business in 1890s, Red Wing, Minnesota.

Northwestern Products: (see Electric Push-M-Up)

Norton, Andrew: In business as a silversmith in early 1800s, Goshen, Connecticut.

Norton, Charles P. and Co.: Provided a type of "Army watch" under Federal contract during the Civil War. Brands included European Timekeeper, American Lever, and an English Duplex stop watch. The importing firm was located in New York City.

Norton Pottery: Long-lasting redware pottery operation from 1790s to 1890s in Bennington, Vermont.

Norton, Samuel: Listed as an active silversmith in 1795, Hingham, Massachusetts.

Norton, Thomas: Pennsylvania-born cabinetmaker working in the trade in 1850s, Morgan County, Indiana.

Norwich Arms Co.: A supplier of 25,000 rifled muskets to the U.S. Army during the Civil War, located in Norwich, Connecticut.

Norwich Pottery Works: Producers of stoneware pottery in 1880s and 1890s, Norwich, Connecticut.

Norwood, Richard: Colonial era silversmith active in 1775, New York City.

Noteman, W. W.: Listed as a cabinetmaker doing business in 1850s, Noble County, Indiana.

Noyer (wood): French term for the use of walnut.

Noyes, Samuel: Doing business as a silversmith in early 1700s, Boston, Massachusetts.

Nude (color): A light tan, considered a shade darker than champagne.

Nujol: Nationally advertised product for constipation on the market early in the twentieth century. Marketed by Standard Oil Company.

Nulling (furniture): Reference to a carving decoration on the edge of furniture said to resemble clenched knuckles. Type of trim dates back centuries and originally was applied to border decoration on silver bowls and plates.

Nuremberg ware: Reference to wooden toys made in homes or small factories in the vicinity of Nuremberg, Germany. Applied to certain toys crafted as late as the early twentieth century.

Nut brown (color: Considered to be a light golden brown.

Nutmeg box (silver): Usually a small box made of silver and used in early America to carry whole nutmegs. A grater inside the box allowed for grating the nuts into a powder like substance for cooking or seasoning.

Nutria tan (color): The 1927 Sears catalog classified it was a medium tan.

Nutter, John: Listed as an active clockmaker in 1830s, Mt. Vernon, New Hampshire.

Nutting, Wallace: Exceptional photographer of the early twentieth century. Also noted as antiquarian and author. Nutting's works included the *Windsor Handbook* and *Furniture of the Pilgrim Century.*

Oak commode with three drawers, cabinet door. (*Harris Auction Center*)

Golden oak washstand with marble top. (*Harris Auction Center*)

161

Oak washstand. *(Harris Auction Center)*

N.Y. Condensed Milk Co.: Contracted to supply rations to Federal troops during the Civil War, located in New York City.

Nys, Johannis: An aspiring silversmith in 1720s, Philadelphia, Pennsylvania.

Oak brown (color): A medium golden brown in the 1920s Sears catalogs.

Oakes, Frederick: Silversmith doing business from 1815 to 1825 in Hartford, Connecticut.

Oakley, James: Formerly from North Carolina, active cabinetmaker in 1850s, Huntington County, Indiana.

Oakwood brown (color): Sears considered it to be a medium brown in the 1920s.

Oats, Mitchell: Cabinetmaker born in Ohio and working in his shop in 1850s, Huntington County, Indiana.

Ober, Henry: Noted clockmaker active in 1820s, Elizabethtown, Pennsylvania.

Oberhousen, Nicholas: German-born cabinetmaker doing business in 1850s, Rockport, Indiana.

Obsidian (glass): Volcanic glass found in areas of volcanic activity including Yellowstone National Park in America. Found in assorted colors including red, green, blue, brown, and black. Some such glass was cut into small pieces and polished as gemstones for jewelry.

Occasional table (furniture): A reference to a small multi-purpose table which could be used in many household settings. Prior to the nineteenth century they may have been called whatnot tables.

Ocher: (see Colors, colonial interior)

Odell, Lawrence: Active silversmith listed in 1815, New York City.

Off-hand glass: (see End of day glass)

Ogden, Isaac: Cabinetmaker born in Ohio. Operated a two person shop in 1850s, Rush County, Indiana.

Ogee foot (furniture): A bracket type of foot once used on English and American furniture including bureaus and desk. It was S-shaped in design providing a double curve.

Ogilvie, John: Listed in the silversmith trade around 1760 in New York City.

Ogive: A curving and shallow S-shaped design, usually tapering at the end.

Ogren automobile: Made by the Ogren Motor Car Company in Milwaukee, Wisconsin. In 1922 the company advertised seven different Ogren vehicles including a $5,500 seven passenger sedan.

O'Hara Glass Works: Specializing in pressed glass, the firm was located in Pittsburgh, Pennsylvania. In 1867 their pressed glassware was on exhibit at the Paris Exposition.

Ohio China Company: A maker of pottery products starting in late 1890s, East Palestine, Ohio.

Ohio-type (glass): Reference to a type of Stiegel glass produced in early nineteenth century, Ohio rather than its native Pennsylvania. Historians suggest Stiegel workers may have carried specific glassmaking techniques to Ohio factories.

Ohr, George: Noted art pottery producer from 1880s to early 1900s in Biloxi, Mississippi.

Old burgundy (color): A very dark wine color according to Sears in 1927.

Old Favorite: Brand name of cigars sold in a tin pail during the 1920s. The 14 ounce tin sold for 75¢ via Sears, Roebuck and Company.

Old gold: As the name implies, a dull gold color.

Old ivory (color): The Sears catalog suggested it was simply a yellow cream.

Old rose (color): Said by Sears to be a soft rose with a grayish cast.

Olds, Joshua: Millwright and cabinet-maker in 1840s, Vigo County, Indiana.

Olds Motor Works: Maker of the Oldsmobile in early 1900s, America. Models included touring, light delivery, and heavy delivery. Based in Detroit, Michigan.

Olerick, Frederick: Pennsylvania born cabinetmaker practicing the trade in 1850s, Lafayette, Indiana.

Oliphant, Joseph: Chair maker born in Ohio and working in 1850s, Cass County, Indiana.

Oliphant, Nuttar: Listed as a chair maker in 1850s, Cass County, Indiana.

Olive (color): Simply a dull brown green in the 1920s listings.

Olive drab (color): A regular U.S. Army olive drab shade according to Sears.

Olive gray (color): A dark gray with a green cast.

Olive green (color): A medium green but with a yellow tint.

Oliver, Andrew: Noted silversmith active in 1805, Philadelphia, Pennsylvania.

Oliver, John: A Colonial era clockmaker in 1780s, Charleston, South Carolina.

Oliver, Peter: Listed as a silversmith in early 1800s, Philadelphia, Pennsylvania.

Oliver plow (toy): A "sturdy and realistic" toy model of the Oliver Plow was produced by Arcade Manufacturing in 1927. It was made of cast iron with nickel plated wheels and aluminum plow shares.

Oliver, Welden: Doing business as a clockmaker in 1820s, Bristol, Connecticut.

Olive tan (color): Considered by Sears in the 1920s to be a greenish tan.

Olive (wood): A hard wood with a close grain used mainly for inlays and veneers. Imported from the Mediterranean region, it offered a contrast of light and dark markings while taking a high polish.

Olmstead, Allen: (see Allen's Foot Ease)

Olmstead, Nathaniel: Colonial era silversmith in early 1800s, Farmington, Connecticut. Later doing business as Nathaniel Olmstead and Son.

Olympic Flyer: Toy wagon offered by Sears, Roebuck and Company in 1935. Spoke wheel and disc wheel models were offered.

Oneida Glass: The Oneida Glass and Iron Manufacturing Company began operations in 1809 at Taberg in Oneida County, New York.

Onion pattern: (see Zwiebelmuster ceramics)

Onondaga Pottery Co.: Producers of porcelain and whiteware starting in 1870s Syracuse, New York. Also doing business as Syracuse China Company.

Opal (color): Simply a white color with a reddish cast.

Opalescent (glass): Term for the particular formula which causes heated glass to become non-transparent. The effect is a milky opal-like hue.

Opaque (glass): A glass which generally does not transmit light. Density can vary depending upon formulas applied.

Open back (furniture): Term for chair back with an non-upholstered opening between the rails and the side splats. Also a reference to an eighteenth century decorative open frame on a chair back.

Open-closed mouth (doll): Seeming contradictory reference to a doll with separated lips but no actual opening cut into the doll's mouth. Frequently molded teeth and tongue were also present.

Opp, Reuben: Cabinetmaker born in Pennsylvania, and working in a shop in 1850s, Carroll County, Indiana.

Oak side by side with lower drawer and cupboard.

George Ohr double-handled vase, late nineteenth century. (Skinner Inc.)

George Ohr pottery jug. (Skinner Inc.)

Orange Powder Company: Supplier of gun powder during the Civil War for Federal troops, located in Newburgh, New York.

Orchid (color): Noted by Sears as a delicate light lavender.

Orcutt & Company: Redware and stoneware pottery operation headed by Stephen Orcutt in early 1800s, Whately, Massachusetts.

Oriental Powder Co.: Civil War supplier of gunpowder to the U.S. Army, located in South Windham, Maine.

Orient Buckboard: (See Waltham Manufacturing Company)

Original stencil (furniture): Relating to the design and paint on early chairs and rockers which had been applied by the original artist. Examples included Boston rockers, Hitchcock chairs, and Windsor chairs. The nineteenth century term also applied to tole tin trays which also had been hand painted by the use of a stencil.

Ormolu (furniture): A furniture decorating practice which originated in eighteenth century France. Mounts were cast in bronze or brass and then gilded to appear as gold. The applied decoration was popular in England and some parts of America in the late eighteenth and early nineteenth century. Mirror frames, clock cases, and candelabra were also given ormolu decoration.

Orrery: Clock-like device designed to reflect the movement of planets, and in some cases the phases of the moon. A series of rotating wheels, moving balls, and clock parts provided the motion. The original invention was credited to the Earl of Orrery in England. Many similar devices were later constructed in nineteenth century America.

Osborn, Alfred: Turner and cabinetmaker born in Ohio and working in 1850s, LaPorte, Indiana.

Osborn, William: An active silversmith in 1850s, Providence, Rhode Island.

Osgood, John: A Colonial era silversmith operating in 1790s, Boston, Massachusetts.

Osman, Ira: Chair maker born in New York and working in the trade in 1850s, Bartholomew County, Indiana.

Otis, Jonathan: Listed as active in the silversmith trade in 1750s, Newport, Rhode Island.

Ott & Brewer: Rockingham and porcelain potters doing business in late nineteenth century, Trenton, New Jersey.

Ott, Daniel: Noted silversmith in 1790s, New York City.

Otter, Thomas: Chair maker born in New York and doing business in 1850s, Fayette County, Indiana.

Ott, George: Listed in the silversmith trade in 1805, Norfolk, Virginia.

Ott, John: First of a prominent family of cabinetmakers doing business in nineteenth century, Indianapolis, Indiana. Succeeded in business by son Lewis W. Ott in the 1880s. Eventually the firm became L.W. Ott Manufacturing Company. In 1890 the firm was known as the Ott Lounge Company and located in Chicago, Illinois.

Ottman Bros. & Company: Stoneware pottery in operation during the 1870s and 1880s in Fort Edward, New York.

Ottoman (furniture): Basically an upholstered seat or bench without arms or a back. Originally an item of furniture in eighteenth century Turkey, but later popular in the remainder of Europe and America.

Ouija: Popular early twentieth century board game employing the alphabet and other characters to answer questions. Term was a combination of the French and German words for yes.

Outcault, R. F.: (see Buster Brown)

Oval back (furniture): A reference to the eighteenth century chair designs of George Hepplewhite, which in turn imitated French chairs known as the medallion.

Over glaze (ceramic): Term for the decoration applied over the glazed surface of a ceramic piece.

Over-glaze mark: Denotes the mark applied to pottery or other ceramic ware after the piece has been first glazed in the oven. Often this has been an effort to provide a mark which was not original and therefore not authentic.

Overin, Richard: As of early 1700, a silversmith in New York City.

Overland automobile: Numerous models of the Overland were manufactured in the early 1900s by the Willys-Overland Company in Toledo, Ohio. The five-passenger Overland Model 41 sold for $1,400 in 1910.

Overlay glass: Intricate process initially involving adding contrasting colors to clear glass. Ultimately it included the process of laminating both colored glass and lead to clear glass in order to achieve a certain art glass. Glass factories of the latter nineteenth century often used three pieces of fused glass and obtained a pattern by cutting through the first two outer layers. A very detailed and delicate procedure.

Overlay veneer: Early furniture application in which the cabinetmaker used the direct upper surface of the furniture. Other veneers were typically placed within text of the furniture's surface.

Overman, Thomas: North Carolina-born cabinetmaker working in 1850s, Bartholomew County, Indiana.

Overstuffed (furniture): In early furniture, a reference to a seating piece in which the upholstering completely engulfs the wood frame designed to carry it.

Ovolo (furniture): Cabinetmaking reference to a rounded, convex molding.

Owen, John: Doing business from 1805 to 1830 as a silversmith in Philadelphia, Pennsylvania.

Owens, J. B.: Founder of the Owens Pottery Company which began production in late nineteenth century, Zanesville, Ohio.

Owens Pottery Company: Distinguished art pottery establishment headed by J. B. Owens in 1890s and early 1900s, Zanesville, Ohio.

Owens, Thomas: Active cabinetmaker in 1850s, Montgomery County, Indiana. Born in Kentucky in 1810.

Oxbow chest: (see Yoke-front chest)

Oxford gray (color): A dark gray in the 1920s catalogs listings.

Ox head: (see Bucranium)

Oxidizing: The result of chemical treatment applied to metalwork.

Oyster, Daniel: Noted clock designer who specialized in tall case clocks in late eighteenth and early nineteenth century Pennsylvania.

Oystering (furniture): Term in early cabinetmaking involving a veneer with a cross-sectional grain. Two or more concentric rings, or cylinders with the same center, provided oyster shell-like markings.

Oyster white (color): Billed in Sears as a basic white with a cream cast.

Pachinko: Miniature pinball machine named for arcades of Tokyo. Sold by Montgomery Ward in 1973 for $39.95.

Pacific Clay Company: Noted yellow ware pottery operation in 1890s and early 1900s, Riverside, California.

George Ohr small pottery vase. (Skinner Inc.)

Parian shoulder-head doll, ca. 1870s. (Skinner Inc.)

German Parian doll, ca. 1870s. (Skinner Inc.)

Pacific Pottery Co.: Stoneware pottery establishment doing business during the first half of the twentieth century in Portland, Oregon.

Packard, Joseph: Doing business as a clockmaker in 1815, Rochester, New York.

Pad foot (furniture): Basically a somewhat flat foot used on the cabriole leg of early eighteenth century American and European furniture. The leg curved out at the knee and inward toward the foot. The foot was named for its resemblance to a disk or pad. It was sometimes called a club foot.

Paersch, Adalbert: Credited with the invention of a breech-loading musket with a range of 1,200 yards during the Civil War. Located in New Orleans, Louisiana.

Page, Benjamin: (see Bakewell, Pears and Co.)

Pagoda: Tower-like structure with upswept roofs which decrease in size as they are added to the previous one. Chinese origins.

Painted furniture: Early nineteenth century revival of decorative painting of fashionable furniture as practiced by Lambert Hitchcock and others. Painted furniture had been in vogue from time to time since ancient Egypt.

Painter, John: Noted silversmith in 1735, Philadelphia, Pennsylvania.

Pairpoint glass: Acclaimed product of the Pairpoint Glass Company located in nineteenth century, New Bedford, Massachusetts. Pairpoint glass was used to craft exceptional paperweights and both clear and colored blown items. A special effect was the tear drop or bubble which appeared on knobs and stems of some glass items.

Paisley (textile): Term for a fabric design in the original shawl pattern first crafted in Paisley, Scotland.

Palethorp, Robert Jr.: Listed as active in pewter work in early nineteenth century, Philadelphia, Pennsylvania.

Palisander (furniture): Term once used to describe an early classification of heavy French furniture. Specifically a French word for a type of rosewood.

Palmer and Bacheldor: Listed as a supplier of swords and sabers during the Civil War to Federal forces. Located in Boston, Massachusetts.

Palmer and Haskell: Supplier of horse harnesses to the U.S. government in 1861, based in St. Louis, Missouri.

Palmer, James: Listed as a silversmith in 1815, New York City.

Palmer, John: Occupied as a clockmaker in early 1800, Philadelphia, Pennsylvania.

Palmer-Singer Manufacturing Co.: Produced the racing body Six-Sixty automobile in 1910 for $3,500. The Six-Sixty Gunboat body automobile was priced at $3,900.

Palmette (furniture): Early use in furniture decoration of a design in the form of a palm leaf.

Palmetto green (color): A soft shade of medium grayish green.

Pan-American automobile: Billed as the "American Beauty Car" in 1917, the Pan American was produced by the Pan-American Motors Corporation of Chicago, Illinois. The factory was located in Decatur, Illinois.

Pancho: (see Cisco Kid)

Pancoast, Samuel: Active as a silversmith in 1785, Philadelphia, Pennsylvania.

Panel-back chair (furniture): A term for an early American chair back, also known as a Wainscot chair.

Pansy (color): Considered in the 1920s to be the color of a pansy blossom, a deep purple.

Pantine (doll): An eighteenth century cardboard doll figure popular in France. The images represented famous men and women but entertained children much like paper dolls of later generations.

Papa Biedermeir: (see Biedermeir)

Papboat: Small, shallow dish with a spout for pouring liquids. Ceramic or silver, the dish was used for feeding infants and invalids. It was accompanied by small papboat spoons also used for feeding. Later the term was simply defined as a kind of sauce dish.

Paperweight eyes (doll): Basically doll eyes given a heavy layer of clear glass over a colored base. Overall effect was quite lifelike.

Papier-mâché: Originally a French term for a mixture of paper, glue, resin, and fine sand. It was compressed when wet and as it dried it form a hard surface. At times various lacquering, painting, enameling, and inlaying were added. The mixture was used for containers, furniture, and ultimately a great number of dolls during the nineteenth century.

Parachute doll: Early in the 1940s aviatrix Elvy Kalep produced Pat and Patty Parachute dolls in Jersey City, New Jersey.

Paraffin lamp: (see Vestal lamp)

Paravent: French term for a folding screen.

Parcel-gilding (furniture): A late seventeenth century and early eighteenth century process involving applying gilt to the high parts of a carved design on fine furniture. The remainder of the surface was simply polished. Also see colors.

Parchment: Paper-like material used for a writing surface. It was typically the treated and processed skin of various animals. Even as early as the nineteenth century there were attempts to imitate this original material with forms of ordinary paper.

Parchment (color): In the 1927 Sears listing, a deep cream color.

Parchment panel (furniture): Term also used to describe an early linen-fold panel.

Parian doll: Named for the very fine unglazed clay which first appeared white like Parian marble. Originally crafted in Germany, during the latter nineteenth century, some had blown glass eyes and some were simply painted on the ware.

Parian ware (ceramic): Basically a hard-paste porcelain generally left unglazed. Its origin is credited to Thomas Minton in England. In America the Bennington pottery in Vermont was famous for such ware. It was also referred to as parian marble.

Parker Alarm Clock: Sold in the Sears retail catalog of 1902 at a price of $1.20. Item made by the Parker Clock Company of Meriden, Connecticut.

Parker Brothers (toys): Launched in 1880s, Salem, Massachusetts, prolific maker of children's games including Monopoly. Masterful in the twentieth century for production of hundreds of colorful and educational board games.

Parker, Isaac: A Colonial silver-smith working in 1780s, Deerfield, Massachusetts.

Parker, Snow and Co.: Under contract with the Federal government during the Civil War to provide 15,000 rifled muskets, located in Meriden, Connecticut.

Parke, Solomon: Doing business as Solomon Parke and Company, clockmakers, in 1800, Philadelphia, Pennsylvania.

The Game of Jack Straws from Parker Brothers, 1900s.

Camelot game from Parker Brothers, 1930s.

Parlor lamp with hunting dog scenes. (Harris Auction Center)

Parlor lamp with painted scene of monks. (Harris Auction Center)

Parker, Wilder & Co.: Supplier of military blankets to Federal troops during the Civil War, based in New York City.

Parkman, Charles: Listed as active in the silversmith trade in 1790s, Boston, Massachusetts.

Park, Seth: Colonial era clockmaker in 1790s, Park Town, Pennsylvania.

Parks, John: Colonial era silversmith doing business in 1790s, New York City.

Parlor lamp: Very decorative kerosene lamp of the latter nineteenth century. Typically with artfully painted globes atop one another. Sometimes called Gone with the Wind lamps but such lamps were not in use during the Civil War era of the novel.

Parmalee, Ebenezer: Active as a clockmaker in 1730s, Guilford, Connecticut.

Parmenter, Flavel: Supplier of a bullet-making machine to Federal troops in the 1860s, based in Troy, New York.

Parquetry: Striking application of wood flooring in geometric patterns to form a mosaic. Typically contrasting light and dark woods were used put emphasis on the overall design.

Parrish, James: Supplier of "French flannel Army shirts" during the Civil War era. Located in New York City.

Parrott gun: Power cannon weapon used by both sides during the Civil War. Credited to inventor Robert Parker Parrott, superintendent of the West Point Foundry.

Parrott, Robert Parker: (see Parrott gun)

Parry, John J.: Listed as a clockmaker doing business in 1800, Philadelphia, Pennsylvania.

Parry, Martin: Active silversmith in 1780s, Kittery, Maine.

Parsons, Silas: A noted clockmaker in 1750s, Bristol, Connecticut.

Parsons, William: Listed as a silversmith in 1780s, Boston, Massachusetts.

Partner's desk (furniture): Basically an eighteenth century desk with a wide pedestal and drawers along both sides thus providing a workspace and drawers for two people.

Partridge, Jorace: Doing business as a clockmaker in 1870s, Bristol, Connecticut.

Patapsco Glass Works: (see Baltimore Glass Works)

Patchwork quilt: The use of small pieces of fabric to form a fancy pattern overall as a handmade quilt. Typically light and dark material or patches were used enhance the overall design.

Paten: Small serving dish of silver or pewter used for bread during religious ceremonies. Most round plate-like pieces were engraved, but some were plain.

Patera (furniture): Round or oval medallion design often making use of flower petals or leaves. During the eighteenth and early nineteenth centuries it was carved, painted, or inlaid on neo-classical furniture. It was also used on wall decorations and mirrors.

Pate-sur-pate (ceramic): French term for the slip process of decoration on porcelain. While the process had origins in China, it was perfected on a large scale a the Sevres factory in France. Basically the mid-nineteenth century technique involved decoration through various succeeding coats applied to the contrasting body. The result was then carved to create a low-relief image.

Patience (game): A solitaire-type of card game popular in the Victorian parlor of the nineteenth century.

Patina: Aging surface of metal objects, usually adding to the color and texture to appearance.

Pattern glass: Very popular glass starting with the first half of the nineteenth century. A pressing machine afforded a wide variety of colors and patterns. Among the patterns were animals, flowers, fruits, and geometric designs. Production of pattern glass was extensive in the United States from the 1870s well into the early 1900s.

Patterson, George: Engaged as a silversmith in 1830s, New York City.

Patton, Abraham: Listed as a clockmaker in early 1800s, Philadelphia, Pennsylvania.

Patton, Thomas: Noted silversmith in 1825, Philadelphia, Pennsylvania.

Patty Comfort (doll): A series of cloth muslin dolls were produced with rubber hot water bottles inside. A celluloid head served to cork the water contents. Patty Comfort, Patty Delight, and Kitty Comfort were patented in the early 1900s by Elizabeth Hinchs of Andover, Massachusetts.

Paule and Walton: Civil War era supplier of military blankets to Federal troops, based in St. Charles, Missouri.

Pauline Pottery Company: A maker of pottery and related ware established in 1880s, Edgerton, Wisconsin.

Payne, Lawrence: Colonial period clockmaker in 1750s, New York City.

Paynes' gray (color): A medium gray tinged with blue in the 1920s era.

Peabody, Henry O.: Listed as a supplier of .52 caliber carbines in the 1860s, located in Boston, Massachusetts.

Peabody, Hiram: Listed as a supplier of knives to the Confederate military during the Civil War. Located in Richmond, Virginia.

Peachblow (glass): Highly noted art glass first produced in the 1880s, known for its brilliant tones of deep rose, pink, yellow, and white. It was crafted in exceptional colors at Hobbs Brockunier Company at Wheeling, West Virginia. Other examples were produced at the New England Glass Company and the Mount Washington Glass Works. Shadings and hues varied at each location.

Peach (color): According to Sears, as the name implies a light yellowish pink.

Peachy (doll): Ventriloquist doll with four puppets from Mattel. The 18" doll sold in the early 1970s for $11.99.

Peacock blue (color): Termed a medium blue with a greenish cast during the 1920s.

Peacock motif: Reference to peacock-like or peacock feathered design favored by Tiffany and other Art Nouveau artists.

Pea green (color): Basically a pale grayish green with a yellow cast.

Pear blush (color): In the Sears lexicon a shade darker than flesh.

Pearce, William: Doing business as a silversmith in 1820s, Norfolk, Virginia.

Pearl gray (color): Considered merely a light gray in the Sears catalog.

Pearse, Robert: Pewter artisan of note active in 1790s, New York City.

Pearson, John: Active silversmith in 1790s, New York City.

Pear's Soap: Victorian era toilet soap which was one of the first to be nationally advertised. First sold in jars, later in the nineteenth century it was sold packaged as a soft soap bar. Its advertising extended from magazines to trade cards and often featured smiling children although it was marketed to women.

Pear (wood): Wood noted for its fine grain. Much of the pearwood had a tinge of reddish color, however it varied by region and could have distinctive yellow hue. It was used in some furniture making, but most often as an inlay in selected pieces or veneer.

Painted roses theme on parlor lamp. (Harris Auction Center)

Electrified parlor lamp for modern usage. (Harris Auction Center)

Pewter quart mug by Jacob Whitmore, ca. 1760s. (Skinner Inc.)

expensive but popular in Colonial days for mugs, basins, tankards, and other tableware as an improvement over wooden ware.

Pewtress & Company: Stoneware pottery under the direction of S. L. Pewtress in 1870s and 1880s, New Haven, Connecticut.

Phelps, Charles: Listed as a noted silversmith in 1825, Bainbridge, New York.

Philadelphia Chippendale: Perhaps the ultimate in early American furniture crafted in the style of British designer Thomas Chippendale. Cabinetmakers in this most prosperous Colonial city displayed a middle eighteenth century flare for heavily carved flowing pieces from chests to lowboys. Typically of mahogany or walnut the ornate furniture sold briskly in the middle 1700s.

Philadelphia City Pottery: A pottery operation headed by J. E. Jeffords in 1860s, Philadelphia, Pennsylvania.

Philadelphia Earthenwares: (see Campbell Pottery)

Philip, Louis and Co.: Noted maker of "National Battle Pins" for Federal army and navy forces during the Civil War, based in New York City.

Phillips, Andrew J.: Provider of musical instruments, plates, and belts to Federal army forces during the Civil War, located in New York City. Also spelled Philips.

Philips, James: Operating as a silversmith in 1830s, Cleveland, Ohio.

Phoenix Ironworks: Provided cannons for the Confederate Navy during the Civil War. Located in New Orleans, Louisiana.

Phoenixville Pottery Company: Well regarded Rockingham and yellow ware pottery active during the latter nineteenth century in Phoenixville, Pennsylvania.

Phyfe, Duncan: One of the most noted furniture designers and furniture makers of the very late eighteenth and early nineteenth centuries. A trademark of his New York City operation was often tables with lyre bases or chairs with lyre backs. However his flare for curves, carvings, and composition were legendary. Phyfe remained active into the 1840s, and lived for another decade.

Phyfe, William: Listed as active in the silversmith trade in 1830s, Boston, Massachusetts.

Piano lamp: Basically a floor lamp that could be adjusted for reading of piano music sheets.

Piano stool (furniture): Single seat provided with a screw pivot that could be spun to various heights. Typically round, but also constructed in square and rectangular styles.

Picture clock: Starting around the middle of the eighteenth century these were designs which included the picture of a tower or church containing an actual working clock. Made in Europe into the twentieth century.

Pieced shawl: (see India shawl)

Piecrust edge (furniture): Decorative piecrust-like edge applied to early tea and other tilt-top tables and sometimes

Duncan Phyfe Grecian sofa, ca. 1815. (Skinner Inc.)

other furniture. The crimped or scalloped rendering appeared both in England and America. Later a machine-made version was used on Victorian furniture.

Pie cupboard: (see Pie safe)

Pie knife: (see Fish slice)

Pie peel: Early nineteenth century device for lifting pies from the hearth oven. Long handled metal tool with horseshoe shaped design at the end.

Pierce Bros. & Co.: Granted a Federal government contract to provide military shirts, drawers, and socks during the Civil War. Located in Boston, Massachusetts.

Pierce, Hart: Noted silversmith doing business in 1830s, New York City.

Pierce motorcycle: Motorcycle was first produced in 1906 as part of the Pierce Arrow Motor Company operation. A four-cylinder model on a large frame was produced in 1911. Production ended in 1914.

Pier glass (furniture): Early term used to describe a wall mirror hanging between windows. Typically such mirrors were located above a semi-circular table or pier table.

Pier table: Reference in early American furniture to a table designed to stand in front of a wall space precisely between two windows.

Pie safe (furniture): Popular nineteenth century structure for storing pies and other foodstuffs. Size and design varied but most included pierced-tin panels to allow for ventilation while protecting pies from insects and rodents. Other names include milk safe, food cupboard, wire safe, pie cupboard, milk cupboard, and tin safe.

Pigeon gray (color): Basically a medium gray during the 1920s era.

Pigeonhole (furniture): Described as a division or compartment used in the early bureau, secretary, and stationery case. Later pigeonholes were also featured in various desks including roll-top desks.

Piggin: Service vessel of pewter and wood used in early American taverns and inns as a carrier or dipper. Usually with a bail handle.

Pilaster (architecture): Architectural term for a shallow pier or column projecting slightly from a wall.

Pilaster (furniture): Reference in early cabinetmaking to a slightly projecting pillar. As crafted it generally included an ornamented base or cap. Rather than structural support, its main purpose was for decoration.

Pillar and scroll (furniture): Term for extensive use of flat-section scroll supports in furniture. Such design often included upright pillars. Circa 1830s and 1840s.

Pilotis: An architectural reference to the legs or stilts that supported a building with a raised first floor.

Pincered trailing: (see Quilling)

Pinchin, William: Listed as an active silversmith in 1780s, Philadelphia, Pennsylvania.

Pineapple (furniture): Reference to a popular finial used by American cabinetmakers during the early nineteenth century. It was applied to beds, supporting columns for swivel mirrors, and other pieces. It was said to originally have been a French symbol for hospitality as only selected guests were served the then rare and exotic fruit.

Pine, southern (wood): Regional favorite in many Southern states during the late

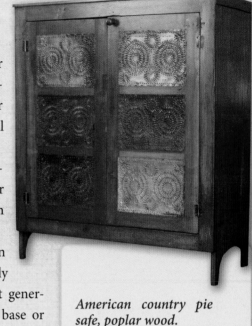

American country pie safe, poplar wood.

Punched tin panel of nineteenth century pie safe.

Brown-painted yellow pine pie safe, early nineteenth century. (Skinner Inc.)

Oak pie safe with two top drawers.

eighteenth and early nineteenth centuries. Again a relatively strong wood, light brown in color when finished. Sometimes it contained reddish pitch stripes.

Pine, white (wood): Basically a common straight-grained softwood. In early America it was used mainly as a secondary wood for drawer sides, backboards, case piece bottoms, and other out-of-sight places. When finished, color varied from light amber to soft yellow.

Pine, yellow (wood): An abundant wood in seventeenth century New England, it was often used in making lids for dower chests and for table tops of various sizes. The relatively hard grain finished into a light brown color.

Pinto, Joseph: Doing business as a silversmith in 1760s, New York City.

Pioneer: (see Westward Ho)

Pioneer postcard: Specific reference to nineteenth century postcards printed prior to the Private Mailing Card Act of 1898.

Pioneer Pottery: (see Brannon, Daniel)

Piping rock (color): Defined by Sears in the 1920s by a single word, gray.

Pipkin: Early American cooking utensil of metal with horizontal handle. In England the term was used for a brass and copper coal hod.

Pirate red (color): Simply a bright red in the early Sears listings.

Pisgah Forest Pottery: A noted art pottery establishment starting in 1914, Arden, North Carolina.

Pitkin, Horace: Doing business as a silversmith in 1830s, East Hartford, Connecticut.

Pitman, Saunders: Doing business as a silversmith in 1770s and 1780s, Providence, Rhode Island.

Pit saw: Early cutting device used both open and framed. Lengthy saw allowed two workers to readily cut in both open pit and from trestle.

Pittman, J. I.: Cartridge box manufacturer for Federal troops during the Civil War, based in New York City.

Pitts, Richard: Noted silversmith in 1740s, Philadelphia, Pennsylvania.

Plant's Mfg. Co.: Listed as maker of Army cartridge revolvers, patented 1859. Located in New Haven, Connecticut.

Plastic Circus Set: Basically a selection of stencils and colored pencils for drawing circus animals. Boxed sets made by Hassenfeld sold in the 1950s for 98¢.

Plasticville, U.S.A.: Toy buildings and accessories produced by Bachmann Bros. in the early 1950s. Rural units, shopping units, and farm units could be added so the town "grows and grows."

Plated ware: Procedure where heavier copper base is covered with a thin layer of silver. Initially it was manually fused and later chemically electroplated.

Platinum (color): As presented by Sears a light gray compared to the color of the precious metal.

Platt, George: Listed during the 1820s as a silversmith in New York City.

Playboy: Name of the steam-lined wagon offered by Sears, Roebuck and Company in 1935. Largest of three sizes sold for $5.95.

Plinth: In architecture a term for the projecting base or pedestal of a column or wall.

Plumbago: Term for a type of miniature portrait drawn on paper with lead pencil during the early eighteenth century. Mostly of British and French origin, the drawings were sometimes given additional tinting to highlight the hair or costume.

Plume (furniture): A fan-like carving on

early furniture mostly applied in England. Typically three to five plumes were used for decoration by eighteenth century cabinetmakers.

Plum (wood): Wood sometimes used by regional cabinetmakers for country furniture. Hardwood with red-brown center and an overall yellowish cast.

Plymouth Rifle: (see Whitney, Eli)

Plywood: Originally a laminated wood produced to provide stronger pierced carving for cabinetmaking. Credited to renowned cabinetmaker John Belter of New York during the middle of the nineteenth century. Laminated plywood was layered with parallel sheets, while later plywood amounted to sheets layered at right angles.

Pokal: Term for German drinking vessel, usually stemmed. The pokal was large and covered.

Polar Bear bank: Gold bronze cast iron bank, about 5" in height, made by Arcade Manufacturing in the 1920s.

Pole screen: Basically a screen used with the early American fireplace. The screen of petit point or tapestry was mounted on a pole which in turn was supported on a tripod base.

Pollak & Sons: Maker of meerschaum smoking pipes for Federal troops during the Civil War, located in 1860s, New York City.

Pollard, A. W. and Co.: Listed as a supplier of military goods to the U.S. government during the Civil War, located in New York City.

Pollard (wood): Term for the growth at the top of a tree. It was said to yield prized figured wood for veneers. The process of cutting back to the trunk of the tree also produced a more bushy growth of foliage.

Polychrome (color): Considered by Sears in the 1920s to be a mixture of colors.

Pomeroy, Noah: Listed as an active clockmaker in 1860s, Bristol, Connecticut.

Pomona Glass: Decorative glass first patented by Joseph Locke in 1885, it was manufactured by the New England Glass Company of Cambridge, Massachusetts. What began as a clear glass was blown and alternatively decorated until it offered a delicate tint in various shades from amber to pale blue.

Pompadour comb: Selection of combs sold in 1902 by Sears, Roebuck and Company. They included turquoise, pearl, and rhinestone settings in similar curved designs. They were priced at 25¢ to 38¢.

Pond, L. W.: Maker of cartridge revolvers for the U.S. Army, patented in 1856. Located in Worcester, Massachusetts.

Pond, Philip: A noted clockmaker in 1840s, Bristol, Connecticut.

Pongee (color): A light tan according to the 1927 Sears catalog.

Pontil mark (glass): Basically the mark left on the bottom of a piece of blown glass prior to the 1850s. It was caused by breaking the piece off of the pontil or punty rod after it had cooled. As methods of glass production improved the "mark" was mostly removed by a polishing process.

Pontypool ware: Term for a tin-plated iron ware which was produced as late as the 1870s. It was manufactured for two centuries and sometimes involved japanning or lacquering. Originally it was made in Pontypool, England.

Poole, Morton: Listed as a Federal contractor for military tents and poles during the Civil War. Located in Wilmington, Delaware.

Poor, Nathaniel: A silversmith in 1830s, Boston, Massachusetts.

Classic pie safe with punched panels.

Pier table of poplar and mahogany, ca 1810. (Skinner Inc.)

Shaker pine cupboard, ca. 1840. (Skinner Inc.)

Popcorn (color): A light canary-like yellow according to mail-order catalogs.

Pope Manufacturing Co.: (see Columbia tricycle)

Pope Motor Car Company: Early 1900s maker of automobiles including "America's greatest car." The firm was located in Toledo, Ohio.

Poplar (wood): Fine grained wood with a pale color, used for inlay in some early furniture.

Porcelain (ceramic): A reference to a ceramic body that is hard and white but also translucent.

Porringer: Round and shallow dish made by American and European craftsmen during the seventeenth and eighteenth centuries. Typically 5" to 6" in diameter, a fancy cut-out handle was often attached to the rim. Usually such pieces were made of pewter or silver.

Portal jamb: Reference in architecture to the straight vertical supporting side of a doorway.

Porter, Edmund: Active as a pewtersmith in 1840s, Taunton, Massachusetts.

Porter, Joseph: Listed as a silversmith in early 1800s, Utica, New York.

Porter, Lincoln: Doing business in the pewter trade in early 1800s, Taunton, Massachusetts.

Porter, Samuel: Producer of pewter ware in early 1800s, Taunton, Massachusetts.

Porter, William: Listed as an active clockmaker in 1820s, Waterbury, Connecticut.

Portland glass: A type of both clear and colored pressed glass once manufactured in Portland, Maine. Among the firm's most notable patterns was the tree of life. Portland glass was produced in the 1860s and early 1870s.

Porto Bello ware: A salt-glaze ware produced during the eighteenth century in the Staffordshire region of England. The grayish white ware made by John Astbury was named in honor of England's capture of the Spanish port.

Portrait doll: Originally said to represent famous women of the Victorian era including Queen Victoria, actress Jenny Lind, and Countess Dagmar. Later a more generalized term.

Posey, Frederick: Noted silversmith doing business in 1830s, Hagerstown, Maryland.

Postament: Term in architecture for the classical base support.

Post-and-beam: Very old reference to a method of construction which involved horizontal beams made to rest on vertical posts or columns.

Postcard: Standard reference to privately printed cards for mailing. It contrasts to the term postal card which applied only the government approved cards provided by the U.S. Postal Service.

Post, Samuel: Listed as an active silversmith in 1750s, New London, Connecticut.

Potter, John: A Colonial period clockmaker in 1780s, Farmington, Connecticut.

Potters Cooperative Company: Group of pottery makers established in 1876 at East Liverpool, Ohio.

Pounce (furniture): Reference to a colored powder used by early crafters of marquetry seeking to copy and mark out designs.

Poutreau, Abraham: Noted silversmith in 1720s, New York City.

Powder blue (color): Sears defined it during the 1920s as a light grayish blue.

Powder horn: During the nineteenth century decorated powder horns for holding musket powder were quite stylish. Using the horn of an ox or cow, hunters and soldiers would apply slogans, scenes, or figures to the surface.

Sometimes the decoration was done by the owner and sometimes by a semi-skilled artist. Often the horns also bore the owner's name.

Powersteel Autolock: Protective device sold in 1917 to prevent auto theft. A wire rope attached to a rear wheel and spring frame. Another attached to the spare tire and rack. They were sold by Broderick and Bascom Rope Co. of St. Louis, Missouri.

Pratt & Letchworth: Leading maker of cast iron toys in late nineteenth century America. Line includes trains, fire fighting wagons, horse-drawn wagons, and military wagons. Originally based in Buffalo, New York.

Pratt, Nathan: Listed as a thriving silversmith in early 1800s, Essex, Connecticut.

Precision Specialties: (see Back-firing Ford)

Pre-Greiner doll: Term for a large papier-mache doll with blown glass eyes, made in 1830s and 1840s, Germany.

Premier automobile: Automobile produced in various models during the early 1900s by the Premier Motor Manufacturing Company in Indianapolis, Indiana. Models in 1910 included the Four-Forty and the Six-Sixty.

Prescott automobile: Product of the Prescott Automobile Manufacturing Company located in early 1900s, New York City. Their steam-powered vehicles included the Doctor's Car.

Prescott, E. A.: Listed as a maker of cartridge revolvers, patented in 1860. Located in Worcester, Massachusetts.

President Eight: (see Studebaker Manufacturing Company)

Press bed (furniture): Early American term for folding bed.

Press cupboard (furniture): An early Colonial cupboard, similar to the court cupboard, with shelves above and compartments or drawers below. The bottom half was used for linen or clothing storage.

Pressed glass: Such glass was produced by machinery starting in the 1820s. Hot glass was forced into an iron mold which resulted in formation of various designs. It provided the basis for all pattern glass which followed.

Pretty Linda (doll): A 16" soft vinyl doll sold in the 1970s with seven extra outfits. Priced at $5.99 in the 1973 Montgomery Ward catalog.

Price, Isaac: An active clockmaker in early 1800s, Philadelphia, Pennsylvania.

Price, John: Listed as an active silversmith in 1760s, Lancaster, Pennsylvania.

Price, Joseph: Doing business as a clockmaker in early 1800s, Baltimore, Maryland.

Primavera (wood): Unlike most darker colored mahogany, primavera was straw-colored light mahogany. Colonial cabinetmakers preferred the darker reddish and brown mahogany and therefore used Central American primavera sparingly.

Prince, Isaac: An active Colonial era clockmaker in 1790s, Philadelphia, Pennsylvania.

Princess Elizabeth (doll): A 1940s doll sold complete with wardrobe and trunk. Advertised as the only "authentic" royal princess doll; complete outfit was $15.

Proctor, William: Listed as a clockmaker in 1750s, New York City.

Projection clock: Reference to a type of magic lantern clock. It this case the time of day is projected on the wall or ceiling. A French novelty in the middle nineteenth century, they were refined in Germany to project the image of the dial and clock hands.

An eighteenth century pine cupboard. (Skinner Inc.)

Paneled cupboard of pine, red painted, eighteenth century. (Skinner Inc.)

Pressed lacy glass dish with scalloped edge, ca. 1840. (Skinner Inc.)

Pressed glass tray from Boston and Sandwich Glass Co., ca. 1830s. (Skinner Inc.)

Prospect Hill Pottery Company: Small pottery firm doing business in 1880s, Trenton, New Jersey.

Protection Wringer: Hand-cranked wringer for washing clothes during the 1920s. Sears sold the latest for tube connection, plus bench wringers.

Proud, Robert: A noted clockmaker active in 1770s, Newport, Rhode Island.

Providence Chandelier Co.: Major seller of fine gas and electric fixtures during the 1890s. A three pound, three light model was $4. Located in Providence, Rhode Island.

Providence Tool Co.: Under contract with the Federal government during the Civil War to provide 70,000 .58 caliber rifled muskets. Located in Providence, Rhode Island.

Prunt (glass): Small diameters of corresponding sized glass pieces. Generally they are applied to the surface of a vessel as decoration and can take on the appearance of berry or pointed cone.

Prussian blue (color): Simply a rich dark blue as noted by the mail-order company in the 1920s.

Pub: An abbreviated term for public drinking house. Acknowledged in Colonial days as English slang, but the American reference of inn or tavern was more accepted in the Colonies.

Pulaski Gun Factory: Provided Mississippi rifles to the Confederate military during the Civil War. Located in Pulaski, Tennessee.

Pullan, R. B.: Granted a patent for military tents in 1861, located in Cumminsville, Ohio.

Pumpkin head doll: A reference to wax head dolls crafted with molded pompadours. The large hair style was covered with a circular comb-like band around the head. Typically such dolls also had large pupil-less dark glass eyes.

Pumpkin pine (wood): Type of white pine native to the eastern coastal areas of America. Wide sections of it from giant pines were used by Colonials for flooring, wall panels, shelving, and even table tops. In New England pumpkin pine was particularly favored because it was pliable yet resistant to warping.

Puncheon: Wood floor created by split logs placed side by side in early American homes.

Puritan furniture: Reference to plain and stark items crafted in New England by Puritan groups. Historically the period runs from 1620 to the early 1700s.

Purpleheart (wood): Term for a dense South America wood used by eighteenth century cabinetmakers for inlays and other furniture ornamentation. It was also called amaranth and violet wood.

Purple lake (color): Interesting 1920s term for a rich transparent purple

Purse, William: Colonial era silversmith from 1790 to 1820 in Charleston, South Carolina.

Putnam, Grace Storey: Best known for the beloved Bye-Lo Baby doll of the 1920s. The infant doll had a bisque head and delicate features.

Putney, Reuben: Noted silversmith doing business in 1820s, Watertown, New York.

Puttee (military): Leather or spiral cloth legging worn by soldiers in the World War I era.

Putto (clock): Clock case decoration like the cherub, a winged celestial being.

Pyramid toaster: Brand of bread toaster sold by S.S. Kresge Co. store in 1913. It toasted four slices at one time and sold for 10¢.

Pyroxylin Baby: Molded baby doll offered by Montgomery Ward catalog in early 1930s. Price was 45¢.

Quadral: Term for four-cornered area, divided into four parts.

Quadrennial: Reference to an event or occurrence every four years.

Quaich: A saucer-like shallow bowl with origins in Scotland. Unlike the single-handled porringer, the quaich had two handles and typically held a serving of oat porridge. Such containers could be made of pewter, silver, or wood.

Quaker: Religious sect in the United States, known as the Society of Friends.

Quaker bath cabinets: Nationally advertised enclosure for "hot vapor" Turkish baths in the 1890s. Cabinet complete with stove and directions was $5 from the World Manufacturing Company of Cincinnati, Ohio.

Quarry: Reference to a small pane of glass used by cabinetmakers for bookcase doors and glazed corner cupboard doors. Originally defined as diamond-shaped, but later used to indicate any small glass pane.

Quarte: French term for a guard in fencing.

Quartered (wood): The cutting of a log in four quarters for use in furniture construction. This was particularly true of quality oak used in the latter nineteenth century. The wood was then cut into parallel boards.

Quartz: Reference to a mineral compound of pure silica.

Quatrefoil: Symbol often carved on early furniture comprised for four lobes or foils and an enclosed circle. Some say the ornamentation represents a flower and four pedals, but interpretations vary.

Queen Anne (furniture): Reference to early eighteenth century furniture developed in England. Mostly made of walnut, its most distinctive feature typically was the curving cabriole leg. Popular motifs included the acanthus leaves and the scallop shell. Corresponding with the reign of Queen Anne, it was also sometimes noted as the Walnut Period.

Queen blue (color): Presented by Sears early in the twentieth century as a medium light blue.

Queen post: Term for one of two vertical timbers in a roof rising from the tie-beam.

Queen's ware (ceramic): Named in honor of Queen Charlotte of England, it was initially a breakfast set. After pleasing the Queen, who ordered a complete service for the royal palace, a full line of the cream-colored ware was put into production. The queenly presentation and full production of the ware was credited to eighteenth century English potter Josiah Wedgwood.

Quervelle, Anthony: Noted cabinetmaker operating in early nineteenth century, Philadelphia, Pennsylvania.

Quest, Samuel: Listed as an active clockmaker in 1820s, Maytown, Pennsylvania.

Quezal (glass): Noted early twentieth century art glass, named for a feathered bird of Latin America. A distinguished iridescent glass produced by the Quezal Art Glass and Decorating Company. The company was said to be comprised mostly of disgruntled former employees of the famed Tiffany glass empire. Among other things makers used actual gold for shading. They were based in Corona, New York.

Quick, G. C.: Issued a Federal government contract for military tents during the Civil War. No located listed.

Quier, William: Indiana born cabinetmaker listed as doing business in 1850s, Wayne County, Indiana.

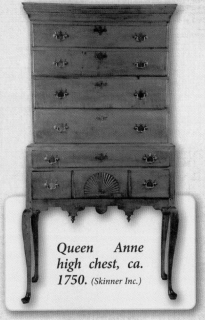

Queen Anne high chest, ca. 1750. (Skinner Inc.)

Queen Anne carved side chair, ca. 1760. (Skinner Inc.)

Queen Anne carved chest of drawers, ca. 1750. (Skinner Inc.)

Picket fence quilt with flower garden.

Array of vintage quilts.

Quilling (glass): Term used to describe the wavy ribbons of glass applied to decorate objects by delicate tooling. Sometimes called pincered trailing.

Quill pen: Homemade writing pen taken from the feathers of a large bird and further sharpened with a knife. Quill pens were gradually replaced by machine-made steel pens.

Quilt: Type of coverlet which is stitched together from pieces of cloth with softer material in between. Of French origin.

Quilting bee: Popular nineteenth century social event involving women of the community joining together in completing a quit. Usually the hostess had previously pieced the quilt into position for the extensive sewing.

Quilting frame: Advancement to quilt-making in the form a large wooden square. Pegs of wood held the four corners of the quilt for the final stages of adding lining, padding top. The tying together of the layers was completed on the frame.

Quimby, Daniel: Active silversmith in 1650, Braintree, Massachusetts.

Quimby, Phineas: Doing business as a clockmaker in 1840s, Belfast, Maine.

Quimby, William: Listed as an active clockmaker in 1830s, Belfast, Maine.

Quinby and Robinson: Suppliers of 32-pound cannon for the Confederate military during the Civil War. Located in Memphis, Tennesee.

Quincy, Henry: A noted clockmaker operating in 1830s, Portland, Maine.

Quintard, Peter: Doing business as a silversmith in 1740s, New York City.

Quirk (furniture): Considered an early reference to a narrow groove of channel molding, sometimes also called a sunken fillet. Method sometimes applied to sideboards.

Quitasol: Initially a Chinese paper parasol, but later a reference to other fashionable parasols including colorful cloth examples. The quitasol was also sometimes called a kittysol.

Quod: Early twentieth century criminal slang for prison.

Quran: The Arabic form of the holy book Koran.

Rabbet (furniture): Early American furniture term for a form of wood joint involving a groove in one piece and a tongue in the other.

Rabbet plane: Basically an early tool for cutting into the sides of boards to allow for overlapping and joining. Fence-like strips served to guide the plane along the board. Other terms for the device were rabbet and rebate.

Rabbit-ear chair: (see Thumb-back chair)

Rachel (color): A dark cream in the catalog's terms, lighter than brunette.

Rachet (furniture): Reference to the gear-like device used in eighteenth century desks or secretaries to raise or lower the writing surface.

Radio: Brand name for various household paints and enamels sold in the early 1900s by S.S. Kresge Co. stores.

Radiogram: Early twentieth century reference to a wireless telegram.

Raggedy Ann: Heavily merchandised cloth character doll during much of the twentieth century. Early in the 1970s Montgomery Ward offered Raggedy Ann dolls, music boxes, toothbrushes, toothpaste dispensers, furniture, folding stroller, playroom furniture, radio, and sleeping bags.

Rails (furniture): Term in early American furniture relating horizontal pieces of wood needed for the construction of framed pieces.

Raingo clock: A foremost maker of early nineteenth century domestic clocks including the Orrery clock was Raingo of Paris. The clock mechanism of the Orrery indicated the motion and position of bodies in the solar system.

Rait, David: Noted silversmith in 1835, New York City.

Rake (furniture): Reference to the degree of angle on a non-vertical part of constructed furniture. Often relating to a chair, desk, or table leg.

Raleigh Bayonet Factory: Supplied Confederate weaponry during the Civil War. Located in Raleigh, North Carolina.

Ralston Shoes: Attractive shoes sold in the 1890s for $4 a pair. Ralston Health Shoe Makers was located in Campello, Massachusetts.

Ralston, William: In practice as a silversmith in 1840s and 1850s, Ashland, Ohio.

Rambler delivery wagon: Produced in the early 1900s in six different models starting at $850. Manufactured by Thomas B. Jeffery Co. in Kenosha, Wisconsin.

Ramsey, John F.: Traveling cabinetmaker known to have worked in Ohio, Kentucky, Louisiana, Missouri, and Indiana early in the nineteenth century. Was listed as active in the trade in 1830s southern Indiana.

Ram's horn (furniture): Cabinetmaking reference to double curved arm supports which gave the appearance of ram's horns.

Randolph, Benjamin: Highly noted late eighteenth century Philadelphia cabinetmaker best known for chairs in the Chippendale style and distinctive Philadelphia highboys.

Range table (furniture): Term describing a rectangular table of the late eighteenth century which could be combined with a similar one to create an extended table surface.

Rankin, William: Granted a patent for military tents in 1861, located in New York City.

Rapp, William: Active clockmaker in 1830s, Philadelphia, Pennsylvania.

Rasch, Anthony: Silversmith in 1810, Philadelphia, Pennsylvania. Later operated as Anthony and Company in 1820.

Rat-claw (furniture): A latter eighteenth century furniture foot in the form of a rat's foot clutching a ball. It was more frequently used by British cabinetmakers than American.

Rat tail hinge: Early wrought-iron strap hinge with a long tapering section. Used on doors and cupboards of Colonial homes said to resemble the tail of a rat.

Rattan Mfg. Co.: (see Dickey seat)

Rauch & Lang Company: Makers of luxury electric automobiles early in the twentieth century. The Rauch and Land Carriage Company was located in Cleveland, Ohio.

Raulet, Samuel: Clockmaker in early 1800s, Monmouth, Maine.

Ravca, Bernard: French maker of cloth dolls during the 1920s. Ravca's costumed dolls were said to represent French peasants in great detail.

Raw sienna (color): Simply a bright and brownish yellow.

Raw umber (color): Considered by Sears to be a dark greenish brown.

Raymond, John: Active silversmith in 1775, Boston, Massachusetts.

Raymond, W. M. and Co.: Supplier of metal burial caskets during the Civil War. Doing business as Fisk's Metallic Burial Casket in Newtown, New York.

Raynes, Joseph: Listed in the silversmith trade in 1835, Lowell, Massachusetts.

Rea, Archelaus: A Colonial period clockmaker operating in 1790s, Salem, Massachusetts.

Raggedy Ann and Andy cloth dolls from Knickerbocker Toy Company, ca. 1970s.

Real photo postcard, early 1900s.

REO Motor Car advertisement, 1906.

Engravings by Paul Revere in 1774 issue of Royal American Magazine. (Skinner Inc.)

Read and Dickson: Listed as supplier of military lances for Confederate forces during the Civil War. Based in Mississippi.

Read and Son: Noted as providers of swords and sabers briefly during the Civil War. Located in Boston, Massachusetts.

Real photo: Reference in postcards to the use of an actual photograph on the front. The back was the usual postcard form, often with an indication of the type of film as well.

Recamier (furniture): Basically a daybed or similar long chair designed for reclining. Emerged from the eighteenth century French style which was more or less a couch with a high end. Sometimes called a chaise lounge, and during the Victorian era a fainting couch.

Rectilinear: Term for a pattern of very straight lines.

Rector, W. H.: Cabinetmaker working in 1830s, Goshen, Indiana.

Redd, Daniel: Pennsylvania-born cabinetmaker listed as working in a furniture factory in 1830s, Logansport, Indiana.

Red filler (furniture): Early cabinetmaking reference to a Spanish brown pigment of furniture finish. Mixed with linseed oil and thinned turpentine, it was frequently used on country-made pieces early in the nineteenth century.

Red gum (wood): Straight-grained wood of moderate strength sometimes referred to in early America as bilsted. When finished the color varied from dark brown to reddish brown. In seventeenth century New York it was often selected for chests or used in combination with oak. Infrequently it was used for chairs and basic tables.

Red Ryder: (see Daisy air rifle)

Redware (ceramic): Term for ceramic ware which was produced in various shades of red from a dark black to a lighter yellow reddish shade. It was low-fired, soft, porous, and coarse-grained.

Red Wing Potteries: Highly regarded art pottery and stoneware producer from 1870s to 1960s in Red Wing, Minnesota.

Redwood (wood): Sometimes known as sequoia, the burls of redwood were sometimes used for decorating furniture or as veneers. When applied it had a reddish brown hue.

Reed, Andrew W.: Cabinetmaker and operator of a shop in 1820s, Indianapolis, Indiana.

Reeder, John: Noted 1835 silversmith in Philadelphia, Pennsylvania.

Reed, Ezekiel: (see Cut nail machine)

Reeding (furniture): A popular eighteenth century furniture decoration involving raised parallel lines which were just above the surface or flush to the edge. Usually applied to table legs, it was considered just the opposite of fluting.

Reed, Isaac: Colonial era silversmith working in 1775, Stanford, Connecticut.

Reed, John: Ohio-born cabinetmaker working in 1850s, Adams County, Indiana.

Reed, Robert M.: Founder of Antique and Collectible News Service. Distinguished author of several books and thousands of magazine articles.

Reed, Stephen: Distinguished clockmaker in 1830s, New York City.

Reed Toy Company: A noted nineteenth century maker of colorful lithographed toys. Line included circus-related paper items, pull toys, and various construction sets. The W.S. Reed Toy Company was based in Leominster, Massachusetts. Major production was from the 1870s into the 1890s.

Rees, Fitzpatrick Capt.: Provided Confederate military with knives during the Civil War. Located in Natchez, Mississippi.

Reeve, Powell: Chair maker born in Kentucky and doing business in 1850s, Warren County, Indiana.

Reeves, D. S.: Listed as an active clockmaker in 1830s, Philadelphia, Pennsylvania.

Reeves, Stephen: Listed as a silversmith 1765 to 1775 in Burlington, New Jersey.

Refectory table (furniture): Reference to a long narrow table similar to dining room table used in monasteries.

Regas automobile: Made by the Regas Automobile located in Rochester, New York. In 1904 their air-cooled automobile of the same name sold for $1,500.

Regency era (furniture): Makes reference to styles of furniture made generally from the 1790s to the 1820s in England.

Reid Manufacturing Company: Maker of two models of the Chainless Wolverine automobile in the early 1900s. Firm was based in Detroit, Michigan.

Reindeer bank: Reindeer image bank offered as a Christmas-related item in the 1920s by Arcade Manufacturing Company. Banks were over 6" tall, cast iron, and trimmed in gold bronze

Reindeer brown (color): This was a dark tannish brown in the Sears listings.

Reindeer tan (color): Somehow slightly lighter than Reindeer brown, a dark tan.

Reinecker, Samuel: Cabinetmaker born in Pennsylvania and working in 1850s, Vermillion County, Indiana.

Reinthal and Newman: Noted early twentieth century postcard publisher, particularly of noted artists and special greetings.

Relief carving (furniture): Process involved carving so the design is raised above the background, or cut in relief. Various styles were termed low relief or high relief.

Remington, E.: Supplied the Federal government with 40,000 rifled muskets and 10,000 Zouave rifles during the Civil War. Located in Ilion, New York.

Remmey, Henry: Headed the Remmey & Family pottery specializing in stoneware and porcelain in nineteenth century, Philadelphia, Pennsylvania.

Renaissance period: Reference to that period in European history which saw a revival of interest in ancient Roman and Greek cultures. Basically a span from 1450 to 1650. It gave rise to extensive ornamentation including acanthus leaves, medallions, and fancy beadings.

Reo Motor Car Co.: Makers of the Reo Touring Car and other vehicles during the early 1900s at a factory in Lansing, Michigan. Reo Runabout sold for $650 in 1905.

Repoussé (metal): Embossing-like process for decorating metal. Images and designs were done in relief by special tools used to hammer the piece from the back. This elaborate process was usually reserved for application of silver or gold.

Reseda green (color): In the Sears catalog a medium grayish green.

Rest bed (furniture): One of many terms for an early chaise lounge, couch, or day bed. Typically ornamental and available for daytime use.

Restoration period: Latter seventeenth century era in England during the rule of Charles the Second. Decorative arts involved luxurious upholstery on chairs and day beds, elaborately carved walnut, and fancy turnings on various

Movie poster of Roy Rogers, 1939.

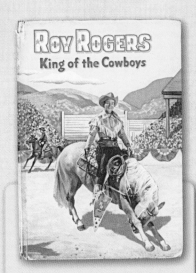

Roy Rogers book by Whitman Publishing, 1956.

Roy Rogers Chuck Wagon, early 1950s.

Early 1900s catalog illustration of an oak rolltop desk.

pieces. Much of it reflected French and Flemish influences.

Reta doll: (see Adele doll)

Reticule: Purse-like cloth or leather bag used to carry needlework. In order to keep her hands busy a nineteenth century woman carried handiwork in the reticule when visiting others.

Revere, Paul: America's most famous silversmith also immortalized in the poem by Henry Wadsworth Longfellow. Revere rose from the rank of tradesman to become a noted crafter of silver late in the eighteenth century. Revere was equally skilled at copper plating.

Reynolds, John: Pennsylvania-born cabinetmaker, listed as working in a shop in 1850s, Columbus, Indiana.

Reynolds, Theodore: Doing business as a silversmith in 1835, Philadelphia, Pennsylvania.

Rham, Phillip: Under contract to provide various cannon carriages and caissons for the Confederate military. Located in Richmond, Virigina.

Rhein, Dan: Cabinetmaker operating a shop in 1840s and 1850s, Lafayette, Indiana.

Rheinstrom Brothers: (see Danziger Magen Bitters)

Rhode Island school: Reference to furniture making during the eighteenth century by the families of Job Townsend and John Goddard in Newport, Rhode Island. The style of case furniture was especially noted for block fronts usually in the form of panels.

Rhoder, George: French-born cabinetmaker who is listed as working in 1850s, Indianapolis, Indiana.

Riband back (furniture): Originally a ribbon-like decoration used on chair backs by British designer Thomas Chippendale in the eighteenth century.

Typically involving carving of bows, knots, and ribbon swirls into the wood.

Ribbon mark (ceramic): Reference to the printed or stamped ribbon-shaped mark on a ceramic piece.

Ribbon stripe (furniture): Reference to straight band appearing in the grain of high quality woods such as mahogany and walnut. Early cabinetmakers prized such stripes to highlight their work.

Rice and Wright: Manufacturer of military cannons for the Confederate cause during the Civil War. Located in Florence, Alabama.

Rice, Joseph: Enterprising silversmith active from 1820 to 1850 in Albany, New York.

Rice, Phineas: In the clockmaker trade in 1830s, Charlestown, Massachusetts.

Richards & Sons: Supplier of cigar holders and pipes to Federal troops during the Civil War, located in 1860s, New York City.

Richardson, C. G.: Recorded as being an active pewtersmith in early nineteenth century, Cranston, Rhode Island.

Richardson, Francis: A noted clockmaker in 1730s, Philadelphia, Pennsylvania.

Richardson, George: Noted as a pewter artisan doing business in 1820s, Boston, Massachusetts.

Richardson, Richard: A Colonial era silversmith in 1795, Philadelphia, Pennsylvania.

Richards, Samuel: Active silversmith 1785 to 1815 in Philadelphia, Pennsylvania.

Richards, William H.: Granted an 1861 patent for knife-fork-spoon combination utensil for military use, located in Newton, Massachusetts.

Richie Donut: (see Entenmann dolls)

Rich, John: Enterprising clockmaker active in 1820s, Bristol, Connecticut.

Richmond, Franklin: Listed as an active

clockmaker in 1820s, Providence, Rhode Island.

Richmond Straight Cut: Nationally advertised brand of cigarettes sold in the early twentieth century. A tin of 50 sold for 40 cents in 1917.

Rich, Obadiah: Noted silversmith active from 1830 to 1850 in Boston, Massachusetts.

Richter Company (toys): Best noted as maker of Anchor Building Bricks, a whole range of construction items. Based in Germany their educational toys were popular in the late nineteenth century and well into the twentieth century. Anchor trademark appeared on most products.

Rider, John: Designer of the Rider's Tent Knapsack for the Federal military during the Civil War.

Ridgeway, John: Ardent silversmith doing business in early 1800s, Boston, Massachusetts.

Ridgeway ware: Fine grade of earthenware produced by early nineteenth century English potter Job Ridgeway. Most noted product was a dark blue ware known as The Beauties of American Series. Individual pieces in the set bore rose and leaf and medallion borders and were exported exclusively for the American market.

Ridgewood Manufacturing: Manufacturer of the Ridgewood Smoking Case for the U.S. military during the Civil War. Located in New York.

Rigaree (glass): Reference to narrow parallel ribbons of glass with ladder rung-like indentations. A decoration involving fine tooling.

Rigden, Thomas: A pewter producer of note in early nineteenth century, Philadelphia, Pennsylvania.

Riker, Peter: Listed as a silversmith from 1805 to 1815 in New York City.

Riker theater bus: Exceptional twin-motored vehicle capable of hauling 13 passengers plus more on the rooftop, produced by the Riker Company in 1901.

Riley, John: Accomplished clockmaker in early 1800s, Philadelphia, Pennsylvania.

Rinceau (furniture): Early use of interlacing acanthus leaves and flowers in border design of furniture.

Rineer, Aaren: New Jersey-born cabinetmaker producing furniture in 1850s, Franklin County, Indiana.

Ripley, Monot: Born in 1790s Massachusetts, listed as working as a cabinetmaker in 1850s, Madison County, Indiana.

Risley & Son: Pottery operation headed by Sidney Risley in middle nineteenth century, Norwich, Connecticut.

Rittenhouse, David: Active Colonial era clockmaker during 1750s in Philadelphia, Pennsylvania.

Ritter, A. J.: Under contract during the Civil War to provide writing kits in the form of a portable desk and checkerboard combination. Located in Rahway, New York.

Ritter, Richard: Doing business as a silversmith in 1790s, New York City.

Road roller (toy): Huber Road Roller, a cast iron toy, made by Hubley Toys of Lancaster, Pennsylvania. It was nearly 8" long and came with a spring motor.

Robbins, George & Co.: Supplier of canteens, corks, and straps to Federal troops during the Civil War, located in New York City.

Roberts, Frederick: Active silversmith in 1770s, Boston, Massachusetts.

Roberts, Gideon: Noted as a clockmaker in early 1800s, Bristol, Connecticut.

Roberts, James: Cabinetmaker who operated a shop with four employees in 1850s,

Rookwood ceramic pieces.
(Harris Auction Center)

Rookwood art pottery vase, ca. 1880s. *(Skinner Inc.)*

Rosewood veneer on Federal mahogany sideboard, ca. 1810. (Skinner Inc.)

Lafayette, Indiana. Roberts was born in Pennsylvania.

Roberts, Larkin: Doing business as a cabinetmaker in 1850s, Morgan County, Indiana. Born in Kentucky.

Robertson Art Tile Company: Doing business in 1880s, Morrisville, Pennsylvania.

Roberts, William: Colonial period clockmaker doing business in 1790s, Philadelphia, Pennsylvania.

Robinson, Benjamin: Enterprising silversmith in 1820s, Philadelphia, Pennsylvania.

Robinson, E.: Under contract with the Federal government during the Civil War to supply 30,000 rifled muskets, located in New York City.

Robison Arms Manufactory: Produced Sharps model carbines for confederate military during the Civil War, located in Richmond, Virginia.

Roby, C. and Co.: Civil War supplier of military knives, swords, and sabers to the U.S. Army, located in West Chelmsford, Massachusetts.

Roby, Joseph: Listed as a pewtersmith in 1780s, Boston, Massachusetts.

Rocaille: Another term for the highly decorative middle eighteenth century ornamentation of rococo.

Rock maple: (see Curly maple)

Rockee (furniture): Basically an early American settee on rockers apparently made for mother and baby. While mother rocked the infant could be contained nearby by a railing of upright spindles. The rockee was also sometimes called a lullaby rocker or a mammy rocker.

Rockery (furniture): Term for naturalistic rock work carved upon more elaborate gilded mirror frames by early furniture makers.

Rocket: Brand of baseball sold by S.S. Kresge Co. stores early in the twentieth century. Price was 5¢.

Rocking chair (furniture): A chair of American origin which emerged in the late eighteenth century, initially as regular chairs with curved runners attached to the legs. By the early 1800s rockers were popular in the new country.

Rockingham ware (ceramic): Remarkable lead glaze ware developed by potter Edward Butler in 1750s, England. The ware's initial yellow and brown colors in the form of teapots and other kitchenware appealed to the public. Soon similar ware was in full production in England and America.

Rockwell, Samuel: Doing business as a silversmith from the 1820s to the 1840s in New York City.

Rocky, David: Pennsylvania-born cabinetmaker working in 1850s, Noble County, Indiana.

Rococo: Highly decorative use of shells, rocks, flowers, and other nature-based forms originating in middle-eighteenth century Europe. Chests and chairs were covered with such items; mirrors and clocks were even carved and gilded in tribute to the lavish style.

Rodarmel, Oscar: Indiana-born cabinetmaker working with Samuel Rodarmel in 1850s, Daviess County, Indiana.

Roe, James: Engaged as a silversmith in 1770s, Kingston, New York.

Roe (wood): Reference to the spotty appearance of a figure in some types of wood.

Rogers and Spencer: Contracted to the U.S. government during the Civil

War for the manufacture of percussion revolvers. Located in Utica, New York.

Rogers, Augustus: Noted silversmith active in 1820s, Boston, Massachusetts.

Rogers group (ceramic): Term for plaster figurines produced in the 1880s by a group headed by John Rogers. The popular sculptures, usually brown in color, each bore the Rogers mark. Late in the nineteenth century the statuettes of people in daily life appeared in American homes everywhere.

Rogers, Isaac: A noted clockmaker in 1820s, Marshfield, Massachusetts.

Rogers, Roy: Singing star of the twentieth century western movies. Many toys and items produced under his name.

Rogers, William: Connected to the silversmith trade in 1820s, Hartford, Connecticut.

Rognon (furniture): French term for a kidney-shaped desk used in the eighteenth century.

Roll top (furniture): Desk or secretary equipped with a flexible hood or lid which could be drawn or rolled down to close the opening.

Romayne work (furniture): A reference to the image of human heads carved upon roundels or medallions as ornamentation.

Romney, John: Active as a silversmith in 1775, New York City.

Rookwood (ceramic): High quality yellow ware with a blue and brown underglaze decoration. First produced in 1879 under the direction of Maria Longworth Nichols Storer in Cincinnati, Ohio. Skilled artists ultimately provided an enduring and popular ware with hundreds of designs and shadings.

Rookwood Pottery: Ultimate art pottery producers from 1880s to 1950s in Cincinnati, Ohio.

Roosevelt, Nicholas: Doing business as a silversmith in 1730s, New York City.

Roper Steam Carriage: An 1860s invention of Sylvester Roper doing business in Roxbury, Massachusetts. The vehicle was coal-powered and carried two passengers.

Rose, Anthony: Listed as an active silversmith in 1760s, New York City.

Rose (color): As defined by the Sears catalog during the 1920s, simply a deep pink.

Rose beige (color): A medium tan according to Sears with a rose cast.

Rose blonde (color): A dark gray with a rose tint, a shade lighter than rose taupe.

Rose blush (color): A light sand shade with a brick cast according to Sears.

Rose breath (color): Basically a light rose as noted by the Sears list in 1927.

Rose carving (furniture): Flowered design added to Victorian furniture denoting loyalty to the House of Tudor in England. The rose motif was typically applied to chairs and sofas of rosewood, mahogany, and walnut.

Rose, Daniel: Listed as an active clockmaker in 1830s, Reading, Pennsylvania.

Roseman, Joseph: Chair maker born in New Jersey and active in the trade in early 1820s, Vincennes, Indiana.

Rose pearl (color): Considered to be simply a very deep pink.

Rose pink (color): A shade of pink with a notable rose cast.

Rose taupe (color): In the 1920s it was presented as a dark gray with a rose cast.

Roseville Pottery: A leading art pottery operation started in 1890s, Zanesville, Ohio.

Rose (wood): Actually a group of tropical woods which offered up the faint scent

Recessed leaf design on Roseville planter.

Roundabout chair in Queen Ann style, ca. 1750s.

Royal Tourist True Blue vehicle from Royal Motor Car Co., 1905.

of roses when freshly cut. Typically finely grained with a reddish-brown color, such woods took a high polish. Striking but somewhat brittle, it was used sparingly throughout the nineteenth century.

Rosewood (color): Presented as a deep rose with a soft brownish tone.

Ross, Allen: Under Federal government contract to provide military boots during the Civil War era. Located in Sing Sing, New York.

Roswell, Bartholomew: A noted silversmith in 1805, Hartford, Connecticut.

Roteras, Philip: Cabinetmaker born in Germany and listed as working in 1850s, Vigo County, Indiana.

Rotten stone: Term used for a soft, powdered stone used with oil in connection with the polishing of furniture.

Roudebush, Henry: Potter operating in 1815, Montgomery County, Pennsylvania.

Rouen pottery: Early French majolica crafted in Italian style at Rouen, France. Centuries of production continued into the nineteenth century.

Roughish (doll): (see Googly eyes)

Roundabout (furniture): Eighteenth century chair intended for corner use. Typically a three-legged armchair with a rounded back which extended around both sides. Spindles or solid splats formed the back and jointed the seat to the top piece.

Roundel (glass): Term for early glass of round shape used for door light or window pane. Disk-like and often in medallion form.

Rouse, William: Silversmith in 1840s, Charleston, South Carolina.

Rouyer, C. A.: Provider of military uniform buttons to Confederate forces in the Civil War, doing business in New Orleans, Louisiana.

Royal automobile: Vehicle manufactured by the Royal Motor Car Company in early 1900s Cleveland, Ohio. Their 1906 Model G sold for $3,500.

Royal blue: The standard bright blue in 1920s Sears catalogs.

Royal Flemish (glass): Resembling stained glass and involving quality art glass in group panels. The panels are colored and separated by lines of heavily raised enamel.

Royal Motor Car Co.: Makers of the Royal Tourist "true blue" automobile in the early 1900s. Based in Cleveland, Ohio, the company sold the Tourist for $3,000 in 1905.

Royal Tourist: (see Royal Motor Car Co.)

Roycrafters: (see Arts & Crafts)

Rubay Company: Makers of European-style automobiles early in the 1920s, based in Cleveland, Ohio. Production ended in 1924.

Rubber Clothing Co.: A supplier of rubber blankets to the U.S. Army during the Civil War, located in New York City.

Rubber Farm Set: Made by Auburn Rubber. The box it came in converted into a barn and shed. Rubber figures included farmer, horse, wagon, and tractor. In 1952 the set sold for $2.98.

Rubina (glass): Late nineteenth century art glass shading which flowed from clear to a pale ruby at the edges.

Rubina verde (glass): Late nineteenth century art glass shading of reheated gold glass. It established shading from a pale greenish-yellow color to strong cranberry color.

Ruby (color): Defined during the 1920s era as a deep rich red.

Ruby pink (color): Simply presented by Sears as a dark pink.

Ruby red (color): Somehow considered by Sears to be the same as the color ruby.

Rufus lion: A plush 1970s doll produced by Animal Fair. A talking version spoke phrases like, "be kind to animals." The Animal Fair pet series of plush figures also included Henry the puppy, Jacob the turtle, and a Patterpiller.

Rule joint (furniture): Term for hinged joint used between a table top and its added leaf. Once in place it prevented any open space on the surface.

Rule, Robert: A Colonial era silversmith in 1780s, Boston, Massachusetts.

Rumsey, Daniel: Active in the silversmith trade in 1730s, Newport, Rhode Island.

Runabout automobile: (see Studebaker Brothers)

Runner (furniture): Reference to a chair's wooden support or rung. Also reference to the strips for sliding a drawer.

Rush seat (furniture): Basically a woven seat from broom-like rush strands. Harvested from marshes, long-stemmed rushes proved pliable and comfortable for nineteenth century furniture. Rush seats, such as those used in Hitchcock chairs, were said to be more expensive and labor-intensive than plank seats.

Russell, A. J. & J. L.: Stoneware pottery producers doing business in 1860s and 1870s, West Troy, New York.

Russell, George: An active clockmaker and silversmith located in 1830s, Philadelphia, Pennsylvania.

Russell, Major John: Engaged in the clockmaking traded in 1760s, Deerfield, Massachusetts.

Russell, Moody: Engaged in the silversmith trade 1730s to 1750s in Barnstable, Massachusetts.

Russell, Stephen H.: Granted a patent for military-related canteen filter and drinking tube in 1861, located in Boston, Massachusetts.

Russet (color): A reddish brown as defined in the 1920s Sears color listings.

Russian violet (color): Just another name for purple according to the Sears catalog listings.

Rust (color): As the name implies, the color of actual rust.

Rustic (furniture): Early twentieth century style reflecting rural retreats and mountain lodges. Simple, rough, and often incorporating pine or hickory.

Rustic brown (color): Oddly a medium reddish brown according to the mail-order catalog terms.

Ruth Doll: Popular doll featured in the Billy and Ruth Catalog of the 1950s. The doll had a vinyl plastic body and "miracle hair" of saran. Standing 20" tall it came in a complete outfit including hair ribbon and sold for $9.95.

Rutter, Moses: Listed as engaged in clockmaking in early 1800s, Baltimore, Maryland.

Ruttan, Marie: (see Columbian doll)

Ryerson, Lattimore: Active silversmith in 1760s, York, Pennsylvania.

Saber leg (furniture): Cabinetmaking reference to the saber-like perpendicular curve on the front leg of an early chair.

Sable (color): Presented as dark tan in the 1920s catalogs.

Sack back (furniture): Term for an early American double-back Windsor chair.

Sacramento Pottery: Stoneware pottery operation in 1860s and 1870s, Sacramento, California.

Sadd, Harvey: Doing business as a clockmaker and silversmith in 1820s, New Hartford, Connecticut.

Saddle seat (furniture): Thick Windsor chair seat which was scooped out to allow for the buttocks. Makers claimed its form resembled the pommel of a riding saddle.

Sadiron: Basically a flat iron with a detachable handle allowing it to be removed while the actual metal base was heated. This was an advancement over the entirely

Rustic chair, ca. 1920, from Old Hickory Chair Company.

Hexagon-shaped pressed glass salt cellar.

Heavy glass, rectangular salt cellar.

metal flat iron which required a protective cover when handled.

Sadler, Philip: Silversmith in early 1830s, Baltimore, Maryland.

Sad ware: Term for pewter pots and other implements made for holding liquids during the fourteenth and fifteenth centuries by members of the Pewterers' Guild Hall in London, England. The workers themselves were known as sad ware men.

Safford, Henry: Listed as a silversmith 1800 to 1810 in Lima, Ohio.

Sailor blue (color): A deep rich blue according to Sears, lighter than navy.

Sailor doll: Both Sailor girl and Sailor boy dolls were sold in the 1902 Sears, Roebuck and Company catalog. Both had solid eyes and bisque head. Each wore a sailor costume complete with cap.

Salamander Works: Name of a pottery undertaking established in 1848, New York City.

Salem rocker (furniture): Early nineteenth century New England rocker, often with stenciled decoration. The top rail was usually scrolled. Similar to the Boston rocker but somewhat earlier in popularity.

Salem secretary (furniture): Cabinet with a writing compartment or a breakfront bookcase. The recessed upper section usually had two doors, and the lower section was fitted with drawers. Also called a gentleman's secretary.

Salmon (color): Ranked in the 1920s as a medium yellowish tan.

Salom, Pedro: (see Morris & Salom Electrobat)

Salt cellar: Container of salt, usually glass, which was typically placed near the most honored place at the dining table. In the Victorian era smaller individual salt cellars were available to all.

Salt glaze (ceramic): A glaze achieved by adding rock salt into the kiln used for preparing stoneware.

Saltire (furniture): A term in early cabinetmaking for the X-shaped stretcher used in furniture construction.

Salver: Metal tray, usually of silver or pewter, used for passing ceremonial bread at religious services.

Sam Browne belt: Reference to the military belt worn by officers in the American and British armies during the World War I era.

Sam Cobra: (see Johnny West)

Sampler (folk art): Particularly popular crafting of needlework in early nineteenth century America. Young women were required to refine their embroidering skills with letters of the alphabet, scenes, or bits of wit. Better results were then framed and hung on the wall. In Europe the practice dated back to the 1500s.

Samuel, Bell: Potter in redware and stoneware during the 1840s and 1850s in Strasburg, Virginia.

Samuels, A. R.: A glassmaker operating in 1850s, Philadelphia, Pennsylvania. Samuels made designs of bottles with Masonic emblems, and marked them with his initials.

Sandalwood: A close-grained hardwood with a musky aroma, it ranged from dark red to yellowish-brown in color. It was used sparingly by early cabinetmakers other than for decorative veneers.

Sand (color): Simply a light tan in the 1927 Sears mail-order catalog.

Sandell, Edward: Listed as an active clockmaker and silversmith in 1820s, Baltimore, Maryland.

Sands, Stephen: Colonial era clockmaker doing business in 1770s, New York City.

Sandwich (glass): Noted production of the Boston and Sandwich Glass Company in nineteenth century, Massachusetts.

Great amounts of blown and molded glass were made in the early years, later colored glass, and etched and enameled glass was added to production. Hundreds of patterns of pressed glass were made at the operation starting in the 1840s. Distinguished items include lamps, perfume bottles, and vases. The plant closed due to labor problems in 1888.

Sanford, Frederick: Doing business as a silversmith in 1830s, Nantucket, Massachusetts.

Sanford, Ransom: A noted clockmaker in 1840s, Plymouth, Connecticut.

Santa: (see Nast, Thomas)

Santos Dumont auto: (see Columbus Motor Vehicle Co.)

Sap green (color): Noted by Sears as a vivid light green.

Sappanwood: Exotic wood used for furniture making in the seventeenth and eighteenth century, Dutch colonies. Mainly from Java, Ceylon, and India it was said to resemble Brazil wood.

Sapphire blue (color): A bright blue in the Sears extensive listing of colors.

Sargeant, Ensign: Noted as a silversmith in 1820s, Boston, Massachusetts.

Sargeant, Joseph: Clockmaker in 1830s, Hartford, Connecticut.

Sarson and Roberts: Suppliers of 5,000 rifled muskets to Federal forces during the Civil War, located in New York City.

Satan: (see Johnny West)

Satin (glass): Tinted glassware of the late nineteenth century. Makers used hydrofluoric acid fumes to finely etch it. The acid application provided the glass with its satin-like texture. Satin glass was produced in many American plants in the late 1800s.

Satin (wood): Light honey-colored

hardwood with a very fine grain. During the eighteenth century cabinetmakers imported this relatively rare wood for inlays. Most of the wood came from Ceylon and India initially, and later partially from the West Indies.

Sauerbier, H.: Listed as a Federal government supplier of swords and sabers during the Civil War. Locations in New York City and Newark, New Jersey.

Sausage turning (furniture): A nineteenth century furniture-making term regarding the production of sausage-like elongated pieces.

Sauterne (color): Considered to be a very light tan during the 1920s by Sears and Roebuck.

Savage, John: Doing business as a silversmith in 1820s, Raleigh, North Carolina.

Savage, R.: Contracted with the Federal government to supply 25,000 rifled muskets, located in Middletown, Connecticut.

Savage Repeating Firearms Co.: Contracted with the federal government to produce percussion revolvers during the Civil War. Located in Middletown, Connecticut.

Savery, William: Highly noted Philadelphia cabinetmaker of the middle eighteenth century. Savery crafted elaborate highboys, lowboys, and other pieces in the heavily ornamented style of England's Thomas Chippendale.

Sawbuck (furniture): Term for an early table with legs in X-form. The top was a long and narrow top supported by an X-frame at each end.

Sawhorse: (see Trestle table)

Sawin, John: A noted clockmaker active in 1830s, Boston, Massachusetts.

Saxon Six: Automobile of the early 1900s produced by the Saxon Motor

Salt glazed stoneware jar, ca. 1840s. (Skinner Inc.)

Needlework sampler dated 1806, contemporary frame. (Skinner Inc.)

Sandwich glass standards and punty lamp, ca. 1860s.
(Skinner Inc.)

Satinwood tea caddy, ca. 1810.

Car Corporation of Detroit, Michigan. Advertised price in 1916 was $815, considerably less than most brands.

Sayre, Joel: Noted as a silversmith in 1800, New York City.

Scallop (furniture): Reference to a carved ornament on furniture which resembled a escalloped shell.

Scarab: Elaborate beetle-like design in the style of an ancient Egyptian charm. Usually jeweled or carved stone.

Scarlet (color): Simply a very bright red among Sears catalog colors.

Scarlet Lake (color): Not differentiated from scarlet by Sears, again a very bright red.

Scarret, Joseph: Colonial era silversmith in 1780s, Philadelphia, Pennsylvania.

Schaghticoke Power Co.: Civil War supplier of gunpowder to the U.S. government, located in Schaghticoke, New York.

Schalk, George: Maker of rifled muskets, and a 1861 supplier to Pennsylvania military, located in Pottsville, Pennsylvania.

Schell, Jacob: Doing business as a pottery in 1830s, Tylers Port, Pennsylvania.

Schickel motorcycle: Norbert Schickel obtained a U.S. patent for a two-cylinder motorcycle in 1905. The Schickel Motor Cycle Company was in full operation in 1912 at Stamford, Connecticut. The company closed in 1924 after making some 1,000 motorcycles.

Schiefflin, P. and D.: Major importer of swords and sabers for military use during the Civil War. Contracts in 1861 called for 5,000 cavalry sabers, 2,000 musicians swords, and 3,000 non-commissioned swords. Located in New York City.

Schilling's Auto Camp: A double bed size shelter fitted into the body of an

automobile and advertised in 1917. The waterproof canvas product offered "absolute privacy." The L.F. Schilling Company was located in Salem, Ohio.

Schloemer-Toepfer Carriage: Remarkable self-propelled vehicle crafted by Gottfried Schloemer and driven on the streets of Green Bay, Wisconsin, in 1892. Assistance for the project, which included wooden tires encased in hard rubber, came from Frank Toepfer.

Schoenhut Company (toys): Major manufacturer of wood-jointed toy figures beginning in the 1890s. Based in Philadelphia, Pennsylvania, the firm became a prolific maker of dolls, puzzles, circus wagons, dollhouses, and various figures through the 1930s.

Schoenhut doll: Early twentieth century dolls made of wood. Additionally they were crafted with steel springs and swivel joints which allowed for movement of the doll's joints right down to ankles and wrists. Every Schoenhut doll had two holes in the bottom of each foot so the doll could be placed upright in an accompanying stand. Styles varied from infant to little boy and little girl.

Schriner, Martin: Doing business as a clockmaker in 1820s, Lancaster, Pennsylvania.

Schubarth, Casper: Under contract with the Federal government to provide 9,500 rifled muskets during the Civil War, located in Providence, Rhode Island.

Schuyler, Hartley and Graham: A leading supplier of military goods during the 1860s to the U.S. government, located in New York City.

Schuylkill Glass Works: Glass operation established near Philadelphia around 1806. The works made flint glass and bottles. Among the green and white bottles were pocket bottles, quart, and half gallon sizes. The works closed in 1823.

Schweinfurt, John G.: Redware pottery producer in latter nineteenth century New Market, Virginia.

Schwin, Ignaz: (see Henderson motorcycle and Excelsior motorcycle)

Sconce: Metal candleholder complete with a support for hanging on the wall. A shield somewhat directed the light. Most were made of tin or brass, although some were silver. Fancier sconce devices were mirrored which reflected even greater light.

Scott, John: Listed as a silversmith in 1750s, Albany, New York.

Scott's Emulsion: Sold as a cod-liver oil food supplement in the 1890s. Offered help to the "thin, weak, nervous, and pale." Druggists sold a 50¢ size and a $1 size.

Screen table: Lady's desk with the addition of a screen set behind the desk surface. In the late eighteenth century it protected the user from the hazards of the fireplace. When not in use the screen slid into a slot opening.

Scrimshaw (folk art): Carving on whale's teeth and bones as applied by mostly nineteenth century sailors. A sharp tool was used to engrave scenes, objects, ships, and sometimes slogans. Once completed India ink was rubbed on the incised design to blacken it.

Scroddled ware: Term for mottled earthenware, sometimes called agate ware. Typically pottery made from different colored clays. Mainly used for making bowls, jugs, and pitchers.

Scroll foot (furniture): Term for fashionable eighteenth century chair legs which end in the shape of a carved scroll.

Scroll top (furniture): Reference in early American secretary furniture to the swan-neck curves on either side of the top. Typically decorated with a center finial.

Scrutoire (furniture): Reference to a early bureau or writing desk, of French origin. Used in eighteenth century England and America.

Seal brown (color): As noted in the Sears catalogs of the 1920s, a dark brown.

Seamless Clothing Co.: Makers for seamless overcoats for the U.S. Army and Navy during the Civil War. Located in New York City.

Sears, Matthew: Noted silversmith in 1830s, New York City.

Sears Motor Buggy: One of only two motor cars sold directly by the Sears, Roebuck and Company. A high-wheeler sold from 1908 to 1912 via crated mail-order. Price for the Sears Model L was $495.

Searson, John: A noted clockmaker active in 1760s, New York City.

Sears tool chest: In the early 1900s Sears, Roebuck and Company offered tool chests with the mail-order firm's name in large letters on the inside lid. The chests, sold empty, were made of chestnut black walnut moldings. Depending on design and drawers prices varied from $3 to $7.

Seaweed marquetry: Basically forms of marine life depicted on early furniture through interlaced and delicate designs of inlay.

Sebring Pottery Company: Pottery making operation which was established in 1880s, Sebring, Ohio.

Secor Company (toys): A maker of metal mechanical toys in the 1870s and 1880s. Typically the animated figures had clockwork movements. Eventually

Satinwood secretary bookcase, late eighteenth century.
(Skinner Inc.)

Schilling's Auto Camp advertisement, 1917.

Schoenhut Company's line of wooden animal figures. (Harris Auction Center)

the business, based in Bridgeport, Connecticut, was acquired by Ives, another clockwork toy maker.

Secretary (furniture): Early term for a fall-front desk complete with a bookcase above and perhaps drawers. Accompanying doors might have fancy glass or elaborately carved wood. Few could afford the best of the secretaries.

Sedge (color): A very dark reddish tan color in the Sears lexicon of the early twentieth century.

Seebass Brothers: Listed as a supplier of military goods during the Civil War to the U.S. government, located in New York City.

Seely, Edgar: Granted a patent for gun capper in 1861, Brookline, Massachusetts.

Selden Road Wagon: Self-propelled vehicle invented by George B. Selden in late 1870s, Rochester, New York. It incorporated a two-cycle engine and a liquid fuel tank. Patented granted in 1885.

Seligman, William & Co.: Provided military uniforms and overcoats to Federal troops during the Civil War. Located in New York City.

Sellers and Company: Listed as active in the pewter trade in 1830s, Cincinnati, Ohio.

Semmons & Co. Opticians: Maker of telescopes for the army and navy in 1860s, New York City.

Seneca Glass Company: Small factory located in Morgantown, West Virginia during the 1890s. Firm made souvenir tumblers with patriotic designs in 1896.

Senorita Pearls: Brand of artificial pearls sold by Sears and Roebuck in the early 1920s. Sold in superior quality and fine quality grades.

Sepia (color): Listed as basically brown in the Sears and Roebuck catalogs.

Seroco Refrigerator: Sold by Sears, Roebuck and Company and issued in new patterns in 1902. They were made of solid quarter sawed oak with beveled panels on front and sides. The ice receptacle held 125 pounds of ice. The apartment house models ranged from $27 to $36 in price.

Serpentine (furniture): A reference to the double-curved, bow-like front surface of some pieces of early furniture. Decorative device was used on bureaus, chests, and commodes primarily.

Serrurerie: French term for wrought iron.

Serving table (furniture): Early reference to the side table used to hold tableware and linen in the dining room. Typically the serving table was higher than the dining table. Prior to serving table was the serving board, later it developed into the sideboard.

Settee (furniture): Early furniture reference to a light seat with a low back and arms. It was sometimes upholstered, usually provided seating for two persons.

Settle (furniture): Initially an all-wood bench with wide high ends and a high straight back. A frequent use was for seating in front of the hearth to deter drafts.

Seveignes, Jacques: Silversmith in 1820s, New Orleans, Louisiana.

Severn ware: (see Chesapeake Pottery)

Sevres ware: High-quality soft-paste porcelain first produced in 1740s, France. The King of France financed the venture which later manufactured a hard-paste porcelain as well. Typically the noted Sevres wares were white, transparent, and flawless in appearance.

Sewing table: A later term for what were originally described as work tables. Typically small, with one or more drawers. Some were accompanied with a lid top.

Seymour & Company: Pottery producing operation headed by Israel Seymour in nineteenth century, Troy, New York.

Seymour, Joseph: Doing business in the silversmith trade as Joseph Seymour and Company in 1875, Syracuse, New York.

Seymour, Robert: A Colonial period clockmaker at work in 1760s, Wilmington, Delaware.

S.F.B.J. (doll): Official initials of the French doll making syndicate of the 1890s which dominated the market for a time.

Sgraffito (pottery): Method of pottery decoration. After firing the surface is scraped into intricate patterns, exposing the color of the clay beneath it.

Shaded marquetry (furniture): Craftsmen used hot sand to create the effect of shading marquetry in early cabinetmaking.

Shadow box: Generally a box or frame for displaying individual items or a picture. Usually glass covered.

Shagreen: Treatment for leather with origins in Persia. Initially hides of the camel or horse were used, however shark skin and hides of other animals were used in various regions. Small, hard seeds were worked into the hide when moist and allowed to dry, leaving indentations on the hide surface. The material was then treated with copper filings and other materials to create a green background. The finished leather was used in the eighteenth century for knife handles, snuff boxes, watchcases, and other fancy trinkets.

Shaker (furniture): Rather plain but highly functional furniture crafted by members of Shaker religious sect in the United States. Mainly during the nineteenth century group in various parts of the country produced chairs, desks, rockers, tables, and other high-quality furniture.

Shaler, Reuben: Maker of cartridges for Federal troops in 1860s, Madison, Connecticut.

Sharon (color): A color defined by Sears as a deep and bright rose.

Sharp, George: Active as a silversmith in 1850s, Philadelphia, Pennsylvania.

Sharps and Hankins: Suppliers of .52 caliber carbines to the U.S. Army starting in 1861, located in Philadelphia, Pennsylvania.

Sharps, C.: Maker of breech-loading percussion rifles, supplier to Berdan's Sharpshooters and some militia units during the Civil War.

Shaving cups: Sold in S.S. Kresge Co. stores nationwide for 10¢ each in the early 1900s.

Shaving mug: Cup-like device used to hold hot water and soap for shaving. Such mugs usually also had a compartment for the face lathering brush. Early shaving mugs were made of pewter or tin, or combinations of both. Later shaving mugs were ceramic and sometimes quite decorative.

Shaving table (furniture): Chippendale era dressing table with a basin, spring-up mirror, and hinged side piece, often with drawers and compartments.

Shaw, Edward: Listed as a silversmith in 1820s, Philadelphia, Pennsylvania.

Shawnee Pottery: Highly regarded art pottery producers from 1930s to 1960s in Zanesville, Ohio.

Shearman, Robert: Clockmaker in early 1800s, Philadelphia, Pennsylvania.

Sheet metal: A reference to any type of metal rolled into a thin plate for making toys and other objects.

Shell gray (color): Sears and Roebuck defined it in the 1920s as similar to pearl gray.

Catalog illustration from Schuyler, Hartley & Graham's, 1864.

Scott's Emulsion trade card, ca. 1880s.

Scrimshaw whale's tooth, early to mid-nineteenth century. (Skinner Inc.)

Victorian era walnut cylinder secretary. (Harris Auction Center)

Shell pink (color): A deep yellowish pink as noted in the catalogs of the 1920s.

Shell top (furniture): Term for the round top on an early cupboard designed to resemble a shell.

Shenango China Company: Pottery operation doing business in 1880s, New Castle, Pennsylvania.

Shepard and Company: Glassmaking firm located in Zanesville, Ohio. The company made bottles including some with the American eagle design. Some were marked with the letters "S. & Co."

Shepard Hardware Company (toys): Hardware store that eventually produced cast iron toys in the 1880s. Based in Buffalo, New York, they specialized in clever mechanical banks and similar toys. I. & E. Stevens purchased the firm in the 1890s.

Shepard's Lighting: Top quality brand ice cream freezer sold by Sears, Roebuck and Company in 1902. It offered a "lightning quad-automatic" scraper, a cast iron cover, steel bottom, and cedar tub. Sizes varied from two quarts up to 20 quarts.

Sheraton style (furniture): Reference to the eighteenth century furniture designs of English cabinetmaker Thomas Sheraton. Sheraton's designs strongly influenced Federal Period furniture making in America. Basically Sheraton favored straight line design over curves, and durable over delicate. In 1790 Sheraton included an assortment of furniture designs in the published book, *The Cabinetmaker's and Upholsterer's Drawing Book*.

Shethar, Samuel: Doing business as a silversmith in 1800 Litchfield, Connecticut.

Shield back (furniture): Carved or ornamented shield-like chair back based on the original delicate design by England's George Hepplewhite in the eighteenth century. Typically the side chair or dining chair had a double-curved top rail and the seat was upholstered.

Shields, Caleb: Active as a silversmith in 1775, Baltimore, Maryland.

Shoemaker, Charles: Listed as a silversmith in 1820s, New York City.

Shopshire, Robert: A Colonial era silversmith in 1780s, Baltimore, Maryland.

Short boot: (see Bootee)

Short, Joseph: Overcoat and tent maker for Federal troops during the Civil War, based in New York City.

Shoulder-head (doll): Reference to a doll having a shoulder and head of the same material. A china head doll for example might have a bisque or porcelain shoulder-head but a cloth body.

Shoulder plate (doll): Term for the shoulder-head doll with an attached rather than solid frame head. The attached head then could move slightly or swivel on the shoulder plate. Examples included some parian dolls, early china head dolls, and French fashion dolls.

Show wood (furniture): Early term used by cabinetmaker in reference to wood left exposed after careful upholstering. Typically this area included the legs, apron, and arms. Quality hardwoods such as mahogany or walnut were used in show areas while less expensive woods were used where covered by upholstering.

Shreve, Standwood and Company: Noted as suppliers of swords and sabers to Federal government during the Civil War. Located in Boston, Massachusetts.

Shurlite flashlight: A 1920s brand of flashlight and supplies sold by Sears, Roebuck and Company. Most advertised as containing fiber nickel.

Sicard, Jacques: (see Sicardo ware)

Sicardo ware (ceramic): Metallic luster American art pottery with dark iridescent grounds produced by Weller Pottery in early twentieth century, Zanesville, Ohio. The designs and foreboding colors of brown, green, and purple were credited to French potter Jacques Sicard.

Sickles and Company: Makers of cavalry cartridge boxes for Federal troops during the Civil War, based in St. Louis, Missouri.

Sideboard (furniture): Initially a serving table beside the main dining table. By the eighteenth century the sideboard had open shelves for storing particular dining items. Later doors and drawers added to its gradual refinement.

Sidewalk bike: (see Big Wheel and Long-horn bike)

Signature play kitchen: Brand name for selection of "pretend" kitchen items including range, sink, refrigerator-freezer, kitchenette, and counter top sold by Montgomery Ward in the early 1970s.

Signature Zig-Zag: Brand name for toy electric sewing machine offered in the 1973 Montgomery Ward catalog. Complete with plastic and metal head, the outfit was $22.88.

Silver (color): Sears in the 1920s considered it to be a very light gray.

Silver gray (color): Seemingly redundant it was listed by Sears as also light gray, the color of silver.

Silver moon (color): A romantic term for what Sears declared was just gray in the 1920s editions.

Silver muskrat (color): Colored with both dark and light gray markings, resembling fur.

Silvertown Balloons: Top selling automobile tire of the 1920s. A product of the B.F. Goodrich Rubber Company in Akron, Ohio.

Silver white (color): Sears defined it was white with a silver cast.

Simkins, William: Listed as a silversmith in 1750s, Boston, Massachusetts.

Simmons, G. W. and Brother: Sword and saber supplier during the Civil War. Located in Philadelphia, Pennsylvania.

Simmons, Peter: Doing business as a silversmith in 1815, New York City.

Simon & Halbig: Renowned doll makers in late nineteenth century and early twentieth century, Grafenhain, Germany.

Simplex automobile: The Simplex six cylinder chassis sold for $6,000 in 1916. Bodies were made to order by the Simplex Automobile Company in New York City.

Sinclair, F. A.: (see Common Sense chair)

Sinnett, John: A noted clockmaker in 1770s, New York City.

Six back (furniture): Early American furniture term denoting a ladder-back chair with exceptional six horizontal slats. Typically most such chairs had five or fewer slats.

Six-43: (see Moon automobile)

Six-Sixty: (see Marion-Handley)

Size: (see Enamel [furniture])

Skillet: Early term for a cast iron frying pan. Also sometimes called a spider.

Skinner, John: Doing business in the pewter trade in 1780s and 1790s, Boston, Massachusetts.

Skinner, Thomas: Listed as a silversmith in 1750s, Marblehead, Massachusetts.

Skiver (furniture): Term for split hide material which was cut into a thin layer of leather and then used for lining table tops.

Skookum dolls: (see McAboy, Mary)

Slant-front (furniture): Denotes a desk

Hepplewhite style secretary, ca. 1800. (Skinner Inc.)

Shaker red-painted settee, ca. 1830s. (Skinner Inc.)

Painted and stenciled pine settle, ca. 1830s. (Harris Auction Center)

Pair of Sevres style cobalt blue ground porcelain palace vases, ca 1880s. (Skinner Inc.)

or secretary with a writing section enclosed by a slanting lid.

Slat-back (furniture): Early chair, also known as a ladder-back, with one or more horizontal slats or rails.

Slate (color): Basically a medium light gray in the 1920s mail-order catalogs.

Sleep eyes (doll): An achievement in doll making involving eyes that moved when the doll was moved. Basically sleep eyes were operated by weights which gave the illusion of the doll closing its eyes to sleep and opening them to awake.

Sleepy Hollow chair (furniture): Late nineteenth century upholstered chair said to have a deeply curved back and hollow seat. The chair, with low arms or even without arms, was designed for comfort. The name lent itself to New York state origins.

Sleigh bed (furniture): A sleigh-like bed with curved or scrolled headpiece and footboard. Basically an Americanized version of the Empire Period bed which originated in France. Usually made of mahogany and often accompanied by a sleight-front bureau during the early nineteenth century.

Slip decorated: Term for raised decoration of clay applied to a ceramic piece.

Slipper chair (furniture): Victorian era upholstered chair for use in the bedroom. Most were small with low arms and seat.

Slipware (ceramic): A term regarding the use of slip, a liquid mixture of water and fine clay, as a decorative technique on ceramic wares, in particularly redware. Slip coating was a pottery practice in eighteenth century England.

Smith, Aaron: Doing business as a clockmaker in 1830s, Ipswich, Massachusetts.

Smith, A. E.: Producer of redware and stoneware pottery in the nineteenth century, Norwalk, Connecticut.

Smith and Cleghorn: Prolific supplier of the Confederate military including knapsacks, sword belts, saddles, and leggings. Doing business in Macon, Georgia.

Smith and Company: Active pewter operation doing business in 1830s, Philadelphia, Pennsylvania. Hallmark often included name, axe, and square.

Smith and Wesson: Major producer of cartridge revolvers from 1850s to 1870s. Located in Springfield, Massachusetts.

Smith, Celia & Charity: Designers of lithographed cloth dolls in late 1800s and early 1900s, Ithaca, New York.

Smith, D. M. (doll): Founder of the D.M. Smith Company makers of wooden dolls in the 1870s and 1880s. Some had swivel composition heads. Based in Springfield, Vermont.

Smith, Ebenezer: Colonial era silversmith in 1790s, Brookfield, Connecticut.

Smith, Ella (doll): Noted maker of the so-called indestructible doll or Alabama baby. Smith maintained a small doll factory during the first quarter of the twentieth century in Roanoke, Alabama.

Smith, Fife and Company: A pottery operation in 1830s, Philadelphia, Pennsylvania.

Smith, Gilbert: Supplier of some 30,000 .50 caliber carbines to the U.S. Army in the 1860s, located in Buttermilk Falls, New York.

Smith, Henry: Active clockmaker in 1815, Waterbury, Massachusetts.

Smith, H. M.: Producer of cannon carriages and caissons for the Confederate military. Located in Richmond, Virginia.

Smith, James T. & Co.: Supplier of military equipment including pans and hatchets to Federal troops during the Civil War, based in New York City.

Smith, J. A. Adams: Maker of military equipment including pans and hatchets for Federal troops during the Civil War, based in Batavia, New York.

Smith, John: Granted a U.S. government contract in 1861 to provide gunpowder, located in Kingston, New York.

Smith, J. W.: Maker of military tents for Confederate forces during the Civil War. Located in Memphis, Tennessee.

Smith, Kline & French Co.: (see Eskay's Alburmenized Food)

Smith Mfg. Co.: (see Dyke-s Beard Elixir)

Smith Pottery: Operated by Joseph Smith in 1760s, Bucks County, Pennsylvania.

Smith-Philips China Company: Pottery making operation in 1840s, East Liverpool, Ohio.

Smith, Richard: Doing business as a silversmith in 1830s, Louisville, Kentucky.

Smith, Washington: Stoneware potter active in mid-nineteenth century, New York City.

Smith, W. H.: Known to make military belt buckles for Federal troops in the Civil War, based in Brooklyn, New York.

Smith, William: A distinguished clockmaker active in 1840s, New York City.

Smith, Willoughby: Headed a pottery operation in 1860s, Womelsdorf, Pennsylvania.

Smokey Bear: Popular character doll during the 1970s. Montgomery Ward offered several different versions of the woodland legend from 15" to 37" tall. Additionally there was a talking Smokey Bear and a sleeping bag.

Smoking case: (see Ridgewood Manufacturing)

Snake foot (furniture): Foot on early furniture such as a tripod candle stand, in the shape of a snake head.

Snitzel knife: (see Drawknife)

Snoopy Sniffer: Toy dog featured in Billy and Ruth Catalog of 1952. Black and white dog made "woof-woof" sound when pulled along. Made of solid wood by Fisher-Price, it was 16½" long.

Snow, Jeremiah: Listed as an active silversmith in 1810, Williamsburg, Massachusetts.

Snow white (color): Not the Disney character, but a pure white like snow in the 1920s.

Snuff box: Decorative box for carrying powdered tobacco leaves in the eighteenth and nineteenth centuries. Typically oval or rectangular in shape, they were small enough to be carried in the pocket or purse. Material for the container varied from carved wood to precious metal, and cover adornment could include mother-of-pearl or tortoise shell.

Socket-head (doll): Reference to the tampering of a doll's head into the neck joint. Consequently the socket fit allowed the head to move above the shoulder.

Socle: Architectural reference to a foundation block, usually a base of pedestal.

Soda-lime (glass): Considered the same as lime glass, less brilliant that lead glass. Term applied to clear and patterned

Shaker oval-shaped boxes, late nineteenth century. (Skinner Inc.)

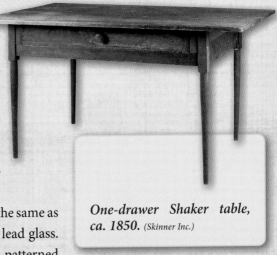

One-drawer Shaker table, ca. 1850. (Skinner Inc.)

Three-drawer Shaker blanket box, ca. 1848. (Skinner Inc.)

A nineteenth century shaving mug with brush.

glass. Adding of soda and other ingredients allowed the substance involved in glassmaking to melt a lower temperatures.

Sofa (furniture): A reference to the upholstered couch or daybed starting with the Louis XIV era in France.

Sofa table (furniture): Originally a reference to the eighteenth century Thomas Sheraton style of a small table with flaps at each end.

Soft paste: An eighteenth century porcelain type of material that was translucent and fragile. Basically a white clay combined with other materials such as bone ash. It lent itself to fine decorative china as it readily absorbed applied colors.

Somes, Brown and Company: Military goods provider to the U.S. government during the Civil War, located in New York City.

Sonner, Samuel: Redware potter in latter nineteenth century, Strasburg, Virginia.

Souers, Christopher: Listed as an active clockmaker in 1720s, Philadelphia, Pennsylvania.

South Bend: Brand name for stylish pocket watch of the early twentieth century. In 1917 their 19-jewel model retailed at $28.75. The South Bend Watch Company was located on Studebaker Street in South Bend, Indiana.

Southern Porcelain Manufacturing: Pottery-making operation first established in 1850s, Kaolin, South Carolina. Founded by Wm. H. Farrar and specializing in porcelain and whiteware.

Southwestern Foundry: Supplier of rifles to Confederate forces during the Civil War. Located in Wytheville, Virginia.

South Ferry Glass: (see Corning Glass Works)

Space Cadet (doll): A character doll produced in the early 1950s by the H & H Doll Manufacturing Corporation of New York City.

Spade foot (furniture): Ending for a tapered leg of early furniture much like a garden spade. During the eighteenth century English designer George Hepplewhite made a somewhat rectangular spade foot for many chairs and tables.

Spandrel (architecture): Historically the space between the arch and its frame, or the curving space between two arches.

Spandrel (clock): Term for the triangular space on each of the four corners of early clock faces. Initially a brass ornament was applied to each spandrel. Later, when painted dial clocks came into fashion, the spandrel was also painted.

Spanish gold (color): An enchanting term for a deep orange gold.

Sparking lamp: Term identified with whale oil lamps and early nineteenth century courtship. The small lamp, comparable to the squat lamp or tavern lamp, held less fuel and therefore offered minimal light and burned out sooner. It was said to be a favorite of young ladies when courted or romanced by a male visitor.

Spark Plug: (see Barney Google)

Sparrow, Henry: Noted silversmith in 1810, Philadelphia, Pennsylvania.

Spatterware (ceramic): Reference to pottery crafted in the first half of the nineteenth century that was spattered or sponged with color and decorated by hand. Various colors were applied to white earthenware made in England and exported to America.

Speedwell Motor Company: Makers of the Speedway Roadster and other automobiles during the early twentieth century. Based in Dayton, Ohio.

Speer, Isaac: Active as a silversmith in 1840s, Newark, New Jersey.

Spence, John: Doing business in the clockmaking trade in 1820s, Boston, Massachusetts.

Spencer, C. M.: Manufacturer of various caliber carbines during the Civil War for state militia and the U.S. Army, doing business in South Manchester, Connecticut.

Spice mill: Small wooden box used for grinding spices in the kitchen. Most were square, but the design varied.

Spider (kitchenware): Term once used in New England for a cast iron skillet. Originally the spider or skillet had three legs, later models were adapted for kitchen ranges and were without legs.

Spindle (furniture): Term for turned section of wood used in early chair backs. Spindles may be straight or tapered.

Spinet: Term for an early stringed instrument. A forerunner of the pianoforte which was the original name for the piano.

Spinner, David: Recorded as a potter of redware in early 1800s, Milford Township, Pennsylvania.

Spinning Jenny: Reference to a latter eighteenth century machine which ultimately allowed several threads to be woven at one time in the making of cloth. The spinning jenny was an invention of James Hargreaves who named the device for his daughter, Jenny.

Spinning wheel: Popular Colonial era device for spinning yarn or thread. In operation a large wheel provided the drive for a single spindle. It was operated by foot-power. Nearly every household had one.

Splat (furniture): An early term for the central, vertical member of a chair back.

Splice: A long handled shovel-like tool used in Colonial times for removing bread and other baked goods from the brick oven in the fireplace. Such a tool with a wide flat end was also sometimes called a peel.

Splint seat (furniture): Basically a chair seat with elements of hickory or oak woven basket-like into a form for sitting.

Spoke dog: A wheelwright's tool, long and narrow, used for pulling wheel spokes into place.

Sponge decoration (ceramic): Reference to applying a thin coating of clay with a cloth or sponge.

Spool bed (furniture): A nineteenth century term for a wooden bed crafted with turned spindles similar to that of end to end spools. Bureaus were also sometimes made with spool turnings.

Sprigged (ceramic): Reference to ceramic ware which was ornamented with small thin pieces of clay cemented into the body with slip — a mixture of water and fine clay. Jasperware was one example.

Spring chair (furniture): Rocking or revolving chair crafted in mid-nineteenth century with heavy metal coil springs. Patented by American Chair Company of Troy, New York.

Victorian era oak sideboard.
(Harris Auction Center)

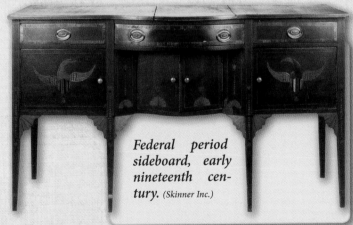

Federal period sideboard, early nineteenth century. *(Skinner Inc.)*

Simon & Halbig doll, ca. 1890s.

Spring-driven (toy): Term for a mechanism sometimes used in power toys. Basically stamped-tinplate gears were put into motion by an unwinding spring.

Springfield doll: Reference to wooden dolls crafted in 1870s and 1880s, Springfield, Vermont. The earlier makers were identified as Joel Ellis and Mason & Taylor.

Spring green (color): Nifty term during the 1920s for a light, bright green.

Sprogell, John: A Colonial era clockmaker in 1790s, Philadelphia, Pennsylvania.

Sprouls, Meeker and Co.: Maker of cavalry cartridge boxes for Federal troops during the Civil War, based in New York City.

Spruce (wood): Softwood with straight grain. Early in the nineteenth century it was used for a range of things from table tops to schoolmaster's desks. It usually finished in a light brown to yellow color. Red filler paint was sometimes incorporated with its use.

Spur (ceramic): Term for slits which separated individual earthenware pieces during firing. Up to three spur marks often appeared on older ware usually in the form of blisters or spots in the glaze.

Squab (furniture): An early term for a chair's or couch's loose cushion seat.

Squibb, E. R.: Physician who crafted most of the medicines used by the U.S. Army during the Civil War. Located in Brooklyn, New York.

Staats, Adam: Noted as operating a stoneware pottery in mid-eighteenth century, Greenwich, Connecticut.

Chippendale mahogany slant front desk, ca. 1770.
(Skinner Inc.)

Stadermann, John: A provider of military goods to the U.S. Army during the Civil War, located in New York City.

Stadler & Bros.: A supplier of military uniforms and U.S. Army clothing during the Civil War era. Located in Cincinnati, Ohio.

Staffordshire (ceramic): Initially a reference to ceramic products crafted in the Staffordshire section of England. Basically this area of about ten miles was the site of numerous potteries particularly during the eighteenth and nineteenth centuries. Among the hundreds of talented potters who once labored there were Josiah Spode and Josiah Wedgwood.

Stage coach clock: The large, long-pendulum wall clock used in stage coach stops and hotels during the eighteenth century. Typically housed in a wooden case about two feet wide.

Stamped mark (ceramic): The mark printed on a ceramic piece.

Standard Eight automobile: Early 1920s product of the Standard Steel Car Company in Pittsburgh, Pennsylvania. Their vestibule sedan sold for $5,000 and their roadster was $3,400 in 1921.

Standing cup: Historically a stylish cup for wine drinking by royalty and the wealthy in old England. Finer standing cups were made of gold, but lesser materials were sometimes used. Hannap was the term for a covered standing cup.

Stanhope automobile: (see Studebaker Brothers and G.N. Pierce Co.)

Stanton, Daniel: Doing business as a silversmith in 1760s, Stonington, Connecticut.

Staples, John Jr.: A Colonial era silversmith in 1780s, New York City.

Star Cars: Low-cost automobiles offered in the 1920s by Durant Motors in New York City. In 1924 their touring car was priced at $540.

Star Encaustic Tile Company: Established in 1880s, Pittsburgh, Pennsylvania.

Star Pottery: Stoneware pottery establishment doing business from 1880s to early 1900s in Elmendorf, Texas.

Starr, Eben T.: Supplier of 20,000 carbines to the U.S. Army during the Civil War, located in Yonkers, New York.

Starr, Frederick: Active clockmaker in 1830s, Rochester, New York.

State Military Works: Provided carbines, muskets, and ammunition to the Confederate military during the Civil War. Located in Greenville, South Carolina.

Stationary eyes (doll): These were set or fixed doll eyes which did not move.

Staton, John: Provided military knives to Confederate forces during the Civil War. Located in Scottsville, Virginia.

Staunton Ordnance Depot: Provided cartridge boxes and bayonet scabbards to Confederate military during the Civil War. Located in Staunton, Virginia.

Steamboat: Brand of regular playing cards offered early in the twentieth century by S.S. Kresge Co. stores.

Steamboat bank: Cast iron bank with Arcade above the paddle wheel. Model made in the 1920s by Arcade Manufacturing Company was 7½" long with gold bronze finish.

Stearns automobile: Manufactured by the F. B. Stearns Company in early 1900s, Cleveland, Ohio.

Stecher Lithograph Co.: Early twentieth century publisher of notable postcards, particularly artist-signed holiday themes. Based at Rochester, New York.

Steel (color): Ranked by Sears and Roebuck in the 1920s as a medium light gray.

Steele, James: Active as a silversmith in 1850s, Rochester, New York.

Steeple clock: A once popular shelf clock with spire-like or steeple top and similar pointed finials at either side. Immediately below the face of the clock was typically a painted picture on glass doors. The majority of these clocks were made in Connecticut from the 1850s to the 1870s.

Stein, Abraham: Noted clockmaker active in early 1800s, Philadelphia, Pennsylvania.

Stencil decoration (ceramic): The use of a brush and a cutout pattern to decorate the potter's thin coating clay.

Stenciled furniture: Stylish decoration applied to early American furniture. Typically a stencil pattern made of cloth or heavily coated paper was used. Painting or bronzing powers were brushed through the open areas around the stencil to create the design. Throughout the nineteenth century gold leaf was dominate in stencil painting, but other colors were also used.

Stephens, George: Listed in 1800 as a silversmith in New York City.

Stephens, Tams & Company: Whiteware pottery operation doing business in 1860s, Trenton, New Jersey.

Stereopticon: A latter nineteenth century device which projected and magnified transparent pictures in a room. Glass slides, known as stereopticon slides were used. The stereopticon was considered an upgrade of the earlier popular magic lantern.

Stereoscope: The rage of every fashionable Victorian parlor, the device was an optical instrument for viewing a double-

Smokey Bear plastic hat made by Tonka.

A nineteenth century sofa with rosewood trim. (Harris Auction Center)

Early nineteenth century sofa with carved wood trim. (Harris Auction Center)

Staffordshire pottery, Death of Munroe, early 1800s. (Mint Museum)

picture. Viewing through the dual lenses offered a unique three-dimensional image. Stereoscopes were so popular in the late nineteenth century and early twentieth century that tens of thousands of stereoscopic views were marketed from foreign lands to nearby street scenes.

Sterling (metal): Originally an English term for a quality silver with an alloy added. In the United States an 1865 federal law required certain items of silver bear this mark. Prior to that time American silver might be marked "coin," with the maker's initials, or entirely unmarked. Sterling silver was typically mixed with a small amount copper alloy.

Sterling Pottery Company: Ironstone pottery establishment launched in early 1900s, East Liverpool, Ohio.

Sterling, Stansbury & Co.: Manufacturer of knapsacks and other items for Federal troops during the Civil War, based in St. Louis, Missouri.

Steuben glass: Highly regarded art glass first crafted in 1903, Corning, New York. The design of stunning crystal glasses and tableware was largely the work of Frederick Carder. One of the best known designs in Steuben glassware was Aurene which was similar to Tiffany's Favrile.

Stevens Company (toys): Major manufacturer of cast iron toys in the nineteenth century and early twentieth century. Brothers John and Elisha Stevens formed the company in Cromwell, Connecticut. Eventually the enterprising firm marketed hundreds of different toys including banks, bell toys, cannons, cap pistols, and wagons. Some production continued in the 1930s.

Stevens-Duryea: A sleek automobile in the $4,500 to $6,000 range in 1913. A product of the Stevens-Duryea Company of Chicopee Falls, Massachusetts.

Stevens, Simon: Supplier of altered and rifled carbines for U.S. troops in 1861, located in New York City.

Stewart, Arthur: Engaged as an active clockmaker in 1830s, New York City.

Stewart, C. W.: Active silversmith in 1850s, Lexington, Kentucky.

Stick chair (furniture): A term for a those seventeenth and eighteenth century chairs made almost entirely of turned members and spindles. Some turner chairs and some Windsor chairs were in this cabinetmaking category.

Stickney, Moses P.: Listed as engaged in the clockmaking trade in 1820s, Boston, Massachusetts.

Stiegel glass: Finely crafted glass with delicate decoration made under the direction of Henry William Stiegel in 1765, Manheim, Pennsylvania. The more refined pieces, which found an early market in nearby Philadelphia, bore jewel-like colors with an occasional flare of enamel. Colors mainly ranged from clear to amber, blue, and green. The factory closed less than ten years after its start.

Stiff wrist (doll): Pertaining to early dolls in which the forearms extended to the fingertips omitting any wrist joint separation. Also known as straight or unbroken wrists.

Stiles, Benjamin: Doing business as a silversmith in 1830s, Woodbury, Connecticut.

Stillman, Samuel: Noted silversmith in 1850s, Hartford, Connecticut.

Stillson, David: A leading clockmaker in 1840s, Rochester, New York.

Stippling: Reference to the use of the brush, pen, or tool for painting, drawing, or punching dots to form a decorative pattern. Sometimes a special tool was used.

Stoddard-Dayton limo: The Stoddard-Dayton limousine sold for $3,800 in 1909. The seven passenger vehicle was produced by the Dayton Motor Company of Dayton, Ohio.

Stokel, John: Engaged as a clockmaker in 1830s, New York City.

Stone, Adam: Doing business as a silversmith in 1805, Baltimore, Maryland.

Stone (color): Sand-like light tan according the 1927 Sears listing of colors.

Stone Marten (color): A full brown but with a white tinge.

Storm, E. C.: Active in 1815 as a silversmith in Rochester, New York.

Stoutenburg, Luke: Noted silversmith in 1735, Charleston, South Carolina.

Stout, James: As of 1825 a silversmith in New York City.

Stout, John: Rockingham and stoneware potter active in 1870s and 1880s, Ripley, Illinois.

Stowell, Abel: A noted clockmaker active in 1790s, Worcester, Massachusetts.

Stow, Solomon: Listed as an active clockmaker in 1830s, Southington, Connecticut.

Strange, Jireh: Doing business as a pewter craftsman in 1800s, Taunton, Massachusetts.

Strange, Joseph: Listed as active in the pewter trade during the 1800s, in Taunton, Massachusetts.

Strapwork (furniture): This amounted to a carved ornamentation used on furniture to resemble cut furniture. It was used during the sixteenth and seventeenth centuries and then revised during the late eighteenth century. Basically it involved bands which were frequently interlaced. A variation was also used on ceilings and screens.

Stratford-le-Bow: (see Bow china)

Stratton, Buck & Co.: (see Bridgeton, New Jersey)

Stratton, Charles: Doing business as a clockmaker in 1820s, Worcester, Massachusetts.

Stratton, John: Maker of cavalry bugles and other musical instruments for Federal troops during the Civil War, located in 1860s, New York City.

Strauss Manufacturing (toys): Extensive maker of colorfully lithographed tin toys, usually mechanical. Millions of the mechanical toys were sold worldwide in the 1920s.

Straw hat: Sears and Roebuck offered the Palm Beach special straw hat in 1923 for $2.25. Available in cream or bronze tan.

Street and Hungerford's Foundry: Produced Parrott guns for Confederate military during the Civil War. Located in Memphis, Tennessee.

Street and Smith: (see Diamond Dick Jr. Weekly)

Stretcher (furniture): Basically the cross rungs or connecting pieces on early chairs and tables. The specific type of stretchers varied including the box stretcher, X and Y stretchers, and Windsor chair type H stretcher.

Striker, George: Doing business in as a silversmith in 1830s, New York City.

Stringing (furniture): Contrasting inlay involving thin band of wood or line.

Struktiron (toy): Term for a line of structural steel parts to be assembled in Erector toy-like fashion. Made by Ives in early 1900s America.

Stucco: Reference to a fine plaster-like substance used for modeled decoration.

Staffordshire pottery, Dandies, ca. 1800s. (Mint Museum)

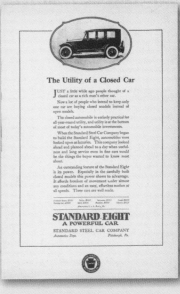

Standard Eight automobile advertisement, 1921.

It was first made popular by designer Robert Adams during the late eighteenth century. Also see compo.

Studebaker Brothers: Noted maker of early 1900s automobiles including gasoline powered touring car and electric Runabout, Victoria Phaeton, and Stanhope.

Studebaker Manufacturing Company: Major maker of automobiles during the first half of the twentieth century, based in South Bend, Indiana. Best sellers during the 1920s included the Erskine Six, President Eight, and the Commander Sedan. Previously a maker of horse carriages.

Studley, David: A noted clockmaker working in 1830s, Hanover, Massachusetts.

Stump bed (furniture): Reference to a rather plain eighteenth century bed lacking any headboard or decorated posts. The bed offered only stumps of wood at its four corners and was found in inns or modest homes.

Sturdivant, Lewis: Supplier of rifles to the Confederate military. Located in Talladega, Alabama.

Stutz automobile: High quality sports car product of the Stutz Motor Car Company of America. In the early 1920s, their Speedway Series autos were priced from $2,400 to $3,400. The maker was based in Indianapolis, Indiana.

Sucket fork: Dual dining device, usually made of silver, providing a fork at one end and a spoon at the other. Designed for eating sweetmeats during the seventeenth century, which were then known as suckets. Such sweetmeats were eaten dry or wet and therefore diners had the option of a fork or spoon.

Sugar tongs: Device, usually silver, for moving lumps of sugar at the table from container to cup. Lump sugar was

first introduced to the tea table in the late eighteenth century.

Sulphide medallion: Reference to a portrait cameo made of specially prepared ceramic material to be enclosed in the base of a glass object such as a paperweight. Apsley Pellatt of England was credited with the 1819 patent.

Sulphume: Sold in the 1890s as a treatment for weak kidneys and rheumatism and a cure for all skin diseases. The dissolved sulphur was also sold as Sulphume soap for 75¢ a box.

Sumner Armory: Known to have been a source of rifles and other weaponry for the Confederate military. Located in Gallatin, Tennessee.

Sunderland ware: A ware initially produced in the town of the same name in Wales. Most noted of this early nineteenth century manufacture was pink luster. Other colorful ware extended from mottled purple to a delicate rose.

Sunflower blanket: Reference to a handwoven woolen blanket which was embroidered with large sunflowers.

Sunken fillet: (see Quirk)

Sunrise (color): Defined in the Sears listings of the 1920s as silver with a pink cast.

Supertone: The Sears, Roebuck and Company brand for musical instruments during the 1920s. Included guitars, mandolins, banjos, and ukuleles. Also saxophones and drums.

Sure Oven: (see Mayflower Stove)

Suter, C. & Company: Provided rifles during the Civil War to the Confederate military. Located in Selma, Alabama.

Sutherland, D. J.: Military equipment maker for Federal troops during the Civil War, based in Philadelphia, Pennsylvania.

Sutherland, Samuel: A supplier of military knives to Confederate soldiers

Wooden stereoscope viewer, ca. 1910.

Stereoscope view of San Francisco fire-earthquake, dated 1906.

during the Civil War. Located in Rich-mond, Virginia.

Sutton, Robert: Enterprising clockmaker doing business in 1820s, New Haven, Connecticut.

Swag: An early term for a type of suspended or swinging ornament. Typically it involved the use of flower or fruit motifs in drapery of festoons.

Swan, Benjamin: An active clockmaker in 1820s, Haverhill, Massachusetts.

Swan, Caleb: Colonial era silversmith in 1775, Boston, Massachusetts.

Swan Hill Pottery: Rockingham and yellow ware pottery operation in mid-nineteenth century, South Amboy, New Jersey.

Swan Neck: (see Gooseneck)

Sweeney, John: Active as a silversmith in 1820s, Geneva, New York.

Sweeter, Henry P.: A Colonial silversmith active in 1770s, Worcester, Massachusetts.

Sweetgum: (see Bilsted wood)

Sweetie Pea: (see Del Monte Corporation)

Sweet Marie: (see Newell cloth doll)

Sweetpea (color): Considered in the 1920s to be a shade between a pink and an orchid.

Swell-front (furniture): Reference to the swell or convex front of early furniture. Initially a more complex design instituted by England's George Hepplewhite and Thomas Sheraton on bureaus and chests.

Swing clock: Rather unusual eighteenth century clock involved a cupid which swung back and forth on a swing as part of the pendulum.

Switchel jug: Basically a large stoneware container used to keep cool a drink mixture known as switchel. During the nineteenth century farm field workers were supplied with the thirst quencher on hot days. It was comprised of cool spring water, vinegar for tartness, molasses for sweetening, and ginger for flavoring.

Syberberg, Christian: Listed as an active clockmaker in 1760s, New York City.

Sycamore (wood): A popular wood in England during the eighteenth century where cabinetmakers used it for inlay and termed it harewood. It was used less frequently in America although it was considered a hardwood with a dense maple-like grain. Typically it provided a light brown finish.

Symmes, John: Doing business as a silversmith in 1760s, Boston, Massachusetts.

Syng, Daniel: Active silversmith in 1820s, Lancaster, Pennsylvania.

Syng, Philip: Noted silversmith in 1700, Philadelphia, Pennsylvania.

Syracuse China Co.: (see Onondaga Pottery Co.)

Syracuse Stoneware Co.: Stoneware firm briefly in operation in late 1890s, Syracuse, New York.

Tab-and-slot: In toy making, a reference to joining lithographed tinplate parts. Small flaps were inserted into corresponding narrow openings of another piece. The flaps were then simply bent to secure joining.

Taber, William: Active silversmith in 1830s, Philadelphia, Pennsylvania.

Table chair (furniture): Term for an eighteenth century armchair with a hinged broad table top arm. It could be lowered for use from the back.

Table croquet: Boxed amusement sold in early twentieth century S.S. Kresge Co. stores. Included mallets, balls, and tape.

Tabouret (furniture): Originally a French term for a low upholstered stool.

Taffeta (glass): Another type of iridescent carnival glass. Produced during the late nineteenth and early twentieth century.

J. E. Stevens Company's Chief Big Moon cast-iron bank, ca. 1890s.

Studebaker automobile advertisement, 1905.

Tambour desk attributed to John Seymour, ca. 1800. (Skinner Inc.)

Tallassee Armory: Muskets and carbines were supplied to Confederate forces via this site. Located in Tallassee, Alabama.

Tallbott and Brother: Makers of cannon carriages and caissons for Confederate military during the Civil War.

Tallboy (furniture): High chest of drawers supported by a second set of drawers below. In early American furniture, the term for such a piece was a highboy. In England it was called a tallboy.

Tamarack tan (color): Described during the 1920s as a medium tan.

Tambour (furniture): Basically the attachment of a flexible shutter or so-called desk-fall. The method in the eighteenth century involved gluing thin strips of wood to a linen backing. Later the backing was a heavier canvas material. At one point desks with the attachment were called tambour desks.

Tampico: Brand name for 1913 nail brush sold by S.S. Kresge Co. for 5¢.

Tan (color): A light brown according to Sears' early catalogs.

Tangerine (color): Consider a bright reddish orange in mail-order terms.

Tankard: A hinged-lid vessel for drinking in early American taverns. Typically made of silver or pewter, it had a broad base and a heavy handle. Such a container with straight sides usually held about a quart of ale or beer.

Tanner, N. B.: One of the few sources of smoothbore muskets for Confederate forces. Located in Bastrop, Texas.

Tanner, Perry: Silversmith in 1840s, Cooperstown, New York.

Tansu (furniture): Reference to a decorative Japanese chest with stylish hinged and elaborate doors.

Tany, Jacob: Operating a pottery business in 1790s, Bucks County, Pennsylvania.

Tappey and Lumsden: In 1861 the firm produced a revolving cannon for the Confederate military. Located in Petersburg, Virginia.

Tappit-hen: Drinking vessel of various sizes with origins in Scotland. Usually made of pewter, containers varied in size from a pint to about three quarts. A hinged cover connected to the thumb piece and handle. Unlike the straight sided tankard, the tappit-hen had tapering sides and a broad base. Like the tankard they usually held ale which could be served warm or cold.

Tarocchi: (see Tarock)

Tarock: A trick-taking game using a deck of tarot cards. Also called tarocchi.

Tarpley carbine: A .52 caliber breech-loading carbine invented by Jere Tarpley of Greensboro, North Carolina. Tarpley was granted a patent by the Confederate government in 1863.

Tarpley, Garrett and Co.: Maker of Tarpley carbines for the Confederate military during the Civil War. Located in Greensboro, North Carolina.

Tarvia: Brand name for nationally advertised roadway covering sold to prevent dust. Marketed early in the twentieth century by the Barrett Company.

Taster: Two-handled vessel, usually silver, used by royalty for tasting wine. Tasters were usually heavily engraved and held about one cup of liquid.

Taunton Britannia Manufacturing Company: Producing pewter and Britannia ware starting in 1830s, Taunton, Massachusetts.

Taupe (color): In the 1927 Sears catalog it was a brownish gray.

Taupe gray (color): Distinctive gray with a brownish cast, according to Sears.

Tavern table (furniture): Frequently seen in eighteenth century America either in oval or rectangular top form. Typically made of maple or pine, stretchers were used to strengthen the legs.

Taylor, Samuel: A noted clockmaker doing business in early 1800, Philadelphia, Pennsylvania.

Taylor, Thomas: Noted silversmith in 1730s, Providence, Rhode Island.

Tazza (glass): Reference to a shallow bowl crafted of luxury glass. The Venetian style glass was characteristic of the Renaissance style and included bowls as well as vases.

Tea caddy: Initially a container for valued tea during the seventeenth century. Early tea caddies were of sturdy construction and fitted with lock and key. Later as tea became less expensive, the caddy became more of a fancy container of materials ranging from china to silver. Eventually the caddy became a tea canister.

Teak wood: A strong and dark wood from a family of Asian trees. Known for its resistance to decay and moisture, it was used in the Far East for furniture. In America however it was largely used for smaller, novelty items.

Teapoy (furniture): Basically a small, eighteenth century three-legged table with a compartment for storage of tea just below the top. While smaller that most tables, it held special focus when tea was served.

Teasmade clock: (see Tea time clock)

Tea time clock: Fascinating combination of alarm clock and mechanical device which boiled water in a kettle and then poured into a teapot. It was electrically powered and sometimes called the Teasmade clock.

Tea urn: Type of kettle which held hot water and was part of the tea service.

Initially such urns had two handles and a lid, plus a lower spigot. Later urns included a burning lamp to keep the water heated.

Teco ware: (see American Terra-Cotta and Ceramic Company)

Teddy Bear bank: Made with the single word "Teddy" across the side. Cast iron and 4" long from Arcade Manufacturing Company during the 1920s.

Ten Cent Novelettes: (see Elliott, Thomes & Talbot)

Tenny, William: Colonial era clockmaker active in 1790s, Nine Corners, New York.

Tent bed: Smaller version of a four-poster bed with a low hanging canopy. Basically a tent-like field bed.

Terhune, John: Supplier under Federal government contract for military bootees during the Civil War. Located in Newark, New Jersey.

Terra cotta (ceramic): Reddish-brown earthenware, usually unglazed. Used for early pottery items, and later for certain selected baked or dried earthenware.

Terry Clock Company: Prolific family of clockmakers doing business in nineteenth century, Pittsfield, Massachusetts.

Terry, John R.: Produced military uniform caps for Federal troops during the Civil War. Located in New York City.

Terry, Wilbert: Active silversmith in early 1800s, Enfield, Connecticut.

Tester bed (furniture): Term for a particular high-post bed with a full canopy. The four posts of the tester bed could be covered with various fabrics including lace or in some cases a light wood.

Tête-à-tête (furniture): A nineteenth century term for a small sofa or love seat. The piece was arranged so that

Hepplewhite style tambour desk, ca. 1790.
(Skinner Inc.)

Eighteenth century pewter tankard, made in America.
(Skinner Inc.)

Tea caddy with lock, ca. 1840.

Chippendale tilt-top tea table, late eighteenth century. (Skinner Inc.)

one person sat facing in one direction while the companion seat faced in the opposite direction. Basically the back formed a small S-curve. Often they were made of mahogany with seats and backs finely upholstered.

Thaxter, J. B.: Maker of military cap boxes for Federal troops during the 1860s, based in Hand, Maine.

Theorem painting: Term for painting, frequently on textiles, involving elements of paper. Typically the paper pieces bore openings in the shape to be painted.

Thibault, Felix: Engaged in the silversmith trade in 1815, Philadelphia, Pennsylvania.

Thistle glass: Term for a short-stemmed glass of the late eighteenth and early nineteenth centuries used for serving brandy or whiskey. It was first used in Scotland around 1780. Its name was derived from the thistle, a native flower of that country. The base of the glass was said to be cut to resemble the flower itself.

Thomas China Company: Manufacturer of pottery products. Established in 1890s, Lisbon, Ohio.

Thomas Flyer: (see Thomas Motor Company)

Thomas, Joseph: Active clockmaker in 1830s, Philadelphia, Pennsylvania.

Thomas, Joseph: Maker of bullet molds for the Confederate military during the Civil War. Located in Memphis, Tennessee.

Thomas Motor Company: Maker of automobiles during the early 1900s in Buffalo, New York. Every Thomas automobile was guaranteed to go 60 miles per hour.

Thomas, Seth: Operated the highly regarded Seth Thomas Clock Company in 1850s, Thomaston, Connecticut.

Thomas, William: A Colonial era silversmith in 1775, Trenton, New Jersey.

Thompson, Benjamin: (see Astral lamp)

Thompson, William: A noted clockmaker and silversmith active in early 1800s, Baltimore, Maryland.

Thonet, Michael: (see Bentwood furniture)

Thor motorcycle: Early twentieth century motorcycle make in Aurora, Illinois. See also Aurora Tool Co.

Thornton, Henry: Doing business as a silversmith in 1820s, Providence, Rhode Island.

Thread glass: Reference to a decidedly decorative glass with threads of differing colors. Typically the contrasting colors of threading decorated bottle necks, pitchers, plate rims, and parts of vases.

Three fold clock: Basically a traveling clock. Made of leather, metal, or plastic it could be fitted on to a hinged central panel. Two outer parts could be closed around the center clock panel. A popular twentieth century medium.

Thrift stamp: Term for a 25¢ non-interest bearing stamp used during World War I, redeemable in certain amounts for war savings stamps.

Thumb-back chair (furniture): Term for the bent thumb shape of some early nineteenth century chair backs. Typically this was a kitchen chair with four to five upright spindles. Such chairs were also called rabbit-ear chairs.

Thumbpiece: Singular part of the lid of a drinking vessel, allowing the lid to be raised by thumb's pressure.

Thumbprint (glass): Reference to the thumbprint-like impression left on certain pattern glass.

Tidy: (see Anti-Macassar)

Tiemann, Geo. & Co.: Suppliers of medical field cases for use by surgeons during the Civil War. Located in New York City.

Tierce: Old English term for a measure of commercial wine. Originally it amounted to 42 gallons, after the 1820s it defined about 35 gallons of wine.

Tier table (furniture): Small, round serving table with two or more shelves or surfaces. The bottom surface is the larger one.

Tiffany glass: World-famous glass manufactured by the L.C. Tiffany Company starting in the late nineteenth century. Most striking was the iridescent glass which ranged from deep blue to purple and green to a yellow-gold. Most true Tiffany glass was marked Tiffany Favrile, L.C. Tiffany, or L.C. T. Other firms attempted to make similar glass.

Tiger lily (color): It was like the flower according to Sears and Roebuck, a deep salmon shade.

Till (furniture): Term for a secret compartment built into early furniture for hiding valuables. The compartment was often in the form of a small drawer. Cabinetmakers typically added one or more such tills to desks and secretaries which could hold cash or jewels.

Tilt-top table: Tripod supported table with the top hinged to allow it to tip into a vertical position.

Timolet's Vapor Bath: The U.S. government granted a contract to Timolet's Vapor Bath during the Civil War. The sulphur and medicated vapor bath was a treatment for rheumatism, chills, fevers, colds, and other illnesses of soldiers and sailors. The product was produced in New York City.

Tinder & Company: Supplier of coffee extract for soldier's rations during the Civil War, located in New York City.

Tinderbox: Reference to a portable box made of tin and used to store linen

tinder, flint, steel, and other materials needed to light a fire in early American households. See chuck muck.

Tin glaze (ceramic): Use of tin oxide in pottery to render an oddly opaque glaze.

Tingley, Samuel: Active silversmith in 1775, New York City.

Tin safe: (see Pie safe)

Tip-Top Bread: (see Cisco Kid)

Toaster: In early America a toaster included wrought iron used for holding slices of bread. The device had a long handle and feet to fix it into position in an open fire.

Tobey, G. R.: New York City based supplier of swords and sabers during the Civil War.

Toby jug (ceramic): English drinking vessels featuring the caricature of a human face and head. Aimed to amuse and entertain such bright-colored jugs or mugs were usually fashioned at potteries in the Staffordshire region of that country.

Todd, George: Supplier of Mississippi rifles to the Confederate government during the Civil War. Located in Montgomery, Alabama.

Toddler Toys: (see Gould's Coaster)

Todd, Richard: Listed as doing business as a clockmaker in 1830s, New York City.

Toepfer, Frank: (see Schloemer-Toepfer Carriage)

Toilettinette, black (furniture): Victorian term for lady's toilet table.

Toledo automobile: Made during the early 1900s by the Pope Motor Car Company in Toledo. Ohio. Advertised price in1905 was $3,200.

Tole ware: French term for decorated tinware used for early household utensils, trays, pitchers, teapots, and scones. Typically such tole ware had a lacquered finish which was applied to tin-plated

Theorem watercolor on paper, nineteenth century.
(Skinner Inc.)

Theorem watercolor on velvet, nineteenth century.

Tiffany bronze and favrile glass lamp. (Skinner Inc.)

Tucker Alarm Till, made in Indianapolis, Indiana.

Stove top non-electric toaster, ca. early 1900s.

iron. In England a similar decorated tinware was known as pontypool.

Tomboy Tot: A 15" stand alone doll offered by Montgomery Ward in the early 1930s. Price was $1.

Tomes, Melvain and Co.: Civil War supplier of military goods to the U.S. government, located in New York City.

Tompkins, Edmund: Active Colonial silversmith in 1780s, Waterbury, Connecticut.

Tompkins, George: A noted maker of clocks in 1820s, Providence, Rhode Island.

Tonneau: Early twentieth century term for an open automobile with seats for two in front and a large rear seat for three or more. See Electric Vehicle Company.

Tootsietoy: (see Dowst)

Topaz (color): Noted with a single word in the 1920s listings — yellow.

Top rail (furniture): On early American furniture, the topmost cross piece on the back of a chair.

Torchere table (furniture): Reference to a small table of French design used for a candle stick or candelabrum. Usually decorated with gilt and fine carvings.

Tormoehlen, Dorothy: One of the models for the Morton Salt girl. See Mary Anderson.

Tortoise (color): Regarded as a medium tan in early Sears catalogs.

Tortoise-shell ware: An effort to decorate eighteenth century earthenware by various English potters including Thomas Thieldon. The mostly highly regarded was the brown mottling in the image of true tortoise shell. However other colors were also created using light applications of oxide on the body of a ware.

Touch mark: Term for the mark of the maker applied to metal.

Tower, Ruben: Clockmaker in 1815, Plymouth, Massachusetts.

Townsend, David: A Colonial period clockmaker active in 1790s, Philadelphia, Pennsylvania.

Tozer, Junis: In the silversmith trade in 1850s, Rochester, New York.

Traffic sign (paperweights): Cast iron traffic sign paperweights were produced in the 1920s by Arcade Manufacturing Company in Freeport, Illinois. The series, 4" to 6" tall, also included a police officer.

Transfer-printing: Reference to the process in which a printed design is transferred to the surface of a ceramic piece.

Transistor clock: Made available around 1960, this timepiece used transistors instead of mechanical switches of earlier days. It was battery-operated.

Translucent (glass): Term for a particular glass which is not entirely clear but allows some limited light to pass through its surface.

Transogram: (see Little Country Doctor kit)

Traprock: (see Basalt)

Trask, Israel: Active as a pewter craftsman during the first half of the nineteenth century in Beverly, Massachusetts.

Trask, John: Active in the pewter trade from the 1820s to 1840s in Boston, Massachusetts.

Trask, Oliver: Pewtersmith of note doing business in nineteenth century, Beverly, Massachusetts.

Travertine: Reference to a porous and cream-colored Italian marble used in construction as a facing material.

Tray table (furniture): Term for an early folding table which was designed to hold a large tray for formal serving of tea during the day.

Tredegar Iron Works: Produced a rifled cannon for the Confederate military during the Civil War. Located in Richmond, Virginia.

Tree of life: Decorative element dating from as early as the seventeenth century. A floral stylized pattern applied in Asian works. Mainly, but not limited to, textiles.

Trelon, Weldon and Weil: French source of military uniform buttons for some Confederate forces, located in Paris, France.

Trencher: Early term for a wooden plate before pewter plates replaced them at the dining table. At one time or another both pewter and china plates were sometimes designated as trenchers. The trencher salt meanwhile was a open salt container placed at each individual's trencher plate. Trencher salts were sometimes footed and were made of glass, pewter, or silver.

Trenton Pottery Company: Pottery established in 1865 at Trenton, New Jersey.

Trestle table: A very early form of table which basically involved a long, usually oblong board, supported by a braced frame. The frame, often composed of two posts with feet, was sometimes called a trestle and later a sawhorse.

Tricky Trolley: An 8" long toy trolley with push down pole to operate. Made of plastic by Mattel. A 1952 Billy and Ruth catalog item priced at $1.

Tripod table (furniture): Basically an early pedestal table with three legs. Most had small round tops.

Triptych (furniture): A three-paneled work of art with individual pieces connected with hinges. Pronounced trip-tick.

Trivet: Basically a metal or iron support of hot dishes on an early American table. Most had cast iron or wrought iron grids with feet for holding hearth heated pots and kettles.

Trompe l'oeil: French term for a seeming three-dimensional look on paintings and other decorations. Giving the illusion of depth to an image.

Troth, James: Noted as a silversmith in 1800, Pittsburgh, Pennsylvania.

Trott, John P.: Active silversmith in early 1800, New London, Connecticut.

Troxel, Samuel: Redware potter doing business in 1820s and 1830s, Montgomery County, Pennsylvania.

Tru-Flesh: (see Miss Ducky)

Truk-Mixer (toy): This cast iron toy was marketed by Hubley Toys during the 1930s. The truck bore the raised letter Truk-Mixer name just below the mixing barrel. It was red and green and 8" in length.

Trumbull, Richard: A noted silversmith in 1765, Boston, Massachusetts.

Trumpet leg (furniture): Early reference to the upturned trumpet-like outline of a turned leg of furniture.

Trundle bed: Term for a low bed designed to slide under a larger bed for daytime storage. Trundle beds often had casters or rollers to accommodate movement. Used mainly for children, they were sometimes called truckle beds.

Trunnel: Originally a hand-carved wooden nail, sometimes also called a tree nail. This form was used for fastening boards together when metal versions were either too costly or too scarce, or both.

Tryron, George W.: Supplier of military knives during the 1860s to the U.S. government, located in Philadelphia, Pennsylvania.

Tuckaway table: Unusual name for an early table which occupied little space when closed. The table had a narrow center, two drop leaves, and pivoting legs.

Tucker (ceramic): Noted American porcelain manufacturer doing business in

Minton toby jug, 1868, England. (Skinner Inc.)

Sam Weller toby jug, made in Germany.

Morton Salt pocket mirror depicting little girl and umbrella. Dorothy Tormoehlen was one of the models for the Morton Salt girl.

Carved ivory triptych, late nineteenth century Germany. (Skinner Inc.)

early nineteenth century, Philadelphia, Pennsylvania.

Tucker, Daniel: Doing business as a silversmith in 1780s, Portland, Maine.

Tudor period: A reference to furniture crafted in the English era from Henry VII in 1485 to Queen Elizabeth in 1603. It embraced late phases of the Gothic style and the early Renaissance phase.

Tudor rose: Originally a carved rose in furniture or other woodwork. It characterized the early Tudor period.

Tulip (glass): Notable flower-like three-lobed motif in pressed glass pattern.

Tuller, William: Active clockmaker during the 1790s in New York City.

Turell, Samuel: Noted Colonial era clockmaker in 1790s, Boston, Massachusetts.

Turkey red (color): Basically a very bright red from the mail-order selections.

Turkeywork (textile): Defined as a form of then stylish seventeenth century embroidery work.

Turkish rocker (furniture): An American-made rocker of the late nineteenth century which may have originated in Turkey. The upholstered chair was mounted on a spring-based platform frame which provided a rocking movement.

Turk's Head: Type of muffin pan offered by S.S. Kresge Co. stores early in the twentieth century. Pans with fluted cups came in two sizes.

Turnbull, Slade & Co.: Supplier of military blankets during the Civil War to Federal troops, located in New York City.

Turn button: In early cabinetmaking, a term for a piece which substituted for a latch. The wooden button was generally oblong and loosely attached with a nail or screw.

Turner & Sibley: Cavalry equipment

manufacturer for Federal troops during the Civil War, based in Chicago, Illinois.

Turquoise (color): A light blue with a greenish cast.

Turquoise (furniture): French reference to a fully-cushioned daybed or settee with high ends and no back. Popular in the Louis XV period.

Tuska, P. H.: Provider of Federal issue swords and sabers during the Civil War. Located in New York City.

Tuttle, Bethuel: Listed as a silversmith in 1800, New Haven, Connecticut.

Two-handed tray: (see Waiter)

Two-tone mount (doll): A contrasting color of the dolls lips and their painted outline. Usually with the outline being the darker of the two.

Tyler, Andrew: A silversmith active in 1725, Boston, Massachusetts.

Tyler, David: Colonial era silversmith in 1775, Boston, Massachusetts.

Tyler Ordinance Works: Listed as a source of rifles, canteens, and ammunition to the Confederate military during the Civil War. Located in Tyler, Texas.

Tyron, E. K. & Co.: A supplier of altered Austrian muskets in 1861 to Federal troops. Located in Philadelphia, Pennsylvania.

Ubelin, Frederick: Active Colonial era silversmith in 1775, Philadelphia, Pennsylvania.

Uhlan: Once a term for a lancer or light cavalry soldier in the German army.

Uhler & Gabriel: Furniture making shop operated by John Uhler and John Gabriel in 1850s, Covington, Indiana.

Uhler, John: Cabinetmaker doing business in 1850s, Fountain County, Indiana.

Ullery, George: Listed as a turner and chair maker working in 1850s, Kosciusko County, Indiana.

Ullman Manufacturing Co.: Noted publisher of early twentieth century postcards, particularly artist-signed greetings and historic events.

Ulrich, Valentine: Listed as an active clockmaker in 1760s, Reading, Pennsylvania.

Ultramarine: A beautiful and lasting blue pigment.

Umber (color): Considered brownish or olive-brown color.

Unbroken wrist (doll): (see Stiff wrist)

Uncle Don: New York City radio program mainly of the 1930s and 1940s. Premiums included song sheet, various pin back buttons, booklets, and still banks.

Uncle Scrooge: Proud and prosperous uncle of the Donald Duck family. Mostly a second banana to Donald and the rest. Uncle Scrooge did foster decades of premiums, toys, figurines, and print collectibles.

Uncle Wiggily: Originally an early twentieth century comic strip character, Uncle Wiggily Longears eventually gained even more enduring fame as a board game. Uncle Wiggily was also featured in books, china, puzzles, and other items throughout the twentieth century.

Uncle Wip: A children's radio show broadcast from 1920s and 1930s, Philadelphia, Pennsylvania. Affiliated with Gimbel's Department stores, its premiums included membership certificate, pin back buttons, book, and badge.

Underbid: Reference to offering less than the current amount at an auction.

Underbracing (furniture): Early American cabinetmaking term for necessary stretchers attached to a chair, table, or similar furniture for additional strength. Simple but decorative designs included H-shapes, Y-shapes, and X-shape stretchers.

Underdog: Television cartoon hero of the 1960s and 1970s. The caped canine generated fan club membership cards, mugs, club ring, school book bags, and even a wristwatch.

Under glaze decoration (ceramic): A reference to the potter's application of decoration to the bisque surface before the application of the ultimate glaze.

Underhill, Andrew: Noted silversmith in 1780s, New York City.

Underhill, Clarkson: Tennessee born cabinetmaker doing business in 1850s, Wayne County, Indiana.

Underhill, Thomas: Listed as a silversmith in 1780s, New York City.

Underwood, Andrew: Pennsylvania born cabinetmaker doing business in 1850s, Elkhart County, Indiana.

Underwood, H. & Son: Stoneware pottery in operation in 1880s, Calhoun, Missouri.

Underwood, J. A.: Stoneware potter in 1860s, Fort Edward, New York.

Underwood, John: Colonial era silversmith in 1795, Philadelphia, Pennsylvania.

Underwood, Joseph: Ohio-born chair maker who worked in 1840s, Indianapolis, Indiana, and in 1850s, Versailles, Indiana.

Undivided back: Postcard reference, see divided back.

Unguent: A term for an ointment used for treatment on the surface of the body.

Unicycle: An acrobat's cycle with just a single wheel.

Union Arms Co.: Listed as a manufacturer of percussion revolvers in the 1860s, located in Newark, New Jersey.

Union Car Works: Listed as a maker of military knives for Confederate troops during the Civil War. Located in Portsmouth, Virginia.

Union Glass Works: Supplier of gunpowder during the Civil War to the

Enterprise Manufacturing Co. trivet.

Triangular cast-iron trivet, nineteenth century.

U.S. government, located in New Durham, New York. Also see Kew-Blas.

Union Manufacturing Co.: Major supplier of Bowie knives and saber bayonets to the Confederate military during the Civil War. Located in Richmond, Virginia.

Union Manufacturing Company: A clockmaking firm active in 1840s, Bristol, Connecticut.

Union Porcelain Works: Porcelain operation started in 1860s, Greenpoint, New York.

Union Products: Noted maker of plastic holiday items and other related products. Based in Leominister, Massachusetts.

United States Pottery: Well noted pottery operation of various wares in 1850s, Bennington, Vermont.

Universal table (furniture): An eighteenth century breakfast table which could also be converted into a dining table later in the day. Typically it contained two leaves which could fit beneath main table surface when not in use.

Upholder (furniture): An eighteenth century term for the particular cabinetmaker who specialized in upholstering.

Upland cotton (textile): Reference to a cotton with a short fiber.

Urey, John: Chair maker working with John Cutter in 1850s, Carroll County, Indiana.

Urn (furniture): A design as a finial or center motif for a chair back especially popular on high-quality furniture crafted in the 1700s. The decorative design was said to originate with Greek and Roman architecture and emerged from time to time including the fifteenth century and the eighteenth century.

Union Products Company plastic witch riding a broom, ca. 1950s.

Urn table (furniture): Term for a small English table used for serving tea during the eighteenth century.

Utensil: Term for an implement, particular one used for domestic or culinary purposes.

Utica Glass Works: Relatively obscure glassmaking operation started in 1810 or 1811, Utica, New York. Operation ceased shortly after opening and was soon abandoned.

Vail and White: Noted cabinetmaking operation which included J. J. Vail in 1840s, Madison, Indiana.

Vail, Elijah: Noted silversmith in 1840s, Troy, New York.

Vail, J. J.: Listed as an active cabinetmaker in 1850s, Madison, Indiana.

Valance (furniture): An early reference to the horizontal drapery of a tester top or canopy of a four-poster bed. Later the term came to designate instead the horizontal piece of any drapery arrangement placed over the mantle or windows.

Valentine Dolls: (see Perfect Baby)

Valentine, John W.: Cabinetmaker working in 1850s, Henry County, Indiana.

Valentine, Lyman: New York born chair maker active in 1850s, Mishawaka, Indiana.

Vallee, Antoine: Listed as an active silversmith in 1820s, New Orleans, Louisiana.

Vanall, John: Colonial era silversmith in 1750s, Charleston, South Carolina.

Van Bergen, John: A Colonial silversmith in 1795, Albany, New York.

Van Briggle Pottery: Highly regarded art pottery operation starting in early 1900s, Colorado Springs, Colorado.

Van Brunt, James: Under contract to make knapsacks and haversacks for Federal troops during the Civil War, based in Brooklyn, New York.

Vance Faience Pottery: Rockingham, stoneware, and whiteware producers in late nineteenth century, Tiltonville, Ohio.

Van Cleave, Joseph: Bayonet scabbard, and other military equipment maker for Federal troops during the Civil War, based in Newark, New Jersey.

Van Cleave, Matthias: Kentucky-born cabinetmaker who operated a furniture shop in 1850s, Crawfordsville, Indiana.

Van Dyke brown (color): In the 1920s Sears describes this as a deep rich brown.

Van Dyke, Joseph: Cabinetmaker listed as working in 1820s, Brookville, Indiana.

Van Dyke, Richard: Noted as a silversmith in 1750s, New York City.

Van Horn, Bevrod: Listed as an active cabinetmaker in 1850s, Dearborn County, Indiana.

Van Horn, David: Early 1800s silversmith in Philadelphia, Pennsylvania.

Van Hoy, John: Indiana-born cabinetmaker working in 1850s, Martin County, Indiana.

Vanhuis, Hezakiah: Indiana-born cabinetmaker doing business in 1850s, Wayne County, Indiana.

Vanity Flossy: (see Flossie Flirt)

Vanleer, Sam and Co.: Supplier of powder flasks and power horns for the Confederate military. Located in Nashville, Tennessee.

Vanolite: A mineral common in crystal form which provided an ax-like edge when flattened.

Van Pelt, I. and J.: Produced cannon carriages and caissons for the Confederate military. Located in Petersburg, Virginia.

Van Pelt, Nicholas: Ohio-born cabinetmaker engaged in the trade with Robert McTeer in 1850s, Carroll County, Indiana.

Van Riper, Tunis: Active silversmith in 1820s, New York City.

Van Ripper, P. V.: Listed as a maker of cartridge boxes for Federal troops during the Civil War, based in Patterson, New Jersey.

Van Sickler & Forby: Firm supplied the Federal military with uniforms, socks, shirts, and drawers during the Civil War era. Located in Albany, New York.

Van Vleit, B. C.: Doing business as a clockmaker in 1830s, Poughkeepsie, New York.

Van Voorhis, Daniel: Silversmith in early 1800s, Philadelphia, Pennsylvania.

Van Wegeman, John: Listed as an active clockmaker in 1840s, Oxford, New York.

Vanwyck, T. J.: Supplier of wall tents and hospital tents to the Federal military during the Civil War.

Vaseline glass: Victorian era glass with a greenish-yellow tint of Vaseline salve. Originally it was said to have been made with amounts of uranium. Its tint is somewhat changeable under certain lights. A British term for the glass is lemonescent.

Vase splat (furniture): Term for the vase-shaped chair back piece applied by cabinetmakers on Queen Anne style chairs in the eighteenth century.

Vase turnings (furniture): Early reference to vase-shaped chair turnings, particularly as seen on Windsor chairs.

Vaughan, William: Kentucky-born cabinetmaker working in the 1850s in Brownsburg, Indiana.

Veal, John: Active silversmith in 1830s, Columbia, South Carolina.

Veazie, Joseph: Operating as a clockmaker in early 1800s, Providence, Rhode Island.

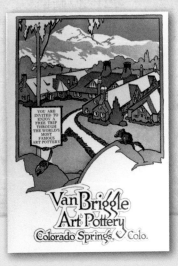

Van Briggle Art Pottery tourist guide, ca. 1930s.

Victorian parlor table with marble top. (Harris Auction Center)

Victorian lady's desk with lift top.
(Harris Auction Center)

Veder, Nicholas J.: Native of New York listed as a working chair maker in 1850s, Fayette County, Indiana.

Veil pin: (see Bar pin)

Vellum (paper): A reference to parchment-like paper. Originally a term for writing material using the skin of a farm animal.

Velocipede: Reference to a light carriage propelled by the feet. An original form of the bicycle.

Velvet brown (color): Simply put a soft brown.

Veneer (furniture): Reference to the layer or layers of figured wood glued together crosswise, upon solid or built-up wood. The practice, in variations, was a part of furniture making for centuries.

Venetian glass: Considered by many to be the highest form glassmaking, it dates to 1083 Venice, Italy. Around 1268 glassmaking artists were segregated to the nearby island of Murano. Rigid laws were passed to prevent workers from going to other countries, but rewards were tempting. Over the centuries Venetian glass remained blown glass. It was traditionally lightweight, fragile, and delicate. Selections included colored and clear glass, gold-trimmed, crackled surfaces, and other novelties. During the nineteenth century the industry was revived and some production continued.

Venetian red (color): According to the early mail-order catalogs a bright light red.

Venturine: A powder made of fine gold and used for japanning.

Verback, John: Occupied as an upholster in 1850s, New Albany, Indiana.

Verd-antique: Early term for green incrustation on ancient copper and brass coins. Also reference to a beautiful mottled marble.

Verdigris (color): Described by Sears in the 1920s as a medium green.

Verditer: A blue or green pigment.

Vermiel: A French term for silver plated. Originally used in the eighteenth century for the silver gilt used on candelabrum.

Vermont Glass Factory: A glassmaking operation established around 1813 in Salisbury, Vermont.

Vermont Novelty Works: (see Ellis, Britton & Easton)

Vermont Toy Works: Produced wooden dolls for the commercial market in 1870s, Springfield, Vermont. Dolls with painted features and jointed body designed there by Joel Ellis.

Vernis Martin: Name for a highly regarded eighteenth century varnishing or lacquering process developed by two French coach painters. It provided furniture and other objects with a deep and brilliant translucent effect starting in the 1730s and continuing for many decades. Accounts say the formula, particularly green flecked with gold, disappeared with the death of Simon Martin.

Vernon, John: Listed as a silversmith in 1800, New York City.

Vernon, Nathaniel: Active silversmith in early 1800s, Charleston, South Carolina.

Verre eglomise (furniture): Reference to painted glass used as decorative inserts on early furniture. Eglomise coined from the name of French designer Jean-Baptiste Glomi.

VertiBird Ship: Detailed toy rescue ship complete with helicopter in 1973 Montgomery Ward catalog. The replica of a Coast Guard cutter also came with a space capsule, astronaut, and life raft. It operated on batteries and retailed at $11.66.

Vesta Accumulator Company: Maker of the Vesta Storage Battery for early 1900s automobiles. Based on Michigan Avenue in Chicago, Illinois.

Vestal lamp (furniture): Basically a latter nineteenth century kerosene lamp set on a base and stand. The glass shade and chimney were raised above the fuel container. Known as a paraffin lamp in England.

Vibro-Roll: (see Gee-I-Jeep)

Vickers, Christian: Virginia-born cabinet-maker working in the Allen & Vickers shop in 1850s, Covington, Indiana.

Vickers, James: Ohio born cabinetmaker working in 1850s, Allen County, Indiana.

Vickers' metal: Sometimes called white metal but with a silver-like appearance. It was credited by James Vickers of England. Vickers' metal was basically an alloy of antimony, copper, tin, and zinc, and often bore the maker's mark. It was more or less superceded by Sheffield plate in England.

Victoria: An early term for a type of carriage for two persons.

Victoria auto: (see Woods Motor Vehicle Company)

Victoria coupe: (see Dayton Friction Toy Company)

Victorian era: Reference to era covered by the reign of Queen Victoria in England. Generally it pertains to furniture, china, clothing, glassware, silverware, and jewelry made during that time from 1837 to 1901.

Victorian Phaeton: Electric automobile manufactured in the early 1900s by Studebaker Brothers Manufacturing Company in South Bend, Indiana.

Victor Razor: One of the many brands sold by Sears, Roebuck and Company "for private use" during the early 1900s. The shaving razor came with a fancy celluloid handle and sold for $1.95.

Victrola: Specific brand of the Victor Talking Company early in the twentieth century. Styles varied in price from $10 to $400. The electric Victrola XVII was $300 in 1917.

View-Master: Popular viewing device which used a vast variety of round reels. Early in the 1970s the Montgomery Ward catalog offered the standard viewers as well as lighted talking viewers, and a View-Master projector.

Views: Regarding post-cards with a reference to images of people and places, usually of a specific area or region.

Views in New York: (see Fay, Theodore)

Vincennes (ceramic): Term for soft-paste porcelain manufactured in France from the 1730s through the 1750s.

Vincent, Richard: Early 1800s silversmith active in Baltimore, Maryland.

Vines, Daniel: Pennsylvania born cabinetmaker working in 1850s, Warren County, Indiana.

Vinette: Reference to the decorative use of a continuous ornamental band of leaves and tendrils by early cabinetmakers.

Vinton, David: A noted clockmaker active in 1790s, Providence, Rhode Island.

Vin Vitae: Sold as "the wine of life" by Sears, Roebuck and Company in 1902. Advertised as "the perfect tonic stimulant for the tired, weak and sick of all classes." Price for a "large bottle" was 69¢.

Victorian era marble top commode. (Harris Auction Center)

Two Sawyer View-Master viewers, ca. 1950s.

View-Master reel list catalog, 1950.

Early twentieth century view postcard of harbor at Everett, Washington.

Violet (color): As the name implies, a bluish lavender.

Violet wood: (see Amarinth)

Violin bottle (glass): Violin-shaped bottle or flask made primarily in the Midwest United States during the nineteenth century in various colors. Originally they were designed to hold about a pint of whiskey. Some sources credit Ohio glasshouses for the first green and brown violin bottles. Sometimes called fiddle bottles, they were made into the very early 1900s.

Violin flask: (see Bellow flask & Violin bottle)

Virgin white (color): As presented by the Sears catalogs in the 1920s, a pure white.

Visite (textile): French term for a light lace or silk cape for summer wear.

Vitrine (French): Reference to an early glazed cupboard crafted in France. Often included a glass top for display and a table-like compartment below.

Vliet, Daniel: New Jersey-born cabinetmaker doing business with Samuel Rodarmel in 1850s, Daviess County, Indiana.

Vodrey Bros.: Pottery producing Rockingham and yellow ware starting in 1850s, East Liverpool, Ohio.

Vodrey Pottery Company: A producer of pottery in 1850s, East Liverpool, Ohio.

Vogler, John: Noted silversmith operating in 1820s, Salem, North Carolina.

Vogt, John: Enterprising clockmaker operating in 1760s, New York City.

Voider: An eighteenth century English term for a tray used in carrying utensils to and from the table.

Voight, Sebastian: A Colonial period clockmaker working in 1780s, Philadelphia, Pennsylvania.

Voight, Thomas: Active clockmaker in 1820s, Philadelphia, Pennsylvania.

Volkmar Pottery: Pottery production firm in 1870s, Greenpoint, New York.

Voss, Lorenzo: Tennessee-born cabinetmaker who was active in the trade in 1850s, Lawrence County, Indiana.

Voss, William: Cabinetmaker, born in Tennessee, engaged in furniture making in 1850s, Lawrence County, Indiana.

Vulcanite: The result of changing India-rubber into a hard and non-elastic substance.

Vulpinite: Term for a variety of gypsum susceptible to a fine polish.

Waddill, Noel: Doing business as a silversmith in 1780s, Petersburg, Virginia.

Wade and Ford: Makers of medical instruments and Wood's General Operating case for use by the U.S. Army during the Civil War. Located in New York City.

Wade, Nathaniel: A noted clockmaker in early 1800s, Stratford, Connecticut.

Wadsworth, Jeremiah: An accomplished clockmaker working in 1820s, Georgetown, South Carolina.

Wadsworth, Lester: Pewter craftsman active in the trade in 1830s, Hartford, Connecticut.

Wady, James: Listed as an active clockmaker in 1750s, Newport, Rhode Island.

Wagner Model: Type of baseball glove sold under the J.C. Higgins brand by Sears, Roebuck and Company in 1923. Both left and right-handed models were sold for $4.20 each.

Wagoner, F. C.: Listed as a supplier of knapsacks and haversacks for Federal troops during the Civil War, based in New York City.

Wagon jack: Early American device for wagon wheel repair. Hand cranked, much like the modern automobile jack, but long handled and made almost entirely of wood.

Wagon seat: Early farm wagon seat made of hickory or other very durable wood. Such seats, perhaps with rush or splint cushioning, were portable. They could be placed into the wagon when the entire family needed transportation to town or church. Commercially they were made in eastern states and sold in rural regions nationwide.

Wagon-spring clock: Early clock fitted with a leaf spring similar to that used at the time in wagons. Attributed to Joseph Ives in early 1800s America. Such springs provided motive power in place of a mainspring or weight.

Wag-on-the wall: Term used in the United States for an early wall clock in which the pendulum and weights were open to view.

Wainscot chair (furniture): Basically a sixteenth and seventeenth century chair with a predominate back panel. While the seat and back were made of solid panels, the legs followed the Jacobean style of that era. Sometimes a cushion was added to the hard wooden seat of the wainscot chair.

Waiter: Sometimes a term for an early two-handled tray. Mostly crafted of silver, but sometimes pewter.

Waite, William: Active silversmith in 1760s, Wickford, Rhode Island.

Walch, J.: Listed as a maker of percussion revolvers patented in 1859. Located in New York City.

Walker, A. J.: Doing business as a clock-maker in 1830s, Brockport, New York.

Walker, Hannah: Listed as a silversmith in 1815, Philadelphia, Pennsylvania.

Walker, Izannah: Highly regarded maker of wood and fabric dolls in 1870s and 1880s, Central Falls, Rhode Island.

Wallace and Chetwynd Pottery Company: A manufacturer of pottery ware in 1880s, East Liverpool, Ohio.

Wallace, William: Active silversmith in 1800s, Westerly, Rhode Island.

Wall furniture: Early reference to furniture intended to be used up against a wall. Included were bookcases, chests, cupboards, and similar pieces.

Wallis and Rice: Suppliers of Mississippi rifles to Confederate forces. Located in Talladega, Alabama.

Walnut (wood): Remarkably richly grained hardwood which was the wood of choice for many early cabinetmakers it America. Quite popular during the Queen Anne and Chippendale periods. Finished color varied from a reddish brown to a deeper chocolate brown. During the Victorian era, black walnut was somewhat favored and used in connection with an acid wash to stain.

Walter, Joseph: Noted silversmith in 1830s, Baltimore, Maryland.

Waltham Manufacturing Company: Maker of early 1900s automobiles including the two speed Orient Buckboard which was priced at $425. The company was located in Waltham, Massachusetts.

Walton, Daniel: Active silversmith in 1810, Philadelphia, Pennsylvania.

Wanamaker, John: (see Deptartment Store game)

Ward, Ambrose: A Colonial silversmith in 1790s, New Haven, Connecticut.

Ward Escort: Brightly colored portable manual typewriter sold in 1973 by Montgomery Ward. The yellow-colored manual was $58.88. The blue-colored portable electric version was $159.88.

Ward, H. B.: Listed as pewter producer in 1820s, Guilford, Connecticut.

Walnut leather top table in Eastlake style. (Harris Auction Center)

Walnut commode, latter eighteenth century. (Skinner Inc.)

Ward, James: An active pewtersmith in 1790s, Hartford, Connecticut.

Ward, John: Listed as a silversmith in 1805, Middletown, Connecticut.

Ward, Lewis: Doing business as a clockmaker in 1830s, Salem Bridge, Connecticut.

Ward, S. M. and Co.: Supplier of battle pins for soldiers and sailors and other ornamentation during the Civil War, based in New York City.

Ward, Thomas: A noted clockmaker in 1820s, Baltimore, Maryland.

Warner, Andrew: Noted silversmith in 1825, Baltimore, Maryland.

Warner, Caleb: Listed as an active silversmith in 1820s, Salem, Massachusetts.

Warner, Cuthbert: Listed as an active clockmaker in early 1800s, Baltimore, Maryland.

Warner, James: Noted as a maker of percussion revolvers, first patent granted in 1851. Supplier of military carbines for the U.S. Army during the 1860s, based in Springfield, Massachusetts.

Warner, Wm.: Noted nineteenth century stoneware and Rockingham potter in West Troy, New York.

Warren, Benjamin: Noted silversmith in 1810, Philadelphia, Pennsylvania.

Warwick China Co.: Whiteware pottery doing business in late nineteenth century, Wheeling, West Virginia.

Washburne & Philbrook: Under contract with the Federal government for military tents during the Civil War. Located in Camden, Maine.

Washington Pottery: (see American Art China Works)

Washstand (furniture): Starting in the eighteenth century a term for any small table stand or sometimes a commode used to support a water-bearing wash basin. Very popular late nineteenth century mail-order furnishing.

Wasp waist (doll): Reference in some adult dolls to the extremely narrow or so-called cinched-in waist.

Wassail bowl: By tradition the bowl filled with spiced ale and used on New Year's Day.

Waterbury Button Co.: A major supplier of military buttons to Federal troops during the Civil War, based in New York, New York.

Waterford (glass): High quality cut-glass first manufactured in late 1720s, Waterford, Ireland. Brilliant, heavy, and known for a distinctive ring — it became a popular export to America. Particularly significant were Waterford bowls and decanters. Some items were noted for their smoky or blue-gray color.

Water gilding: Early furniture decorating method involving ormolu (metal furniture mounts) and adding thin deposits of gold and mercury.

Waterhouse, A: (see Eaton Hall Chair)

Water leaf (furniture): Decorative device used on eighteenth furniture in the form of an elongated laurel leaf. Such an ornamental detail was used chiefly on George Hepplewhite and Thomas Sheraton furniture.

Waters, A. H.: Listed as a maker of rifled muskets during the Civil War. Credited with making the 1861 rifled musket marked Millbury. Located in Millbury, Massachusetts.

Watkins and Slaughter: Provided infantry equipment to Federal troops during the Civil War, based in Indianapolis, Indiana.

Watkins, James: Active silversmith in 1840s, Philadelphia, Pennsylvania.

Watson, E. P.: Granted a Civil War era

patent for spur carrier and boot-drawer (boot jack), located in New York City.

Watson Wagon Co.: Early twentieth century maker of Watson Wagons, trailers, and motor trucks. Based in Canastota, New York.

Watts, John: A Colonial era silversmith in 1790s, New York City.

Waverly Electric: Automobile produced in the early 1900s by the Pope Motor Car Company of Indianapolis, Indiana. Price in 1907 was $1,600.

Wax inlaying: Treatment of incised work on early furniture with a type of colored wax.

Wax polish: Term for early form of wood polishing involving only beeswax and turpentine. Generally replaced by other types of polish in the eighteenth century.

Wayne automobile: Made during the early 1900s by the Wayne Automobile Company in Detroit, Michigan. The four cylinder Model B sold for $2,000.

Way, S. H.: Potter working in redware in 1860s, Eola, Oregon.

Weatherley, James: Contracted to supply horse harness to the U.S. Army in 1861, located in Cincinnati, Ohio.

Weaver, Nicholas: Active silversmith in 1820s, Utica, New York.

Webb, Edward: Listed as a silversmith in 1820s, Boston, Massachusetts.

Webber singing doll: A rather complex doll which required a bellows to activate organ reeds. Patented in 1882 by William Weber of Medford, Massachusetts, it was manufactured by the Massachusetts Organ Company. The wax-head doll came in three sizes.

Webb odometer: Early 1900s product of the Webb Company located in New York City. The firm also manufactured the Webb speed indicator.

Webster, Henry: Noted silversmith in 1830s, Providence, Rhode Island.

Wedgwood (ceramic): Historic eighteenth century English pottery noted for its quality and variations. The firm may be most famous for basalt which credited to the genius and talent of Joseph Wedgwood. The distinguished firm also made cream ware, jasperware, salt glaze, Parian, and redware over the years.

Weeden engine: Leading brand of toy horizontal engine sold for children by Sears, Roebuck and Company in the early 1900s. Various models came with a brass boiler fueled by alcohol. The most elaborate double engine Weeden sold for $3.50.

Weeden Manufacturing (toys): A company which excelled at the production of steam-powered toys for decades starting in the 1880s. Based in New Bedford, Massachusetts, Weeden continued to make transportation-related toys into the early 1930s.

Weed, Nathan: Listed as a supplier of Bowie knives for the Georgia military during the Civil War.

Weekend Barbie: (see Euro Disney)

Weiss, F. W.: Granted a U.S. patent in 1861 for a Federal army military cloak. Located in Mount Vernon, California.

Welch, Elisha: Involved in clockmaking as the Elisha Welch Company in 1850s, Bristol, Connecticut.

Welch, James: Noted as a supplier of military knives for Confederate forces during the Civil War. Located in Richmond, Virginia.

Welch, John: Pewter artisan of note in 1790s, Boston, Massachusetts.

Welch, W. W.: Under contract with the Federal government to provide 17,000

Queen Anne walnut bureau table. (Skinner Inc.)

Wash stand with two drawers and curtained shelf.

Wedgwood solid pale blue Jasper vase, ca 1780. (Skinner Inc.)

rifled muskets during the Civil War. Located in Norfolk, Connecticut.

Weldon, C. & J.: British source of military uniform buttons for some Confederate troops, located in London, England.

Weldon, Oliver: A noted clockmaker active in 1820s, Bristol, Connecticut.

Weller Pottery: Highly regarded art pottery operation from 1890s to 1940s in Zanesville, Ohio.

Weller, S. A.: Founder of pottery making company established in 1890s Zanesville, Ohio.

Welles, Alfred: Listed as an active silversmith in 1840s, Hebron, Connecticut.

Wellington cloth doll: A cloth doll constructed over a wire frame, covered with stockinet and stuffed with cotton batting. It was patented in 1883 by Martha Wellington of Brookline, Massachusetts.

Wellsville China Co.: Early 1900s whiteware pottery operation in Wellsville, Ohio.

Wells, William: Doing business in the silversmith trade in 1760s, Hartford, Connecticut.

Welsh dresser (furniture): Originally a reference to a dresser used in the dining room. It offered cabinet storage compartments below and shelves above for display of prized china and pewter.

Wendlinger, C.: Source of military uniform buttons to the Confederacy during the Civil War, doing business in Richmond, Virginia.

Wentworth, Jason: Active silversmith in 1840s, Boston, Massachusetts.

West End Pottery: Active whiteware pottery from 1890s to the 1930s in East Liverpool, Ohio.

Westermeyer, Henry: Colonial silversmith in 1790s, Charleston, South Carolina.

Western Stoneware Company: Stoneware pottery operation starting in early 1900s, Monmouth, Illinois.

Westervelt, John: Listed as a silversmith in 1840s, Newburgh, New York.

Westward Ho (glass): Striking nineteenth century pressed glass pattern depicting scenes on the western frontier. Originally called Pioneer. Acid provided a frosted or satin finish.

Wet: Prohibition era reference to a location allowing the sale of liquor. Also a term defining a person opposed to prohibition.

Whartenby, Thomas: Listed as Thomas Whartenby and Company Silversmiths in 1850s, Philadelphia, Pennsylvania.

What-not shelf (furniture): Term for a tier of shelves supported by turned posts. While they were said to have originated in eighteenth century France, they were highly popular in American homes during the Victorian era for display of small china and various other trinkets. Particular design varied from standing flat against a wall, hanging upon the wall, or fitted into a corner. Walnut or walnut stained were most popular in the late Victorian era. Also see Etagere.

Whatnot table: (see Occasional table)

Wheat ears: Early cabinetmaking term for the carving of ears of wheat in low relief as a furniture decoration.

Wheatley & Co.: (see Cincinnati Art Pottery)

Wheaton, Caleb: Listed as an active clockmaker in 1830s, Bristol, Connecticut.

Wheeler, Edward: (see Deadwood Dick)

Wheeling (glass): A reference to prized art glass produced in nineteenth century Wheeling, West Virginia. Additionally William Leighton was credited with the improved soda-lime process for glassmaking in the 1860s at the Hobbs Brockunier and Company.

Wheeling Pottery Company: Active whiteware pottery establishment from the 1870s to early 1900s in Wheeling, West Virginia.

Wheelock, C. E.: Noted early twentieth century publisher of state capitol and presidential postcards. Based at Peoria, Illinois.

Whieldon, Thomas: (see Agate ware)

Whimsy: Toy or other object produced by the maker on a whim, and intended to amuse or entertain the recipient.

Whippet automobile: Launched as a "finger-tip control" automobile in 1929, it was a product of Willys-Overland Inc. in Toledo, Ohio. The Whippet Four Coach was priced at $535 that year.

Whipple, Arnold: Listed as an active silversmith and clockmaker in 1820s Providence, Rhode Island.

Whirl-I-Gig: Toy airplane with a gun-like operating device. The action of pulling the trigger kept the propeller revolving. Nickel plated, it was sold by Hubley Toys in the 1930s.

Whisk broom holder: Outfit for crafting such an item complete with cotton material for 10¢ in 1900s S.S. Kresge Co. stores.

Whist: Card game popular in early America involving four players and 52 cards, somewhat related to the game of bridge.

Whitaker, Josiah: Doing business in the clockmaking firm of Josiah Whitaker and Company in 1820s, Providence, Rhode Island.

White, Edward: Noted silversmith in 1760s, Ulster County, New York.

White elephant: An item one does not know what to do with. From the parable of a king who sent a white elephant to a rival. The rival's wealth was destroyed attempting to maintain the elephant in royal style.

White, John G.: Listed as a maker for gun carriages for the Confederate military. Located in Macon, Georgia.

White metal: Reference to tin-based or lead-based alloy once often used to make small toys. The material allowed for finely detailed castings.

White Mountain Freezer Co.: (see Frozen dainties)

White, Rollin: Supplier of cartridges to the Federal military in 1860s, Davenport, Iowa.

Whitescarver, Campbell & Co.: Provided Mississippi rifles during the Civil War to Confederate forces. Located in Rusk, Texas.

White, Sebastian: A Colonial era clockmaker active in 1790s, Philadelphia, Pennsylvania.

White Sewing Machine Co.: Makers of the White steam-powered automobile during the early 1900s. Company was located in Cleveland, Ohio.

White, Silas: A Colonial era silversmith in 1780s, New York City.

White's Pottery: Operation headed by Noah White which produced stoneware from the nineteenth century to the early 1900s in Utica, New York.

White steamer: This remarkable steam-powered vehicle was a product of the White Sewing Machine Company in 1901. Gasoline fueled the boiler, but water converted the steam to power the vehicle.

White walnut: (see Butternut wood)

Whiteware (ceramic): The result of a combination of earthenware and ironstone.

White, William: Supplier of military hatchets to Federal troops during the Civil War, located in Newark, New Jersey.

Weller Pottery's Dickens-ware including portrait of Abraham Lincoln. (Harris Auction Center)

Weller Pottery vase signed by artist F. Ferrell, dated 1897. (Skinner Inc.)

Early twentieth century Weller Pottery vase. (Skinner Inc.)

Westward Ho platter by Gillinder & Sons, ca. 1880.

Whitewood: Another term for popular wood or tulip wood. A softwood with a clear grain that varied in color from gray to yellow. On occasion it was used for case pieces and as a secondary piece for tables and some chairs. Country cabinetmakers sometimes used the wood entirely for blanket chests and cupboard.

Whitney doll carriage: Whitney brand of the 1940s offered two sizes of fiber doll carriages; also an upholstered wood version. Prices varied from $8 to $18.95.

Whitney, Eli: Maker of rifled muskets during the Civil War for the U.S. Army and the State of Connecticut. Credited with making the Plymouth rifle. Located in Whitneyville, Connecticut.

Whitney Glass Works: Glassmaking operation begun in 1837, Glassboro, New Jersey. Thomas H. Whitney purchased an existing firm and in 1840 took in his brother Samuel Whitney naming it Whitney Brothers. The company became the Whitney Glass Works in 1887. Among other things they produced log-cabin whiskey bottles, campaign bottles, and Jenny Lind bottles over the decades.

Whitney, M. F.: Listed as a silversmith in 1820s, Schenectady, New York.

Whittemore, A. O.: Recorded as a stoneware potter doing business in latter nineteenth century, Havana, New York.

Whittmore & Co.: Supplier of military uniform felt hats to Federal troops during the Civil War era. Located in St. Louis, Missouri.

Wick: Used in kerosene lamps and earlier, the wick was a woven flat band of cotton. It was submerged in the kerosene or other burning fluids to transport a steady flame.

Wicker (furniture): Reference to chairs and tables crafted by a weave of small twigs and slightly larger flexible lengths of wood. Small items including baskets and screens were also made in this manner.

Wiggins, Thomas: Doing business as a clockmaker at Thomas Wiggins and Company in 1830s, Philadelphia, Pennsylvania.

Wilcox, Alvin: Active redware potter in 1840s, West Bloomfield, New York.

Wilcox, Cyprian: Noted clockmaker active in 1820s, New Haven, Connecticut.

Wild Baby: Doll dressed in a grass skirt with brown skin, 8½" tall. Offered in the Montgomery Ward catalog of 1931 for 75¢.

Wildes, Thomas: Known to be doing business in pewter crafting in 1830s, New York City.

Wildey, Spence: (see Kookie doll)

Wild honey (color): A light brown according to the 1920s references.

Wildt, Wm.: A provider of military uniform buttons to Confederate troops during the Civil War, based in Richmond, Virginia.

Wilkens Toy Company: Starting early in 1890s the firm was successful at marketing cast iron, tinplate, and pull toys. Earlier as the Triumph Wringer Company it also sold washing machines. Although ownership changed in the mid-1890s, production continued for many years. Shortly before the 1920s it became the Kingsbury Toy Company.

Wilkeson, H. W.: Eagle plate and carbine sling maker for Federal troops during the Civil War, based in Springfield, Massachusetts.

Wilkinson, W. M. & Co.: Cavalry cartridge box maker for Federal troops during the Civil War, based in Springfield, Massachusetts.

Willard, Aaron: Listed as doing business as a clockmaker in early 1800, Grafton, Massachusetts.

Willard, Alexander: Established clockmaker in 1820s, Ashby, Massachusetts.

Willard, James: Doing business as a silversmith in 1815, East Windsor, Connecticut.

Willcox, Alvan: Active as a silversmith in 1820s, New Haven, Connecticut.

Will, George W.: A noted pewter designer in early nineteenth century, Philadelphia, Pennsylvania.

Will, Henry: Prominent pewter craftsman from 1760s to 1780s in New York City.

William and Mary Period: Specific reference to style of furniture developed in England during the 1685 to 1725 reign of King William and slightly beyond. Importance was placed on upholstery and needlework was popular for chair seats. Brass mounts were in favor for important pieces. Introduced and accepted as stylish were kneehold desks, hooded top secretaries, spooned-backed chairs. Accounts say the highboy first appeared in America during this period.

William Brunt Pottery Company: Doing business as a pottery maker in 1850s, East Liverpool, Ohio.

Williams, Charles: Active silversmith in 1820s, New York City.

Williams, David: Listed as doing business as a clockmaker in 1820s, Newport, Rhode Island.

Williams, E. C.: Granted a patent for portable military tents in 1861. Located in Jersey City, New Jersey.

Williamson, David: Listed as holder of a patent on .50 caliber military carbines during the Civil War, located in Brooklyn, New York.

Williams, R. S.: Crafted a machine gun for Confederate forces during the Civil War. The weapon, with a range of 2,000 yards was used at the Battle of Seven Pines. Williams was located in Covington, Kentucky.

Williams, Ruth: (see Darcy doll)

Willington Glass Company: The glassmaking operation began in the 1830s in West Willington, Connecticut. It was operated by Gilbert Turner and Company before being sold to a new concern in 1847. It continued to make hollow ware, bottles, and pickle bottles until the early 1870s.

Willis, Stillman: Listed as a silversmith in 1820s, Boston, Massachusetts.

Willits Manufacturing Company: Basically a pottery operation in 1880s, Trenton, New Jersey.

Willow pattern: Romantic motif pattern used on chinaware starting in the eighteenth century. Despite many variations, the overall style and character remained. Most designs were in blue, but there were a few other colors. Legend has the Chinese scene dealing with a daughter fleeing her father's garden to join her lover across a bridge. Sometimes two birds are seen flying over the treetops. The willow pattern was produced by many potteries over the years.

Wills St. Claire automobile: Quality six-cylinder car made for the luxury market during the 1920s. Wills Sainte Claire Incorporated was located in Marysville, Michigan.

Will, William: Maker of pewter ware in early 1800s, Philadelphia, Pennsylvania. Hallmark is often initials within a rectangle.

Willys-Overland Inc.: (see Whippet auto)

Wilma: (see Flintstones)

Wilmot, Thomas: Noted silversmith in 1840s, Charleston, South Carolina.

White Steam Car advertisement, 1905.

Whiting and Davis mesh purse with enameled design, 1920s.

Windsor side chair with fan back, ca. 1800. (Skinner Inc.)

Windsor armchair with braced back, ca. 1780. (Skinner Inc.)

Wilson, Hosea: Engaged in the clockmaking trade in 1815, Baltimore, Maryland.

Wilson, James: A Colonial era silversmith in 1770s, Trenton, New Jersey.

Wiltberger, Christian: Active silversmith in 1820s, Philadelphia, Pennsylvania.

Windmill (toy): Arcade Manufacturing produced a toy windmill in Freeport, Illinois, during the late 1920s. It was 26" high and had wheels 7" in diameter. It was decorated in red, white, and blue enamel.

Window jamb: Term in architecture for the straight, vertical supporting side of a window.

Window seat (furniture): A middle-eighteenth century reference to a small upholstered bench or stool fitted into an alcove or window recess. Typically the seat was covered with pillows above a lid which lifted to storage.

Windslow, Edward: Listed as a silversmith in early 1700s, Boston, Massachusetts.

Windsor chair (furniture): Very significant chair linked to the immediate vicinity of Windsor Castle in England. Accounts put them in America as early as middle of the eighteenth century, starting in Philadelphia. Varied designs included the brace-back, comb-back, fan-back, hoop-back, rod-back, and writing-arm. Favored woods in America were ash, birch, and hickory. Seats were often crafted of pine. Such chairs remained popular into the 1830s.

Wine (color): Described as a very dark rich red.

Wine cooler (furniture): During the eighteenth century metal-lined tubs were used to cool bottles of wine. The round-shaped coolers stood on four short legs, and were seen in fashionable English homes.

Wine table (furniture): Reference to an unusual horseshoe-shaped table placed in front of the fireplace. A curtain protected it from the heat. Typically a small wine decanter sat on a pivoting arm allowing access to all seated at the table.

Wingate, Fred: Listed as an active clockmaker working in 1800, Augusta, Maine.

Wing chair (furniture): An upholstered easy chair with a high back and elongated "wings" atop each side. As early as the latter seventeenth, century it had other names including the forty-wink chair, grandfather chair, and the saddle-back chair.

Winged claw (furniture): A decorative carving used on early nineteenth century Empire style furniture. Often added to the feet of elaborate Empire sofas.

Wingender & Brother: Pottery works in early nineteenth century, Haddonfield, New Jersey.

Wings (toy): Target game produced in the 1940s by Parker Brothers. Outfit included large board with enemy planes and two toy rifles. Price was $2.80.

Winnebago motor home: Toy vehicle in the image of the popular selling Winnebago Motor Home. Made by Tonka with steel body and plastic top, it included two jointed dolls. Total price in 1973 was 14.99.

Winsch, John: Highly notable early twentieth century postcard publisher based in New York City. Known for quality holiday postcards using exceptional artists.

Winter Iron Works: Listed as a supplier of Mississippi rifles to the Confederate military. Located in Montgomery, Alabama.

Winton automobile: Motor vehicle of several different models manufactured early in the twentieth century. The Winton Motor Carriage Company was located in Cleveland, Ohio.

Winton Motor Carriage Co.: Early 1900s maker of automobiles located in Cleveland, Ohio. Their best model with hinged glass front canopy sold for $2,500.

Wire-eyed doll: Term used to describe wax dolls whose "sleeping" or closing eyes were manipulated by a wire connection at the waist of the doll.

Wire safe: (see Pie safe)

Wistar glass: Quite rare glass produced at the Wistarberg Glass Factory in New Jersey under the direction of Caspar Wistar, a German immigrant. Wistar opened the factory around 1717 specializing in plain colors and the occasional three-colored piece. Shades of green, brown, and blue were used to make the characteristic Wistarberg glass. Thin threads of glass were wound spirally at the top to form a wavy design. Chief products included bottles, bowls, drinking glasses, and pitchers.

Witch ball: During the Victorian era balls of blown glass were used for decoration and to hang on a cord from the ceiling or the mantelpiece. In various forms and colors, they were said to ward away witches and other evil sprits. Produced in late nineteenth century glass factories, they were popular in many American homes.

Witch doll: Reference to the witch and wizard dolls made in the 1880s Vermont by Mason and Taylor. Such dolls were jointed with wooden and later metal pins. The head and body were attached with a toggle joint — allowing them to separate at a sharp angle.

Withe: Blacksmith's early tool, used to hold up tools such as chisels. Usually made of hazelwood.

Withington, Daniel: Listed as an active silversmith in 1840s, Ashland, Ohio.

Wm. Rogers Manufacturing: Company which provided military knives to the U.S. government during the 1860s, located in Hartford, Connecticut.

Wolfe and Company: Maker of cannon guns for the Confederate military during the Civil War. Located in New Orleans, Louisiana.

Wolfe, Francis: Listed as a silversmith in 1830s, Philadelphia, Pennsylvania.

Wolverine automobile: (see Reid Manufacturing)

Wolverton, G.A. & Co.: Under Federal governmental contract to provide military uniforms and shoes during the Civil War. Located in Albany, New York.

Wood, Benjamin: Noted silversmith in 1830s, New York City.

Wood brown (color): Simply a mail-order medium brown.

Wood choker: Multiple four-in-one mouse trap listed in 1913 S.S. Kresge Co. catalog.

Woodcock, E. P.: Granted a 1863 patent for pack-saddle used for carrying litters of wounded during the Civil War. Located in New York City.

Woodcock, Isaac: A Colonial era silversmith operating in 1780s, Wilmington, Delaware.

Woodcut: An early printing technique used solid blocks of wood. The woodcut was typically made of season hardwood and aided in transferring an image onto paper. Some form of the woodcut was used as early as the 1500s and as late as the nineteenth century. Eventually the woodcut was replaced with copper and steel engravings.

John Winsch postcard, dated 1911.

Wonder Woman record album cover from Power Records, 1975.

Woven coverlet from Indiana, dated 1850.

Writing arm Windsor chair.
(Skinner Inc.)

Wood, David: A noted clockmaker in early 1800s, Newburyport, Massachusetts.

Wood, G. and Co.: Maker of camp stools, camp cots, chests, and button molds for the Confederate military during the Civil War. Located in Macon, Georgia.

Woodruff, Barnet & Co.: Maker of knapsacks for Federal troops during the Civil War, based in New York City.

Woodruff, Enos: Doing business in the silversmith trade in 1830s, Cincinnati, Ohio.

Woods, Freeman: Colonial period silversmith in 1790s, New York City.

Woods Motor Vehicle Company: Early 1900s maker of electric automobiles including the Brougham, Landaus, and Victoria. Company was located in Chicago, Illinois.

Woodward, Antipas: Listed as a silversmith in 1790s, Middletown, Connecticut.

Woolsack: A wool sack used as a seat, said to be used by the Lord Chancellor of England.

Woolsey, Frank: Stoneware potter doing business in 1880s and 1890s, Benton, Arkanas.

Worcester porcelain: Historic porcelain produced by Dr. John Wall at the Worcester Pottery Works in 1750s England. Noted for its faint greenish-white tint, it was incorporated with transfer printing by the 1770s. The most successful transfer colors including black, brown, purple, red, and underglaze blue. Under the later ownership of Thomas Flight, the company added the prefix Royal after gaining permission from England's king. Royal Worcester then became known for delicate coloring and fine forms.

World Manufacturing Co.: (see Quaker bath cabinets)

Worman, Ely & Co.: Company granted a 1864 patent for military type knife-fork-spoon utensil, located in Philadelphia, Pennsylvania.

Woven coverlet: Distinguished hand-loomed bed covering dating from America's Colonial era. Over the decades blue and white coverlets were the most traditional. However brown, green, red, and even yellow dyes were used. Early examples used home-grown wool and vegetable dyes. Originally the coverlets included two sewn together strips, each about 30" in width.

W.P.F.: Initials for West Point Foundry during the Civil War era. See also Parrott Gun.

Wriggins, Thomas: Engaged in the clockmaking business as Thomas Wriggins and Company in 1830s, Philadelphia, Pennsylvania.

Wriggled work (pewter): Noted style of engraving on pewter jugs and tankards during the eighteenth century. Pewter craftsmen used a chisel to apply the wriggling design while slightly rocking the piece. This practice was popular with German and Dutch pewter workers, but seldom used in England and America.

Wright and Son: Pottery headed by Franklin Wright, specializing in stoneware in 1850s and 1860s, Taunton, Massachusetts.

Wright, William: Silversmith in 1750s, Charleston, South Carolina.

Writing armchair (furniture): The use of a flat, broad arm to accompany a chair to allow for a steady writing surface. Early Windsor examples offered a detachable writing arm. Later the writing arm was a fixed part of the overall chair. Also see tablet chair.

Wyer, Eleazer: Listed as an active silversmith in early 1800s, Portland, Maine.

Wynn, Christopher: Colonial era silversmith active in 1770s, Baltimore, Maryland.

Xanthein (color): Describes a hue yellowish in color.

Xantho: Based on the Greek word for yellow, or yellow fruit.

X-chair: Basically a folding chair with ancient origins. The chair's folding frame in the form of the letter X were found in Rome, Greece, Egypt, and in other civilizations that followed. A similar frame was also used in nineteenth century America.

Xeres: A sherry or wine first exported from Spain.

Xiphoid: Reference to something sword-shaped.

Xmas: Frequently used abbreviation for Christmas on early twentieth century postcards.

X-Men: Comic book figures first introduced in the 1960s, and later revived in the 1970s. Numerous comic books and a popular cartoon show prompted plastic badges, cereal boxes, and highly sought rings.

Xylograph: Term for the impression created by an engraving on wood.

Xylonite: Described as a type of pressed gun-cotton with an ivory color, used for making combs and similar items.

Xyst: Athletic hall or covered portico used in ancient Greece.

Xyster: Bone scraping surgical instrument.

X-stool: Leather-covered stool incorporating the X form of folding design. Ancient origins and records of usage through the ages. Eventually cloth covering replaced leather on the stools. Versions of x-chairs and x-stools were featured by leading cabinetmakers of the eighteenth century and as portable seating for outdoor events in the nineteenth century.

X-stretcher: Generally a crossed stretcher that was used on chairs and tables to provide support. Such stretchers were shaped like the letter X.

Yacca wood: The wood of a tree of Jamaica, one used for cabinetwork.

Yad Kids: Assortment of illustrated postcards offered by S.S. Kresge Co. stores early in the twentieth century. Price was six for 5¢.

Yak lace: Reference to a very coarse lace.

Yale & Company: Enterprising pewter firm operating in early 1800s, Wallingford, Connecticut. Known to use eagle and stars in various hallmarks.

Yale Touring Car: (see Kirk Manufacturing Company)

Yankee: Denotes an American, sometimes more specifically from the North or a New England. Used by Massachusetts farmer Jonathan Hastings to note quality: a Yankee chair for example.

Yankee ax: Distinctive name for American designed double-bit ax. One side was razor sharp for fine work while the other side was used for rougher work. Popular in the mid-nineteenth century.

Yankee Doodle: Melody based on English ditty, dating back to 1625.

Yanolite: A mineral commonly in crystal form, ax-like when edges are flattened.

Yardlong Print: Popular artists and leading publishers combined efforts to produce long and narrow prints early in the twentieth century. Some framed examples were a full 36", others were less long.

Yardstick: Stick three feet in length and used for measuring. Frequently used in the twentieth century to deliver advertising messages on wooden versions.

Yarn: (see Homespun)

Xmas Wishes postcard, early 1900s, made in U.S.A.

Framed yard prints, early twentieth century. (Harris Auction Center)

Yearbook photograph of Elvis Presley.

Yataghan: A dagger-like, double curved saber.

Yearbook: Annual accounting of activities and personalities at a school or university. Treasured when containing mention of future celebrities or professional athletes.

Yellow cab (toy): Bestselling toy made by Arcade Manufacturing Company in Freeport, Illinois. Offered in three lengths in 1927, from 5" to 9". Made of cast iron. Also see checker cab.

Yellow Coach (toy): Double deck Yellow Coach was manufactured in the late 1920s by Arcade. It resembled transportation units in larger cities. Made of cast iron, it came with rubber tires and dual wheels.

Yellow Kid: Originally a comic strip of the 1890s created by the talented artist Richard Outcault. The Kid became one of the advertising icons of the early twentieth century and promoted numerous projects from chewing gum and candy to games and soap collectible items included pin back buttons, trade cards, posters, and a cloth doll.

Yellow ochre (color): A medium light yellow according to Sears in 1927.

Yellow parlor coach (toy): Long 13" transportation vehicle made by Arcade in the late 1920s. Made of cast iron it came brightly painted and rubber tires were optional.

Yellow ware (ceramic): Term for earthenware with a distinct yellow glaze.

Yelvington, Thomas: Cabinetmaker active in 1850s, Wayne County, Indiana.

Yeomans, Elijah: Noted silversmith in 1790s, Hadley, Massachusetts.

Yergus, Christopher: Doing business as a cabinetmaker in 1850s, Wayne County, Indiana.

Yettons, Randell: A silversmith in 1740s, Philadelphia, Pennsylvania.

Yew (wood): Hard wood of reddish-brown color used by cabinetmakers for inlay and veneering. The close-grained wood was favored as early as the seventeenth century for its resistance to decay and wear.

Y-level: Reference to an instrument for measuring heights and distances.

Yoder, John: Virginia born cabinetmaker active in the trade in 1850s, Miami County, Indiana.

Yogi Bear: Delightful animation created by Hanna-Barbera starting in 1959. Highly popular as a cartoon character in the 1960s and 1970s. Yogi's image appeared on comic books, cereal boxes, lunch boxes, records, and other collectible items.

Yoke: Reference to hollowed timber used to connect two draught oxen together. Also a term for a wooden frame fitted to a person's shoulders for carrying purposes.

Yoke-front chest (furniture): Chest of drawers with a reverse serpentine front in the eighteenth century. The center was concave while sides swelled out. Also sometimes known as an oxbow chest.

Yokum, Mammy: Comic strip mother of Li'l Abner character during much of the twentieth century.

York, Cyrus: Enterprising cabinetmaker in 1850s, Indianapolis, Indiana.

York, J. P.: Ohio-born cabinetmaker at work in 1850s, Franklin County, Indiana.

Yorkshire chair (furniture): Carved side chair with seventeenth century origins in Yorkshire, England. Similar to the American panel and wainscot chairs, they were typically made of oak. In most the front legs were turned and made with stretchers for additional support.

Youle, George: Listed as doing business in the pewter trade in early nineteenth century, New York City.

Youle, Thomas: Operated as a pewter craftsman in early 1800s, New York City. Records show the business was continued into the 1820s by his widow who was unnamed.

Young America: A brand of revolver sold in the 1902 Sears, Roebuck and Company catalog. Young America revolvers made by Harrington and Richardson were sold as a ladies' revolver and a self cocker revolver, among others.

Young, Alexander: Listed as an active silversmith in 1850s, Camden, South Carolina.

Young, Bartlett: Listed as an active cabinetmaker along with Elijah Gossett in 1850s, Salem, Indiana.

Young, Edward: Ohio born cabinetmaker active in the trade in 1850s, Elkhart, Indiana.

Young, Ephraim: Listed as a cabinetmaker in 1850s, Hendricks County, Indiana.

Young, John: Noted chair maker doing business in 1840s, Rising Sun, Indiana.

Youngman, Jacob: Noted cabinet maker working in 1850s, Shelby County, Indiana.

Young, R. & Z.: Operators of a chair factory in 1850s, Ohio County, Indiana.

Young, Samuel: Virginia born cabinetmaker who was active in 1850s, Crawford County, Indiana.

Youngs, Ebenezer: An established clock maker doing business in 1780s, Hebron, Connecticut.

Young, S. H.: Cartridge box manufacturer for Federal troops during the Civil War, based in Newark, New Jersey.

Young, William: Listed as a cabinetmaker engaged in the trade in 1850s, Whitley County, Indiana.

Young, Zebulon: Chair maker born in New York and doing business in 1850s, Ohio County, Indiana.

Yufts: Term for a type of Russian leather.

Yule: Meaning Christmas, but some attribute its original meaning to have been December.

Yule card: An early name for the Yuletide Christmas card.

Yule log: A huge log of wood put on the hearth fire at Christmas.

Zaccho: Reference to the lowest part of the pedestal of a column.

Zaffre (ceramic): An early name for a type of intense blue cobalt color used in early pottery making. At times a small quanity of the zaffre blue was mixed with the glaze for a more effective decoration.

Zahn, G. M.: Listed as a silversmith in 1840s, Lancaster, Pennsylvania.

Zane, Jesse: Noted Colonial period silversmith in 1790s, Wilmington, Delaware.

Zanella (textile): Reference to a mixed twilled fabric once used for covering umbrellas.

Zane Pottery: Art pottery doing business from 1920s to the early 1940s in South Zanesville, Ohio.

Zanesville glass: One of the earliest Midwest glass factories was started in 1815, Zanesville, Ohio. Initially the White Glassworks firm made clear hollow ware and windowpanes. Later production included colored glass used in bottles and certain hollow ware. The operation closed in 1848.

Zanesville Stoneware Co.: Prolific stoneware pottery established in 1880s, Zanesville, Ohio.

Zappler clock: Reference to an early nineteenth century clock made in Austria. It had a small pendulum which moved in front of the dial. Some Zapplers had two pendulums moving in opposite directions.

Yogi Bear and Boo Boo Bear by Hallmark.

Mammy Yokum comic strip character doll.

233

Zorro hat and other Disney hats advertisement, 1957 Walt Disney Magazine.

Zax: Early tool used for cutting roofing slate, and for making nail holes.

Zebra wood: (see Coromandel wood)

Zeigler, Jonas: Ohio born cabinetmaker working in 1850s, De Kalb County, Indiana.

Zemule: The result of a hybrid breeding of a donkey and a zebra.

Zeotrope (toy): British-made moving picture toy of the 1830s. Illustrated paper moved through slits of a drum to provide simulated movement.

Zeppelin: Reference to a type of German dirigible balloon credited to Count Zeppelin.

Zimmerman, H. G.: Early twentieth century publisher of comical postcards. Based in Chicago, Illinois.

Zimmerman, J. C.: Maker of Bowie knives for Georgia military during the Civil War.

Zimmerman, Joseph: Listed as operating a cabinet shop in 1850s, Hendricks County, Indiana.

Zinc: Bluish-white metal, use for making many mid-twentieth century toys.

Zinck, George C.: Cabinetmaker prolific in producing stands, bureaus, and desks in 1850s, Clark County, Indiana.

Zinck, J. C.: Germany born cabinetmaker doing business in 1850s, Clark County, Indiana.

Zinck, Leonard: German born cabinetmaker producing goods in 1850s, Clark County, Indiana.

Zincograph: The impression made from a zinc plate.

Zincography: Practice of drawing from or printing upon zinc plates.

Zinc Stearate: An antiseptic dusting powder for infants sold in the 1920s. Price of a large round container was 17¢.

Zinc white (color): Called a pure bright white by early Sears mail-order catalogs.

Zircon: Term for a heavy, hard, and sparkling mineral.

Zither: A stringed instrument more popular in central Europe than America. However, examples of the autoharp-like device were featured in the 1902 Sears, Roebuck and Company catalog. Strings were stretched across the flat box of the instrument.

Zittel & Company: Stoneware pottery active from 1870s to early 1900s in Waco, Kentucky.

Zoebisher, C. A. & Son: Possible contractor with the federal government for providing musical instruments during the Civil War. Located in 1860s New York City.

Zofra (textile): Reference to an early Moorish carpet.

Zoom (aviation): To climb at an angle greater than the maximum climbing angle by virtue of initial excess of speed.

Zopfstil (furniture): A German term for the rococo style of decorative furniture in the middle of the eighteenth century.

Zorro: An amazing fictional caped hero popular from time to time throughout the twentieth century. Featured in a silent movie of the 1920s, and later as movie serials in the 1930s and 1940s, a television series in the 1950s, and full-length films in the decades that followed. Namesake for many premiums and collectibles from pin back buttons and lunch boxes to playsuits and a wristwatch.

Zouave: Reference to the Arab dress of soldiers of the light infantry corps of the French army. Later a type of fancy dress worn by some Federal soldiers during the Civil War. Outfits included baggy pants and leggings plus stylized hats and jackets. Mostly New York and Pennsylvania units.

Zsolnay (ceramic): A decorative ceramic chinaware made during the nineteenth century in Hungary. The factory opened in 1850 and eventually produced ornate and highly decorated tableware and vases.

Zuni: Reference to a particular tribe of Pueblo Indians in New Mexico.

Zwiebelmuster (ceramic): A remarkable china with blue in-glazed decoration whose origins date to the eighteenth century. Often referred to onion pattern china because of a fruit-shape motif mistaken for an onion.

Zymometer: An instrument once used in determining the degree of fermentation in different liquids.

Zythum: Term for an ancient beer-like beverage made from malt and wheat.

Also from Robert & Claudette Reed:
Vintage Postcards for the Holidays,
2nd Edition

Everyone has a favorite holiday, and they are all celebrated in this sweeping collection of vintage postcards. Christmas, Halloween, Valentine's Day, Easter, and other holidays are all memorialized in authentic postcards nearly a century old. More than 850 color images present the greeting selections of long ago in exquisite detail. This new and expanded edition features many vintage holiday postcards not included in the first edition, plus additional chapters such as April Fool's Day and Arbor Day. Authors Robert and Claudette Reed have carefully arranged this fascinating volume chronologically to provide reading and viewing through all the seasons of the year. A final special section includes early twentieth century postcards, paying tribute to birthdays, graduations, and other special occasions. You won't want to miss this exciting second edition of *Vintage Postcards for the Holidays*.

Item #6837 · ISBN: 978-1-57432-476-1 · 8½ x 11 · 368 Pgs. · PB · $24.95

Bibliography

Allmen, Diane. *The Official Identification and Price Guide to Postcards.* New York, House of Collectibles, 1990.

Arrowsmith, Robert, PHD, Peck, Harry Thurston, PH.D., Litt., D., LLD. *Webster's School and College Dictionary.* Chicago, Willcox & Follett The Educational Book House, 1926.

Barber, Edwin Atlee, A.M., PH.D. *The Pottery and Porcelain of The United States.* New York, G.P. Putnam's Sons, 1909.

Barlow Ronald S. *The Great American 1879 – 1945 Antique Toy Bazaar 5,000 Old engravings from original trade catalogs.* California, Windmill Publishing Company, 1998.

Bishop, Robert, Weissman, Judith Reiter, McManus, Michael, and Niemann, Henry. *The Knopf Collectors' Guides to American Antiques Folk Art Paintings, Sculpture & Country Objects.* New York, Chanticleer Press, Inc., 1983.

Black, Howard Jr. *Fell's Collector's Guide to Valuable Antiques.* New York, Frederick Fell Inc. 1963.

Black, Howard R. Jr. *The Collector's Guide to Valuable Antiques.* New York, Grosset & Dunlap, 1963.

Bond, Harold Lewis. *An Encyclopedia of Antiques.* New York, Tudor Publishing Co., 1944.

Butler, Joseph T. *American Antiques 1800 – 1900 — A Collector's History and Guide.* New York, The Odyssey Press, 1965.

Carle, Donald de, F.B.H.I. *Watch & Clock Encyclopedia.* New York, Bonanza Books, 1950.

Cescinsky, Herbert and Hunter, George Leland. *English and American Furniture.* New York, Garden City Publishing Company, Inc. 1929.

Christopher, Catherine. *The Complete Book of Doll Making & Collecting.* New York, The Greystone Press, 1949.

Cole, Ann Kilborn. *Antiques How to Identify, Buy, Sell, Refinish, and Care for Them.* New York, David McKay Company, Inc. 1957.

Comstock, Helen. *The Concise Encyclopedia of American Antiques.* New York, Hawthorn Books, Inc. 1965.

Cook, John W. and Klotz, Heinrich. *Conversations with Architects.* New York, Praeger Publishers, 1973.

Cowie, Donald and Henshaw, Keith. *Antique Collector's Dictionary.* New York, Gramercy Publishing Company, 1962.

Cox, Warren E. *The Book of Pottery and Porcelain.* New York, Crown Publishers, 1944.

Coysh, A.W. *The Antique Buyer's Dictionary of Names.* New York, Praeger Publishers, 1970.

Davidson, Marshall B. *The American Heritage History of Antiques from the Civil War to World War I*. New York, American Heritage Publishing Co., Inc., 1969.

———. *The American Heritage History of Antiques from Revolution to the Civil War*. New York, American Heritage Publishing Co., Inc. 1969.

Doane, Ethel. *Antiques Dictionary*. Massachusetts, Maine, The Anthoensen Press, Portland, Maine, 1949.

Drepperd, Carl W. *First Reader for Antique Collectors*. New York, Garden City Books, 1946.

Drepperd, Carl W. *Primer of American Antiques*. New York, Doubleday, Doran & Company, Inc., 1944.

Eberlein, Harold Donaldson, and McClure, Abbot. *The Practical Book of American Antiques*. New York, Halcyon House , 1916.

Freeman, Ruth S., B.S. *Encyclopedia American Dolls*. Watkins Glen, Century House, 1972.

Hake, Ted. *Official Hake's Price Guide to Character Toys, 5th Edition*. New York, House of Collectibles, 2004.

Hornung, Clarence P. *100 Great Antique Automobiles*. New York, Harry N. Abrams, Inc. 1968.

Ketchum, William, Jr. *The Knopf Collectors' Guides to American Antiques Pottery & Porcelain*. New York, Alfred A. Knopf, 1983.

Lavitt, Wendy. *The Knopf Collectors' Guides to American Antique Dolls*. New York, Alford A. Knopf, 1983.

Lockwood, Sarah M. *Antiques*. New York, Doubleday, Page & Company, 1926.

Lord, Francis A. *Civil War Collector's Encyclopedia Arms, Uniforms, and Equipment of the Union and Confederacy*. New York, Castle Books, 1963.

McClinton, Kathaine Morrison. *Antiques of American Childhood*. New York, Bramhall House, 1970.

Meine, Franklin J. *Webster's Encyclopedic Dictionary, A Library of Essential Knowledge*. Chicago, Columbia Educational Books, Inc., 1941.

Moore, N. Hudson. *Old Glass, European and American*. New York, Tudor Publishing Co., 1924.

Ormsbee, Thomas H. *Field Guide to Early American Furniture*. Boston, Little, Brown and Company, 1951.

Papert, Emma. *The Illustrated Guide to American Glass*. New York, Hawthorn Books, Inc. 1972.

Pegler, Martin M. *Discovering Antiques, The Story of World Antiques*. New York, Crown Publishers, Inc. 1966.

Reed, Robert. *Bears & Dolls in Advertising, Guide to Collectible Characters and Critters*. Norfolk, Antique Trader Books, 1998.

Bibliography

Reif, Rita. *The Antique Collector's Guide to Styles and Prices.* New York, Hawthorn Books, Inc., 1970.

Savage, George. *Dictionary of Antiques.* New York, Praeger Publishers, Inc., 1970.

Schweitzer, John C. *The ABC's of Doll Collecting.* New York, Sterling Publishing Co., Inc. 1981.

Singleton, Esther. *The Furniture of Our Forefathers.* New York, Doubleday, Page & Company, 1922.

———. *The Collecting of Antiques.* New York, The Macmillan Company, 1941.

Sloane, Eric. *A Museum of Early American Tools.* New York, Ballantine Books, 1964.

St. George, Eleanor. *Old Dolls.* New York, Gramercy Publishing Company, 1950.

Walters, Betty Lawson. *Furniture Makers of Indiana, 1793 to 1850.* Indianapolis, Indiana Historical Society, 1972.

Watson, Richard. *Bitters Bottles.* New York, Thomas Nelson & Sons, 1965.

Webster, Noah LL.D. *New Websterian Dictionary 1912.* New York, Syndicate Publishing Company, 1912.

Webster, William G. and Wheeler, William A. *A Dictionary of the English Language.* New York, Ivison, Blakeman & Company, 1867.

Whitton, Blair. *The Knopf Collectors' Guides to American Antiques Toys.* New York, Alfred A. Knoph, 1984.

Yates, Raymond F. *The Antique Collector's Manual: A Price Guide and Data Book.* New York, Harper & Brothers Publishing, 1952.

Catalogs

Arcade Toys, Number 33, Arcade Manufacturing Company, Freeport, Ill, 1927.

Billy and Ruth America's Famous Toy Children 1952 Miller's, Copyrighted by L. A. Hoeflich 1952, Headquarters in PA.

Christmas Joy, Montgomery Ward 1973 Christmas Catalog, Kansas City, MO.

Hubley Cast Iron Toys catalog #3, The Hubley Manufacturing Company, Lancaster, Pennsylvania.

Kresge's Katalog of 5 cent & 10 cent Merchandise, S. S. Kresge Company, Detroit, 1913.

Sears, Roebuck and Co. Catalogue 1902, Chicago, IL.

Sears, Roebuck and Co. Catalogue 1927, Chicago, IL.

Sears, Roebuck Catalogue 1923, Thrift Book of a Nation, Edited by Joseph J. Schroeder, Jr., Illinois, DBI Books, Inc.

The Great American 1879 – 1945 Antique Toy Bazaar, Edited & Arranged by Ronald S. Barlow, El Cajon, Windmill Publishing Company, 1998.

Turn-of-the-Century, Dolls, Toys and Games, The Complete Illustrated, Carl P. Stirn Catalog from 1893, New York, C.P. Stirn.

more great TITLES from collector books

GLASSWARE & POTTERY

7362 American Pattern Glass Table Sets, Florence/Cornelius/Jones......................$24.95
6326 Collectible Cups & Saucers, Book III, Harran................................$24.95
6331 Collecting Head Vases, Barron................................$24.95
7526 Collector's Encyclopedia of Depression Glass, 18th Ed., Florence................$19.95
6629 Collector's Encyclopedia of Fiesta, 10th Ed., Huxford................$24.95
5609 Collector's Encyclopedia of Limoges Porcelain, 3rd Ed., Gaston................$29.95
5842 Collector's Encyclopedia of Roseville Pottery, Vol. 2, Huxford/Nickel................$24.95
6646 Collector's Ency. of Stangl Artware, Lamps, and Birds, 2nd Ed., Runge................$29.95
7029 Elegant Glassware of the Depression Era, 12th Edition, Florence................$24.95
6126 Fenton Art Glass, 1907 – 1939, 2nd Edition, Whitmyer................$29.95
6320 Gaston's Blue Willow, 3rd Edition................$19.95
6127 The Glass Candlestick Book, Vol. 1, Akro Agate to Fenton, Felt/Stoer................$24.95
7353 Glass Hen on Nest Covered Dishes, Smith................$29.95
6648 Glass Toothpick Holders, 2nd Edition, Bredehoft................$29.95
6562 The Hazel-Atlas Glass Identification and Value Guide, Florence................$24.95
5840 Heisey Glass, 1896 – 1957, Bredehoft................$24.95
7534 Lancaster Glass Company, 1908 –1937, Zastowney................$29.95
7359 L.E. Smith Glass Company, Felt................$29.95
5913 McCoy Pottery, Volume III, Hanson/Nissen................$24.95
6135 North Carolina Art Pottery, 1900 – 1960, James/Leftwich................$24.95
6335 Pictorial Guide to Pottery & Porcelain Marks, Lage................$29.95
6925 Standard Encyclopedia of Carnival Glass, 10th Ed., Edwards/Carwile................$29.95
6476 Westmoreland Glass, The Popular Years, 1940 – 1985, Kovar................$29.95

DOLLS & FIGURES

6315 American Character Dolls, Izen................$24.95
7346 Barbie Doll Around the World, 1964 –2007, Augustyniak................$29.95
6319 Barbie Doll Fashion, Volume III, 1975 – 1979, Eames................$29.95
6221 Barbie, The First 30 Years, 2nd Edition, Deutsch................$24.95
6134 Ency. of Bisque Nancy Ann Storybook Dolls, 1936 – 1947, Pardee/Robertson................$29.95
6825 Celluloid Dolls, Toys & Playthings, Robinson................$29.95
6451 Collector's Ency. of American Composition Dolls, Vol. II, Mertz................$29.95
6546 Collector's Ency. of Barbie Doll Exclusives, 3rd Ed., Augustyniak................$29.95
6636 Collector's Ency. of Madame Alexander Dolls, 1948 – 1965, Crowsey................$24.95
6473 Collector's Ency. of Vogue Dolls, 2nd Ed., Izen/Stover................$29.95
6563 Collector's Guide to Ideal Dolls, 3rd Ed., Izen................$24.95
6456 Collector's Guide to Dolls of the 1960s and 1970s, Vol. II, Sabulis................$24.95
6944 Complete Gde. to Shirley Temple Dolls and Collectibles, Bervaldi-Camaratta................$29.95
7028 Doll Values, Antique to Modern, 9th Ed., Edward................$14.95
7360 Madame Alexander Collector's Dolls Price Guide #32, Crowsey................$14.95
7536 Official Precious Moments Collector's Guide to Figurines, 3rd Ed., Bomm................$19.95
6467 Paper Dolls of the 1960s, 1970s, and 1980s, Nichols................$24.95
6642 20th Century Paper Dolls, Young................$19.95

JEWELRY & ACCESSORIES

4704 Antique & Collectible Buttons, Volume I, Wisniewski................$19.95
6122 Brilliant Rhinestones, Aikins................$24.95
4850 Collectible Costume Jewelry, Simonds................$24.95
5675 Collectible Silver Jewelry, Rezazadeh................$24.95

7529 Collecting Costume Jewelry 101, 2nd Edition, Carroll................$24.95
7025 Collecting Costume Jewelry 202, Carroll................$24.95
6468 Collector's Ency. of Pendant & Pocket Watches, 1500 – 1950, Bell................$24.95
6554 Coro Jewelry, A Collector's Guide, Brown................$29.95
4940 Costume Jewelry, A Practical Handbook & Value Guide, Rezazadeh................$24.95
5812 Fifty Years of Collectible Fashion Jewelry, 1925 – 1975, Baker................$24.95
6330 Handkerchiefs: A Collector's Guide, Guarnaccia/Guggenheim................$24.95
6833 Handkerchiefs: A Collector's Guide, Volume 2................$24.95
6464 Inside the Jewelry Box, Pitman................$24.95
7358 Inside the Jewelry Box, Volume 2, Pitman................$24.95
5695 Ladies' Vintage Accessories, Bruton................$24.95
1181 100 Years of Collectible Jewelry, 1850 – 1950, Baker................$9.95
6645 100 Years of Purses, Aikins................$24.95
6942 Rhinestone Jewelry: Figurals, Animals, and Whimsicals, Brown................$24.95
6038 Sewing Tools & Trinkets, Volume 2, Thompson................$24.95
6039 Signed Beauties of Costume Jewelry, Brown................$24.95
6341 Signed Beauties of Costume Jewelry, Volume II, Brown................$24.95
6555 20th Century Costume Jewelry, 1900 – 1980, Aikins................$24.95
4850 Unsigned Beauties of Costume Jewelry, Brown................$24.95
4955 Vintage Hats & Bonnets, 1770 –1970, Langley................$24.95

FURNITURE

6928 Early American Furniture: A Guide to Who, When, and Where, Obbard................$19.95
3906 Heywood-Wakefield Modern Furniture, Rouland................$18.95
7038 The Marketplace Guide to Oak Furniture, 2nd Edition, Blundell................$29.95

TOYS & MARBLES

2333 Antique & Collectible Marbles, 3rd Ed., Grist................$9.95
6649 Big Book of Toy Airplanes, Miller................$24.95
7523 Breyer Animal Collector's Guide, 5th Ed., Browell/Korber-Weimer/Kesicki................$24.95
7527 Collecting Disneyana, Longest................$29.95
7356 Collector's Guide to Housekeeping Toys, Wright................$16.95
7528 Collector's Toy Yearbook, Longest................$29.95
7355 Hot Wheels, The Ultimate Redline Guide Companion, Clark/Wicker................$29.95
6466 Matchbox Toys, 4th Ed., 1947 to 2003, Johnson................$24.95
6638 The Other Matchbox Toys, 1947 to 2004, Johnson................$19.95
7539 Schroeder's Collectible Toys, Antique to Modern Price Guide, 11th Ed................$19.95
6650 Toy Car Collector's Guide, 2nd Ed., Johnson................$24.95

PAPER COLLECTIBLES & BOOKS

6623 Collecting American Paintings, James................$29.95
7039 Collecting Playing Cards, Pickvet................$24.95
6826 Collecting Vintage Children's Greeting Cards, McPherson................$24.95
6553 Collector's Guide to Cookbooks, Daniels................$24.95
1441 Collector's Guide to Post Cards, Wood................$9.95
6627 Early 20th Century Hand-Painted Photography, Ivankovich................$24.95
6936 Leather Bound Books, Boutiette................$24.95
7036 Old Magazine Advertisements, Clear................$24.95
6940 Old Magazines, 2nd Ed., Clear................$19.95
3973 Sheet Music Reference & Price Guide, 2nd Ed., Guiheen/Pafik................$19.95

1.800.626.5420 Mon. – Fri. 7 am – 5 pm CT   Fax: **1.270.898.8890**

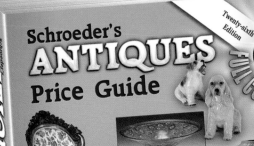